11/25/78

PS:

I intended
to get you candles.
What I wanted wasn't
available, so we can
light this on a
snowy evening.

With all my love,
Rick

The Native Muse

The Native Muse

THEORIES OF AMERICAN LITERATURE
Volume I

Edited with Notes and Commentary by
RICHARD RULAND

 A DUTTON PAPERBACK

E. P. Dutton & Co., Inc. : : *New York* : : *1976*

For Susan, Paul, Michael, and Joseph

Contents

Preface

Goethe was fascinated by America, so much so that he collected striking comments on the United States that happened to come his way. In 1819 he found these remarks in *Blackwood's Edinburgh Magazine:*

> There is nothing to awaken fancy in that land of dull realities; it contains no objects that carry back the mind to the contemplation of early antiquity; no mouldering ruins to excite curiosity in the history of past ages; no memorials, commemorative of glorious deeds, to call forth patriotic enthusiasm and reverence; it has no traditions and legends and fables to afford materials for romance and poetry; no peasantry of original and various costume and character for sketches of the pencil and the subjects of song; it has gone through no period of infancy; no pastoral state in which poetry grows out of the simplicity of language, and beautiful and picturesque descriptions of nature are produced by the constant contemplation of her. . . . The fact is undeniable, that hitherto they have given no proof whatever of genius in works of invention and fancy, and unless we allow that the failure is owing to the want of proper subjects to awaken it, and proper materials to nourish it, in the manner above shewn; or that it is displayed in a different sphere, we must agree with Buffon and Raynal, that the human mind has suffered a deterioration by being transported across the Atlantic.

For the journalist, this indictment explained why America had no literature and would perhaps never have any—the argument was to echo through the nineteenth century and become enshrined in the famed apology of Henry James. But for Goethe this apparent freedom from the past seemed a great asset: "America, you have it better," he wrote in 1827, for you have "no basalt," no established underlayer of precedent and assumption to limit the future. During the first century of the Republic, this hopefulness served as steady counterpoint to the confident assertions of those who—like H. L. Mencken years later—believed that Americans were destined to be no more than hewers of wood and drawers of water for the race. "In America we are free of artistic traditions," notes a reader of *The Nation* in the 1880's. "Our freedom begets license, it is true. We do shocking things; we produce works of architecture irremediably bad; we try crude experiments that result in disaster. Yet somewhere in this mass of ungoverned energy lies the principle of life. A new spirit of beauty is being developed and perfected, and even now its first achievements are beginning to delight us. They spring out of the past but they are not tied to it; they study the traditions but they are not enslaved by them."

There are often several other books lying close beside the one which finally emerges; they may represent different ways of answering the questions posed or alternate uses to which the materials under consideration might be put. Sometimes related matters can be combined, but there always comes a moment when one must make a choice between two or more inviting alternatives. The review articles, prefaces, verses, lectures and essays collected in these two volumes seek in one way or another to extend the historical debate over the existence of a native literature; they touch upon the nature of that literature, either actual or potential. I have tried to focus on answers that have been offered to the question, how can our literature be made unmistakably American? The line between theories of American literature and theories of literature or poetics which happen to be advanced by Americans is not always a sharp one, and I have doubtless strayed across it more than once. But an anthology of literary and critical theory written in America would be quite another book. Similarly, these pieces often begin as comments on literary nationalism, and this entire collection should be placed within the context of that exhaustive controversy. But that index to the self-consciousness of a developing culture has been adequately investigated; I could not have proceeded without these investigations, as I indicate below, but I have tried not to repeat them. I have been primarily interested, in short, not in the nature of American nationality or the desirability or possibility of an indigenous culture, but in theoretical and practical advice on how Americans—as Americans—should write: in what diction, with what form, on what subjects, for what audience, after what models, to what purpose? I have pursued this interest not, I hasten to add, because I believe Americans should aspire to such national individuation, but because so many of my compatriots have thought so and have sought and received advice on how to accomplish their goal.

A few of my selections are already familiar. I have included Bradford's decision to adopt the plain style, Franklin's account of his literary apprenticeship, Tocqueville on the natural subject for a democratic poet, Hawthorne on the difficulties an American writer must face, and Emerson on the wide range of the native author's opportunities. For those who use this book for reference, it may prove helpful to have these widely reprinted statements available in a single place. My central aim, however, has been to place them in a richer context than they usually enjoy. When they are seen simply as contributions to a continuing and noisy public debate, they lose their aura of isolated, inexplicable (but now somehow prototypical) utterance and regain the flavor of topicality and public pertinence they originally had. My view of these materials as participating in the flow of cultural dialogue has dictated the loose chronological order of the contents. And while most readers may not read from cover to cover, the thematic groupings which occasionally disrupt this chronology, the frequent cross reference to individual or concept, and the cumulative nature of my brief headnotes all reflect my efforts to provide a readable narrative. I have tried, that is, to mold these historical documents into a coherent essay on America's self-conscious effort to develop a native aesthetic sensibility.

The material has resisted my efforts in two ways. The controversy was repetitive; a few recommendations and complaints were so obvious that they played what was apparently felt to be a necessary part in statement after statement. And those statements, moreover, rarely confine themselves conveniently to a single, coherent discussion. Many begin as reviews which embrace implicitly the program of William Ellery Channing: "We shall use the work prefixed to this article as ministers are sometimes said to use their texts. We shall make it a point to start from, not the subject of our remarks." I have edited these selections both to bring together relevant portions of verbose magazine essays and to limit repetition to a representative yet endurable degree. Since one essay seldom comments intentionally on another, the recurrence of ideas and even of words and phrases is itself a historical phenomenon worth noting. A reader of the whole volume may well be struck by echoes of theme and variation that are almost musical. This, I would argue, is no accident, nor is it the result of elaborate distortion and arrangement on my part. One does not have to insist on the existence of a unified national mind or character to recognize that ideas develop within a cultural context and that such development is often both repetitive and cumulative. And it is also, at least in the present case, responsive. What at first appears simply repetitious may not only carry an earlier statement forward or in a different direction entirely, it may also introduce a familiar assertion as defense against a new attack. The cultural conversation I seek to document frequently warmed to argument, argument not only between compatriots but between Americans and their close observers in England and France as well. When Sydney Smith asked in the *Edinburgh Review,* "In the four quarters of the globe, who reads an American book?", the entire subject took on new urgency, and everything that had been said had to be said once more. I have sought to avoid excision which would obscure this aspect of my subject; I have tried in addition to preserve the flavor of the original essays, even straying on occasion from my topic when the interest of the material seemed to warrant such editorial irresponsibility.

My assumption that these materials are most accurately represented in a continuous narrative accounts for the physical form of this anthology. Most of my selections are from magazines, many of them by anonymous hands and untitled. Rather than separate these statements with incomplete and what for many would be distracting bibliographic data, I have reserved this information for a full Table of Contents and used simple numerals both to space my selections and to indicate the relevant entry in the Contents. I have relegated such authorial identification as I could collect to the same place; most of the essays gain little for the modern reader from the unfamiliar names of their authors, and where the name is a famous one, it often seems to distract attention from the work itself and from the context provided by neighboring essays. Some of the more obscure contributors to this volume are identified at the back of the book. Whatever information seems essential to each selection, however, is included in the headnote, and since the date of publication is occasionally a noteworthy aspect of the story, I provide at the end of each item the most accurate date I could determine.

The very effort to see the remarks sampled here as connected discourse serves to emphasize a central feature of the narrative: it is, ultimately, a story without a climax. While what we have come to regard as an American literary tradition was taking shape, it was accompanied by heated discussion of its theoretical needs and implications. But there is little reason to assume that the two developments had any more than a casual relationship. Early assessments of contemporary writing rarely discussed the authors we now find most interesting, and when they did they were not likely to take a position many today would occupy. It cannot be claimed therefore that the persistent debate had much direct influence on the particular books and authors we now value. But its participants took it very seriously, revealing as they wrote their hopes for their nation and its art. And so a few conclusions can be drawn from this collection which elucidate the cultural basis of the literature we do have.

From the very first our concern with national identity is implied in Bradford's choice of the plain style. The way one wrote said important things about what kind of man one was. Franklin's insistence on clarity and succinctness merely secularizes Bradford's assumptions into an assertion of good judgment and commercial trustworthiness. Both regard style as utilitarian and, in a sense, substantive. And the implications of manner and material remain a question of national concern when the goals become more aesthetic in the nineteenth century. In the documents collected here, this concern illuminates the well-known laments of Hawthorne and James and helps explain both our early dependence on the romance and the profound influence of the new directions pointed by Emerson. Indeed, the persistent adulation of Addison, Goldsmith, and Pope says a good deal about American taste, the reputation of Irving and Longfellow, and the angry reception given Whitman. The extraordinary popularity of both Irving and Cooper points first to the provincial's hunger for recognition in every sphere of activity—a hunger which made of Scott a model and Sydney Smith a nemesis—but once Irving and Cooper won acceptance, the question became one of theory: how is their achievement to be carried forward, what is to be imitated or avoided?

What the present collection emphasizes is how quickly the individual writer was cast as mentor, how persistently his work was turned into a model for a native art. It is perhaps only in this context that we can account for the hortatory tone which pervades Emerson's aesthetic theorizing, a tone Whitman acknowledged in striving to make his life and his poetry an appropriate response. It is not too much to see in Whitman's every utterance an explicit reply to the queries on his nation's art raised repeatedly since the earliest days of the colonies. Brownson's remarks in 1864, however, suggest that the questions persisted. Whitman had proposed his answer, but—as Volume II will illustrate—it was not to be the only one.

I am grateful to all those studies and collections which have provided historical perspective, suggested materials, or served as models for the shape an anthology may take. Among the more helpful works I have utilized which will lead the interested reader further into my subject and its peripheries are Perry Miller, *The Raven and the Whale, The Transcendentalists: An Anthology,* and *The Puritans* (with Thomas H.

Johnson); Howard Mumford Jones, *The Theory of American Literature;* Robert Spiller, *The American Literary Revolution, 1783–1837;* Kay S. House, *Reality and Myth in American Literature;* Benjamin T. Spencer, *The Quest for Nationality: An American Campaign,* and "An American Literature Again," *Sewanee Review,* LVII (1949), 56–72; William B. Cairns, "British Criticisms of American Writings, 1783–1815," and "British Criticisms of American Writings, 1815–1833," *University of Wisconsin Studies in Language and Literature,* I (1918), 1–97, and XIV (1922), 1–319; Robert Whitney Bolwell, "Concerning the Study of Nationalism in American Literature," *American Literature,* X (January, 1939), 405–416; Harry Hayden Clark, "Literary Criticism in the *North American Review, 1815–1835,*" *Transactions of the Wisconsin Academy of Sciences, Arts, and Letters,* XXXII (1940), 299–350; and C. Hugh Holman, "Introduction," *Views and Reviews in American Literature, History and Fiction: First Series* by William Gilmore Simms, vii–xxxvii.

I want to express particular gratitude to my colleague, student, and friend, Herbert Zarov, who helped with sources and prepared the biographical notes, and to Barbara, who sustains a wonderful interest in an American mind.

On these bleak climes by Fortune thrown,
Where rigid *Reason* reigns alone,
Where lovely *Fancy* has no sway,
Nor magic forms about us play—
Nor nature takes her summer hue
Tell me, what has the muse to do?—

Philip Freneau   [1788]

These are the gardens of the Desert, these
The unshorn fields, boundless and beautiful,
For which the speech of England has no name. . . .

William Cullen Bryant   [1832]

We have not yet any poetry which can be said
to represent the mind of our world. The poet
of America is not yet come. When he comes,
he will sing quite differently.

Ralph Waldo Emerson   [1850]

Folks of all sorts and of every degree;
Snob And Snip and haughty grandee;
Duchesses, Countesses, fresh from their tea;
And Shopmen, who only read books for a spree,
Halloo'd and hooted and roar'd 'cross the sea,
            'Be grand! be grand!
            Let your lines expand!
We'll take nothing small from so monstrous a land!'

C. M. Kirkland   [1853]

The Native Muse

꩜ *William Bradford was one of the leaders of the migration to New England, and he served the colony as governor with brief interruption from 1621 until his death in 1657. In 1630 he began his history of Plymouth, one of the first in a long list of American books written to glorify the values of the fathers by way of reprimand to a distracted and ungrateful later generation. The following lines begin his book:*

1 ꩜

OF PLYMOUTH PLANTATION and first of the occasion and inducements thereunto; the which, that I may truly unfold, I must begin at the very root and rise of the same. The which I shall endeavour to manifest in a plain style, with singular regard unto the simple truth in all things; at least as near as my slender judgment can attain the same. . . .

Since his argument for the significance of the Pilgrim mission depends on his theory of history, Bradford starts with a "root and rise" which places the seventeenth-century Saints in dramatic opposition to Satan and satanic popery. By eschewing the ornate diction and elaborate locution of the courtly tradition and adopting the plain style, he seeks to reenforce the "simple truth" of his historical interpretation. The need to separate Pilgrim virtue from High Church decadence thus led to one of the first efforts to adopt a style suited to the particular needs of the colonies.

The Preface to the Bay Psalm Book further reflects the New England colonists' respect for what is here called the "common style" of most Old Testament books. For if "God's Altar needs not our polishings" the casting of the Psalms into rhythmic and rhymed English requires careful justification. It now seems certain that this Preface was written by John Cotton. Cotton's conversion to Puritanism helps illustrate the theological implications of style. He enjoyed a growing reputation as a preacher in the English church when he came to see "that the plain style was the saving style, and he realized that he must abandon his elegant oratory. But as the time approached for him to preach at St. Mary's and he received indications that the usual anticipatory crowd would be on hand to hear his display, he had to strive manfully to put down his doubts. . . . He went through with his plan." The style of his discourse effectively announced his change of faith: "Many of his listeners pulled their caps about their ears, astonished undergraduates looked in amazement at the fellows who had enthusiastically herded them to the church, and the hum of approval, the preacher's version of applause, did not break the silence after his conclusion."[1]

2

The singing of Psalms, though it breathe forth nothing but holy harmony and melody, yet such is the subtilty of the enemy and the enmity of our nature against the Lord and His ways, that our hearts can find matter of discord in this harmony, and crotchets of division in this holy melody. For there have been three questions especially stirring concerning singing. First, what psalms are to be sung in churches? whether David's and other scripture psalms or the psalms invented by the gifts of godly men in every age of the church. Secondly, if scripture psalms, whether in their own words, or in such meter as English poetry is wont to run in? Thirdly, by whom are they to be sung? whether by the whole church together with their voices? or by one man singing alone and the rest joining in silence, and in the close of saying amen.

[1] Larzar Ziff, *The Career of John Cotton* (Princeton, N.J.: Princeton University Press, 1962), p. 32.

Touching the first, certainly the singing of David's psalms was an acceptable worship of God, not only in his own, but in succeeding times, as in Solomon's time 2 *Chron.* 5. 13; in Jehosaphat's time 2 *Chron.* 20. 21; in Ezra's time *Ezra* 3. 10, 11; and the text is evident in Hezekiah's time they are commanded to sing praise in the words of David and Asaph, 2 *Chron.* 29, 30; which one place may serve to resolve two of the questions (the first and the last) at once . . .

If the singing David's psalms be a moral duty & therefore perpetual, then we under the New Testament are bound to sing them as well as they under the Old. And if we are expressly commanded to sing Psalms, Hymns, and spiritual songs, then either we must sing David's psalms, or else may affirm they are not spiritual songs, which being penned by an extraordinary gift of the Spirit, for the sake especially of God's spiritual Israel, not to be read and preached only (as other parts of holy writ) but to be sung also; they are therefore most spiritual, and still to be sung of all the Israel of God. . . .

Obj. 1. If it be said that the Saints in the primitive Church did compile spiritual songs of their own inditing, and sing them before the Church. 1 *Cor.* 14, 15, 16.

Ans. We answer first, that those Saints compiled these spiritual songs by the extraordinary gifts of the spirit (common in those days) whereby they were enabled to praise the Lord in strange tongues, wherein learned *Paraeus* proves those psalms were uttered, in his Comment on that place (verse 14) which extraordinary gifts, if they were still in the Churches, we should allow them the like liberty now. Secondly, suppose those psalms were sung by an ordinary gift (which we suppose cannot be evicted) doth it therefore follow that they did not, and that we ought not to, sing David's psalms? Must the ordinary gifts of a private man quench the spirit still speaking to us by the extraordinary gifts of his servant David? There is not the least foot-step of example, or precept, or colour reason for such a bold practice.

Obj. 2. Ministers are allowed to pray conceived prayers, and why not to sing conceived psalms? Must we not sing in the spirit as well as pray in the spirit?

Ans. First because every good minister hath not a gift of spiritual poetry to compose extemporary psalms as he hath of prayer. Secondly, suppose he had, yet seeing psalms are to be sung by a joint consent and harmony of all the Church in heart and voice (as we shall prove) this cannot be done except he that composeth a psalm, bringeth into the Church set forms of psalms of his own invention; for which we find no warrant or precedent in any ordinary officers of the Church throughout the scriptures. Thirdly, because the book of psalms is so complete a System of psalms, which the Holy-Ghost himself in infinite wisdom hath made to suit all the conditions, necessities, temptations, affections, &c. of men in all ages (as most of all our interpreters on the psalms have fully and particularly cleared), therefore by this the Lord seemeth to stop all men's mouths and minds ordinarily to compile or sing any other psalms (under colour that the occasions and conditions of the Church are new) &c. for the public use of the Church, seeing, let our condition be what it will, the Lord Himself hath supplied us with far better. . . .

As for the scruple that some take at the translation of the book of psalms into meter, because David's psalms were sung in his own words without meter, we answer: First, there are many verses together in several psalms of David which run in rhythms . . . which shews at least the lawfulness of singing psalms in English rhythms.

Secondly, the psalms are penned in such verses as are suitable to the poetry of the Hebrew language, and not in the common style of such other books of the Old Testament as are not poetical. Now no protestant doubteth but that all the books of the scripture should by God's ordinance be extant in the mother tongue of each nation, that they may be understood of all; hence the psalms are to be translated into our English tongue. And if in our English tongue we are to sing them, then as all our English songs (according to the course of our English poetry) do run in meter, so ought David's psalms to be translated into meter that so we may sing the Lord's songs as in our English tongue so in such verses as are familiar to an English ear—which are commonly metrical. And as it can be no just offence to any good conscience to sing David's Hebrew songs in English words, so neither to sing his poetical verses in English poetical meter. Men might as well stumble at singing the Hebrew psalms in our English tunes and not in Hebrew tunes, as at singing them in English meter, which are our verses, and not in such verses as are generally used by David according to the poetry of the Hebrew language. But the truth is, as the Lord hath hid from us the Hebrew tunes, lest we should think ourselves bound to imitate them, so also the course and frame (for the most part) of their Hebrew poetry, that we might not think ourselves bound to imitate that, but that every nation without scruple might follow as the graver sort of tunes of their own country songs, so the graver sort of verses of their own country poetry.

Neither let any think that for the meter's sake we have taken liberty or poetical license to depart from the true and proper sence of David's words in the Hebrew verses; no, but it hath been one part of our religious care and faithful endeavour to keep close to the original text. . . . We have therefore done our endeavour to make a plain and familiar translation of the psalms and words of David into English meter, and have not so much as presumed to paraphrase to give the sense of his meaning in other words. . . . We have with our English Bibles (to which next to the Original we have had respect) used the Idioms of our own tongue instead of Hebraisms, lest they might seem English barbarisms. . . .

If therefore the verses are not always so smooth and elegant as some may desire or expect, let them consider that God's Altar needs not our polishings (Exod. 20) for we have respected rather a plain translation than to smooth our verses with the sweetness of any paraphrase, and so have attended Conscience rather than Elegance, fidelity rather than poetry, in translating the Hebrew words into English language, and David's poetry into English meter; that so we may sing in Sion the Lord's songs of praise according to his own will, until he take us from hence, and wipe away our tears, & bid us enter into our master's joy to sing eternal Halleluiahs.

[1640]

Although the previous passage refers to singing, its main concern is the need to assure orthodoxy through accuracy of translation. Thomas Hooker's comments on style in A Survey of the Summe of Church-Discipline *reaffirms Puritan rejection of ornate decoration for its own sake in favor of the didactic utility of "plainesse."*

3

That the discourse comes forth in such a homely dresse and course habit, the Reader must be desired to consider, It comes *out of the wildernesse,* where curiosity is not studied. Planters if they can provide cloth to go warm, they leave the cutts and lace to those that study to go fine.

As it is beyond my skill, so I professe it is beyond my care to please the nicenesse of mens palates, with any quaintnesse of language. They who covet more sauce then meat, they must provide cooks to their minde. It was a cavill cast upon *Hierom,*[1] that in his writing he was *Ciceronianus non Christianus:* My rudenesse frees me wholly from this exception, for being Λόγῳ Ἰδιώτης,[2] as the Apostle hath it, if I would, I could not lavish out in the loosenesse of language, and as the case stands, if I could answer any mans desire in that daintinesse of speech, I would not do the matter that Injury which is now under my hand: *Ornari res ipsa negat.*[3] The substance and solidity of the frame is that, which pleaseth the builder, its the painters work to provide varnish.

If the manner of the discourse should occasion any disrellish in the apprehension of the weaker Reader, because it may seem too *Logicall, or Scholasticall,* in regard of the *terms* I use, or the way of dispute that I proceed in, in some places: I have this to professe,

That plainesse and perspicuity, both for matter and manner of expression, are the things, that I have conscientiously indeavoured in the whole debate: for I have ever thought writings that come abroad, they are not to dazle, but direct the apprehension of the meanest, and I have accounted it the chiefest part of Iudicious learning, to make a hard point easy and familiar in explication. . . .

[1648]

[1] St. Jerome.
[2] Ignorant of the Word.
[3] That a work needs decoration argues weakness of structure.

﹥ *In Michael Wigglesworth's praise of eloquence the argument centers once again on utility. But there is an obvious distance between getting as close to David as possible through translation and a use of rhetoric that "wil make a very block understand." The plain style then, even as Wigglesworth writes it, might hope for eloquence so long as it continues to serve truth.*

4 ﹤

How sweetly doth eloquence even inforce trueth upon the understanding, and subtly convay knowledge into the minde be it never so dull of conceiving, and sluggish in yeelding its assente. So that let a good Oratour put forth the utmost of his skill, and you shall hear him so lay open and unfould, so evidence and demonstrate from point to point what he hath in hand, that he wil make a very block understand his discourse. Let him be to giue a description of something absent or unknown; how strangely doth he realize and make it present to his hearers apprehensions, framing in their mindes as exact an idea of that which they never saw, as they can possibly have of any thing that they have bin longest and best acquainted with. Or doth he take upon him to personate some others in word or deedes why he presents his hearers not with a lifeless picture, but with the living persons of those concerning whom he speaks. They see, they hear, they handle them, they walk they talk with them, and what not? Or is he to speak about such things as are already known? Why should he here discourse after the vulgar manner, and deliver his mind as a cobler would doe: his hearers might then have some ground to say they knew as much as their oratour could teach them. But by the power of eloquence ould truth receivs a new habit. though its essence be the same yet its visage is so altered that it may currently pass and be accepted as a novelty. The same verity is again and again perhaps set before the same guests but drest and disht up after a new manner, and every manner season'd so well that the intellectuall parts may both without nauseating receiv, and so oft as it doth receiv it still draw some fresh nourishing virtue from it. So that Eloquence giues new luster and bewty, new strength new vigour, new life unto trueth; presenting it with such variety as refresheth, actuating it with such hidden powerful energy, that a few languid sparks are blown up to a shining flame.

And which is yet more: Eloquence doth not onely reviue the things known but secretly convay life into the hearers understanding rousing it out of its former slumber, quickning it beyond its naturall vigour, elevating it aboue its ordinary conception. There are not onely objects set before it, but ey's (after a sort) giuen it to see these objects in such wise as it never saw. Yea it is strengthened as to apprehend that which is taught it, so of it self with enlargment to comprehend many things which are not made known unto it. Hence it comes to pass that after the hearing of a wel-composed speech livelily exprest the understanding of the Auditor is so framed into the mould of Eloquence, that he could almost goe away and compose the like himself either upon the same or another subject. And whats the reason of this? why his mind is transported with a kind of rapture, and inspired with a certain oratoric fury, as if the oratour together with his words had breathed his soul and spirit into those that hear him.

These and the like effects hath Eloquence upon the understanding. But furthermore 'tis a fit bait to catch the will and affections. For hereby they are not onely layd in wait for, but surprized: nor onely surprized, but subdued; nor onely subdued, but triumphed over. Yet Eloquence beguil's with such honesty, subdues with such mildness, triumphs with such sweetness: that here to be surprized is nothing dangerous, here to be subject is the best freedom, this kind of servitude is more desireable then liberty. For whereas our untractable nature refuseth to be drawn, and a stiff will scorn's to be compel'd: yet by the power of wel-composed speech nature is drawn against the stream with delight, and the will after a sort compelled with its owne consent. Altho: for a time it struggle and make resistance, yet at length it suffer's it self to be vanquish't, and takes a secret contentment in being overcome.

In like manner, for the affections. Look as a mighty river augmented with excessiue rains or winter snows swelling above its wonted channel bear's down banks and bridges, overflows feilds and hedges, sweeps away all before it, that might obstruct its passage: so Eloquence overturn's, overturn's all things that stand in its way, and carrys them down with the irresistible stream of its all controuling power. Wonderful it were to speak of the severall discoverys of the power in severall affections: wonderfull but to think in generall, how like a blustering tempest it one while driues before it the raging billow's of this troubled Ocean: how other whiles (as though it had them in fetters) it curb's and calm's the fury at a word. And all this without offering violence to the party's so affected; nay with a secret pleasure and delight it stirs men up to the greatest displeasure and distast. Doth it affect with grief? why to be so grieved is no grievance. doth it kindle coales, nay flames of fiery indignation? why those flames burn not, but rather cherish. doth it draw tears from the eys? why even tears flow with pleasure. For as is wel sayd by one upon this point In omni animi motu etiam in dolore est quaedam jucunditas.[1] So potently, so sweetly doth Eloquence command. and of a skilfull oratour in point of the affections that may be spoken really, which the Poet affirmeth fabulously of Æolus god of the winds. . . .

But I need instance no more. some of you I hope will by this time assent unto what has bin hitherto prov'd that Eloquence is of such useful concernment and powerfull operation. But methinks I hear some still objecting. 'Tis very true Eloquence is a desirable thing, but what are we the better for knowing its worth unless we could hope our selues to attain it? It is indeed a right excellent indowment but 'tis not every capacity, nay scarce one of a hundreth that can reach it. How many men of good parts do we find that yet excel not here? Cicero indeed, a man in whom vast understanding and naturall fluent facility of speech conspire together; no marvail if he make judges weep and princes tremble. But to what purpose is it for a man of weak parts and mean abilitys to labour after that which he is never like to compass? Had we not as good toss our caps against the wind as weary out our selves in the pursuit of that which so few can reach to?   /

An. To these I would answer first, the reason why so few attain it is because there [are] few that indeed desire it. hence they run not as if they ment to win, they pursue not as if they hop't to overtake. But let me answer them with Turner's words upon this very argument Negligentiam nostram arguit, qui cum non possimus. quod debemus, optimus, nolumus quod possimus, benè. We cannot do what we would therefore will not doe what we may. This savours of a slouthful sistem. Because we cannot keep pace with the horsemen, shall we refuse to accompany the footmen? Because we cannot run, shall we sit down and refuse to goe? we cannot reach so far as our selues desire and as some others it may be attain, shall we not therefore reach as far as our endeavours may carry us? Because we cannot be Oratores optimi, do we content our selues to be Oratores Pessimi?

And as for those that have most excell'd in this kind, whence had they their excellency? they did not come declaming into the world: they were not born with orations in their mouths: eloquence did not sit upon their

---

[1] In every activity of the spirit, yea even in sorrow, there is a certain pleasure.

lips whilest they lay in their cradles: neither did they suck it in from their mothers brests. But if you examine the matter you shall find that by incredible paines and daly exercise, they even turn'd the cours of nature into another channel, and cut out a way for the gentle stream of Eloquence, where naturall impediments seem'd altogether to deny it passage. . . .

[1650]

⧫ These two pieces by Cotton Mather illustrate once again how quickly the quest for religious purity led to literary theory. Mather was so dissatisfied with earlier renderings of the Psalms that he prepared his own translation, Psalterium Americanum. *Free of the "Clink" and "Lace" of rhyme, he has—he remarks with typical modesty—supplied "ALL that the Holy Spirit of God has dictated."*

5 ⧫

OUR Poetry has attempted many Versions of the PSALMS, in such *Numbers* and *Measures,* as might render them capable of being *Sung,* in those grave *Tunes,* which have been prepared and received for our *Christian Psalmody.* But of all the more than twice Seven Versions which I have seen, it must be affirmed, That they *leave out* a vast heap of those rich things, which the Holy SPIRIT of GOD speaks in the Original Hebrew; and that they *put in* as large an Heap of poor Things, which are intirely *their own.* All this has been meerly for the sake of preserving the *Clink* of the *Rhime:* Which after all, is of small consequence unto a Generous *Poem;* and of none at all unto the Melody of *Singing;* But of how little then, in *Singing unto the Lord!* Some famous pieces of Poetry, which this Refining Age has been treated withal, have been offered us in 𝕭𝖑𝖆𝖓𝖐 𝖁𝖊𝖗𝖘𝖊. And in 𝕭𝖑𝖆𝖓𝖐 𝖁𝖊𝖗𝖘𝖊 we now have the Glorious Book of Psalms presented unto us. The PSALMS fitted unto the *Tunes* commonly used in the Assembles of our *Zion:* But so fitted, that the *Christian Singer* has his Devotions now supplied, with ALL that the Holy SPIRIT of GOD has dictated, in this Illustrious and Cælestial Bestowment upon His Church in the World; and there is NOTHING BESIDES the pure Dictates of that Holy SPIRIT imposed on him. Now, True PIETY, Thou shalt be Judge, whether such a *Divine matter* for thy *Songs* thus disencumbered from every thing that may give them any *Humane Debasements,* be not really to be preferred before any Compositions thou hast ever yet been entertain'd withal. Doubtless, the more that any are desirous to offer unto the Glorious GOD what is purely *His Own,* and the more concerned that any are to have their *Worship* entirely Regulated and Animated, by the SPIRIT OF GOD, the more agreeable to them, will be such an *Instrument of Devotion,* as is here prepared. Tho' the *Hymns* have not the Trifle of *Rhime,* as a Lace to set them off, yet they are *all Glorious within,* which is the thing that

Manly Christianity has its eye most upon; and in the *Spiritual Songs* thus enjoyed and improved, thou mayst most hope to have the Holy Spirit of God, who indited them, *speaking* unto thee, even such Things as *cannot be uttered*.

But that our **Cantional** may be furnished with a superabundance, and the Faithful be plentifully feasted with *Angels Food,* Behold, an Addition of Passages Collected in Metre, (but still as exactly translated) from some *other parts* of the Sacred Scriptures, to answer the various occasions of Christianity.

For the *New Translation* of the Psalms, which is here endeavoured, an *Appeal* may be with much Assurance made, unto all that are Masters of the **Hebrew Tongue**, whether it be not much more agreeable to the *Original,* than the *Old* one, or than any that has yet been offered unto the World. Perhaps there is more Liberty taken here in Translating the *First Verse* of the *Psalter,* than almost any Verse in the whole Book beside. It keeps close to the *Original;* and even when a *word of supply* is introduced, it is usually a needless Complement unto the *care of exactness,* to distinguish it at all, as we have done, with an *Italica-Character;* for it is really in the Intention and Emphasis of the *Original.* Yea, the just *Laws of Translation* had not been at all violated, if a much greater Liberty had been taken, for the beating out of the Golden and Massy *Hebrew* into a more *Extended English.* For, it may be observed, if you Translate a *French Book,* suppose, into *English,* you turn it into *English Phrase,* and make not a *French English* of it; For, *Il fait froid,* for instance, you do not say, *It makes Cold,* but, *It is Cold.* We have tied our selves to *Hebraisms,* more scrupulously, than there is real occasion for. . . .

Most certainly, our Translation of the Psalms, without the Fetters of *Rhime* upon it, can be justly esteemed no prejudice to the Character of *Poetry* in the performance. For indeed, however it is now appropriated, according to the true sense of the Term, to *Rhythme* it self a *Similis Desinentia,* or, a *likeness of sound* in the last Syllables of the Verse, is not essential. Old *Bede* will give you such a Definition of *Rhythme,* and bring other Authorities besides *Austins* for it, that *Scaliger* thereupon holds, all *Verses* wherein Regard is had unto the *Number of Syllables,* to have a claim unto it. Be that as the Criticks on the Term shall please, our *Translation* is all in *Metre;* and really more tied unto *Measure,* than the *Original* appears to have been, by all the Examinations that have as yet been employ'd upon it. . . .

I am therefore strongly of the Opinion, That the *Poesie* of the Ancient *Hebrews,* knew no *Measure,* but that of the unknown *Music,* wherein it was to be accommodated. Our PSALMS in the *Hebrew,* are not so much *Metrical* as *Musical;* And hence, the very Inscriptions of them sometimes intimate, that there was a sort of *Melody,* unto which they were adapted. It is true, the *Oriental Nations* at this day, have their *Metred Poetry;* But it is of a late Original. However, 'tis very certain, that all the skill in the World, will hardly find the Rules of that *Metred Poetry* observed with any exactness in the Songs of the Sacred Scriptures. There is little value to be set on the Authority, of either *Philo,* or *Josephus,* and after them, of *Jerom,* who quotes *Origen* and *Eusebius* for it, when they go to resolve the *Hebrew Poesie,* into I know not what, *Lyricks* and *Hexameters.* And therefore it may be hoped, that our Version may be released from the *Chime* of a, *Similis Desinentia,* without being censured for *Unpoetical.* The *Sublime Thought,* and the *Divine Flame,* alone is enough, to challenge the Character of *Poetry* for these Holy Composures. And if any *Beauties* be wanting, 'tis owing to the lowness of the *Language,* whereinto a strict and close *Translation,* is what we are here tied unto. . . .

[1718]

Mather's interest in verse led him to discuss poetry and style in his handbook for divinity students, Manuductio ad Ministerium. *The distance between 1640 and 1720 is demonstrated in Mather's recognition here of secular literature. He works cautiously toward linking the Bible with a classical tradition and recognizes poetry as a valid respite from hours of study: "I cannot wish you a soul that shall be wholly unpoetical." Even relaxation, of course, must be to good purpose. It must be temperate and well advised, and it must ultimately serve the serious business of the student—hence the warning against the devil's library and the ignorance of contemporary reviewers.*

6

. . . Poetry, whereof we have now even an *Antediluvian* piece in our hands, has from the beginning been in such request, that I must needs recommend unto you some acquaintance with it. Though some have had a soul so unmusical, that they have decried all verse as being but a meer playing and fiddling upon words; all versifying, as if it were more unnatural than if we should chuse dancing instead of walking; and rhyme, as if it were but a sort of morisce-dancing with bells: yet I cannot wish you a soul that shall be wholly unpoetical. An old Horace has left us an art of poetry, which you may do well to bestow a perusal on. And besides your lyric hours, I wish you may so far understand an epic poem, that the beauties of an Homer and a Virgil may be discerned with you. As to the moral part of Homer, it is true, and let me not be counted a Zoilus[1] for saying so, that by first exhibiting their gods as no better than rogues, he set open the flood-gates for a prodigious inundation of wickedness to break in upon the nations, and was one of the greatest apostles the devil ever had in the world. Among the rest that felt the ill impressions of this universal corrupter, (as men of the best sentiments have called him,) one was that overgrown robber, of execrable memory, whom we celebrate under the name of Alexander the Great; who by his continual admiring and studying of his Iliad, and by following that false model of heroic virtue set before him in his Achilles, became one of the worst of men, and at length inflated with the ridiculous pride of being himself a deity,

[1] I.e., a spiteful critic.

exposed himself to all the scorn that could belong to a lunatic. And hence, notwithstanding the veneration which this idol has had, yet Plato banishes him out of a common-wealth, the welfare whereof he was concerned for. Nevertheless, custom or conscience obliges him to bear testimonies unto many points of morality. And it is especially observable, that he commonly propounds prayer to heaven as a most necessary preface unto all important enterprizes; and when the action comes on too suddenly for a more extended supplication, he yet will not let it come on without an ejaculation; and he never speaks of any supplication but he brings in a gracious answer to it. I have seen a travesteering high-flier, not much to our dishonour, scoff at Homer for this; as making his actors to be like those whom the English call dissenters. . . .

. . . Nevertheless, it is observed, that the Pagans had no rules of manners that were more laudable and regular than what are to be found in him. And some have said, it is hardly possible seriously to read his works without being more disposed unto goodness, as well as being greatly entertained. To be sure, had Virgil writ before Plato, his works had not been any of the books prohibited. But then, this poet also has abundance of rare antiquities for us: and such things, as others besides a Servius, have imagined that they have instructed and obliged mankind, by employing all their days upon. Wherefore if his Æneid, (which though it were once near twenty times as big as he has left it, yet he has left it unfinished,) may not appear so valuable to you, that you may think twenty-seven verses of the part that is the most finished in it, worth one and twenty hundred pounds and odd money, yet his Georgics, which he put his last hand to, will furnish you with many things far from despicable. But after all, when I said, I was willing that the beauties of these two poets might become visible to your visive faculty in poetry, I did not mean that you should judge nothing to be admittable into an epic poem, which is not authorized by their example; but I perfectly concur with one who is inexpressibly more capable to be a judge of such a matter than I can be; that it is a false critic who, with a petulant air, will insult reason itself, if it presumes to oppose such authority.

I proceed now to say, that if (under the guidance of a Vida) you try your young wings now and then to see what flights you can make, at least for an epigram, it may a little sharpen your sense, and polish your style for more important performances; for this purpose you are now even overstocked with patterns, and——*Poemata passim,*[2] you may, like

---

[2] Writing poetry occasionally.

Nazianzen, all your days make a little recreation of poetry in the midst of your painful studies. Nevertheless, I cannot but advise you. Withhold thy throat from thirst. Be not so set upon poetry, as to be always poring on the passionate and measured pages. Let not what should be sauce, rather than food for you, engross all your application. Beware of a boundless and sickly appetite for the reading of the poems which now the rickety nation swarms withal; and let not the Circæan cup intoxicate you. But especially preserve the chastity of your soul from the dangers you may incur, by a conversation with muses that are no better than harlots: among which are others besides Ovid's Epistles, which for their tendency to excite and foment impure flames, and cast coals into your bosom, deserve rather to be thrown into the fire, than to be laid before the eye which a covenant should be made withal. Indeed, not merely for the impurities which they convey, but also on some other accounts; the powers of darkness have a library among us, whereof the poets have been the most numerous as well as the most venemous authors. Most of the modern plays, as well as the romances, and novels and fictions, which are a sort of poems, do belong to the catalogue of this cursed library. The plays, I say, in which there are so many passages that have a tendency to overthrow all piety, that one, whose name is Bedford, has extracted near seven thousand instances of them, from the plays chiefly of but five years preceding; and says awfully upon them, They are national sins, and therefore call for national plagues; and if God should enter into judgment, all the blood in the nation would not be able to atone for them. How much do I wish that such pestilences, and indeed all those worse than Egyptian toads, (the spawns of a Butler, a Brown, and a Ward,[3] and a company whose name is legion!) might never crawl into your chamber! The unclean spirits that come like frogs out of the mouth of the dragon, and of the beast; which go forth unto the young people of the earth, and expose them to be dealt withal as the enemies of God, in the battle of the great day of the Almighty. As for those wretched scribbles of madmen, my son, touch them not, taste them not, handle them not: thou wilt perish in the using of them. They are the dragons, whose contagious breath peoples the dark retreats of death. To much better purpose will an excellent but an envied Blackmore feast you, than those vile rhapsodies (of that *Vinum dæmonum*) which you will find always leave a taint upon your mind, and among other ill effects, will sensibly indispose you to converse with the holy oracles of God your Saviour.

[3] Samuel Butler, Thomas Brown, Edward Ward.

But there is, what I may rather call a parenthesis than a digression, which this may be not altogether an improper place for the introducing of.

There has been a deal of a-do about a style; so much, that I must offer you my sentiments upon it. There is a way of writing, wherein the author endeavours that the reader may have something to the purpose in every paragraph. There is not only a vigour sensible in every sentence, but the paragraph is embellished with profitable references, even to something beyond what is directly spoken. Formal and painful quotations are not studied; yet all that could be learnt from them is insinuated. The writer pretends not unto reading, yet he could not have writ as he does if he had not read very much in his time; and his composures are not only a cloth of gold, but also stuck with as many jewels as the gown of a Russian ambassador. This way of writing has been decried by many, and is at this day more than ever so, for the same reason that, in the old story, the grapes were decried, that they were not ripe. A lazy, ignorant, conceited set of authors, would persuade the whole tribe to lay aside that way of writing, for the same reason that one would have persuaded his brethren to part with the incumbrance of their bushy tails. But however fashion and humour may prevail, they must not think that the club at their coffee-house is all the world; but there will always be those, who will in this case be governed by indisputable reason: and who will think that the real excellency of a book will never lie in saying of little; that the less one has for his money in a book, it is really the more valuable for it: and the less one is instructed in a book, and the more superfluous margin and superficial harangue, and the less of substantial matter one has in it, the more it is to be accounted of. And if a more massy way of writing be ever so much disgusted at this day, a better gust will come on, as will some other thing, *quæ jam cecidere*.[4] In the mean time, nothing appears to me more impertinent and ridiculous than the modern way (I cannot say, rule; for they have none!) of criticising. The blades that set up for critics, I know not who constituted or commissioned them!—they appear to me, for the most part, as contemptible as they are a supercilious generation. For indeed no two of them have the same stile; and they are as intolerably cross-grained, and severe in their censures upon one another, as they are upon the rest of mankind. But while each of them, conceitedly enough, sets up for the standard of perfection, we are entirely at a loss which fire to follow. Nor can you easily find any one thing wherein they agree for their stile, except perhaps a perpetual care to give us jejune and empty

[4] Which (discourse) now to cut short.

pages, without such touches of erudition (to speak in the stile of an ingenious traveller) as may make the discourses less tedious, and more enriching to the mind of him that peruses them. There is much talk of a florid stile obtaining among the pens that are most in vogue; but how often would it puzzle one, even with the best glasses, to find the flowers! And if they were to be chastised for it, it would be with much the same kind of justice as Jerom was, for being a Ciceronian. After all, every man will have his own stile, which will distinguish him as much as his gait: and if you can attain to that which I have newly described, but always writing so as to give an easy conveyance unto your ideas, I would not have you by any scourging be driven out of your gait; but if you must confess a fault in it, make a confession like that of the lad unto his father while he was beating him for his versifying.

However, since every man will have his own stile, I would pray that we may learn to treat one another with mutual civilities and condescensions, and handsomely indulge one another in this as gentlemen do in other matters.

I wonder what ails people that they cannot let Cicero write in the stile of Cicero, and Seneca write in the (much other!) stile of Seneca; and own that both may please in their several ways.—But I will freely tell you, what has made me consider the humourists that set up for critics upon stile as the most unregardable set of mortals in the world, is this! Far more illustrious critics than any of those to whom I am now bidding defiance, and no less men than your Erasmus's and your Grotius's, have taxed the Greek stile of the New Testament with I know not what solecisms and barbarisms; and how many learned folks have obsequiously run away with the notion! whereas it is an ignorant and an insolent whimsey which they have been guilty of. It may be (and particularly by an ingenious Blackwall, it has been) demonstrated, that the gentlemen are mistaken in every one of their pretended instances; all the unquestionable classics may be brought in to convince them of their mistakes. Those glorious oracles are as pure Greek as ever was written in the world; and so correct, so noble, so sublime is their stile, that never any thing under the cope of Heaven, but the Old Testament, has equalled it. . . .

[1726, 1789]

⊰ Mather Byles' satire offers a model for American writing as it attacks excess. It suggests the condescending good sense and wit of the British coffeehouse, the satiric urbanity America came to value in Franklin and Irving. With the weakening of religious fervor, insistence on the purity of colonial autonomy disappeared. For close to a century the New World would borrow its literary materials from the Old and thereby demonstrate the provincialism which was to obsess literary theorists in the nineteenth century.

7 ⊱

As one great Design of many of the Entertainments in our *Magazine,* is to cultivate *polite* Writing, and form and embellish the Style of our ingenious Countrymen: So, Instead of a Preface to this Volume, we ask Leave to give the following Piece of *Criticism.*

> *Clamorem immensum tollit, quo pontus et omnes*
> *Intremuere undæ, penitusque exterrita tellus*
> *Italiæ, curvisque immugiit Ætna cavernis.*   Virg. Æneid.[1]

There have been innumerable Authors, from *Aristotle's Rhetorick* to *Longinus's Treatise of the Sublime,* and from thence down to the Compiler of our modern *Horn-book,* who have written Introductions to the Art of Polite Writting. Every one that can just distinguish his Twenty Four Letters sets up for a Judge of it; as all who are able to flourish a Goose's Quill, pretend to be Masters of that Secret. The noblest Productions have given Birth to many a supercillious Caveller; Criticks of all Sizes and Dimensions have nibled round the divinest Pages; and Ignorance and Conceit have endeavoured to shake down the most beautiful Structures, in order to build themselves a Reputation out of the Ruins. A superiour Genius, though he seems to kindle a wide Horizon of Light all about him, and is admired by the understanding Part of Mankind, yet he must expect to be the Occasion of a great many Absurdities, with which the unknowing and envious will strive to satyrize him: As the Sun scatters Day through a whole Frame of Worlds, but yet may, in some

[1] He raises a mighty roar, whereat the sea and all its waves shuddered and the land of Italy was affrighted far within, and Aetna bellowed in its winding caverns (III, 672–674).

particular Spots, raise a Fog, or hatch a Nest of Vermin. To conclude, the Science of correct Writing having been a Subject exhausted by so many able Hands, and seeing all the Rabble of Scriblers are such indisputable Proficients in it; not to mention my own Incapacity for such an Undertaking; I shall not be so vain as to offer my Thoughts upon it: But I shall apply my Labours at this Time, to an Ornament of a contrary Nature, which is a Theme intirely New, Namely, *The Art of writing Incorrectly*.

This, I take it, is a Work that I am excellently well qualified for, and I doubt not but to convince the World that I am a perfect Master of my Subject. In the Prosecution of this useful Design, I shall show the Excellency of Incorrect Writing in general; I shall lay open the several Artifices, by which a Man of competent Abilities, may, with proper Application, attain to a tolerable Degree of Perfection in it; I shall produce pertinent Examples from Writers of undoubted Eminence in that improving Science: And in the last place, I may possibly address the World with a very pathetick Exhortation, to follow the Instructions which I shall give them, in order to accomplish themselves in the Art of Incorrect Writing. In short, I intend to entertain the Publick, with a regular Criticism upon Nonsense.

Authors of this Kind may be divided into two Classes, generally known under the Denomination of the *Bombastick* and the *Grubstreet*. The latter of these Characters is easily attained, provided a Man can but keep himself from thinking, and yet so contrive Matters, as to let his Pen run along unmolested over a Sheet of White Paper, and drop a convenient Quantity of Words, at proper Intervals on it. A Person who is acquainted with this Secret, may, with great Facility and Composure of Mind, furnish himself with a comfortable Stock of Reputation, as often as he finds it requisite. This he might do, as without any Ruffle to his own Tranquility, so neither would it prove the least Disturbance to his Readers: For while he flow'd along with that unmeaning Softness, every one within the Warble of his Accents would undoubtedly dissolve away in a supine Indolence, and, (as a late Musical Author of this Species has very tenderly expressed it) be *hush'd into lulling Dreams*.

I shall, perhaps, dedicate some future Essay to the Incouragement of these worthy Gentlemen, but at this Time I intend to consider those my ingenious Fellow-Labourers, who deviate into the contrary Extream; I mean the Admirers of Bombast and Fustian.

These Writers, to avoid the Imputation of low and flat, blow up every Subject they take in Hand beyond its natural Dimensions; and nothing will please them that is not big and boisterous, wild and irregular. They wonderfully delight in Noise and Clamour; a Rattle of Words, and an Extravagance of Imagination, they look upon as the Perfection of Rhetorick; and are Transported beyond themselves, at the Tumult and Confusion that bellows through a Hurricane of Nonsense. In short, that which Men of this Turn applaud as the Masterpiece of good Writing, differs from the *true Sublime,* as a Boy's artificial Kite, wadling among the Clouds at the End of a Skein of Pack-thread, does from the natural Flight of an Eagle, towering with steddy Pinions up the Sky, and bearing full upon the Sun.

If this false Taste prevails amongst us, we shall quickly prove such a Generation of Blusterers, that our Country will resemble the Cave of *Æolus,* where the Winds make their general Rendezvous, and battel and clash together in an eternal Din and Uproar. For my own Part, I look upon it to be the Duty of every one, as far as in him lies, to lend his Assistance in banking out this Inundation of Sound, which, if it finds a clear Passage, will not fail to overwhelm us in a Deluge of Folly and Absurdity.

A Friend of mine who writes in this exorbitant Style, Mr. *Richard Stentor* by Name, shall be the Hero of the present Essay. Mr. *Stentor* as to his exterior Figure, is one of the portliest Mortals that have flourished in our World, since *Goliah* over-top'd the *Philistian* Army. He is moderately speaking, Nine Foot high, and Four in Diameter. His Voice is not unlike the Roar and Rapidity of a Torrent foaming down a Mountain, and reverberated amongst the neighbouring Rocks. The Hurry of Vociferation with which he drives along in the Heat of an Argument, imitates the Thunder of a Cart-load of Stones poured out upon a Pavement. He was educated in a Ship of War, and one would imagine he learnt the Notes of his Gamut, from the various Whistlings of a Tempest thro' the Rigging of his Vessel. I was once so unadvised as to offer my Dissent from one of his Opinions; but I had better have held my Tongue: He turned upon me, and rung me such a Peal of Eloquence, that had I not made off with the greatest Precipitation, would have gone near to have stun'd, and made me deaf all my Days. Nay, I have cause to think my Hearing has been never the better for it to this Moment.

This is a short Description of his external Accomplishments; as to the Qualifications of his Mind, they will be best perceived, by a Transcript I shall here make, from an Oration he formerly composed in *Praise of Beacon Hill.* I must inform my Readers, that it was conceived as he stood upon the Summit of that little Mount, one Training-Day, when, as he has since owned to me, the Drums and Musquets assisted his Inspiration, and augmented and deepend the Rumbling of his Periods. It begins in the following Manner—

The gloriously-transcendent, and highly-exalted Precipice, from which the sonorous Accents of my Lungs resound with repeated Echoes, is so pompous, magnificent, illustrious, and loftily-towering, that, as I twirle around my Arm with the artful Flourish of an Orator, I seem to feel my Knucles rebound from the blew Vault of Heaven, which just arches over my Head. I stand upon an amazing Eminence that heaves itself up, on both sides steep and stupendous! high and horrendous! The spiry Teneriffe, the unshaken Atlas, or Olympus divine and celestial, when compared to this prodigious Mountain, sink to Sands, and dwindle to Atoms. It is deep-rooted in its ever-during Foundations, firm as the Earth, lasting as the Sun, immoveable as the Pillars of Nature! I behold from this awful and astonishing Scituation, the concave Expanse of uncreated Space, stretch itself above: and the Land and Ocean below, spreading an Infinitude of Extension all about me. But what daring Tropes and flaming Metaphores shall I select, O aspiring Beacon! to celebrate Thee with a suitable Grandeur, or exalt thee to a becoming Dignity? How does it shoot up its inconceivable Pinnacle into the superior Regions, and blend itself with the cerulian circum-ambient Æther! It mocks the fiercest Efforts of the most piercing Sight, to reach to its impenetrable Sublimities. It looks down upon the diminish'd Spheres; the fixt Stars twinkle at an immeasurable Distance beneath it; while the Planets roll away, unperceived, in a vast, a fathomless Profound! *****

By this little Quotation from Mr. *Stentor's* Panegyrick on Beacon Hill, my Reader will in some Measure be able to judge of his Manner of thinking, and expressing himself. It appears plainly that he heaps his Subject with improper and foreign Thoughts; that he strains those Thoughts into the most unnatural and ridiculous Distortions; and, last of all, that he clouds them with so many needless supernumerary Epithets, as to fling the whole Piece into this unaccountable Huddle of Impertinence and Inconsistency. *Richard* is mighty fond of great sounding Words, and, let his Topick be what it will, he has perpetual Recourse to them upon all Emergencies. He once took it in his Head to be in Love, and wrote a Poem to his Mistress on that delicate Passion: But instead of the gentle Flow of Harmony which any one would reasonably have expected, and which is indeed essential to Compositions of that Kind, his Numbers stalked along as sturdy and outragious as in any other of his Performances. I my self counted in Fifty Six Lines of it, three *Celestials*, eight *Immortals*, eleven *Unboundeds*, six *Everlastings*, four *Eternities*, and thirteen *Infinites;* Besides *Bellowings, Ravings, Yellings, Horrors, Ter-*

ribles, Rackets, Hubbubs, and *Clutterings,* without Number. But what pleased me the most of any of my Friend's Compositions, was, *A Poetical Description of a Game at Push-pin.* Sure, thought I, when I read the Title, there can be nothing very loud and impetuous upon so trivial a Matter as This. How I was surprized out of my mistake, my Reader will in some Measure conceive, when he understands that the first Distich of the Poem runs thus,

> *Rage, fire, and fury in my bosom roll,*
> *And all the gods rush headlong on my soul.*

He then proceeded to compare the Pins to two Comets, whose Heads, as he expressed it, enlightned the boundless Desarts of the Skies with a bloody Glare, and threw behind them the ruddy Volumes of their tremendous Trains, into the tractless Wastes of Immensity. When the Pins met in the Progress of the Game, for a Similitude, he supposed the two Continents to be tossed from their Foundations, and encounter, with a direful Concussion, in the midst of the briny *Atlantick:* or rather, *says he,* as if two Systems of Worlds, Suns, Planets and all, should be hurled resistless one against another, and dash a horrible *Chaos,* from the general Ruins of Matter, and Wrecks of a whole Universe. He concluded the Poem with the following Lines, which I look upon to be the most finished Pattern of this Sort of Productions, that I have any where met with; whether I consider, the Uncouthness of the Language, the Ruggedness of the Style, or the Disproportion and Extravagance of the Images. Speaking of the Pins he says,

> *The Bars of Brass, harsh-crashing, loud resound,*
> *And jarring discords rend th' astonish'd ground.*
> *So when aloft dire hurricanes arise,*
> *And with horrendous shatterings burst the skies,*
> *Dread ghastly terrors drive along in crowds,*
> *And hideous thunder howls amongst the clouds;*
> *Eternal whirlwinds on the ocean roar,*
> *Infinite earth-quakes rock the bounding shore.*

I shall conclude these Remarks upon Bombast, with an Observation which I ought in Justice to make, in favour of those who fall into it; *viz. That no Person can be a considerable Proficient this way, who has not a good Share of natural Powers and Abilities.* Hence, when we see a Young Man delivering himself in this warm Manner, he is to be regarded as a good *Genius* run wild, for want of Cultivation from Study, and the Rules of Art: And it follows, that should such a juvenile Writer, take proper

Methods to improve his Mind, in innuring himself to a close Way of
Reasoning, and by conversing with the best Authors, however defective he
might be in this Particular at first, he would in the End make a chaste
and excellent Writer. Thus it happened to the immortal *Virgil,* whose
divine *Æneid* once shot itself into so great a Luxuriance, as to be near
twenty Times as Large as it appears at this Day. As his Imagination
cooled by Years, and his Judgment ripened, and hasted on to Maturity, his
Style dropped the false Glare of Ornaments, and shone with an equal
Purity and Elegance; His Thoughts learned to proportion themselves to
his Subject, and cast themselves into that exact Symmetry of Arrangement
and Disposition, in which they now charm us; And, in a word, a new
Beauty began to dawn in every Line of that exquisite Work which conse-
crates his deathless Fame to the Admiration of all Posterity.

[1745]

⊰ These three excerpts capture the essence of post-Puritan literary theory in America. The lines from Richard Lewis' dedication are the first I have found which compare Europe and America and suggest the difficulties facing the American artist—the lament more familiar in Hawthorne and James. Nathaniel Evans asks the question many were to echo, would America ever have an art of her own? Evans' lines would seem to answer in the negative, for he leans heavily on the pastoral conventions of Europe, but a more accurate prediction can be seen in Byles' stanzas. He rejects praise for himself because he has only responded—as his lines attest—to the inspiration of Pope. British fashion was always delayed in crossing the Atlantic; enthusiasm for Pope ran higher and lasted longer in America than in England. The devotion to Addison and Pope apparent in the writing of Byles, Franklin, and Freneau reflects the theoretic assumptions that were to persist for nearly a century.

8 ⋋

. . . Nor *Here,* expect such *"soft enchanting Strains,"*
As once You heard on fair ITALIAN PLAINS;
Where, the kind Climate does the Muse inspire ⎫
With Thoughts sublime, and gay poetic Fire; ⎬
Where VIRGIL, OVID, HORACE, struck the Lyre: ⎭
Who still demand our Wonder, and our Praise;
Nor spite, nor Time, shall ever blast their Bays.

There PAINTURE breathes, *There* STATUARY lives,
And MUSIC most delightful Rapture gives:
There, pompous Piles of *Building* pierce the Skies,
And endless Scenes of *Pleasure* court the Eyes.
While *Here,* rough Woods embrown the Hills and Plains,
Mean are the *Buildings,* artless are the *Swains:*
"To raise the Genius," W E no Time can spare,
A *bare Subsistence* claims our utmost Care. . . .

[1728]

29

9 ⮌

. . . Shall fam'd Arcadia own the tuneful choir,
And fair Silicia boast the matchless lyre?
Shall Gallia's groves resound with heav'nly lays,
And Albion's poets claim immortal bays?
And this new world ne'er feel the muse's fire;
No beauties charm us, or no deeds inspire?
O Pennsylvania! shall no son of thine
Glow with the raptures of the sacred nine?
Ne'er rouze the soul, by strokes of magic kind,
Just war to wage, or humanize mankind;
With sweetest sounds the virgin's soul control,
Or in Elysium wrap the lover's soul?

"Fir'd with the thought, I court the Sylvan muse,
Her magic influence o'er me to diffuse;
Whilst I aspire to wake the rural reed,
And sing of swains, whose snowy lambkins feed
On *Schuylkill's* banks, with shady walnuts crown'd,
And bid the vales with music melt around." . . .

[1758]

10 ⮌

. . . But Oh! forbear, thy lavish Tongue be tame,
Nor flush my Features with a conscious Flame,
Justice demands that I th' Applause refuse:
Not I, but mighty Pope inspir'd thy Muse.
He, wondrous Bard! whose Numbers reach our Shore,
Tho' Oceans roll between, and Tempests roar:
Hush'd are the Storms, and smooth the Waters lie,
As his sweet Musick glides harmonious by;
Ravish'd, my Ear receives the heav'nly Guest,
My Heart high-leaping, beats my panting Breast:
Thro' all my Mind incessant Rapture reigns,
And Joys immortal revel in my veins.
So the soft SYRENS *warbled o'er the Main,*

And so ULISSES' *Soul took Wing to meet the Strain.*
O Pope! thy Fame is spread around the Sky,
Far as the Waves can flow, far as the Winds can fly!
Hail! Bard triumphant, fill'd with hallow'd Rage,
Sent from high Heav'n to grace the happy Age:
For thee a thousand Garlands shall be wove,
And ev'ry Clime project a laurel Grove;
Thy Name be heard in ev'ry artful Song,
And thy loud Praise employ each tuneful Tongue.
Ev'n my young Muse the noble Theme would take,
And lisp imperfect what she cannot speak.
'Tis Pope, my Friend, that guilds our gloomy Night,
And if I shine 'tis his reflected Light:
So the pale Moon, bright with her borrow'd Beams,
Thro' the dark Horrors shoots her silver Gleams.
Pope's are the Rules which you, my Friend, receive,
From him I gather what to you I give.
When I attend to his immortal Lyre,
I kindle instant with a sacred Fire;
Now here, now there, my Soul pursues his Song,
Hurried impetuous by his Pow'r along:
My Pulse beats thick, urg'd by my driving Blood,
And on my Breast I feel the rushing GOD.
But when to you I would the Flames convey,
In my cold Hands the holy Fires decay.
As when your Hand the Convex-Glass displays,
It close collects some scatter'd solar Rays;
Tho' cold the Glass, where'er its Focus aims,
The Object smokes, it reddens, and it flames:
So Pope, thro' me, shines full upon your Muse;
So cold *my* Breast; and so *your* Bosom glows. . . .

[1744]

Noah Webster was one of America's most influential authorities on language and style. The paragraphs which follow indicate where America was to look for its models and help explain the great popularity of Franklin's prose.

11

The great Sidney wrote in a pure stile, yet the best models of purity and elegance are the works of Sir William Temple, Dr. Middleton, Lord Bolingbroke, Mr. Addison and Dean Swift. But a litle inferior to these are the writings of Mr. Pope, Sir Richard Steele, Dr. Arbuthnot, with some of their cotemporaries. Sir William Blackstone has given the law stile all the elegance and precision of which it is capable. Dr. Price and Dr. Priestley write with purity and Sir William Jones seems to have copied the ease, simplicity and elegance of Middleton and Addison.

But how few of the modern writers have pursued the same manner of writing Johnson's stile is a mixture of Latin and English; an intolerable composition of Latinity, affected smoothness, scholastic accuracy and roundness of periods. The benefits derived from his morality and his erudition will hardly counterbalance the mischief done by his manner of writing. The names of a Robertson, a Hume, a Home and a Blair almost silence criticism, but I must repeat what a very learned Scotch gentleman once acknowledged to me, "that the Scotch writers are not models of the pure English stile." Their stile is generally stiff, sometimes very awkward, and not always correct.[1] Robertson labors his stile and sometimes introduces a word merely for the sake of rounding a period. Hume has borrowed French idioms without number; in other respects he has given an excellent model of historical stile. Lord Kames' manner is stiff; and Dr. Blair, whose stile is less exceptionable in these particulars, has however introduced into his writings several foreign idioms and ungrammatical phrases. The Scotch writers now stand almost the first for erudition, but perhaps no man can write a foreign language with genuine purity.

[1] Dr. Witherspoon is an exception. His stile is easy, simple and elegant. I consider Dr. Franklin and Dr. Witherspoon as the two best writers in America. The words they use and their arrangement appear to flow spontaneously from their manner of thinking. The vast superiority of their stiles over those of Gibbon and Gillies is owing to this circumstance, that the two American writers have bestowed their labor upon *ideas* and the English historians upon *words*.

Gibbon's harmony of prose is calculated to delight our ears, but it is difficult to comprehend his meaning and the chain of his ideas, as fast as we naturally read, and almost impossible to recollect them at any subsequent period. Perspicuity, the first requisite in stile, is sometimes sacrificed to melody, the mind of a reader is constantly dazzled by a glare of ornament or charmed from the subject by the music of the language. As he is one of the *first,* it is hoped he may be the *last,* to attempt the gratification of our *ears* at the expense of our *understanding.*

Such however is the taste of the age; simplicity of stile is neglected for ornament, and sense is sacrificed to sound.[2] . . .

[1789]

[2] The same taste prevailed in Rome under the Emperors, when genius was prostituted to the mean purposes of flattery. "It must be acknowledged indeed, that after the dissolution of the Roman republic, this art began to be perverted by being too much admired. Men grew excessively fond of the numerous stile, and readily sacrificed the strength and energy of their discourse to the harmony of their language. Pliny the younger often complains of this contemptible affectation: And Quintilian speaks of certain prose writers in his time, who boasted that their compositions were so strictly numerous, that their hearers might even beat time to their measures. And it should seem that even in Tully's time, this matter was carried to excess; since even then the orators dealt so much in numbers, that it was made a question, wherein they differed from the Poets."—Mason's Essay on the Power and Harmony of Prosaic Numbers. Introduction, page 4.

This was an abuse of the art. Melody should be studied, but not principally.

⤐ For Benjamin Franklin, that secular Puritan, American style became an emblem of directness, efficiency, industry, and commercial trust. Its aim was effectiveness: "With all true Judges, the simplest Stile is the most beautiful"; "no piece can properly be called good, and well written, which is void of any Tendency to benefit the Reader, either by improving his Virtue or his Knowledge." Franklin's plain style is a model of American prose at its best, but as the first and last selection illustrate, his assumptions led to little interest in poetry. Fortunately for lovers of Emmeline Grangerford, however, Franklin's prose aesthetic dictated burlesque as a means of discussing contemporary American verse.

12 ⤐

I approv'd the amusing one's self with Poetry now and then, so far as to improve one's language, but no farther. . . . It was proposed that we should each of us, at our next meeting, produce a piece of our own composing, in order to improve by our mutual observations, criticism, and corrections. As language and expression were what we had in view, we excluded all considerations of invention by agreeing that the task should be a version of the eighteenth Psalm. . . .

[1771]

. . . But as Prose Writing has been of great Use to me in the Course of my Life, and was a principal Means of my Advancement, I shall tell you how in such a Situation I acquir'd what little Ability I have in that Way.

There was another Bookish Lad in the Town, John Collins by Name, with whom I was intimately acquainted. We sometimes disputed, and very fond we were of Argument, and very desirous of confuting one another. Which disputacious Turn, by the way, is apt to become a very bad Habit, making People often extreamly disagreable in Company, by the Contradiction that is necessary to bring it into Practice, and thence, besides souring and spoiling the Conversation, is productive of Disgusts and perhaps Enmities where you may have occasion for Friendship. I had caught it by reading my Father's Books of Dispute about Religion. Persons of good Sense, I have since observ'd, seldom fall into it, except Lawyers, University Men, and Men of all Sorts that have been bred at Edinborough. A Question was once some how or other started between Collins and me, of the Propriety of educating the Female Sex in Learning, and their Abilities for Study. He was of Opinion that it was improper; and that they were naturally unequal to it. I took the contrary Side, perhaps a little for Dispute sake. He was naturally more eloquent, had a ready Plenty of Words, and sometimes as I thought bore me down more by his Fluency than by the Strength of his Reasons. As we parted without settling the Point, and were not to see one another again for some time, I sat down to put my Arguments in Writing, which I copied fair and sent to him. He answer'd and I reply'd. Three or four Letters of a Side had pass'd, when my Father happen'd to find my Papers, and read them. Without entring into the Discussion, he took occasion to talk to me about the Manner of my Writing, observ'd that tho' I had the Advantage of my Antagonist in correct Spelling and pointing (which I ow'd to the Printing House) I fell far short in elegance of Expression, in Method and in Perspicuity, of which he convinc'd me by several Instances. I saw the Justice of his Remarks, and thence grew more attentive to the *Manner* in Writing, and determin'd to endeavour at Improvement.

About this time I met with an odd Volume of the Spectator. It was the third. I had never before seen any of them. I bought it, read it over and over, and was much delighted with it. I thought the Writing excellent, and wish'd if possible to imitate it. With that View, I took some of the Papers, and making short Hints of the Sentiment in each Sentence, laid them by a few Days, and then without looking at the Book, try'd to compleat the Papers again, by expressing each hinted Sentiment at length and as fully as it had been express'd before, in any suitable Words, that should come to hand.

Then I compar'd my Spectator with the Original, discover'd some of my Faults and corrected them. But I found I wanted a Stock of Words or a Readiness in recollecting and using them, which I thought I should have acquir'd before that time, if I had gone on making Verses, since the continual Occasion for Words of the same Import but of different Length, to suit the Measure, or of different Sound for the Rhyme, would have laid me under a constant Necessity of searching for Variety, and also have tended to fix that Variety in my Mind, and make me Master of it. Therefore I took some of the Tales and turn'd them into Verse: And after a time, when I had pretty well forgotten the Prose, turn'd them back again. I also sometimes jumbled my Collections of Hints into Confusion, and after some Weeks, endeavour'd to reduce them into the best Order, before I began to form the full Sentences, and compleat the Paper. This was to teach me Method in the Arrangement of Thoughts. By comparing my work afterwards with the original, I discover'd many faults and amended them; but I sometimes had the Pleasure of Fancying that in certain Particulars of small Import, I had been lucky enough to improve the Method or the Language and this encourag'd me to think I might possibly in time come to be a tolerable English Writer, of which I was extreamly ambitious.

[1771]

13 🖎

To the Printer of the *Gazette*.

There are few Men, of Capacity for making any considerable Figure in Life, who have not frequent Occasion to communicate their Thoughts to others in *Writing;* if not sometimes publickly as Authors, yet continually in the Management of their private Affairs, both of Business and Friendship: and since, when ill-express'd, the most proper Sentiments and justest Reasoning lose much of their native Force and Beauty, it seems to me that there is scarce any Accomplishment more necessary to a Man of Sense, than that of *Writing well* in his Mother Tongue: But as most other polite Acquirements make a greater Appearance in a Man's Character, this however useful, is generally neglected or forgotten.

I believe there is no better Means of learning to write well, than this of attempting to entertain the Publick now and then in one of your Papers. When the Writer conceals himself, he has the Advantage of hearing the Censure both of Friends and Enemies, express'd with more Impartiality. And since, in some degree, it concerns the Credit of the Province, that such Things as are printed be performed tolerably well, mutual Improvement seems to be the Duty of all Lovers of Writing: I shall therefore frankly communicate the Observations I have made or collected on this Subject, and request those of others in Return.

I have thought in general, that whoever would write so as not to displease good Judges, should have particular Regard to these three Things, viz. That his Performance be *smooth, clear,* and *short:* For the contrary Qualities are apt to offend, either the Ear, the Understanding, or the Patience.

'Tis an Observation of Dr. Swift, that modern Writers injure the Smoothness of our Tongue, by omitting Vowels wherever it is possible, and joining the harshest Consonants together with only an Apostrophe between; thus for *judged,* in it self not the smoothest of Words, they say *judg'd;* for *disturbed, disturb'd,* &c. It may be added to this, says another, that by changing *etb* into *s,* they have shortned one Syllable in a multitude of Words, and have thereby encreased, not only the *Hissing,* too offensive before, but also the great Number of Monosyllables, of which, without great Difficulty, a smooth Sentence cannot be composed. The Smoothness of a Period is also often Hurt by Parentheses, and therefore the best Writers endeavour to avoid them.

To write *clearly,* not only the most expressive, but the plainest Words should be chosen. In this, as well as in every other Particular requisite to Clearness, Dr. Tillotson is an excellent Example. The Fondness of some Writers for such Words as carry with them an Air of Learning, renders them unintelligible to more than half their Countrymen. If a Man would that his Writings have an Effect on the Generality of Readers, he had better imitate that Gentleman, who would use no Word in his Works that was not well understood by his Cook-maid.

A too frequent Use of Phrases ought likewise to be avoided by him that would write clearly. They trouble the Language, not only rendring it extreamly difficult to Foreigners, but make the Meaning obscure to a great number of English Readers. Phrases, like learned Words, are seldom used without Affectation; when, with all true Judges, the simplest Stile is the most beautiful.

But supposing the most proper Words and Expressions chosen, the Performance may yet be weak and obscure, if it has not *Method.* If a Writer would *persuade,* he should proceed gradually from Things already allow'd, to those from which Assent is yet with-held, and make their Connection manifest. If he would *inform,* he must advance regularly from Things known to things unknown, distinctly without Confusion, and the lower he begins the better. It is a common Fault in Writers, to allow their Readers too much Knowledge: They begin with that which should be the Middle, and skipping backwards and forwards, 'tis impossible for any one but he who is perfect in the Subject before, to understand their Work, and such an one has no Occasion to read it. Perhaps a Habit of using good Method, cannot be better acquired, than by learning a little Geometry or Algebra.

Amplification, or the Art of saying Little in Much, should only be allowed to Speakers. If they preach, a Discourse of considerable Length is expected from them, upon every Subject they undertake, and perhaps they are not stock'd with naked Thoughts sufficient to furnish it out. If they plead in the Courts, it is of Use to speak abundance, tho' they reason little; for the Ignorant in a Jury, can scarcely believe it possible that a Man can talk so much and so long without being in the Right. Let them have the Liberty then, of repeating the same Sentences in other Words; let them put an Adjective to every Substantive, and double every Substantive with a Synonima; for this is more agreeable than hauking, spitting, taking Snuff, or any other Means of concealing Hesitation. Let them multiply Definitions, Comparisons, Similitudes and Examples. Permit them to make a Detail of Causes and Effects, enumerate all the Consequences, and express one Half by Metaphor and Circumlocution: Nay, allow the Preacher to tell us whatever a Thing is negatively, before he begins to tell us what it is affirmatively; and suffer him to divide and subdivide as far as *Two and fiftiethly.* All this is not intolerable while it is not written. But when a Discourse is to be bound down upon Paper, and subjected to the calm leisurely Examination of nice Judgment, every Thing that is needless gives Offence; and therefore all should be retrenched, that does not directly conduce to the End design'd. Had this been always done, many large and tiresome Folio's would have shrunk into Pamphlets, and many a Pamphlet into a single Period. However, tho' a multitude of Words obscure the Sense, and 'tis necessary to abridge a verbose Author in order to understand him; yet a Writer should take especial Care on the other Hand, that his Brevity doth not hurt his Perspicuity.

After all, if the Author does not intend his Piece for general Reading, he must exactly suit his Stile and Manner to the particular Taste of those he proposes for his Readers. Every one observes, the different Ways of Writing and Expression used by the Different Sects of Religion; and can readily enough pronounce, that it is improper to use some of these Stiles in common, or to use the common Stile, when we address some of these Sects in particular.

To conclude, I shall venture to lay it down as a Maxim, *That no Piece can properly be called good, and well written, which is void of any Tendency to benefit the Reader, either by improving his Virtue or his Knowledge.* This Principle every Writer would do well to have in View, whenever he undertakes to write. All Performances done for meer Ostentation of Parts, are really contemptible; and withal far more subject to the Severity of Criticism, than those more meanly written, wherein the

Author appears to have aimed at the Good of others. For when 'tis visible to every one, that a Man writes to show his Wit only, all his Expressions are sifted, and his Sense examined, in the nicest and most ill-natur'd manner; and every one is glad of an Opportunity to mortify him. But, what a vast Destruction would there be of Books, if they were to be saved or condemned on a Tryal by this Rule!

Besides, Pieces meerly humorous, are of all Sorts the hardest to succeed in. If they are not natural, they are stark naught; and there can be no real Humour in an Affectation of Humour.

Perhaps it may be said, that an ill Man is able to write an ill Thing well; that is, having an ill Design, and considering who are to be his Readers, he may use the properest Stile and Arguments to attain his Point. In this Sense, that is best wrote, which is best adapted to the Purpose of the Writer.

I am apprehensive, dear Readers, lest in this Piece, I should be guilty of every Fault I condemn, and deficient in every Thing I recommend; so much easier it is to offer Rules than to practise them. I am sure, however, of this, that I am Your very sincere Friend and Servant.

[1733]

14 ✍

. . . We lived happily together in the Heighth of conjugal Love and mutual Endearments, for near Seven Years, in which Time we added Two likely Girls and a Boy to the Family of the Dogoods: But alas! When my Sun was in its meridian Altitude, inexorable unrelenting Death, as if he had envy'd my Happiness and Tranquility, and resolv'd to make me entirely miserable by the Loss of so good an Husband, hastened his Flight to the Heavenly World, by a sudden unexpected Departure from this.

I have now remained in a State of Widowhood for several Years, but it is a State I never much admir'd, and I am apt to fancy that I could be easily perswaded to marry again, provided I was sure of a good-humour'd, sober, agreeable Companion: But one, even with these few good Qualities, being hard to find, I have lately relinquish'd all Thoughts of that Nature.

At present I pass away my leisure Hours in Conversation, either with my honest Neighbour Rusticus and his Family, or with the ingenious Minister of our Town, who now lodges at my House, and by whose Assistance I intend now and then to beautify my Writings with a Sen-

tence or two in the learned Languages, which will not only be fashionable, and pleasing to those who do not understand it, but will likewise be
very ornamental. . . .   Silence Dogood
                                                              [1722]

> *Give me the Muse, whose generous Force,*
>   *Impatient of the Reins,*
> *Pursues an unattempted Course,*
>   *Breaks all the Criticks Iron Chains.*   Watts.

To the Author of the *New-England Courant*.

Sir,

It had been the Complaint of many Ingenious Foreigners, who have
travell'd amongst us, *That good Poetry is not to be expected in New-
England*. I am apt to Fancy, the Reason is, not because our Countreymen
are altogether void of a Poetical Genius, nor yet because we have not those
Advantages of Education which other Countries have, but purely because
we do not afford that Praise and Encouragement which is merited, when
any thing extraordinary of this Kind is produc'd among us: Upon which
Consideration I have determined, when I meet with a Good Piece of New-
England Poetry, to give it a suitable Encomium, and thereby endeavour to
discover to the World some of its Beautys, in order to encourage the
Author to go on, and bless the World with more, and more Excellent
Productions.

There has lately appear'd among us a most Excellent Piece of Poetry,
entituled, *An Elegy upon the much Lamented Death of Mrs. Mehitebell
Kitel, Wife of Mr. John Kitel of Salem, &c*. It may justly be said in its
Praise, without Flattery to the Author, that it is the most *Extraordinary*
Piece that ever was wrote in New-England. The Language is so soft and
Easy, the Expression so moving and pathetick, but above all, the Verse
and Numbers so Charming and Natural, that it is almost beyond
Comparison,

> *The Muse disdains*
>   *Those Links and Chains,*
> *Measures and Rules of vulgar Strains,*
> *And o'er the Laws of Harmony a Sovereign Queen she reigns.**

* Watts.

I find no English Author, Ancient or Modern, whose Elegies may be compar'd with this, in respect to the Elegance of Stile, or Smoothness of Rhime; and for the affecting Part, I will leave your Readers to judge, if ever they read any Lines, that would sooner make them *draw their Breath* and Sigh, if not shed Tears, than these following.

> *Come let us mourn, for we have lost a Wife, a Daughter, and*
> *a Sister,*
> *Who has lately taken Flight, and greatly we have mist her.*

In another Place,

> Some little Time *before she yielded up her Breath,*
> *She said, I ne'er shall hear one Sermon more on Earth.*
> *She kist her Husband some little Time before she expir'd,*
> *Then lean'd her Head the Pillow on, just out of Breath and tir'd.*

But the Threefold Appellation in the first Line

> *a Wife, a Daughter, and a Sister,*

must not pass unobserved. That Line in the celebrated Watts,

> GUNSTON *the Just, the Generous, and the Young,*

is nothing Comparable to it. The latter only mentions three Qualifications of *one* Person who was deceased, which therefore could raise Grief and Compassion but for *One.* Whereas the former, (*our most excellent Poet*) gives his Reader a Sort of an Idea of the Death of *Three Persons,* viz.

> *a Wife, a Daughter, and a Sister,*

which is *Three Times* as great a Loss as the Death of *One,* and consequently must raise *Three Times* as much Grief and Compassion in the Reader.

I should be very much straitned for Room, if I should attempt to discover even half the Excellencies of this Elegy which are obvious to me. Yet I cannot omit one Observation, which is, that the Author has (to his Honour) invented a new Species of Poetry, which wants a Name, and was never before known. His Muse scorns to be confin'd to the old Measures and Limits, or to observe the dull Rules of Criticks;

> *Nor Rapin gives her Rules to fly, nor Purcell Notes to sing.* Watts.

Now 'tis Pity that such an Excellent Piece should not be dignify'd with a particular Name; and seeing it cannot justly be called, either *Epic, Sapphic, Lyric,* or *Pindaric,* nor any other Name yet invented, I presume it may, (in Honour and Remembrance of the Dead) be called the KITELIC. Thus much in the Praise of *Kitelic Poetry*.

It is certain, that those Elegies which are of our own Growth, (and our Soil seldom produces any other sort of Poetry) are by far the greatest part, wretchedly Dull and Ridiculous. Now since it is imagin'd by many, that our Poets are honest, well-meaning Fellows, who do their best, and that if they had but some Instructions how to govern Fancy with Judgment, they would make indifferent good Elegies; I shall here subjoin a Receipt for that purpose, which was left me as a Legacy, (among other valuable Rarities) by my Reverend Husband. It is as follows,

A RECEIPT to make a New-England Funeral ELEGY.

For the Title of your Elegy. Of these you may have enough ready made to your Hands; but if you should chuse to make it your self, you must be sure not to omit the Words *Aetatis Suae,* which will Beautify it exceedingly.

For the Subject of your Elegy. Take one of your Neighbours who has lately departed this Life; it is no great matter at what Age the Party dy'd, but it will be best if he went away suddenly, being *Kill'd, Drown'd,* or *Froze to Death.*

Having chose the Person, take all his Virtues, Excellencies, &c. and if he have not enough, you may borrow some to make up a sufficient Quantity: To these add his last Words, dying Expressions, &c. if they are to be had; mix all these together, and be sure you *strain* them well. Then season all with a Handful or two of Melancholly Expressions, such as, *Dreadful, Deadly, cruel cold Death, unhappy Fate, weeping Eyes,* &c. Have mixed all these Ingredients well, put them into the empty Scull of some *young Harvard;* (but in Case you have ne'er a One at Hand, you may use your own,) there let them Ferment for the Space of a Fortnight, and by that Time they will be incorporated into a Body, which take out, and having prepared a sufficient Quantity of double Rhimes, such as, *Power, Flower; Quiver, Shiver; Grieve us, Leave us; tell you, excel you; Expeditions, Physicians; Fatigue him, Intrigue him;* &c. you must spread all upon Paper, and if you can procure a Scrap of Latin to put at the End, it will garnish it mightily; then having affixed your Name at the Bottom, with a *Mœstus Composuit,* you will have an Excellent Elegy.

N.B. This Receipt will serve when a Female is the Subject of your Elegy, provided you borrow a greater Quantity of Virtues, Excellencies, &c. Sir, Your Servant, SILENCE DOGOOD

[1722]

❧ *Crèvecoeur appealed to Europe's interest in America by masquerading as a simple American farmer responding to requests for information from abroad. The following selection begins in the center of a discussion between the farmer, his minister, and the farmer's wife—whose remarks at one point seem close to Hawthorne's quip that some would say he had as well be a fiddler as a writer. Crèvecoeur's style belies the roughhewn naïveté he attributes to his farmer, but the letter does illustrate the virtues civilization expected from the untutored Western writer, virtues later claimed by "Walt Whitman—rough."*

15 ❧

. . . The art of writing is just like unto every other art of man; . . . it is acquired by habit, and by perseverance. That is singularly true, said our minister, he that shall write a letter every day of the week, will on Saturday perceive the sixth flowing from his pen much more readily than the first. I observed when I first entered into the ministry and began to preach the word, I felt perplexed and dry, my mind was like unto a parched soil, which produced nothing, not even weeds. By the blessing of heaven, and my perseverance in study, I grew richer in thoughts, phrases, and words; I felt copious, and now I can abundantly preach from any text that occurs to my mind. So will it be with you, neighbour James; begin therefore without delay; and Mr. F. B.'s letters may be of great service to you: he will, no doubt, inform you of many things: correspondence consists in reciprocal letters. Leave off your diffidence, and I will do my best to help you whenever I have any leisure. Well then, I am resolved, I said, to follow your counsel; my letters shall not be sent, nor will I receive any, without reading them to you and my wife; women are curious, they love to know their husband's secrets; it will not be the first thing which I have submitted to your joint opinons. Whenever you come to dine with us, these shall be the last dish on the table. Nor will they be the most unpalatable, answered the good man. Nature hath given you a tolerable share of sense, and that is one of her best gifts let me tell you. She has given you besides some perspicuity, which qualifies you to distinguish interesting objects; a warmth of imagination which enables you to think with quickness; you often extract useful reflections from objects which presented none to my mind: you have a tender and a well meaning heart, you love description, and your pencil, assure yourself, is not a bad one for the pencil of a farmer; it seems to be held without any labour; your mind is what we called at Yale college a *Tabula rasa,* where spontaneous and strong impressions are delineated with facility. Ah, neighbour! had you received but half the education of Mr. F. B. you had been a worthy correspondent indeed. But perhaps you will be a more entertaining one dressed in your simple American garb, than if you were clad in all the gowns of Cambridge. You will appear to him something like one of our wild American plants, irregularly luxuriant in its various branches, which an European scholar may probably think ill placed and useless. If our soil is not remarkable as yet for the excellence of its fruits, this exuberance is however a strong proof of fertility, which wants nothing but the progressive knowledge acquired by time to amend and to correct. It is easier to retrench than it is to add; I do not mean to flatter you, neighbour James, adulation would ill become my character, you may therefore believe what your pastor says. Were I in Europe I should be tired with perpetually seeing espaliers, plashed hedges, and trees dwarfed into pigmies. Do let Mr. F. B. see on paper a few American wild cherry trees, such as nature forms them here, in all her unconfined vigour, in all the amplitude of their extended limbs and spreading ramifications—let him see that we are possessed with strong vegetative embryos. After all, why should not a farmer be allowed to make use of his mental faculties as well as others; because a man works, is not he to think, and if he thinks usefully, why should not he in his leisure hours set down his thoughts? I have composed many a good sermon as I followed my plough. The eyes not being then engaged on any particular object, leaves the mind free for the introduction of many useful ideas. It is not in the noisy shop of a blacksmith or of a carpenter, that these studious moments can be enjoyed; it is as we silently till the ground, and muse along the odoriferous furrows of our low lands, uninterrupted either by stones or stumps; it is there that the salubrious effluvia of the earth animate our spirits and serve to inspire us; every other avocation of our farms are severe labours compared to this pleasing occupation: of all the tasks which mine imposes on me ploughing is the most agreeable, because I can think as I work; my mind is at leisure; my labour flows from instinct, as well as that of my horses; there is no kind of difference between us in our different shares of that operation; one of them keeps the furrow, the other avoids it; at the end of my field they turn either to the right or left as they are bid, whilst I thoughtlessly hold and guide the plough to which they are harnessed. Do therefore, neighbour, begin this correspondence, and persevere, difficulties

will vanish in proportion as you draw near them; you'll be surprised at
yourself by and by: when you come to look back you'll say as I have often
said to myself; had I been diffident I had never proceeded thus far. Would
you painfully till your stony up-land and neglect the fine rich bottom
which lies before your door? Had you never tried, you never had learned
how to mend and make your ploughs. It will be no small pleasure to your
children to tell hereafter, that their father was not only one of the most
industrious farmers in the country, but one of the best writers. When you
have once begun, do as when you begin breaking up your summer fallow,
you never consider what remains to be done, you view only what you
have ploughed. Therefore, neighbour James, take my advice; it will go
well with you, I am sure it will.——And do you really think so, Sir? Your
counsel, which I have long followed, weighs much with me, I verily believe that I must write to Mr. F. B. by the first vessel.——If thee persistest
in being such a foolhardy man, said my wife, for God's sake let it be kept
a profound secret among us; if it were once known abroad that thee
writest to a great and rich man over at London, there would be no end of
the talk of the people; some would vow that thee art going to turn an
author, others would pretend to foresee some great alterations in the welfare of thy family; some would say this, some would say that: Who would
wish to become the subject of public talk? Weigh this matter well before
thee beginnest, James—consider that a great deal of thy time, and of thy
reputation is at stake as I may say. Wert thee to write as well as friend
Edmund, whose speeches I often see in our papers, it would be the very
self same thing; thee wouldst be equally accused of idleness, and vain notions not befitting thy condition. Our colonel would be often coming here
to know what it is that thee canst write so much about. Some would
imagine that thee wantest to become either an assemblyman or a magistrate, which God forbid; and that thee art telling the king's men abundance of things. Instead of being well looked upon as now, and living in
peace with all the world, our neighbours would be making strange sur-
mises: I had rather be as we are, neither better nor worse than the rest of
our country folks. Thee knowest what I mean, though I should be sorry
to deprive thee of any honest recreation. Therefore as I have said before,
let it be as great a secret as if it was some heinous crime; the minister, I
am sure, will not divulge it; as for my part, though I am a woman, yet I
know what it is to be a wife.—I would not have thee, James, pass for what
the world calleth a writer; no, not for a peck of gold, as the saying is. Thy
father before thee was a plain dealing honest man, punctual in all things;
he was one of yea and nay, of few words, all he minded was his farm and

his work. I wonder from whence thee hast got this love of the pen? Had he spent his time in sending epistles to and fro, he never would have left thee this goodly plantation, free from debt. All I say is in good meaning; great people over sea may write to our town's folks, because they have nothing else to do. These Englishmen are strange people; because they can live upon what they call bank notes, without working, they think that all the world can do the same. This goodly country never would have been tilled and cleared with these notes. I am sure when Mr. F. B. was here, he saw thee sweat and take abundance of pains; he often told me how the Americans worked a great deal harder than the home Englishmen; for there he told us, that they have no trees to cut down, no fences to make, no negroes to buy and to clothe: and now I think on it, when wilt thee send him those trees he bespoke? But if they have no trees to cut down, they have gold in abundance, they say; for they rake it and scrape it from all parts far and near. I have often heard my grandfather tell how they live there by writing. By writing they send this cargo unto us, that to the West, and the other to the East Indies. But, James, thee knowest that it is not by writing that we shall pay the blacksmith, the minister, the weaver, the tailor, and the English shop. But as thee art an early man follow thine own inclinations; thee wantest some rest, I am sure, and why shouldst thee not employ it as it may seem meet unto thee.—However let it be a great secret; how wouldst thee bear to be called at our country meetings, the man of the pen? If this scheme of thine was once known, travellers as they go along would point out to our house, saying, here liveth the scribbling farmer; better hear them as usual observe, here liveth the warm substantial family, that never begrudgeth a meal of victuals, or a mess of oats, to any one that steps in. Look how fat and well clad their negroes are.

Thus, Sir, have I given you an unaffected and candid detail of the conversation which determined me to accept of your invitation. I thought it necessary thus to begin, and to let you into these primary secrets, to the end that you may not hereafter reproach me with any degree of presumption. You'll plainly see the motives which have induced me to begin, the fears which I have entertained, and the principles on which my diffidence hath been founded. I have now nothing to do but to prosecute my task— Remember you are to give me my subjects, and on no other shall I write, lest you should blame me for an injudicious choice—However incorrect my style, however unexpert my methods, however trifling my observations may hereafter appear to you, assure yourself they will all be the genuine dictates of my mind, and I hope will prove acceptable on that account. Remember that you have laid the foundation of this correspondence; you well know that I am neither a philosopher, politician, divine, nor naturalist, but a simple farmer. I flatter myself, therefore, that you'll receive my letters as conceived, not according to scientific rules to which I am a perfect stranger, but agreeable to the spontaneous impressions which each subject may inspire. This is the only line I am able to follow, the line which nature has herself traced for me; this was the covenant which I made with you, and with which you seemed to be well pleased. Had you wanted the style of the learned, the reflections of the patriot, the discussions of the politician, the curious observations of the naturalist, the pleasing garb of the man of taste, surely you would have applied to some of those men of letters with which our cities abound. But since on the contrary, and for what reason I know not, you wish to correspond with a cultivator of the earth, with a simple citizen, you must receive my letters for better or worse.

[1782]

Political independence only served to emphasize American cultural provincialism; condescending attacks both at home and abroad seemed to sting all the more as their truth grew increasingly apparent. Jefferson's defense follows a pattern that was to become classic in the next few decades: America may not have a literature as yet, but time will certainly see one develop. And besides, all men must recognize the greatness of those who have already made their contribution in more practical areas. The Freneau verses which follow repeat the lament that America has done little to encourage art. His couplets suggest that Pope's influence remained strong, and even the theater dedication of 1815 merely claims a native platform for Shakespeare and Congreve.

16

. . . So far the Count de Buffon has carried this new theory of the tendency of nature to belittle her productions on this side of the Atlantic. Its application to the race of whites, transplanted from Europe, remained for the Abbé Raynal. "One must be astonished (he says) that America has not yet produced one good poet, one able mathematician, one man of genius in a single art or a single science." "America has not yet produced one good poet." When we shall have existed as a people as long as the Greeks did before they produced a Homer, the Romans a Virgil, the French a Racine and Voltaire, the English a Shakespeare and Milton, should this reproach be still true, we will enquire from what unfriendly causes it has proceeded, that the other countries of Europe and quarters of the earth shall not have inscribed any name in the roll of poets. But neither has America produced "one able mathematician, one man of genius in a single art or a single science." In war we have produced a Washington, whose memory will be adored while liberty shall have votaries, whose name will triumph over time, and will in future ages assume its just station among the most celebrated worthies of the world, when that wretched philosophy shall be forgotten which would have arranged him among the degeneracies of nature. In physics we have produced a Franklin, than whom no one of the present age has made more important discoveries, nor has enriched philosophy with more, or more ingenious solutions of the phænomena of nature. . . .

[1787]

17

. . . Thrice happy Dryden, who could meet
Some rival bard in every street!
When all were bent on writing well
It was some credit to excel:—

Thrice happy Dryden, who could find
A *Milbourne* for his sport designed—
And *Pope,* who saw the harmless rage
Of *Dennis* bursting o'er his page
Might justly spurn the *critic's aim,*
Who only helped to swell his fame.

On these bleak climes by Fortune thrown,
Where rigid *Reason* reigns alone,
Where lovely *Fancy* has no sway,
Nor magic forms about us play—
Nor nature takes her summer hue
Tell me, what has the muse to do?—

An age employed in edging steel
Can no poetic raptures feel;
No solitude's atracting power,
No leisure of the noon day hour,
No shaded stream, no quiet grove
Can this fantastic century move. . . .

[1788]

18

LITERARY IMPORTATION.

However we wrangled with Britain awhile
We think of her now in a different stile,
And many fine things we receive from her isle;
Among all the rest,
Some demon possessed

Our dealers in knowledge and sellers of sense
To have a good *bishop* imported from thence.

The words of *Sam Chandler** were thought to be vain,
When he argued so often and proved it *so plain*
"That Satan must flourish till bishops should reign:"
Though he went to the wall
With his project and all,
Another bold Sammy,† in bishop's array,
Has got something more than his pains for his pay.

It seems we had spirit to humble a throne,
Have genius for science inferior to none,
But hardly encourage a plant of our own:
If a college be planned,
'Tis all at a stand
'Till in Europe we send at a shameful expense,
To send us a book-worm to teach us some sense.

Can we never be thought to have learning or grace
Unless it be brought from that horrible place
Where tyranny reigns with her impudent face;
And popes and pretenders,
And sly faith-defenders
Have ever been hostile to reason and wit,
Enslaving a world that shall conquer them yet.

'Tis folly to fret at the picture I draw:
And I say what was said by a *Doctor Magraw,*
"If they give us their Bishops, they'll give us their law."
How that will agree
With such people as we,
Let us leave to the learned to reflect on awhile,
And say what they think in a handsomer stile.

[1788]

---

* Who laboured for the establishment of an American Episcopacy, previous to the revolutionary war.

† Freneau refers here to Bishop Samuel Seabury of Connecticut, the first Anglican bishop in America. [Ed.]

19 ✍

THE DISTREST THEATRE.*

Health to the Muse!—and fill the glass,—
Heaven grant her soon some better place,
Than earthen floor and fabric mean,
Where disappointment shades the scene:

There as I came, by rumour led,
I sighed and almost wished her dead;
Her visage stained with many a tear,
No HALLAM and no HENRY here!

But what could all their art attain?—
When pointed laws the stage restrain
The prudent Muse obedience pays
To sleepy squires, that damn all plays

Like thieves they hang beyond the town,
They shove her off—to please the gown;—
Though Rome and Athens owned it true,
The stage might mend our morals *too.*

See, *Mopsus* all the evening sits
O'er bottled beer, that drowns his wits;
Were Plays allowed, he might at least
Blush—and no longer act the beast.

See, *Marcia,* now from guardian free,
Retailing scandal with her tea;—
Might she not come, nor danger fear
From *Hamlet's* sigh, or *Juliet's* tear.

The world but acts the player's part†—
(So says the motto of their art)—
That world in vice great lengths is gone
That fears to see its picture drawn.

* Harmony Hall, at Charleston, now demolished.
† *Totus Mundus agit Historionem.*

Mere vulgar actors cannot please;
The streets supply enough of these;
And what can wit or beauty gain
When sleepy dullness joins their train?

A *State* betrays a homely taste,
By which the stage is thus disgraced,
Where, drest in all the flowers of speech,
Dame virtue might her precepts teach.

Let but a dancing bear arrive,
A pig, that counts you four, or five—
And Cato, with his moral strain
May strive to mend the world in vain.

[1791]

20 🖎

Lines

on the

ESTABLISHMENT OF THE NEW THEATRE

and the management of the house being placed
in the hands of Mr. Cooper.—

Quid Sophocles, et Thespis, et Aeschylus utile ferrent
Tentavit quoque, rem si digne vertere posset.—Hor.

This noble pile, superbly great
In *Athens,* might have graced her state,
And rivals all that London claims
From brilliant scenes, and boasted names.

Whate'er the tragic muse affords
Will *here* be told in glowing words:
From magic scenes to charm the eyes
All nature's pictures will arise.

And she, who charms the sprightly throng,
The goddess of the comic song
The muse of laughter, and of jest
Will bring amusement with the rest.

And Cooper, here, who leads the train
Of sorrow, pleasure, pity, pain,
A Roscius, of superior powers,
The modern Garrick now is ours.

He will display on nature's stage
(Or nature copied from her page)
The force of all that Shakespeare writ,
All Otway's grief and Congreve's wit.

With him a chosen band agree
To make the stage what it should be,
The serious moral to impart,
To cheer the mind and mend the heart.

The manners of the age t'improve,
To enforce the power of virtuous love,
Chaste morals in the soul t'implant
Which most admire, and many want.

On such a plan, theatric shows
Do honor to the thespian muse,
Impart a polish to the mind;
Instruct and civilize mankind.

Ye sages who in morals deal,
But all the pleasing side conceal,
From hence confess that morals may
As surely take the brilliant way.

With such an object in our view
Let Thespis all her art pursue,
When autumn brings the lengthening nights
And reason to her feast invites.—

[1815]

⤜ *David Humphreys' On the Happiness of America runs some 678 lines. As he says in the Preface, his purpose is to enumerate the pleasures of American life, among them the rich material available to the poet. This is the first effort I have found to list "the splendid spoils of other times" which America lacks. Unlike Hawthorne, James, and countless others, however, Humphreys anticipates Goethe in regarding liability as asset: Irving's romanticized "mouldering piles" become mere "piles of rubbish."*

21 ⤜

. . . The Americans, whose exertions and sufferings had been rewarded by the acquisition of Independence, were, however, at the end of the war, surrounded with threatening prospects. In these circumstances the writer endeavoured to show his countrymen the superior advantages for happiness which they possessed; to dissipate their gloomy apprehensions, by the exhibition of consolatory anticipations; and to make them think favourably of their own situation when compared with that of other nations. Many circumstances conspired to give facility to the execution of the task he had imposed on himself. The ideas were principally suggested by the peculiarity of our condition. We began our political career, in a great measure, free from the prejudice, and favoured with the knowledge of former ages and other nations. The amiable innocence and simplicity of manners which resulted from the present state of society in America, offered a curious subject for philosophical contemplation. Our minds, imperceptibly impressed with the novelty, beauty, or sublimity of surrounding objects, gave energy to the language which expressed our sensations. While the shades of changing nature, which diversified the scenery through all the intermediate stages of settlement and population, from the rude grandeur of a wilderness to the pleasant landscapes of cultivation, afforded an extensive field for variegated description. To an assemblage of such magnificent images, so proper for poetry, were added, a multitude of incidents derived from the delights of agricultural life, the blessings of enlightened society, and the progress of human improvements. The author, by thus availing himself of circumstances, was enabled to gratify an early and decided propensity for contemplating the beauties of creation, especially under that point of view in which they are most conspicuously beneficial to his fellow men.

[1790]

No feudal ties the rising genius mar,
Compel to servile toils or drag to war;
But free each youth, his fav'rite course pursues,
The plough paternal, or the sylvan muse;
For here exists, once more, th' Arcadian scene,
Those simple manners, and that golden mean:
Here holds society its middle stage,
Between too rude and too refin'd an age:
Far from that age, when not a gleam of light
The dismal darkness cheer'd of Gothic night,
From brutal rudeness of that savage state—
As from refinements which o'erwhelm the great,
Those dissipations which their bliss annoy,
And blast and poison each domestic joy.

What though for us, the pageantry of kings,
Crowns, thrones, and sceptres, are superfluous things;
What though we lack the gaudy pomp that waits
On eastern monarchs, or despotic states;
Yet well we spare what realms despotic feel,
Oppression's scourge, and persecution's wheel.

What though no splendid spoils of other times
Invite the curious to these western climes;
No virtuoso, with fantastic aim,
Here hunts the shadow of departd fame:
No piles of rubbish his attention call,
Nor mystic obelisk, or storied wall:
No ruin'd statues claim the long research:
No sliding columns and no crumbling arch;
Inscriptions, half effac'd, and falsely read,
Or cumbrous relics of th' unletter'd dead:
Yet here I rove untrodden scenes among,
Catch inspiration for my rising song;
See nature's grandeur awfully unfold,
And, wrapt in thought, her works sublime behold!
For here vast wilds, which human foot ne'er trod,
Are mark'd with footsteps of a present God:
His forming hand, on nature's broadest scale,
O'er mountains, mountains pil'd, and scoop'd the vale;

Made sea-like streams in deeper channels run,
And roll'd through brighter heav'ns his genial sun.
In vain of day, that rolling lucid eye
Look'd down in mildness from the smiling sky;
In vain, the germe of vegetation lay,
And pin'd in shades, secluded from the day;
In vain, this theatre for man so fair,
Spread all its charms for beasts or birds of air;
Or savage tribes, who, wand'ring through the wood,
From beasts and birds obtain'd precarious food:
Till great Columbus rose, and, led by heav'n,
Call'd worlds to view, beneath the skirts of ev'n. . . .

[1786?]

≥ *Tyler's Prologue urges acceptance of his play for its use of American materials, but his audience has usually been most pleased by the success with which it imitates English Restoration comedy. Brother Jonathan is a fresh Yankee character, Maria sings of Indians, and Manly triumphs over the Chesterfieldian Dimple in the contrast which gives the play its title, but the work remains nonetheless British. The Prologue does suggest, however, that the need for greater literary autonomy was widely felt; like Tyler's other claims on our applause, the assertion of nationality fast becomes a convention.*

22 ✍

The Subscribers (to whom the Editor thankfully professes his obligations) may reasonably expect an apology for the delay which has attended the appearance of THE CONTRAST; but, as the true cause cannot be declared without leading to a discussion which the Editor wishes to avoid, he hopes that the care and expence which have been bestowed upon this work will be accepted, without further scrutiny, as an atonement for his seeming negligence.

In justice to the Author, however, it may be proper to observe that this Comedy has many claims to the public indulgence independent of its intrinsic merits: It is the first essay of American genius in a difficult species of composition; it was written by one who never critically studied the rules of the drama and, indeed, had seen but few of the exhibitions of the stage; it was undertaken and finished in the course of three weeks; and the profits of one night's performance were appropriated to the benefit of the sufferers by the fire at *Boston*.

These considerations will therefore it is hoped supply in the closet the advantages that are derived from representation, and dispose the reader to join in the applause which has been bestowed on this Comedy by numerous and judicious audiences in the Theatres of *Philadelphia, New-York,* and *Maryland*.

Written by a YOUNG GENTLEMAN *of New-York, and*
Spoken by MR. WIGNELL

Exult each patriot heart!—this night is shewn
A piece, which we may fairly call our own;
Where the proud titles of "My Lord! Your Grace!"
To humble Mr and plain Sir give place.
Our Author pictures not from foreign climes
The fashions, or the follies of the times;
But has confin'd the subject of his work
To the gay scenes—the circles of New-York.
On native themes his Muse displays her pow'rs;
If ours the faults, the virtues too are ours.
Why should our thoughts to distant countries roam,
When each refinement may be found at home?
Who travels now to ape the rich or great,
To deck an equipage and roll in state;
To court the graces, or to dance with ease,
Or by hypocrisy to strive to please?
Our free-born ancestors such arts despis'd;
Genuine sincerity alone they priz'd;
Their minds, with honest emulation fir'd,
To solid good—not ornament—aspir'd;
Or, if ambition rous'd a bolder flame,
Stern virtue throve, where indolence was shame.

But modern youths, with imitative sense,
Deem taste in dress the proof of excellence;
And spurn the meanness of your homespun arts,
Since homespun habits would obscure their parts;
Whilst all, which aims at splendour and parade,
Must come from Europe, and be ready made.
Strange! we should thus our native worth disclaim,
And check the progress of our rising fame.
Yet one, whilst imitation bears the sway,
Aspires to nobler heights, and points the way,
Be rous'd, my friends! his bold example view;
Let your own Bards be proud to copy you!

Should rigid critics reprobate our play,
At least the patriotic heart will say,
"Glorious our fall, since in a noble cause.
"The bold attempt alone demands applause."
Still may the wisdom of the Comic Muse
Exalt your merits, or your faults accuse.
But think not, 'tis her aim to be severe;—
We all are mortals, and as mortals err.
If candour pleases, we are truly blest;
Vice trembles, when compell'd to stand confess'd.
Let not light Censure on your faults, offend.
Which aims not to expose them, but amend.
Thus does our Author to your candour trust;
Conscious, the free are generous, as just.

[1790]

> Brackenridge was a satirist in the great British tradition, and his playful remarks on the simple style comment seriously on American prose. They are, in fact, Franklin's norms set once again in comic frame.

23 *<*

Proceeding with my object; the giving an example of a perfect stile in writing, I come now to the third volume of the work. I well know, that it will not all at once, and by all persons, be thought to be the model of a perfect stile, for it is only the perfectly instructed, and delicately discerning that can discover its beauties: and perhaps none will be more apt to pass them by than the learned of the academies, versed in grammar rules of writing, for there is a greenness in the judgment of the school critics with respect to what is simple and natural in composition.

To illustrate this by analogy. Let a dancing master pass his judgment on the movements of the best bred man in life; and not finding in his position and attitudes, an evident conformity to the lessons of the saltatory art, he will conclude that he has not been taught to move with propriety. He does not know that it is this very circumstance that constitutes the excellence of the movements of the easy and perfectly genteel man; to wit, that when you observe him, it will never once come into your mind that he thinks of his attitudes or positions in the least; but that every movement is just as it happens, and without any intention on his part. Ars est celare artem. To wit; It is the secret of good taste and perfection in behavior to conceal that you ever think of it at all. So it is the most perfect proof of a good stile, that when you read the composition, you think of nothing but the sense; and are never struck with the idea that it is otherwise expressed than every body would express it.

That stile, is not good, where it appears that you have not dared to use a word without thinking a long time whether you ought to use it; that, in the disposition of words, you have carefully studied which ought to go first and which last; and, that your sentence has a cadence which could not come by chance; but is the effect of design and art.

I acknowledge that no man will ever possess a good stile that has not well studied, and exercised himself in writing, selecting with a most perfect delicacy, in all cases, the proper term; but he must go beyond this, and be able to deceive the world, and, never let it come into their heads that he has spent a thought on the subject. But it is not one in five hundred that is born with such sensibility of nerve as to be able to attain with the help of great instruction and practice, a perfect judgment in the use of words. It is for this reason that I am ambitious of the praise of writing well so far as respects language. For it requires no uncommon structure of nerves, or organization of the brain to produce good sense; the mass of mankind is equal to this.

Language, as it is the peculiar gift, so it is the highest glory of our species; and the philologist is to be considered as cultivating the most useful and ornamental of all arts. Pursuing therefore solely the use of words, I do not descend professedly to think of sense; nevertheless, if at any time there should be found ideas that have some consistency and meaning, they may deserve attention, as much as if it was the primary object of my work to express them; for it is not their fault if I set little store by them, and think more of the dress that I put upon them than I do of themselves.

I am happy to find that in the review of this publication, given in Young's magazine, my ideas of the merit of the stile, is recognized, and fully justified. And as my work may be well supposed, to have a much more extensive circulation, and to live longer than that miscellaneous performance, I have thought it not amiss, for the honor of the critics to extract some part of the observations which have been made by them, and which are as follows:

"The author of the work before us, is H. H. Brackenridge, well known in the literary world for his treatise of the oeconomy of Rats, a satirical composition, in which under the veil of allegory, he designates the measures of the federal government; as also for his history of Weazels, in which the same strokes are given to those at the helm of our affairs, in a different fable, and narration. In the present work which he entitles Modern Chivalry, he disowns the idea of any moral or sentiment whatsoever, and proposes stile only as the object of the composition. And to this object, in our opinion, he scrupulously adheres; for though on some occasions, there would seem to be a semblance of idea, yet this we must attribute to the imagination of the reader, just as in looking upon a plaistered wall, attentively for a long time, you will conceive the inequality of the surface, or accidental scratchings, to be the shape of birds and beasts, or the letters of the alphabet. Yet as reason in this case will correct the fancy, and bring to mind that there is really no character or image there, there being none intended; so on a perusal of the work in question, looking a long time for sense, you may at last conceive that you observe some glimmerings of it, yet when you recollect that you have it from the author himself that he means none, you will be sensible that it is nothing more than the accidental combination of words which has given this picture to the mind.

Stile, then, which is his object, must also be ours, in our view of the publication. For, to give a simile; if a manufacturer of cloth, or a taylor that forms it into vestments, should come forward, and produce each his work, to be considered merely as to the manufacture, or making up, without regard to the materials of the woof and warp in the one case, or the wearing in the other, it would be absurd to enquire of these when nothing was proposed to you respecting them, by the artists themselves.

Confining ourselves therefore to the stile of this performance, we observe, that it has what is the first characteristic of excellence; viz. Simplicity. This consists in the choice of the plainest and most familiar words, and in the arrangement of the words in their natural order. There is a great difference between a vulgar term, or phrase, and that which is common, and comes first upon the tongue, in easy and familiar conversation. It is the mistake of this distinction which leads some writers to avoid the phrase that any one would use, and seek out what is uncommon. Hence there appears a variation in the words they put upon paper, from those which they themselves would use in conversation. And why this? Ought not language to be precisely the same whether spoken or written.

Perspicuity is the natural result of simplicity, and needs not to be laid down as a different characteristic. For can there be obscurity in that composition where the most familiar word is used, and that word put in its proper place. This brings to mind the definition of stile by Swift; "proper words in proper places."

There can be nothing more easy than the composition of our author. His writing savours of the skill of an artificer who after many years exercitation in his art, acquires a power of accomplishing his work by a habit of the fingers, independent of any application of the mind. So that while in the stile of others there is an appearance of exertion, here there is what a superficial observer would call carelessness, but which the sound critic will discover to be the result of a perfect mastery of all that relates to language.

It is pretty generally believed that our stile has been constantly degenerating from the time of queen Anne, in whose reign flourished those immortal penmen, Swift, Addison, Arbuthnot, Tillotson, Bolinbroke, &c. If the stile of this author is examined, and compared with those models, it will be found to be in the same pure, simple attic taste. We shall therefore not hesitate to recommend it as a restorer of "all that is correct and beautiful in writing." So far the reviewers.

I have said that I was happy to find that these have had the good taste to find out what I myself had thought of the composition. But as I wish at all times to let the reader, into a knowledge of my real sentiments, I will confess that these are merely words of course with me, and that I was not happy to find my work praised in any respect; because I wished to have a quarrel with the critics; and this not because I love war, abstractedly considered; but because in this case I should have had an opportunity of shewing my polemic talents. Nay, expecting an attack, I had prepared a number of good thoughts in my mind, to be used in my contest with them. What is more I had actually written a copy of verses in the Hudibrastic rhyme and manner, for their use, in which I considered them as muskitoes, or flies of some kind, that were troublesome to men; and though the occasion fails, yet there can be no impropriety in giving to the public those strokes of satire which lay dormant in my mind as these would apply more particularly to an attack upon me; yet the essay being in general terms, it may appear without a particular circumstance to call it forth; merely as a specimen of what I could do had there been occasion for it. And the insertion will be excuseable, when it is considered how painful it is to be frustrated in what we propose as our pleasure. I have known a good man wish to have bad news true, merely because he had related them: and we may conceive a saint vexed at not finding a man dead, when he had digested a funeral sermon in his mind, and was ready to bury him. . . .

[1793]

These two brief excerpts by Charles Brockden Brown open the new century with remarks which are to become extremely familiar. As a novelist, Brown recognized the challenge of American materials and claimed attention for his originality. As the editor of The American Review and Literary Journal, *he acknowledged and tried to explain the slow growth of American literature. (His observation on the importance of the magazines proved prophetic of their significant role in the development of nineteenth-century American culture.)*

24

TO THE PUBLIC

The flattering reception that has been given by the public to Arthur Mervyn has prompted the writer to solicit a continuance of the same favour, and to offer to the world a new performance.

America has opened new views to the naturalist and politician, but has seldome furnished themes to the moral painter. That new springs of action and new motives to curiosity should operate; that the field of investigation opened to us by our own country should differ essentially from those which exist in Europe, may be readily conceived. The sources of amusement to the fancy and instruction to the heart that are peculiar to ourselves are equally numerous and inexhaustible. It is the purpose of this work to profit by some of these sources; to exhibit a series of adventures growing out of the condition of our country. . . .

One merit the writer may at least claim; that of calling forth the passions and engaging the sympathy of the reader by means hitherto unemployed by preceding authors. Puerile superstition and exploded manners, Gothic castles and chimeras, are the materials usually employed for this end. The incidents of Indian hostility, and the perils of the western wilderness, are far more suitable; and for a native of America to overlook these would admit of no apology. These, therefore, are in part the ingredients of this tale, and these he has been ambitious of depicting in vivid and faithful colours. The success of his efforts must be estimated by the liberal and candid reader.

C.B.B.

[1799]

25 ↙

PREFACE

The people of the United States are, perhaps, more distinguished than those of Europe as a people of business; and by an universal attention to the active and lucrative pursuits of life. This habit has grown out of the necessities of their situation, while engaged in the settlement of a new country, in the means of self-preservation, in defending their possessions, in removing the obstacles and embarrassments arising from their colonial condition, and in forming and establishing independent systems of government. When, now that our population is increased, our national independence secured, and our governments established, and we are relieved from the necessities of colonists and emigrants, there is reason to expect more attention to polite literature and science.

Nothing, it is thought, will tend more to excite this attention and to render the pursuits of knowledge more compatible with those of business than those periodical publications which impart information in small portions; by which, men engaged in active occupations may gradually acquire a degree of intellectual cultivation and improvement without any infringement of the time allotted to their customary and necessary concerns.

Much has been said about the claims which the natives of America may urge to the praise of genius and learning. Some European critics hold our pretensions in contempt; and many among ourselves seem inclined to degrade our countrymen below the common level. Their judgment has been formed from very imperfect evidence, and very narrow views, though it must be admitted that we have not contributed our share to the great fund of knowledge and science, which is continually receiving such vast accessions from every part of Europe.

Genius in composition, like genius in every other art, must be aided by culture, nourished by patronage, and supplied with leisure and materials. The genius of the poet, orator, and historian cannot be exercised with vigour and effect without suitable encouragement, any more than that of the artist and mechanic. Neither the one or the other is beyond the sphere of social affections and domestic duties and wants; neither can be expected to produce works of ingenuity and labour without such a recompense as the natural ambition of man and the necessities of his nature and situation demand.

No one is so absurd as to suppose that the natives of America are unfitted by any radical defect of understanding for vieing with the artizans of Europe in all those useful and elegant fabrics which are daily purchased by us. Similar and suitable circumstances would show Americans equally qualified to excel in arts and literature as the natives of the other continent. But a people much engaged in the labours of agriculture, in a country rude and untouched by the hand of refinement, cannot, with any tolerable facility or success, carry on, at the same time, the operations of imagination and indulge in the speculations of Raphael, Newton, or Pope.

The causes, indeed, why the intellectual soil of America is so comparatively sterile are obvious. We do not cultivate it; nor, while we can resort to foreign fields, from whence all our wants are so easily and readily supplied, and which have been cultivated for ages, do we find sufficient inducement to labour in our own. We are united by language, manners, and taste, by the bonds of peace and commercial intercourse, with an enlightened nation, the centre of whose arts and population may be considered as much *our* centre, as much the fountain whence *we* draw light and knowledge through books, as that of the inhabitants of Wales and Cumberland. In relation to the British capital as the centre of English literature, arts, and science, the situation of *New* and *Old-York* may be regarded as the same. It is only the gradual influence of time, that, by increasing our numbers and furnishing a ready market for the works of domestic hands and heads, will at length generate and continue a race of artists and authors, purely indigenous, and who may vie with those of Europe. . . .

[1802]

Some who would solve the problem of American literature turned to recent events of national history. William Dunlap discovered the difficulties attendant upon such a choice and repeats, incidentally, the didactic aims which continued to dominate most writing: "His end . . . he avows, is pleasure to impart, / And move the passions but to mend the heart."

26

More than nine years ago the Author made choice of the death of Major André as the subject of a Tragedy, and part of what is now offered to the public was written at that time. Many circumstances discouraged him from finishing his Play, and among them must be reckoned a prevailing opinion that recent events are unfit subjects for tragedy. These discouragements have at length all given way to his desire of bringing a story on the Stage so eminently fitted, in his opinion, to excite interest in the breasts of an American audience.

In exhibiting a stage representation of a real transaction, the particulars of which are fresh in the minds of many of the audience, an author has this peculiar difficulty to struggle with, that those who know the events expect to see them *all* recorded; and any deviation from what they remember to be fact, appears to them as a fault in the poet; they are disappointed, their expectations are not fulfilled, and the writer is more or less condemned, not considering the difference between the poet and the historian, or not knowing that what is intended to be exhibited is a free poetical picture, not an exact historical portrait.

Still further difficulties has the Tragedy of André to surmount, difficulties independent of its own demerits, in its way to public favor. The subject necessarily involves political questions, but the Author presumes that he owes no apology to any one for having shewn himself an American. The friends of Major André (and it appears that all who knew him were his friends) will look with a jealous eye on the Poem, whose principal incident is the sad catastrophe which his misconduct, in submitting to be an instrument in a transaction of treachery and deceit, justly brought upon him: but these friends have no cause of offence; the Author has adorned the poetical character of André with every virtue; he has made him his Hero; to do which, he was under the necessity of making him condemn his own conduct, in the one dreadfully unfortunate action of his life. To shew the effects which Major André's excellent qualities had upon the minds of men, the Author has drawn a generous and amiable youth, so blinded by his love for the accomplished Briton, as to consider his country, and the great commander of her armies, as in the commission of such horrid injustice, that he, in the anguish of his soul, disclaims the service. In this it appears, since the first representation, that the Author has gone near to offend the veterans of the American army who were present on the first night, and who not knowing the sequel of the action, felt much disposed to condemn him: but surely they must remember the diversity of opinion which agitated the minds of men at that time, on the question of the propriety of putting André to death; and when they add the circumstances of André's having saved the life of this youth, and gained his ardent friendship, they will be inclined to mingle with their disapprobation, a sentiment of pity, and excuse, perhaps commend, the Poet, who has represented the action without sanctioning it by his approbation. . . .

The Poem is now submitted to the ordeal of closest examination, with the Author's respectful assurance to every reader, that as it is not his interest, so it has not been his intention to offend any; but, on the contrary, to impress, through the medium of a pleasing stage exhibition, the sublime lessons of Truth and Justice upon the minds of his countrymen.

PROLOGUE

Spoken by Mr. Martin.

A Native Bard, a native scene displays,
And claims your candour for his daring lays:
Daring, so soon, in mimic scenes to shew,
What each remembers as a real woe.
Who has forgot when gallant André died?
A name by Fate to Sorrow's self allied.
Who has forgot, when o'er the untimely bier,
Contending armies paus'd, to drop a tear.

Our Poet builds upon a fact to-night;
Yet claims, in building, every Poet's right:
To choose, embellish, lop, or add, or blend,
Fiction with truth, as best may suit his end;

Which, he avows, is pleasure to impart,
And move the passions but to mend the heart.

O, may no party-spirit blast his views,
Or turn to ill the meanings of the Muse:
She sings of wrongs long past, Men as they were,
To instruct, without reproach, the Men that are;
Then judge the Story by the genius shown,
And praise, or damn it, for its worth alone.

[1798]

❦ *Literary effort in the new nation seemed always to be looking over its shoulder at the mother country. The great British reviews dominated the American scene. These remarks (probably by Southey) are typical. They are not unfriendly, but their very equanimity suggests the condescension which sensitive Americans found intolerable. American discussion of the national letters should be read as one side of a steady and often heated dialogue with England on the nature and value of American life.*

27 ❦

. . . The first English work written in America was Sandy's Translation of the Metamorphoses; a version, says the translator, 'limned by that imperfect light which was snatched from the hours of night and repose; and doubly a stranger, being sprung from an ancient Roman stock, and bred up in the New World, of the rudeness of which it could not but participate; especially as it was produced among wars and tumults, instead of under the kindly and peaceful influence of the Muses.' Dr. William Vaughan's poem of the Golden Fleece was written in Newfoundland about the same time. Jocelyn, who wrote the New England Rarities, and the account of his two voyages, took over with him a version of part of the Psalms by Quarles, which, if they had received the minister of Boston's approbation, were to have succeeded Sternhold and Hopkins in the New World. The first printing press was set up at Cambridge in 1639. Glover, at whose expense it was established, died on his passage out; the printer's name was Daye. The first thing which was printed was the Freeman's Oath; the second was an Almanack calculated for New England by Pierce, a sea-faring man; the third was the Psalms newly turned into metre. Such were the beginnings of literature among the Anglo-Americans; its progress has not been rapid. No work of distinguished merit in any branch has yet been produced among them; that which lies before us is perhaps one of the most meritorious; and this is of an inferior class.* Their Life of Washington is ill-proportioned, nor can much praise be bestowed upon its execution. Their drama is so bad—as almost to reconcile us to the present state of our own. Of their two best poets,

* Abial Holmes, *American Annals.*

Dwight has failed because he imitated bad models, and Barlow because he formed a bad style for himself. It is no great reproach to the Americans that they have not as yet done more; more ought not to be expected from their circumstances and population. Some blame, however, is due to their government for the little encouragement which it holds out to literature. It is especially incumbent upon a nation which professes to despise factitious distinctions, to acknowledge intellectual rank with every thing short of ostentation, and to set other countries an example by patronizing and promoting those efforts of genius which all civilized nations consider as their proudest boast, and their only permanent glory. . . .

[1809]

The sort of advice an American writer might expect from England is suggested by this review of Barlow's Columbiad *in the* Edinburgh Review.

28

As epic poetry has often been the earliest, as well as the most precious production of national genius, we ought not, perhaps, to be surprised at this goodly firstling of the infant Muse of America. The truth however is, that though the American *government* be new, the *people* is in all respects as old as the people of England; and their want of literature is to be ascribed, not to the immaturity of their progress in civilization, but to the nature of the occupations in which they are generally engaged. These federal republicans, in short, bear no sort of resemblance to the Greeks of the days of Homer, or the Italians of the age of Dante; but are very much such people, we suppose, as the modern traders of Manchester, Liverpool, or Glasgow. They have all a little Latin whipped into them in their youth; and read Shakespeare, Pope and Milton, as well as bad English novels, in their days of courtship and leisure. They are just as likely to write epic poems, therefore, as the inhabitants of our trading towns at home; and are entitled to no more admiration when they succeed, and to no more indulgence when they fail, than would be due, on a similar occasion, to any of those industrious persons.

Be this, however, as it may, Mr Barlow, we are afraid, will not be the Homer of his country; and will never take his place among the enduring poets either of the old or of the new world. The faults which obviously cut him off from this high destiny, may be imputed partly to his country, and partly to his subject—but chiefly to himself. The want of a literary society, to animate, controul and refine, and the intractableness of a subject which extends from the creation to the millennium, and combines the rude mythologies of savages with the treaties and battles of men who are still alive, certainly aggravated the task which he had undertaken with no common difficulties. But the great misfortune undoubtedly is, that Mr Barlow is in no respect qualified to overcome these difficulties. From the prose which he has introduced into this volume, and even from much of what is given as poetry, it is easy to see that he is a man of a plain, strong, and resolute understanding,—a very good republican, and a considerable despiser of all sorts of prejudices and illusions; but without any play or vivacity of fancy,—any gift of simplicity or pathos,—any loftiness of genius, or delicacy of taste. Though not deficient in literature, therefore, nor unread in poetry, he has evidently none of the higher elements of a poet in his composition; and has accordingly made a most injudicious choice and unfortunate application of the models which lay before him. Like other persons of a cold and coarse imagination, he is caught only by what is glaring and exaggerated; and seems to have no perception of the finer and less obtrusive graces which constitute all the lasting and deep-felt charms of poetry. In his cumbrous and inflated style, he is constantly mistaking hyperbole for grandeur, and supplying the place of simplicity with huge patches of mere tameness and vulgarity. This curious inter-mixture, indeed, of extreme homeliness and flatness, with a sort of turbulent and bombastic elevation, is the great characteristic of the work before us. Instead of aspiring to emulate the sublime composure of Milton, or the natural eloquence and flowing nervousness of Dryden, Mr Barlow has bethought him of transferring to epic poetry the light, spar-kling, and tawdry diction of Darwin, and of narrating great events, and delivering lofty precepts in an unhappy imitation of that picturesque, puerile, and pedantic style, which alternately charms and disgusts us in the pages of our poetical physiologist. Infinitely more verbose and less spirited than Darwin, however, he reminds us of him only by his charac-teristic defects; and, after all, is most tolerable in those passages in which he reminds us most of him. . . .

. . . This American bard frequently writes in a language utterly un-known to the prose or verse of this country. We have often heard it reported, that our transatlantic brethren were beginning to take it amiss that their language should still be called English; and truly we must say, that Mr Barlow has gone far to take away that ground of reproach. The groundwork of his speech, perhaps, may be English, as that of the Italian is Latin; but the variations amount already to more than a change of dialect; and really make a glossary necessary for most untravelled readers. As this is the first specimen which has come to our hands of any consider-able work composed in the American tongue, it may be gratifying to our philological readers, if we make a few remarks upon it.

It is distinguished from the original English, in the first place, by a great multitude of words which are radically and entirely new, and as utterly foreign as if they had been adopted from the Hebrew or Chinese; in the second place, by a variety of new compounds and combinations of words, or roots of words, which are still known in the parent tongue; and, thirdly, by the perversion of a still greater number of original English words from their proper use or signification, by employing nouns substantive for verbs, for instance, and adjectives for substantives, &c. We shall set down a few examples of each.

In the first class, we may reckon the words *multifluvian—cosmogyral— crass—role—gride—conglaciate—colon* and *coloniarch—trist* and *contristed—thirl—gerb—ludibrious—croupe—scow—emban—lowe—brume— brumal,* &c. &c.

The second class is still more extensive, and, to our ears, still more discordant. In it we may comprehend such verbs as, to *utilise,* to *vagrate,* to *oversheet,* to *empalm,* to *inhumanise,* to *transboard,* to *reseek,* to *bestorm,* to *ameed,* &c. &c.; such adjectives as *bivaulted, imbeaded, unkeeled, laxed, forestered, homicidious, millennial, portless, undungeoned, lustred,* &c.—*conflicting fulminents;* and a variety of substantives formed upon the same plan of distortion.

The third or last class of American improvements, consists mainly in the violent transformation of an incredible number of English nouns into verbs. Thus we have, 'to *spade* the soil'—'to *sledge* the corn'—and 'to *keel* the water.' We have also the verbs, to *breeze,* to *rainbow,* to *hill,* to *scope,* to *lot,* to *lamp,* to *road,* and to *reroad,* to *fang,* to *fray,* to *bluff,* to *tone,* to *forester,* to *gyve,* to *besom,* and fifty more. Nor is it merely as verbs that our poor nouns are compelled to serve in this new republican dictionary; they are forced, upon a pinch, to do the duty of adjectives also; and, accordingly, we have science distinguished into moral science and *physic* science; and *things* discussed with a view to their *physic* forms and their final ends.

The innovations in prosody are not less bold and meritorious. We have *galaxy* and *platina* with the middle syllable long.

> 'New constellations, new *galaxies* rise.'
> 'The pale *platina* and the burning gold.'

Contents, allied, bombard, and *expanse,* are accented on the first syllable.

> 'Each thro the adverse ports their *contents* pour,' &c.

And *empyrean* is made short in the penult; as in that fine line.

> 'Empalms the *empyrean,* or dissects a gaz.'

The rhimes are equally original;—*plain* rhimes to *man*—*blood* to *God,* and *share* to *war,* in three successive couplets.

Before closing these hasty and imperfect notices of the characteristics of

this new language, it seems proper to observe, that if Mr Barlow's authority is to be relied on, it may also be known from all other tongues by an
utter disregard of all distinction between what we should call lofty and
elegant, and low and vulgar expressions. These republican literati seem to
make it a point of conscience to have no aristocratical distinctions—even
in their vocabulary. They think one word just as good as another, provided its meaning be as clear; and will know no difference, but that of
force and perspicuity. Thus, we hear of rivers that *tap* the upland lakes;
and are told, that, in North America, there are 'hills by hundreds,' of such
a height, that, if set beside them,

> 'Taurus would shrink, Hemodia *strut* no more.'

In the same taste, in an elaborate description of the celebrated feat of
William Tell, our attention is particularly directed to the stretching of his
knuckles as he draws the cord, and to the skill with which *'he picked the
pippin'* off the boy's head. . . .

Our readers, we suspect, have now enough of this performance. As a
great national poem, it has enormous—inexpiable—and, in some respects,
intolerable faults. But the author's talents are evidently respectable; and,
severely as we have been obliged to speak of his taste and his diction in a
great part of the volume, we have no hesitation in saying, that we consider him as a giant, in comparison with many of the puling and paltry
rhymsters, who disgrace our English literature by their occasional success.
As an Epic poet, we do think his case is desperate; but, as a philosophical
and moral poet, we think he has talents of no ordinary value; and, if he
would pay some attention to purity of style, and simplicity of composition, and cherish in himself a certain fastidiousness of taste,—which is not
yet to be found, we are afraid, even among the better educated of the
Americans,—we have no doubt that he might produce something which
English poets would envy, and English critics applaud. . . .

[1809]

The care with which the reviewer examines Barlow's language points to a fundamental American literary problem. One of the most closely reasoned discussions of American English was John Pickering's "Memoir on the Present State of the English Language in the United States of America." Pickering's insistence on constant vigilance reflects his cultural conservatism, but his picture of language alteration and fluidity indicates a surprisingly modern sense of linguistic development.

29

The preservation of the English language in its purity throughout the United States is an object deserving the attention of every American who is a friend to the literature and science of this country. It is in a particular manner entitled to the consideration of the Academy; for, though subjects which are usually ranked under the head of the physical sciences were doubtless chiefly in view with the founders of the Academy, yet as our language is to be the instrument of communicating to the world the speculations and discoveries of our countrymen in science and literature, it seems also necessarily "to fall within the design of the institution"; because, unless that language is well settled and can be read with ease and satisfaction by all to whom it is addressed, our authors will write and publish certainly under many disadvantages though perhaps not altogether in vain.

It is true, indeed, that our countrymen may speak and write in a dialect of English which will be generally understood in the United States; but if they are ambitious of having their works read by Englishmen as well as Americans, they must write in a language that Englishmen can read with facility and pleasure. And if for sometime to come it should not be the lot of many Americans to publish any thing which shall be read out of their own country, yet all who have the least tincture of learning will continue to feel an ardent desire to acquaint themselves with the works of English authors. Let us then for a moment imagine the time to have arrived when Americans shall be no longer able to understand the works of Milton, Pope, Swift, Addison, and the other English authors, justly styled classic, without the aid of a translation into a language that is to be called at some future day the American tongue! By such a change, it is true, our loss would not be so great in works purely scientific, as in those which are usually termed works of taste; for the obvious reason that the design of the former is merely to communicate information without regard to elegance of language or the force and beauty of the sentiments. But the excellencies of works of taste cannot be felt even in the best translations; a truth which, without resorting to the example of the matchless ancients, will be acknowledged by every man who is acquainted with the admirable works in the various living languages.

Nor is this the only view in which a radical change of language would be a loss to us. To say nothing of the facilities afforded by a common language in the ordinary intercourse of business between the people of the two countries, it should not be forgotten that our religion and our laws are studied in the language of the nation from which we are descended; and with the loss of the language we should finally suffer the loss of those peculiar advantages which we now derive from the investigations of the jurists and divines of that country.

But it is often asked among us, do not the people of America now speak and write the English language with purity? A brief consideration of the subject will furnish a satisfactory answer to this question; it will also enable us to correct the erroneous opinions entertained by some Americans on this point and at the same time to defend our countrymen against the charge made by some English writers, of a design to effect a radical change in the language.

As the inquiry before us is a simple question of fact, it is to be determined, like every other question of that nature, by proper evidence. What evidence then have we that the English language is not spoken and written in America with the same degree of purity that is to be found in the writers and orators of England?

In the first place, although it is agreed that there is greater uniformity of dialect throughout the United States (in consequence of the frequent removals of people from one part of our country to another) than is to be found throughout England, yet none of our countrymen, not even those who are the most zealous in supporting what they imagine to be the honour of the American character, will contend that we have not in some instances departed from the standard of the language. We have formed some entirely new words, and to some old ones that are still used in England we have affixed new significations; while others that have long since become obsolete in England are still retained in common use with us. For example: it is admitted by all that the verb *to advocate,* the adjective *lengthy,* and a few others are of American origin; and, that the adjective *clever* and some other words of English origin have been generally used by us in a sense different from their present signification in England. If then, in connexion with these acknowledgments of our own countrymen, we allow any weight to the opinions of Englishmen (who must surely be competent judges in this case) it cannot be denied that we have in many instances deviated from the standard of the language, as spoken and written in England at the present day. By this, however, I do not mean that so great a deviation has taken place as to have rendered any considerable part of our language unintelligible to Englishmen; but merely that so many corruptions have crept into our English as to have become the subject of much animadversion and regret with the learned of Great Britain. And as we are hardly aware of the opinion entertained by them of the extent of these corruptions, it may be useful if it should not be very flattering to our pride to hear their remarks on this subject in their own words. We shall find that these corruptions are censured, not by a few contemptible critics but, so far as the fact is to be ascertained from English publications, by all the scholars of that country who take any interest in American literature. In proof of this I request the attention of the Academy to the following extracts from several of the British Reviews, some of which are the most distinguished of the present day and all of which together may be considered as expressing the general opinion of the literary men of Great Britain. That all the remarks are just, to the extent in which they will naturally be understood, few of our countrymen will be willing to admit.

The *British Critic,* for February 1810, in a review of the Rev. Mr. Bancroft's Life of Washington, says—"In the style we observe, with regret rather than with astonishment, the introduction of several *new* words, or *old* words in a new sense; a deviation from the rules of the English language, which, if it continues to be practised by good writers in America, will introduce confusion into the medium of intercourse, and render it a subject of regret that the people of that continent should not have an entirely separate language as well as government of their own. Instances occur at almost every page; without pains in selecting, the following may be taken as specimens," &c. The Reviewers then mention several words which are all inserted in the Vocabulary annexed to this memoir.

The same Reviewers (in April 1808) in their account of Chief Justice Marshall's Life of Washington, have the following remarks:—"In the writings of Americans we have often discovered deviations from the purity of the English idiom, which we have been more disposed to censure than to wonder at. The common speech of the United States has departed very considerably from the standard adopted in England, and in this case it is not to be expected that writers, however cautious, will maintain a strict purity. Mr. Marshall deviates occasionally, but not grossly," &c.

The *Critical Review* (for September 1809) in remarks upon *Travels through France, by Col. Pinckney,* says of the author's style—"He falls into occasional inaccuracies . . . . . but the instances are rare, and by no means so striking as we have frequent occasions of remarking in most American writers."

The same Reviewers (in July 1807) in speaking of Marshall's Life of Washington, have the following, among other remarks on the style of that work—that "it abounds with many of those idioms which prevail on the other side of the Atlantic."

The *Annual Review,* for 1808, in speaking of the same work, after pointing out several instances of false English (in respect to many of which, however, the Reviewers have been misled by the incorrectness of the English edition of that work, as will be seen in the following Vocabulary,) has the following observations; which, if they had been made in a manner somewhat different, would probably have been more favourably received by those for whose benefit they seem to be intended:—"We have been more particular in noticing these faults in Mr. Marshall's language because we are not at all certain that the Americans do not consider them as beauties; and because we wish, if possible, to stem that torrent of barbarous phraseology, with which the American writers threaten to destroy the purity of the English language."

The *Monthly Reviewers,* in their account of a little work, entitled *A Political Sketch of America,* cite, with approbation, the following passage—"The national language should be sedulously cultivated; and this is to be accomplished by means of schools. This circumstance demands particular attention, for the language of conversation is becoming incorrect; and even in America authors are to be found who make use of new or obsolete words which no good writer in this country would employ." *Monthly Rev. May 1808*

The *Edinburgh Review* for October 1804 (which is the last I shall cite) has the following general observations on this subject:—

"If the men of birth and education in that other England which they are building up in the West will not diligently study the great authors who purified and fixed the language of our common forefathers, we must soon lose the only badge that is still worn of our consanguinity."

The same Reviewers, in their remarks on Marshall's and Ramsay's Lives of Washington, say—

"In these volumes we have found a great many words and phrases which English criticism refuses to acknowledge. America has thrown off the yoke of the British nation, but she would do well for some time to take the laws of composition from the Addisons, the Swifts and the Robertsons of her ancient sovereign. . . . . These remarks, however, are not dictated by any paltry feelings of jealousy or pride. We glory in the diffusion of our language over a new world where we hope it is yet destined to collect new triumphs; and in the brilliant perspective of American greatness, we see only pleasing images of associated prosperity and glory of the land in which we live."

Such is the strong language of the British literati on this subject. And shall we at once, without examination, ascribe it wholly to prejudice? Should we not by such a hasty decision expose ourselves to the like imputation? On the contrary, should not the opinions of such writers stimulate us to inquiry that we may ascertain whether their animadversions are well founded or not? We see the same critics censure the Scotticisms of their northern brethren, the peculiarities of the Irish and the provincial corruptions of their own English writers. We cannot therefore be so wanting in liberality as to think that, when deciding upon the literary claims of Americans, they are governed wholly by prejudice or jealousy. A suspicion of this sort should be the less readily entertained as we acknowledge that they sometimes do justice to our countrymen. The writings of Dr. Franklin, for example, have received their unqualified praise; and a few other American authors have been liberally commended by them. The opinions of these critics too are supported by those of some distinguished men in our own country. Dr. Franklin censures, without reserve, "the popular errors several of our own states are continually falling into," with respect to "expressions and pronunciation." Dr. Witherspoon who, by having been educated in Great Britain and by his subsequent long residence in the United States, was a peculiarly well qualified judge on this subject, remarks:—"I shall also admit, though with some hesitation, that gentlemen and scholars in Great Britain speak as much with the vulgar in common chit chat as persons of the same class do in America; but there is a remarkable difference in their public and solemn discourses. I have heard in this country in the senate, at the bar, and from the pulpit, and see daily in dissertations from the press, errors in grammar, improprieties and vulgarisms, which hardly any person of the same class in point of rank and literature would have fallen into in Great Britain."

With these opinions of such distinguished writers before us, shall we entertain the illiberal jealousy that justice is intentionally withheld from us by our English brethren? Let us rather imitate the example of the learned and modest Campbell who, though he had devoted a great part of a long life to the study of the English language, yet thought it no disgrace to make an apology for his style in the following terms: "Sensible," says he, "of the disadvantages, in point of style, which my northern situation lays me under, I have availed myself of every opportunity of better information in regard to all those terms and phrases in the version, [of the Gospels] of which I was doubtful. I feel myself under particular obligations on this account to one gentleman, my valuable friend and colleague Dr. Beattie who, though similarly situated with myself, has with greater success studied the genius and idiom of our language; and of whom it is no more than justice to add that the acknowledged purity of his own diction is the least of his qualifications as an author. But if, notwithstanding all the care I have taken, I shall be found, in many places, to need the indulgence of the English reader, it will not much surprise me. . . . . The apology which Irenæus, Bishop of Lyons in Gaul in the second century, makes for his language in a book he published in defence of religion, appears to me so candid, so modest, so sensible, at the same time so apposite to my own case, that I cannot avoid transcribing and adopting it:—'Non autem exquires a nobis, qui apud Celtas commoramur, et in barbarum sermonem plerumque avocamur, orationis artem quam non didicimus, neque vim conscriptoris quam non affectavimus, neque ornamentum verborum, neque suadelam quam nescimus'. . . ."[1]

Upon an impartial consideration of the subject then, it seems impossible to resist the conclusion that although the language of the United States has perhaps changed less than might have been expected, when we consider how many years have elapsed since our ancestors brought it from England, yet it has in so many instances departed from the English standard that our scholars should lose no time in endeavouring to restore it to its purity and to prevent future corruption.

This, it is obvious, is to be effected, in the first place, by carefully noting every unauthorised word and phrase; or (as Dr. Franklin many years ago recommended, in his letter to Mr. Webster on this subject[2]) by "setting a discountenancing mark" upon such of them, as are not rendered indispensably necessary by the peculiar circumstances of our country; and, even if we should continue to have a partiality for some of those expres-

---

[1] Cambell's *Four Gospels,* preface, p. 28.
[2] See the word *Improve* in the *Vocabulary* [not included here].

sions, and should choose to retain them, it will always be useful to know them. By knowing exactly what peculiar words are in use with us, we should, among other advantages, have it in our power to expose the calumnies of some prejudiced and ignorant writers who have frequently laid to the charge of our countrymen in general the affected words and phrases of a few conceited individuals;—words and phrases which are justly the subject of as much ridicule in America as they are in Great Britain. As a general rule also we should undoubtedly avoid all those words which are noticed by English authors of reputation as expressions with which they are unacquainted; for although we might produce some English authority for such words, yet the very circumstance of their being thus noticed by well educated Englishmen is a proof that they are not used at this day in England and, of course, ought not to be used elsewhere by those who would speak correct English.

With a view to this important object I have taken some pains to make a collection of words and phrases which I offer to the Academy, not as a perfect list of our real or supposed peculiarities of language but merely as the beginning of a work which can be completed only by long and accurate observation, especially of intelligent Americans who shall have an opportunity of residing in England and of well educated Englishmen who may resort to this country. It has long been the wish of our scholars to see a work of that sort; but, though several words have been occasionally noticed by Dr. Witherspoon, Dr. Franklin, and some others, yet nobody seems to have been willing to undertake the laborious task of making a general collection of them. Seeing no prospect of such a work and observing, with no small degree of solicitude, the corruptions which are gradually insinuating themselves into our language, I have taken the liberty to ask the attention of the Academy to this subject by laying before them the following Vocabulary: a performance which I am sensible is not so worthy of their notice as more time and ability might have rendered it.

In making this Vocabulary I have resorted to all the sources of information in my power and have, under each word, given some of the authorities for and against the use of it. I have also subjoined to some of the words the criticisms of Dr. Franklin, Dr. Witherspoon, and other writers at large, in order that the reader may avail himself of their instructive observations without the trouble of searching for them through the numerous volumes of their works; and in all cases where any word had been noticed by English or American writers, which I had also myself observed, (particularly during my residence in England, where my attention was first drawn to this subject) I have chosen to give it upon their authority rather than my own. Many words will be found in the list which are not in fact of American origin, or peculiar to Americans; but it appeared to me that it would be useful to insert all words the legitimacy of which had been questioned, in order that their claim to a place in the English language might be discussed and settled. Several of the words have been obtained from British Reviews of American publications; and I may here remark how much it is to be regretted that the reviewers have not pointed out all the instances that have come under their notice of our deviations from the English standard. This would be doing an essential service to the cause of literature and be the most effectual means of accomplishing what those scholars appear to have so much at heart—the preservation of the English language in its purity wherever it is spoken.

It has been asserted that we have discovered a much stronger propensity than the English to add new words to the language; and the little animadversion which, till within a few years, such new-coined words have met with among us, seems to support that opinion. With us, every writer takes the liberty to contaminate the language with the barbarous terms of his own tasteless invention; but in England, new words are seldom hazarded even by authors of the highest rank. The passion for these ridiculous novelties among us, however, has for some time past been declining. Our greatest danger now is that we shall continue to use antiquated words which were brought to this country by our forefathers nearly two centuries ago—(some of which too were at that day provincial words in England) and that we shall affix a new signification to words which are still used in that country in their original sense. Words of these descriptions having long been a part of the language, we are not led to examine critically the authority on which their different significations rest; but those that are entirely new, like strangers on their first appearance, immediately attract our attention and induce us to inquire into their pretensions to the rank they claim.

But it is not enough for us to note single words; our idiom, it would seem, is in some degree changed and is in danger of still greater corruptions.[3] At the same time, therefore, that we are "setting a discountenanc-

---

[3] That a radical change in the language of a people so remote from the source of it as we are from England, is not a chimerical supposition will be apparent from the alterations that have taken place among the nations of Europe; of which no instance, perhaps, is more striking than the change and final separation of the languages of Spain and Portugal, notwithstanding the vicinity and frequent intercourse of the people of those two countries.

ing mark" upon unauthorised words, we should assiduously study the language of the best authors, especially Dryden, Swift, and Addison, to the last of whom, Dr. Blair, in his Lectures on Rhetoric, justly applies Quintilian's well-known remark upon Cicero—that "to be highly pleased with his manner of writing is the criterion of a good taste in English style—Ille se profecisse sciat cui Cicero valde placebit;" and of whom Dr. Johnson emphatically says—"whoever would attain a good English style, familiar but not coarse, and elegant but not ostentatious, must give his days and nights to Addison." Dr. Franklin, who informs us in his *Life*, that it was one of the greatest objects of his ambition to write English well, formed his style upon that of Addison; and Franklin is one of the very few American writers whose style has satisfied the English critics. This is the discipline to which the most distinguished scholars of Great Britain have submitted and without which neither they nor the scholars of our own country can acquire and preserve a pure English style. It is related of Mr. Fox, that when speaking of his intended History of England, he said, he would "admit no word into his book for which he had not the authority of Dryden." This determination may perhaps seem at first view to have been dictated by too fastidious a taste or an undue partiality for a favourite author; but unquestionably, a rule of this sort, adopted in the course of our education, (extending, however, to two or three of the best authors,) would be the most effectual method of acquiring a good English style. And surely if Fox found no necessity for any other words than Dryden had used, those authors have little excuse who take the liberty not only of using all the words they can find in the whole body of English authors, ancient and modern, but also of making new terms of their own at pleasure. Who shall have a right to complain of scarcity, where that distinguished orator found abundance? Such standard authors, therefore, should be made the foundation of our English; but as our language like all others is constantly though slowly changing, we should also, in order to perfect our style as we advance to mature age, study those authors of our own time who have made the older writers their models. Every word in the writings of Addison is not now in general use in England; and many words have been adopted since his time and are now sanctioned by all the best writers of that country. Such writers, therefore, as well as their illustrious masters, ought to be diligently read; for we should always remember, that in language, as in the fine arts, we can only attain to excellence by incessant study of the best models.

[1816]

The roots of an American romantic movement can be seen in this plea for independence and defense of inspiration. Edward Tyrell Channing was Boylston Professor of Rhetoric and Oratory at Harvard for thirty years. His belief in "the splendid barbarism" of a nation's literature prepared the way for Emerson and Whitman, and his thesis came eventually to dominate the discussion of the national letters: "What we contend for is that the literature of a country is just as domestick and individual as its character or political institutions. Its charm is its nativeness."

30 &

> "Yet still uppermost,
> Nature was at his heart, as if he felt,
> Though yet he knew not how, a wasting power
> In all things, which from her sweet influence,
> Might tend to wean him."
>
> Wordsworth.

When I lay down the reviews or go home from a party of fashionable criticks, I pity the whole race of authors. If they would be the favourites of the age they live in, they must stand in awe of its opinions and taste, however various or chilling. They are surrounded by tribunals and judges in almost every class; and all put in their claims to special deference and respect. The frivolous and gay, one would think, had no concern with the depths of the heart, nor even with the landscape, any farther than the tints that overlay it. Still they are readers and judges. They lay up a little poetry or wit for conversation's sake, or at least to gild their affectation—and therefore they must be consulted.—Then again, we have exact scholars who require a sustained faultlessness and elegance in every thing. They are shocked with blemishes or occasional dulness and judge a man by failures that are merely accidental and which do not indicate in the least the original cast or defects of his mind. They never look at gleams or regions of clear azure in a sleepy sky. They laugh at foolish simplicity till they cannot discern the real which is very often in the neighbourhood.— There is too, a great middling crowd of readers whose vocabulary of criticism extends little further than to *"unnatural, out-of-life,"* &c.; and words of this sort they are sure to level against every man who ventures upon the marvellous, wild, and unreal. These are the practical men who judge every thing by what they call common sense. They laugh at the folly of encouraging men in the indolent luxuries and unprofitable excesses of imagination and feeling when we were sent here to work, to be useful, to conquer the vices, and bring home the wanderings of the mind.—Other readers, however, are so fastidious and ethereal that they cannot bear to see a Poet in the streets or workshops.

And shall authors then never be allowed to lose sight of the motley race who are to judge them? A heavy day it will be for poetry when society is made the school of genius instead of solitude. You might as well take a man from the quiet, unconfined seclusion in which he has lived and rioted from infancy, and fit up a cell for him in the inquisition, in some large city, where the tread of the tormentor is heard above and the laughter of the world without the walls.

We may differ in our tastes as much as we please. It is a way to encourage all sorts of mind and bring to light every thing fitted for poetry. But we must get out of the bad habit of dictating to great minds and striving to bring them up in our own way. Genius is not willing to be interfered with and told how to work, where to travel, and what to admire. And yet there are men who go so far as to hold up models for imitation and standards of taste for writers of every age and country, let their minds be ever so lofty and original. We shall say a little of this interference, for it appears to be the most mischievous of all.

It may be well for minds of a common cast to read and obey. They may profitably give themselves up all their lives, to the superiour intellects about them. They are not made nor wanted for authors, and they only leave a gap in the busier parts of society when they venture to be such. It is the great men of a country who are to make and support its literature. And to tell such men that they must give their days and nights to any models, ancient or modern, is to destroy the whole worth and character of genius. It is to make men look at creation and society through another man's eyes and communicate all that their hearts labour with by the help of a remembered manner they learnt in the schools. It is to educate different men by one rule and force all minds to one taste and pursuit. It comes in the way of nature and reduces all her irregularities, crooks, and violence, her endless change, into straightness, smoothness, and harmony. It is to make the difference of country, of habits, and institutions wholly ineffectual as to literature, and to bring the native of the mountains and plains, of the inland and coast, to a lifeless similarity of taste.

Where is a mind thus trained to get its food and excitement? It is irksome and exhausting to walk in the dusty track of an earlier traveller, especially when the whole world in "morning freshness" lies open to the observing, intrepid, and ardent. Their refreshment is in toils and adventures of their own seeking. Their imaginations are filled with bright forms of unattained excellence, kindling enthusiasm and hope for a man to dream about when he grows tired of what others have done and burns to make more perfect what he attempts himself. Such men owe their power over the reader chiefly to something all their own in their notice of things, their manner, feelings, partialities, and taste. There is a savour of genius and individuality in all they say. They write from the heart, and we know them every where. They sit alone and work by themselves, leaving friends unconsulted, enemies neglected, and doing nothing merely because it has been pointed out. They speak with freedom and infant fearlessness as if they were alone in the world and had all to themselves. They are never dried up by the fear that nature is failing but feel that something is left for them every where.

The imitator, the man who gets his stock of thought and sentiment of beauty from books, is cautious, constrained, and modelled throughout. Every thing, even to his enthusiasm, seems disciplined and artificial. He will have no sins of overgrowth to repent of. He seems under a careful process of emaciation to keep in the fashion of grace and slenderness. His business is to select and trim where others, with the prodigality of invention, have thrown heaps and masses. He burnishes old jewels or sets them anew and submits cheerfully to other labours about as generous and nourishing to a hungry mind. When he is among the great, either of the living or dead, he does not feel himself in society. He does not come within the touch of greatness. There is no friendly action of other minds on his own—no level on which they can meet and be happy and useful together. He goes as a worshipper, to wonder and obey, not as an equal, to question, value, and surpass. Is this the way to make writers of whom a nation is to be proud or who shall be happy from themselves? The reader will tell you that works fashioned by models, or infected with books, are but old stories, the more tedious for the finish and elegance which is intended to make up for freedom and originality. They have no carelessness nor waste thought about them—no indication that the mind was the lighter and happier for throwing off its constant growth. The writer has the stiff, genteel way of a man who is trying to entertain strangers and is afraid of committing himself, and so prepares himself for the occasion. There is none of that gracious, fearless familiarity which one feels with those of his own home, whom he has seen every hour and whose characters have rather grown upon him than been studied.

If the borrowers and imitators are only encouraged, the swarm will go on thickening. There is enough now in the stores of poetry, heaped up by others, to serve them for ages. They need not once look out of doors to see things for themselves. There are rules for versification, laws of taste, books of practical criticism, and approved standards of language, to make one go right and safely. And surely it is very easy for men (except those who have the indignant freedom of genius,) to write with such helps. Besides, it looks hard now-a-days to be original when so many have already gone over the land of poetry and soiled and made common all that lay on the surface or in secret. Alas, when the world grows rich, heirs will be indolent; and we should not wonder at it. The habit of living on other minds naturally creates a spirit of self indulgence, and at last of weak timidity. Instead of being kindled into effort by what others have done, the heart sinks into cowardly admiration. It is content to relish what it dares not rival. It sets much by a refined, artificial taste, and thinks it enough to be exquisite in criticism and eloquent in praise. You will see idolaters leaning upon the broken columns of ancient Temples or in ecstacies before pictures and statues. The student sits at his window with a book before him, but he never looks out upon the fields. Knowledge must now be drawn from libraries and collections. The difficulties of acquiring which were once encountered are now done away, and with them the wholesome and invigorating labour. We need not confound ourselves any longer in the wastes and thickets which our fathers so eagerly plunged into. We have masters and schools at our very doors, to teach us every thing and to reduce every thing to system and simplicity. Here then is the very mischief of learning—the way to turn great men into confectioners and second-hand caterers. Their minds are surfeited with what other men have said, and toiled hard and all alone, to come at. No wonder that they grow sickly, acquiescing, and unproductive.

Let us just look at one or two ways in which freedom and originality of mind are assailed or endangered. The first is by inculcating an excessive fondness for the ancient classicks and asserting their supremacy in literature. By some means or other the ancients have exerted an enormous influence among literary men, and in nations too that have had hardly any thing of real congeniality with them. And many a lover of his own home, of the domestick fame and character of his country, has in his fits of vexation been tempted to wish that the Barbarians had either done their work more faithfully among the fair fakricks of Greece and Rome or else left those illustrious nations to live and provoke the rest of the world to independent greatness, instead of being their school or nurse. As it now is, the old nations survive in a sort of mixed state of grandeur and desolation. We grow tender among ruins and fragments. We love to soften down the errours and grossness of the fallen and to extol and venerate the remains of their greatness without making a very scrupulous estimate of its real worth. The grave-yard is common ground where the living from every land may come together. There is no rancour nor heart-burning there. We can all give praise with generous complacency when no pretensions are set up. The Romans worshipped Greece after they had conquered her.

Besides, the earliest nations in letters have a sort of patriarchal claim to the reverence of those who come after. Nothing remains of them but their finished and best works. We have no records of their early attempts and failures—nothing to inspire pity, to lessen admiration, or to encourage us when we fail. They seem to have started up at once, as if by an "overnight creation," into elegance and beauty, full of the ease, delight, and earnestness of men who draw directly from nature. They are set off from the earlier world and connected with every after age by appearing to be the very beginners of literature. They become the lights and helps of other nations who are slower and later in attention to the mind. And even when their followers have surpassed their guides, and become quite equal to looking about and making a fortune for themselves, it is still hard to throw off the veneration and deference which all have felt and which gives them something common in their taste, pride, and obligations.

The boy at school (in the best but most complying hours of his life) is set to work upon the ancient classicks. He hears and reads of the god-like people who began and finished the world's literature. This is taken in with his rudiments, and along with it, indifference towards his own language which he acquired as unconsciously as he grew, and thinks too familiar for study or respect, while every thing ancient is brought home to him in solemnity and wonders and fastens itself upon him more closely than his prayers.

The effect of this is, in many cases, to make what is foreign, artificial, and uncongenial, the foundation of a man's literary habits, ambition, and prejudices. It is hardly possible that a man, thus trained and dependent, should not lose self respect and come to think every thing vulgar at home.

But it ought to be remembered that the question is not upon the merits of the ancients, or any models whatever. Men will always settle this matter for themselves according to their own taste and feelings. What we contend for is that the literature of a country is just as domestick and individual as its character or political institutions. Its charm is its nativeness. It is made for home, to be the luxury of those who have the feeling and love of home and whose characters and taste have been formed there. No matter for rudeness, or want of systems and schools. It is enough that all is our own and just such as we were made to have and relish. A country then must be the former and finisher of its own genius. It has, or should have, nothing to do with strangers. They are not expected to feel the beauty of your old poetical language, depending as it does on early and tender associations; connecting the softer and ruder ages of the country, and inspiring an inward and inexplicable joy, like a tale of childhood. The stranger perhaps is only alarmed or disgusted by the hoarse and wild musick of your forests or sea-shore, by the frantick superstition of your fathers, or the lovely fairy scenes that lie far back in the mists of your fable. He cannot feel your pride in the splendid barbarism of your country when the mind was in health and free and the foundations of your character and greatness laid for ever. All these things are for the native. They help to give a character to his country and her literature, and he loves them too well to be concerned at the world's admiration or contempt.

So long then as a country is proud of itself, it will repel every encroachment upon its native literature. Improvements will offer themselves under a thousand forms. Intimacy with other nations, especially if they are polished and the leaders of fashion, will tempt men to imitate them in every thing. But a nation should keep itself at home and value the things of its own household. It will have but feeble claims to excellence and distinction when it stoops to put on foreign ornament and manner, and to adopt from other nations, images, allusions, and a metaphorical language which are perfectly unmeaning and sickly out of their own birth-place. The most polished will be the dreariest ages of its literature. Its writers will be afraid to speak the language that God has given them till they have mingled the rough torrent with the allaying streams of a softer region. A strange idiom will be introduced into style. And the whole literature of a country will be mere gaudy patchwork, borrowed from every region that has any beauty to lend.

It may be well too just to hint that it is not foreign models alone which are to be feared. We must also be shy of ourselves. For men of real genius and independence will sometimes introduce dangerous novelties, and make errours and corruptions popular and contagious, however short-lived they may prove. And besides this, there is good reason to fear that every country, as it falls into luxury and refinement, will be doomed to have an Augustan age, a classical era of its own, when fine writers will determine what shall be correct taste, pure language, and legitimate poetry. A domestick master may not be as alarming as a foreigner, and long before a man has ceased to study and love the early literature of his country, he may expect to hear that the old language is barbarous and obsolete and rejected by all chaste authors who wish to keep the national literature uniform and pure. As to all this, a man must judge for himself. And one would think that if there must be models, a writer would do well to go as near to the original as possible, even to the very fathers of poetry. If there is luxury for him in such society, and if his books can find readers, in spite of the old cast about them, let him turn to the rougher and more intrepid ages of his country, before men troubled themselves about elegance or plan and wrote right on as they felt, even though they were uttering a thought for the first time, feeling probably very little concern whether a softer age laughed at or worshipped them—whether they were to be ranked among the classicks or barbarians of poetry, whether theirs was to be called an Augustan era, or merely the plain old English days of Elizabeth.

[1816]

There were many who asked what materials a native author might draw upon to make his work American. The following address by William Tudor is among the most detailed of the early recipes. Particularly noteworthy is his balanced account of the Indians and his habit, so common in Europe, of comparing them with the heroes of classical antiquity.

31

It has been said that one reason why we have not produced more good poems was owing to the want of subjects and though

> The poet's eye in a fine phrensy rolling,
> Glances from Heaven to earth, from earth to Heaven,

and makes the universe his domain, yet that the appropriate themes of other countries had been exhausted by their own poets and that none existed in ours. Thinking this opinion to be unfounded, the attempt to prove the latter part of it to be so may furnish a theme for this discourse during the few moments that I can presume to solicit your attention.

The early history of illustrious nations has been the source of the great master pieces of poetry: the fabulous ages of Greece are the foundation of the Iliad and Odyssey, and the same period gave Virgil his hero for the Æneid. Many modern epicks have taken the heroes of the earlier periods and revolutions of modern times. The American Revolution may some centuries hence become a fit and fruitful subject for an heroick poem; when ages will have consecrated its principles and all remembrance of party feuds and passions shall have been obliterated—when the inferiour actors and events will have been levelled by time, and a few memorable actions and immortal names shall remain the only monuments to engage and concentrate the admiration of a remote posterity.

From the close of the 16th to the middle of the 18th century many most interesting events took place on this continent and circumstances have concurred with time in casting a shade of obscurity resembling that of antiquity over the transactions of that period; while, by the great revolutions which have since happened, the connexion between those days and our own is interrupted, and they are so disconnected with the present era that no passionate feeling is blended with their consideration; they are now exclusively the domain of history and poetry. All the communities then standing have passed away or exist under new relations. The remarkable Confederacy of Indian tribes under the name of the five nations is extinct. The foundations of the French Empire in America have been torn up, the possessions that were once French are now held by the British, and the English colonies have become an independent nation. All these changes have insulated this portion of history and divested it of the irritation attendant on recent political affairs.

The region in which these occurrences took place abounds with grand and beautiful scenery, possessing some peculiar features. The numerous waterfalls, the enchanting beauty of Lake George and its pellucid flood, of Lake Champlain, and the lesser lakes, afford many objects of the most picturesque character; while the inland seas from Superiour to Ontario, and that astounding cataract whose roar would hardly be increased by the united murmurs of all the cascades of Europe, are calculated to inspire vast and sublime conceptions. The effects too of our climate composed of a Siberian winter and an Italian summer furnish peculiar and new objects for description. The circumstances of remote regions are here blended, and strikingly opposite appearances witnessed in the same spot, at different seasons of the year—In our winters, we have the sun at the same altitude as in Italy, shining on an unlimited surface of snow which can only be found in the higher latitudes of Europe where the sun in the winter rises little above the horizon. The dazzling brilliance of a winter's day, and a moon-light night when the utmost splendour of the sky is reflected from a surface of spotless white attended with the most excessive cold, is peculiar to the northern part of the United States. What too can surpass the celestial purity and transparency of the atmosphere in a fine autumnal day when our vision and our thoughts seem carried 'to the third heaven;' the gorgeous magnificence of their close, when the sun sinks from our view surrounded with varied masses of clouds, fringed with gold and purple, and reflecting in evanescent tints all the hues of the rainbow.[1]

---

[1] There is no climate in the world that presents more remarkable contrasts than that of the middle and northern parts of the United States. Boston, for instance, is in the same latitude with Rome, the cold in winter is occasionally as intense and the snow as deep as at Stockholm and St. Petersburg; but the sun hardly gleams on them in the winter months, while here his rays are shed from the same altitude as in Italy, and interrupts during the day that severity of cold, induced by the prevalence of the winds in the western quarter, coming to us over a continent of such vast extent covered with dense forests which shadow the earth and prevent

A most remarkable feature in the landscape at this same season, and which those who see it for the first time must behold with astonishment, is the singular appearance of the woods; where all the hues of the most lively flowers, the vivid colours of tulips, are given to the trees of the forest, and nature appears in a moment of capricious gayety to have attired the groves in the gaudiest and most fantastick livery. Nothing comparable to this effect can be seen in any part of Europe.[2]

---

the sun from warming and drying its surface. Our climate affords some of the worst and some of the finest weather that can be felt in any part of the world. The spring generally is the most capricious and disagreeable, the autumn the mellowest and most serene. Persons who are in the habit of remarking the appearance of the atmosphere cannot fail of admiring the extreme beauty of the sky at most seasons of the year. To witness the same effects, it is necessary in Europe to get into the same latitudes. The climate of England, modified by an insular situation, and the wide spread cultivation of its surface is peculiarly temperate, but constantly vapoury and humid. France and Germany, colder and warmer than England, are still more temperate than the United States; it is necessary to cross the Alps to find the same bright and beautiful atmosphere that surrounds us. In England it is seldom that any distant object can be seen distinctly, and there is always such a degree of haziness in the air that even neighbouring objects are never so clearly defined as they are under a purer sky; the artists of the Continent commonly reproach the artists of England with carrying this imitation of nature in their own country into their representations of the scenery of others, and in their engravings (the remark was made particularly in criticising that magnificent work, Stuart's Antiquities of Athens,) giving the misty, indistinct outline which they were accustomed to and which is not without its beauties but which was entirely foreign to the appearance of objects in Greece. This same effect of great distinctness, which is common to the south of Europe, may very often be seen here, especially in the summer. Any person may judge of this in a clear day by regarding elevated buildings, looking from the sun and observing with what sharpness and distinctness their edges and angles are marked and how bold the relief and distant the sky recedes. The most careless eye can hardly fail to be struck with the beauty of an evening sky, after sunset, and the appearance of the western horizon when the darkness has encroached on the eastern. On a summer or autumnal evening, when there are no clouds, as the twilight is advancing, the purity, transparency, brilliancy and harmonious subsiding and blending of the warmer tints from where the sun has set, to the fine *chiaro oscuro* of the opposite point, where the shadows of night are approaching, will afford a few minutes of delightful contemplation to the lover of nature. In contending for this splendour of our atmosphere which has sometimes been denied it I am well aware of all its disadvantages and would gladly take a little less brilliance and a little more comfort; but, as we are fully sensible, and are habitually repining at its inconveniences, it is well to know what compensation may be derived from its beauties. To the poet and the artist it is replete with picturesque effect.

[2] This singular and beautiful appearance of the forests is peculiar to this country. It arises partly from the greater variety of trees and perhaps from the early occur-

Many other beauties of inanimate nature might be enumerated, and these just mentioned are only cited as being in a degree peculiar. These extensive and variegated forests afford shelter to a variety of animals, beautiful in form and curious in their habits, such among others, are the beaver and the deer; and to birds of most exquisite plumage. The graceful shape and various species of some of the diminutive quadrupeds, the very abundance of some of these animals, and of certain kinds of birds, which almost darken the air in their flight, serve to enrich and animate the scenery. Prominent among objects of this class, is the king of birds, Jove's own imperial Eagle, the sacred emblem of our country: 'Formed by

---

rence of frosts when the leaves are still vigorous and filled with juices and which may be decomposed by the cold so as to produce these vivid colours; when they might merely fade and be partially changed if their fall was not produced prematurely. The forests in Europe in their autumnal dress have many shades of brown and yellow intermixed, but there is nothing equal to the effect produced here. To select two of our forest trees for instance, the white walnut and the maple, these trees attaining the height of forty feet and upwards and the whole foliage of the former of the brightest yellow and the latter the deepest scarlet. No artist has hitherto ventured to give this appearance in its full effect. There are many features in our forest scenery that are highly beautiful from their variety and strong contrasts. Europeans who have a knowledge and love of botany always admire them. Most of our trees and plants have been transplanted into the nurseries of Europe, and are much in request for all their ornamental plantations. It is not only the aspect of our forests, but the general aspect of our country, which have both been too much neglected by the American poets, who have written their descriptions more from the study of the classick poets of ancient and modern Europe than from meditating on the scenes familiar to them.—A painter who only makes pictures from copying the ideas and style of the great masters, without animating his manner by a study of nature, may produce correct but always cold and dry performances. Descriptive poetry, which borrows the fashion of other countries, however classick its allusions, will be languid and spiritless, it will possess no raciness and can never be rendered interesting. The general physiognomy of the United States is different from that of every country in Europe, its buildings, its cultivation, its natural and artificial objects have many peculiar features. There is no species of cultivation in Europe, not even the vine, except when cultivated on espaliers or pendant between trees, which is seldom seen, that can compare with a field of Indian corn, next to the sugar cane the richest in appearance of all plants. The care and labour which is bestowed on this grain in the Eastern States, the neatness and beauty of its appearance, form a strong contrast with the too careless and neglected appearance of other fields. This is the most splendid of all the gifts of Ceres, and it is difficult to say whether it is most pleasing to the eye in its growing state or at the period of harvest, when the ripened, luxuriant ears are discovered through their faded covering. It would extend this note too far to notice all the objects that may be cited as peculiar in some degree to our scenery.

nature for braving the severest cold, feeding equally on the produce of the sea and of the land, possessing powers of flight capable of outstripping even the tempests themselves; unawed by any but man; and from the etherial heights to which he soars, looking abroad at one glance to an immeasurable expanse of forests, fields, lakes and ocean deep below him, he appears indifferent to the little localities of change of seasons; as in a few minutes he can pass from summer to winter, from the lower to the higher regions of the atmosphere, the abode of eternal cold, and from thence descend at will to the torrid and arctick zones of the earth.'[3] In the same territories are found those enormous bones of animals now extinct that have generated so many fables among the savages and speculations among philosophers; and those extensive fortifications so buried in obscurity that even tradition is silent respecting them;—objects which lead to that musing on former times most propitious to poetry.

Such are some of the subordinate subjects that would be fruitful of allusion and fertile in description to the poet. The human actors on this theatre are still more striking and their history replete with interest and romantick adventure. The English and French were founding extensive empires here and their contiguous possessions produced a century of conflicts which terminated at last in the exclusive power of the former. European affairs were more than once affected by the disputes of these two nations in the regions of Canada, and the decision of the most important contests on the Old Continent has been produced by the issue of operations in the remote wilds of North America. The period also was one of great interest in European annals; France and England were rivals in glory, both in arts and arms.

Between these powers were interposed the Aborigines, who became the allies of these nations and the most efficient part of their force. Before speaking more particularly of them, it will be necessary to deprecate the prejudices naturally entertained on the subject from what we now see. The degenerate, miserable remains of the Indian nations which have dwindled into insignificance and lingered among us as the tide of civilization has flowed, mere floating deformities on its surface, poor, squalid and enervated with intoxicating liquors, should no more be taken for the representatives of their ancestors who first met the Europeans on the edge of their boundless forests, severe and untamed as the regions they tenanted, than the Greek slaves who now tremble at the frown of a petty Turkish tyrant can be considered the likeness of their immortal progeni-

[3] Wilson's Ornithology.

tors, of those immoveable bands, before whom at Platœa, Thermopylæ and Marathon, the whole Persian empire broke and subsided like the waves of the sea against the rocks they defended. To form an idea of what they once were, to see them in the energy and originality of their primitive condition, we must now journey a thousand miles. They possessed so many traits in common with some of the nations of antiquity that they perhaps exhibit the counterpart of what the Greeks were in the heroick ages, and particularly the Spartans during the vigour of their institutions. Their origin has been the source of many theories and conjectures, few of which are more reasonable than the suggestion of Spenser in his Fairy Queen that they are the descendants of the man whom Prometheus animated by stealing fire from Heaven. Whether this race of men could like the Greeks have gradually acquired civilization, or whether they are a distinct species incapable of being tamed, may be uncertain: sudden civilization at least has been shewn to be impossible; they diminish and waste before its progress like snow before the vernal influence. The sublime allegorical painting of Guido,[4] in which Apollo encircled by the hours is chasing night and her shadows over the surface of the globe might almost represent the extinction of our savage precursors before the dawn of science and cultivation. The history of these people then is not less interesting since in a short period they will exist no where else, and even in the next century the Indian warriour and hunter will perhaps only be found on the shores of the Pacifick ocean.

The virtues and vices of the original inhabitants of America have been generally exaggerated by their enemies or admirers. It would be as foolish to vindicate the one as to deny the other; both grew out of their condition: the influence of civilized society destroyed the former and nourished the latter. Their virtues were hospitality, reverence to age, unalterable constancy in friendship, and undaunted fortitude in every species of enterprise and suffering. They lived in a state of proud savage equality and had no esteem for any merit except that which was derived from superiority in the arts of hunting, war, and eloquence. These were their general characteristicks, but the difference between Indian was almost as great as among European nations, and the inferiority of some to others was quite as remarkable as that which exists between civilized people.

Among those who were distinguished, few are more eminent than the confederated tribes which were first known to us under the name of the Five Nations. These nations resided originally in the district where now

[4] In the Rospigliosi Palace at Rome.

stands Montreal. The Algonquins lived more in the interiour. The former were peaceable in their habits and subsisted by cultivating the earth; the latter were warlike and depended on hunting; the two nations were friendly and exchanged their corn and venison. At a certain period, when game was scarce, the Algonquins requested the Five Nations to send them some of their young men to assist in the increased toil of procuring food. These becoming very expert huntsmen, were murdered by the Algonquin employers out of jealousy and apprehension. When complaint was made of this treacherous cruelty, they only blamed the murderers and made some slight presents to the injured people, fearless of the resentment of a nation who subsisted by the effeminate employment, as they esteemed it, of agriculture. The Five Nations determined on revenge, which being discovered by the Algonquins, they resolved to reduce them to absolute obedience by force. In pursuing this scheme, they chased them from their place of living and obliged them to seek shelter in the region between the Hudson and Lakes Erie and Ontario. The Confederacy, goaded by the injustice of their enemies to relinquish their peaceable employments, gradually acquired a knowledge of war and courage to face them; and, though the latter aided by the French had the great advantage of the previous use of fire arms, the Five Nations eventually triumphed and, with the exception of a small number that were driven to the vicinity of Quebec, finally extinguished the Algonquins, one of the most warlike, numerous and politick tribes of North America. Having once acquired the habits and knowledge of war, they extended their dominion with restless ambition till they had either formed alliances with, or reduced to submission, most of the nations between the St. Lawrence, the sea coast, and the Ohio. The Dutch formed a treaty with them in 1609. The English made their first treaty of alliance with them in 1664, which was continued from time to time and never violated. They had also particular treaties with Massachusetts, New-York, Pennsylvania, Maryland and Virginia.

From this slight sketch of their history, it may be imagined that these nations must have held an important part in all the contests between the French and English. Indeed, the affairs of the former were more than once brought to the very brink of destruction by them. At a very critical moment, the English withdrew from the contest by the most positive orders of the Sovereign, which were artfully obtained by the French Ministry, from the bigoted subservience of the Stuarts to the Court of Rome, while, under pretence of religion, the Jesuit Missionaries were promoting the designs of France in that vast scheme of Colossal aggrandizement which, with one foot at New Orleans and the other at Quebec, would have bestrode the Empire of North America.

The actions of these people in war had a strong character of wildness and romance; their preparations for it and celebrations of triumph were highly picturesque. The solemn councils of their Sachems, the war-dance which preceded their expeditions, like the Pyrrhick Dance of antiquity, was full of terrifick expression. Many of their achievements were performed by a few or sometimes only one or two individuals. These were savage in their character and not admitted now in the practice of war among civilized nations and yet such actions may be rendered highly interesting in poetry. What was the nocturnal excursion of Diomed and Ulysses in the 10th book of the Iliad, in which they slew Rhesus, king of the Thracians, with many of his officers in their sleep, and brought away his beautiful horses? what was the enterprise of Nisus and Euryalus in the 9th book of the Æneid, in which they murdered so many in their sleep, and in which Euryalus, by taking from one of them his splendid helmet and belt was afterwards discovered by the moon gleaming on its polished surface, and the death of both occasioned by this spoil? These episodes are two of the finest in those immortal Epicks, yet it is only to the genius of Homer and Virgil that they are indebted for more than may be found in several Indian adventures.

Many of their friendships were as strong as that of the two followers of Æneas: their affection generally for those of their own nation was of the most powerful kind; a proof of this may be found in the speech of a Sachem of the Mohawks to an officer who was hurrying them to undertake an expedition, just after they had returned from holding a Council at Albany, where they had lost by sickness some of their finest young men: 'You seem,' said he 'to think that we are brutes, that we have no sense of the loss of our dearest relations, and some of them the bravest men we had in our nation; you must allow us time to bewail our misfortunes'— They were guilty of ferocious cruelty towards their enemies. Alas! cruelty is not peculiar to savages. They condemned to torture the foes who would have tortured them.—How many Christian nations are free from the reproach at every period of their history of having tortured their own subjects for mere matters of opinion? In war they laid waste the dwellings and cornfields of their enemies and murdered the defenceless.—Is there nothing in the conduct of nations pretending to the highest civilization that will, under this head, interfere with their exclusive claim to barbarism?

That they were not merely hunters and warriours, but sagacious in the management of affairs and capable of deep laid schemes of policy, there are many historical anecdotes to prove. One must suffice on this occasion. The most accomplished statesman of the Italian school could hardly surpass the following perfidious and subtle policy of an Indian Chieftain. In the year 1687, Adario, a very distinguished Sachem of the Hurons, finding that his nation had become suspected by the French on account of the intercourse they had held with the English, determined to recover their good graces by some signal action against the Five Nations, their common foe. For this purpose he left Michilimackinack with an hundred men and called on his way at the fort of Cadaraqui for intelligence. The French, after many attempts, had just succeeded in obtaining from a part of the Five Nations that they would send Ambassadours to Montreal to form a treaty of peace. The French commander informed the Huron Chief of this state of affairs, that the deputies were then on their way, and begged him to return home and attempt no enterprise that might interrupt these favourable prospects.

Surprised at this intelligence, the wily savage was under the greatest concern for his nation, least they should be sacrificed to the French interests if the latter could make peace with the Confederacy. Dissembling his feelings, he left the fort, not to return home as the Commander supposed, but to proceed to a spot where he knew the Ambassadours must pass, to await them. After a short time they made their appearance, guarded by forty young warriors. They were surprised, and all their guards either killed or made prisoners. When these latter were all secured, Adario told them that he had been informed by the Governour of Canada that fifty of their warriors were to pass that way about this period and that he had formed this ambush to intercept them. The deputies, astonished at this perfidy of the French, related the purpose of their journey to Adario; on hearing which he affected the utmost fury and rage at the atrocity which the French government had caused him to commit and swore he would be revenged. Then looking steadfastly on the prisoners, one of whom was Decanesora, a famous Chief of the Oneidas, he said, go, my brethren, I loose your bonds and send you home again, though our nations be at war; I shall never rest easy till the Five Nations have taken their revenge of the French for this treachery.

The Deputies were persuaded by his conduct and told him that he and his nation might make peace with them when they pleased. Adario, who had lost but one man in the affair, took one of theirs as usual to supply his place; then giving them a supply of arms and ammunition, dismissed them. These Chiefs were from the Oneida and Onondagua tribes which had received the Jesuit Missionaries, were the best disposed towards the French, and now returned home most deeply incensed.

One circumstance remained to complete the effect; Adario, on his return, gave up his prisoner to the French officer commanding, who being ignorant of these circumstances, to nourish the hatred between the Five Nations and the Hurons, ordered him to be shot. The Huron Chief called an Indian of the former people to witness this execution of his country-man and the cruelty of the French from which even he was not able to save his own prisoner, and then bid him make his escape and relate what he had seen. The fugitive arrived at the very time when the French had sent to disown Adario in the action he had committed; but this additional circumstance exasperated them so highly that they would listen to no representations. Their thoughts were all bent on revenge. A short time after they made a descent on the island of Montreal, took all the Forts in their way, destroyed, with indiscriminate havock, men, women and children, and reduced the French power in Canada to the very verge of ruin.

As the government of these people was a republick, the practice of eloquence was of the highest importance, since the art of persuasion was a principal source of influence and power. None of the Indian Nations carried the science of speaking to greater perfection, of which there are many proofs on record. The general characteristicks of their style are well known. We have received their speeches under every disadvantage, since they come to us through the medium of ignorant interpreters who were incapable of transfusing the spirit and ornament of one language into the idiom of another when they thoroughly understood neither. The solem-nity of their councils, the dignity and animation of their manner, their style of address, 'Sachems and Warriours,' were all suited to command attention and respect. Colden thus describes one of their orators: 'Decane-sora had for many years the greatest reputation among the Five Nations for speaking and was generally employed as their speaker in their negoti-ations with both French and English: he was grown old when I saw him and heard him speak, he had great fluency and a graceful elocution, that would have pleased in any part of the world. His person was tall and well made, and his features to my thinking resembled much the busto's of Cicero.'[5]

[5] There were many metaphors which were transmitted down among the Indians by the women whose business it was to retain and repeat them from one generation to another. The following remarks on the language and oratory of the Five Nations are taken from Colden's history.

'The people of the Five Nations are much given to speech-making, ever the natural consequence of a perfect Republican government; where no single person has a power to compel, the arts of persuasion alone must prevail. As their best speakers distinguish themselves in their public councils and treaties with other nations, and thereby gain the esteem and applause of their countrymen, (the only superiority

The speeches given by Homer to the characters in the Iliad and Odyssey, form some of the finest passages in those poems. The speeches of these Indians only want similar embellishment to excite admiration. A few fragments of one may serve as a specimen. It was delivered under the following circumstances. James the second, at the solicitation of the French Court, having given orders to the Colonies not to interfere, the French were determined to bring the Five Nations to their own terms. For this purpose the governor of Canada proceeded with a strong force in 1684 to Lake Ontario. The Indian Chiefs had meanwhile been persuaded by the Jesuits to send a deputation to meet him having been promised that they should be cordially received and kindly treated. The French army

---

which any one of them has over the others) it is probable they apply themselves to this art by some kind of study and exercise in a great measure. It is impossible for me to judge how far they excel, as I am ignorant of their language; but the speakers whom I have heard had all a great fluency of words and much more grace in their manner than any man could expect among a people entirely ignorant of all the liberal arts and sciences.

'I am informed that they are very nice in the turn of their expressions, and that few of themselves are so far masters of their language as never to offend the ears of their *Indian* auditory by an unpolite expression. They have, it seems, a certain *urbanitas* or *atticism* in their language, of which the common ears are ever sensible, though only their great speakers attain to it. They are so much given to speech-making that their common compliments to any person they respect at meeting and parting are made in harangues.

'They have some kind of elegance in varying and compounding their words, to which not many of themselves attain, and this principally distinguishes their best speakers. I have endeavoured to get some account of this, as a thing that might be acceptable to the curious; but, as I have not met with any one person who understands their language and also knows any thing of grammar or of the learned languages, I have not been able to attain the least satisfaction. Their present minister tells me that their verbs are varied, but in a manner so different from the *Greek* or *Latin* that he cannot discover by what rule it was done and even suspects that every verb has a peculiar mode. They have but few radical words, but they compound their words without end; by this their language becomes sufficiently copious and leaves room for a good deal of art to please a delicate ear. Sometimes one word among them includes an entire definition of the thing; for example they call *wine, Oneharadesehoengtseragherie,* as much as to say, *a liquor made of the juice of the grape.* The words expressing things lately come to their knowledge are all compounds; they have no labeals in their language, nor can they perfectly pronounce a word wherein there is a labeal; and when one endeavours to teach them to pronounce words, they tell one, they think it ridiculous that they must shut their lips to speak. Their language abounds with gutturals and strong aspirations; these make it very sonorous and bold; and their speeches abound with metaphors, after the manner of the Eastern nations, as will best appear by the speeches that I have copied.'

however became so much weakened by sickness, so many of the soldiers
had died, that all the formidable preparations were rendered useless and
their Commander was unable to prosecute his designs by force. This
situation of the French was well understood by the Indians. When they
met, after many ceremonies the conference was opened with due form, the
parties being drawn up in a circle of which the French officers formed one
half and the Savages the other. The Governor delivered a most arrogant,
menacing speech, to impress them with fear of the tremendous power of
France. Garangula, the Indian speaker on this occasion, was much surprised at the difference of its tone from what he had been led to expect by
the Jesuits and immediately returned an answer of which the following
are extracts. The Indians called the Governor of Canada, Onondio; it was
their custom to give a surname as a mark of honour to the Governor of
each of the Provinces, which was never changed.

'ONONDIO

'I honor you, and the warriors that are with me all likewise honor you.
Your interpreter has finished your speech, I now begin mine. My words
hasten to reach your ears, pray listen to them.

'Onondio, you must have believed when you left Quebec that the sun
had burnt up all the Forests which render our country inaccessible to the
French, or that the Lakes had overflowed their banks and surrounded our
Castles so that it was impossible for us to get out of them. Yes, Onondio,
you must surely have dreamt this, and curiosity to see so great a wonder
has brought you so far. Now you are undeceived, since I and the warriors
here present are come to assure you that the Senekas, Cayugas, Onondagas, Oneidas and Mohawks are yet alive. I thank you, in their name, for
bringing back into their country that Calumet which your predecessor
received from their hands. I congratulate you for your good fortune in
having left under ground that murdering hatchet which has been so often
dyed with the blood of the French. Listen, Onondio, I am not asleep, I
have my eyes open, and that sun which enlightens me discovers to me a
great Captain at the head of a Company of soldiers who speaks as if he
were dreaming. He says that he only came to the Lake to smoke on the
great Calumet with the Onondagas. But Garangula asserts that he sees the
contrary, that it was to have destroyed them if sickness had not weakened
the arms of the French.

'I see Onondio raving in a camp of sick men whose lives the great Spirit
has saved by inflicting this sickness on them. Hear, Onondio, our women
had taken their clubs, our children and old men had carried their bows
and arrows into the heart of your camp if our warriors had not disarmed

them and kept them back when your messenger Oquesse came to our castles. Enough, I say no more on this subject.

'We may go where we please, and carry with us whom we please, and buy and sell what we please. If your allies be your slaves, use them as such, command them to receive no other but your people. This belt confirms my words.

'What I say is the voice of all the five nations; hear what they answer, open your ears to what they speak: The Senakas, Cayugas, Onondagas, Oneidas and Mohawks say, that when they buried the hatchet at Cadaracqui, in the presence of your predecessor, in the centre of the Fort, they planted the tree of peace in the same place to be there carefully preserved, that in place of being a retreat for soldiers, it might become a rendezvous for merchants; that in place of arms and ammunitions of war, beavers and merchandize should only enter there.

'Hearken Onondio, take care for the future, that so great a number of soldiers as appear there do not choak the Tree of Peace planted in so small a fort. It would be a great misfortune if after it had so easily taken root, you should stop its growth and prevent its covering your country and ours with its branches. I assure you in the name of the Five Nations that our warriors shall dance to the Calumet of peace under its leaves, and shall remain quiet on their matts, and shall never dig up the hatchet, till their brethren Onondio, or Corlaer, shall either jointly or separately endeavour to attack the country which the Great Spirit has given to our ancestors. This belt confirms my words, and this other the authority given to me by the Five Nations.'—Then addressing himself to the French Interpreter, he said—'Take courage, Oquesse, you have spirit, speak, explain my words, omit nothing, tell all that your brethren and friends say to Onondio, your Governor, by the mouth of Garangula, who loves you and desires you to accept this present of beaver and take part with him in his feast to which he invites you. This present of beaver is sent to Onondio on the part of the Five Nations.'

This speech may be compared with the celebrated message of the Scythians to Alexander in Quintius Curtius, and it affords materials which, if they were drest in the style of the great Roman Historians, would vie with any that they have transmitted to us; indeed, its figurative language, pungent sarcasm, and lofty tone can hardly be surpassed.

Perilous and romantick adventures,[6] figurative and eloquent harangues,

---

[6] The early history of our country furnishes many characters, adventures and incidents of the strongest interest. Prominent among the former is Capt. John Smith

strong contrasts and important interests, are as frequent in this portion of history as the theatre on which these actions were performed is abundant in grand and beautiful scenery. There are many inferiour circumstances that might contribute appropriate materials for poetry. The armorial bearings of the Indians, their Hieroglyphick writings, and some of their superstitions may be made subservient to poetical effect. For instance, there is in Lake Champlain a high rock against which the waves dash with vehemence and the spray is thrown to a great height. The Savages believed that an ancient Indian resided under this rock, who had power over the winds; to propitiate him they always threw over a pipe, or made some other oblation in passing. A man of distinction among the early Dutch inhabitants of New York, by the name of Corlaer, who was held in such high veneration by the Indians that they treated with him as the Governor of that Province and ever after called the Governor by his name, while on his way to visit the Governor of Canada, ridiculed this

---

whose common and familiar name is the only thing pertaining to his history which is not elevated and heroick. His life is now very rare and the book commands a high price, but a very able abstract of it may be found in Dr. Belknap's American Biography. And there is hardly a marvellous tale on the shelves of any circulating library that can surpass the real adventures of this extraordinary man. From his very infancy to his death, which happened in the middle period of life, his whole career is a series of daring and romantick achievements in many different parts of the world. His reputation appears without stain, and he is a genuine hero of romance, being equally distinguished for the gallantry of love and war. He gave to the northern Cape of Massachusetts bay the name of a Turkish lady who interested herself in his fate, when a prisoner of the Turks; but *Cape Tragabizanda,* afterwards got the name of Cape Ann, which it will no doubt retain, though the other out of regard to Smith might be used in poetry. His name is best known in this country, from his encounters with the father of Pocahontas and the devoted affection of that interesting Indian princess towards him. The character of Standish among the Plymouth colonists; of the Sachem of Mount Hope, and the wars which ended in his destruction: the singular and heroick character of Madame de la Tour of whom some account may be found in Hubbard's history recently published by the Historical Society from an ancient Ms.: the religious fanaticism and intrigues of Mrs. Hutchinson and her supporter in Sir Henry Vane, which caused as much trouble and commotion in the colony of Massachusetts as the Mystical doctrines of Madame Guyon occasioned in Paris and to the Court of Louis 14th. These and many others are interesting materials. The incident mentioned by President Stiles is very striking, of Dixwell one of the regicides suddenly emerging from his concealment, and by his presence animating an infant settlement when suddenly assailed from the Indians to repel the savages, and then returning unnoticed to his retreat; which made many of the people who knew nothing of his concealment regard him as a mysterious being, a good angel sent for their deliverance. If remarkable characters and actions

Indian Eolus. He was drowned directly afterwards by the upsetting of his canoe, which the Indians always attributed to his disrespect for the old man who had the control of the winds. This at least is not more extravagant than Homer's account of the present made by the monarch of Eolia to Ulysses of an assortment of winds secured in bags which being untied by his sailors, a tempest was created that drove them on the coast of the Lestrigons.

There is an ingenious device of Epick poetry that might be here used with great effect. This is the prophetick narration, a prophecy after the facts have occurred. Such is the celebrated Ode of Gray, in which the last of the Bards predicts the misfortunes of Edward's posterity; such are the adventures of Ulysses in the 11th book of the Odyssey, and of Æneas in the 6th book of the Æneid, in which those heroes are told among the shades the future fortunes of their race. The poet might introduce the expedient as his fancy suggested. It may be supposed that a French and

---

are to be found in our history, the scenes where they lived or occurred must be interesting from association of ideas. There are many such, though they have been too much neglected. We have all felt the interest excited by Scott for the scenery he describes in the Lady of the Lake. Its natural beauty is doubtless great—yet, give a bard of equal genius, the spot described in the last volume of the Historical collections as the one chosen by Gosnold in his first voyage—on one of the Elizabeth Islands there is a small lake in which there is a rocky islet where is still to be seen the foundations of the first dwelling erected on these shores by Europeans. The remarkable security of this situation, its natural beauty, the interest attending this attempt to colonize a country which has since played such an important part in the world, make this secluded spot more interesting than the Highland Lake; the time will come when this spot will be visited with as much interest, as the traveller at Rome goes to the Fountain of Egeria.

It would be encroaching too far to dwell longer on these topicks. No prejudice is more common, none more unfounded, none will more certainly be hereafter destroyed, than the one which supposes the early history of our country to be deficient in interest. To a person totally unacquainted with it, the mere mention of the leading circumstances on which it is founded would prove on very slight reflection that it was indeed impossible it should be so. Even saints and miracles may be incorporated in it if such be the taste of the poet. In the 'Lettres edifiantes' published at Paris in 1807, there are the letters of Father Charlevoix and the other Jesuits in Canada relating all the minute circumstances of the deaths of some holy Indian Virgins, who died in the odour of sanctity, and at whose tombs miracles were performed duly attested and sworn to by divers honourable men. Those who wish to investigate this department, may consult, *Smith's Life, Belknap's Biography, Hubbard's history, Colden's history of the Five Nations, La Hontan's Travels, and the histories of Virginia and Massachusetts. Charlevoix Nouvelle France. Lafitau's Mœurs des Sauvages, Adair's American Indians.*

English Officer and an American Colonist should accompany an Indian Sachem deputed by his tribe to consult some Indian sorcerer or divinity; the scene may be in one of those islands of Lake Superiour which some of their traditions represent as the abode of the blest, on shores perhaps untrodden by the foot of man, lone, distant and obscure as those Cimmerian climes in which lay the opening to Tartarus. In seeking for a knowledge of destiny, what wonderful events would be unfolded.

The prescient expounder of fate would declare to the Chieftain of the Five Nations, the alliances, contests, triumphs and utter extinction of his race; that they should disappear with the animals they hunted and the forests that sheltered both—they should vanish before the spirit of civilization, like the mist of the Lakes before the morning sun, and leave no trace of their existence, but in the records of the white men. To the Englishman he would foretell the civil war, the death of Charles on the scaffold, the fanatical austerity of the times, the usurpation of Cromwell, and, at his decease, the restoration of Royalty and the licentious gayety that ensued— the final expulsion of the Stuarts and extinction of that family—the lustre of arts and arms during the reign of Anne; with the subsequent increasing splendour and grandeur of his nation till their empire should extend over both the Indies. To the American Colonist would be foretold the American Revolution, the fame of its heroes and statesmen—he would announce to him the first of these, the man who should be first in war, first in peace, and first in the hearts of his countrymen; the successful issue of the glorious contest for Independence would be predicted and he would be shewn the future greatness, happiness and glory of his country. To the Frenchman he would narrate the conquests, the splendour of the arts and of literature, the bigotry, disasters and miseries of the reign of Louis 14th—the profligacy and corruption of the regency, the loss of their possessions on this continent, and in the last conflict the death of the victorious and the vanquished Generals under the walls of Quebec. The constant increase of luxury and refinement to the era of the Revolution. In revealing that Revolution, he would describe the contagious enthusiasm of hope which would intoxicate all nations at its dawn; the crimes, the horrours and wonderful events that would accompany its progress; and the foul, gloomy despotism that would attend its close.—The King, his family, and his nobles perishing on the scaffold, or withering in exile; religion prohibited, its altars profaned, its ministers proscribed.—France covered with the dust of her ruined palaces and drenched with the blood of her citizens. He would foretell the rapid rise, energetick progress, and portentous grandeur of the great usurper; his ambition, wars, and victories; the ravages committed, the remote regions invaded, the kingdoms overthrown, while

> at his heels
> Lash'd in like hounds, should famine, sword and fire,
> Crouch for employment,

he would predict at the hour of deepest gloom, the reaction of publick feeling, the overwhelming wave of retributive conquest pursuing him back from every country of Europe to his own capital, his abdication, the return of the—but no, plain prose and sober reason are confounded by these events, they must be left to the madness of verse, and the inspiration of the poet.

This is a cursory sketch of some of the scenes and events that would be fruitful in poetry. When we recollect what delightful performances have been composed by one modern poet out of the obscure quarrels of Border Banditti in barbarous ages, how another in thoughts that breathe and words that burn has immortalized the pirates of the Archipelago, much may surely be expected from this region when it shall be explored with the torch of imagination. The materials are rude, yet talent only is wanting to mould and animate them. The same block of marble which in the hands of an artisan might only have formed a step for the meanest feet to trample on, under the touch of genius unfolded the Belvidere Apollo, glowing with divine beauty and immortal youth, the destroyer of the Python, the companion of the Muses, the majestick God of Eloquence and Poetry.

[1815]

John Knapp's essay begins with a reminder that a nation will remain great in memory only if its achievements find literary embodiment. The passage below picks up his argument as he points to the materials which await the American writer and then moves to the familiar question of whether the poet should deal with recent events. Knapp has a remarkably high opinion of the poet's power and social function; appearing as they did in the important North American Review, *his ideas must have had wide influence.*

32

. . . Whatever we have learnt under pleasing emotions is constantly recurring to our thoughts. If we have heard noble actions described in language that charmed our ears, and filled us with transport, shall we not be fonder of reflecting on them and their similitudes; and will they not tend more to give a bias to our dispositions, than if they were related only for the fact's sake, with dry precision and circumstance? None can be blind to the invaluable uses or the dignity of history. Yet how few among the more numerous ranks of the community derive from it any thing to influence their feelings or inform their understandings? It boots nothing what things have happened, if men have no delight in thinking of them. The events and characters, which have distinguished the eras of England are, indeed, well known to the British people, but it is Shakspeare, who has made it a pleasurable thing to be told of them.

It can hardly be doubted, that the American revolution might afford subjects to employ the poet, with success and glory, limited only by his talents. The materials it would furnish are infinite, its characters innumerable, and the scenery of its places full of beauty and grandeur. All ranks of the community took part in it; every station of life was reached by its agitations. The hopes and fears of the remote cultivator and *woodsman,* no less than the busy townsman, the concerns of lovers, their plans for connubial welfare, the prouder calculations of men of property and station, all were at the mercy of the times. Above all, the crisis was brought upon them by their resolute adherence to principles esteemed just.

It is in such periods, that the soul is transformed, and acquires energies unimagined in tamer ages. What calls into motion all our inward powers, those diviner faculties which are proof of our immortality, like the occurrences of perilous and calamitous times? What men are great like those, who have passed through scenes of general distress, and perplexity, and change, and mighty, but almost despaired of deliverance?

When such a union of interests and feelings exists, as binds together all orders and conditions of men; when the hopes and fears, joys and misfortunes, in which we fluctuate, equally toss and swell the bosoms of unnumbered fellow-beings, the sensations and capacities of every individual are mysteriously magnified. A providential interposition seems to work in us a change, so that we can endure and perform what we could not before have passed through in imagination only, without agony of spirit; and at the same time it yields us solemn pleasures of no earthly nature. The soul, perceiving a more congenial quality in outward things, comes forth into full dominion, thoughtless of its garment of flesh, as if to anticipate its disembodied state. So much superior are the enjoyments bestowed by the predominance of this immortal part of us, to those more connected with our animal nature, that the rudest of mankind, who have once been conscious of them, are not only ever fond of the recollection, but often disposed to renew the dangers and commotions, to which they had owed the transient expansion of their faculties.

But, to be thus moved, we need not pass through these dangers ourselves,—there is efficacy in language for the production of equal excitement. Personal experience is not requisite to him whose intelligence may be quickened through sympathies, which the appealing voice of poetry can touch. It is enough and more than enough for the poet, that in times long elapsed, men and elements have contended and wrought overthrow. His materials already abound,—the ravages of armies, plots of the ambitious, assemblies of men with anxious countenances and agitated hearts;— all past ages have endowed him with their ruins and their glories. Say not, that words are of the substance of air. The words of the poet are like the breath of life to him that hears them worthily. They dilate the intellectual frame, and match it to high and vast contemplations:—they call up our whole humanity, and again soothe the troubled affections into a mild, but never lifeless calm.

But, though the elements of poetry are chiefly strong passions and great interests, and consist not with feeble emotions, yet are the tender affections essential in its composition. The poem that does not abound in themes of kind humanity, in the vicissitudes of friendship and love, in scenes and images of innocent joy and pastoral simplicity;—in the soft bird-like music, as well as the trumpet notes of its verses,—cannot be the lasting favourite of any people. These gentle but impressive incidents were copiously supplied by the situation and habits of our population. Even those who were engaged in the most arduous operations, the civil and military heroes of the times, were involved in the various fortunes, and often romantic adventures of heart-formed connexions. Unlike the European military, who, on entering their armies and fleets, like the monk on entering his convent, separate themselves from all domestic interest and feelings, the American soldiery retained in the fort and field every concern and sympathy of the fireside and neighbourhood. Our females, indeed, came not out among them, girt with shining armour, like Artemisia of the Leonidas, Clorinda and Gildippe of the Jerusalem Delivered, or the Maid of Orleans. There were some, however, as private memoirs tell us, who caught the zeal of martial enterprise, and performed deeds, that might, with slight poetic aid, be managed to equal the exploits of those antique heroines. But the poet need not enlist them in his service. Females, that follow the camp in modern wars, scarcely expect the notice of the muses.—Yet our matrons and sisters were exposed to the dangers and often heard the tumult of the contest; for the march of armies was by their own doors, and the battle field not seldom on their patrimonial hills and plains. An acquaintance with such scenes was not, however, an object of their curiosity or ambition.—They also partook in the civil agitations, for the fortunes and rank in life of both the retired and forward depended also on political measures; and they could not but sympathise with their connexions and friends, who were delegated to councils of government, and returned to their families fraught with the anxieties and hopes and resolves of freemen under proscription.

These circumstances will give animation to local descriptions, of which the poetical uses are obvious. If we take any glory in our country's being beautiful and sublime and picturesque, we must approve the work which reminds us of its scenery by making it the theatre of splendid feats and heart-moving incidents. If men's minds are influenced by the scenes in which they are conversant, Americans can scarcely be denied a claim to be inspired with some peculiar moral graces, by their grand and lovely landscapes. But, moreover, it is beneficial to connect our best intellectual associations with places in our own land. In part, we love our country because our minds seem to have been furnished from its surface, and because our most natural and vivid ideas are inseparable from pictures which have it for their groundwork. The places which we have long frequented are the props of our memory:—it fails, and the mind misses its fulness of ideas, when we are absent from them. It is no idle forecasting to consider, whether, in the course of providence, it may not be necessary for this nation to avail itself of the full strength and operation of its patriotic attachments and principles.

Important uses will undoubtedly accrue from the labours of the antiquary and historical collector. They have already attested that the lives and adventures of our predecessors comprehend things interesting to the scholar and philosopher, as well as the patriot. The poet and sentimentalist would no longer lament the want of human incident, if informed by them of the numberless trials and achievements which have marked every league of our unmeasured country. There is no necessity, in our travels through it, to recollect the stories and romances and heroic exploits, which have signalized transatlantic regions of similar localities and features. We need but inquire, and we shall seldom fail, wherever the place, to hear some story that will either touch the heart or lift it with strong emotion.

But it may be questioned, whether the modern origin of the transactions and personages designed for celebration, would not defeat the plans of the poet. The antiquity of our compatriots does not extend to two hundred years; and men are now alive, who may have conversed with the children of those who first arrived on our shore. This circumstance, it is apprehended, would cut off the poet from what has ever been esteemed his peculiar province. It denies him space to employ any of those magnificent beings, the kin of gods, which glorify the times anterior to the date of annals. As it requires a misty atmosphere to elevate into view the distant islands and promontories, which are ordinarily intercepted by the curve of the globe, so is the obscurity of remote time deemed necessary to exhibit the fields of romance and poetry, and their wonder-working inhabitants. It is conceded that history may appeal to our admiration, and secure a passionate interest, although the matters it relates should be of recent occurrence. Herodotus recounted the wars of the Greeks with the Persians in the famed Olympic Assembly, where not a few attended who had been engaged in them, and great numbers who had learnt the principal facts from heroes whose funeral rites they had just performed. He did not, however, refrain from inserting many fables and marvellous traditions, which had doubtless obtained belief in that age. Most of these appear to have been related with the view to expose their untruth or absurdity, and so correct the credulity of the people by the remarks and arguments he subjoined. But they nevertheless had the effect of heightening the interest and ornament of the story. A work under the denomination of history, abounding with similar embellishment, would scarcely be approved at the present day. Yet, for the purposes of moral instruction, as well as entertainment, things real may, without offence, be modified and take their form from the hand of an author not strictly historical; and it is best to leave this to the poet. Characters and events drawn wholly from the imagination, may charm for a moment; but nothing will permanently interest, that is wholly without the sphere of human duties and experience. Traditions and fables are however necessary to poetry. Men delight in listening to them, no less than to recorded truth. In all countries, men have fancied that their first progenitors were empowered to hear the voice of gods and enjoy the personal society of immortals. Therefore, though obscure and susceptible of contradictory meanings, traditions do not cease to be reverenced; for they seem to have proceeded from that favoured ancestry, and to owe to sacrilegious time the loss of what would make them consistent and plain. The poet may interpret them, and illustrate and enlarge their influence upon national character.

A country is undeniably the more endeared by the multitude of its tender and heroical tales and memoirs, fabulous as well as authentic. Let us then not slight even its barbarian annals. Let us not only revisit the dwellings of the European settler exposed to savage incursions, and every variety of affecting vicissitude; but let us hasten to acquaint ourselves with the earlier native. Let us hasten;—for already has the cultivator levelled many a monumental mound, that spoke of more than writings might preserve. Already are the lands cleared of their heaven-planted forests, once hallowed by the visits of the Wakon bird, before she ascended into other regions, indignant at the approach of a race, who knew not the worship of nature. Already are the hills surmounted, and the rocks violated by the iron hammer, which the Indian regarded with distant awe, as the barriers of his 'humble heaven.'—And why should not these vast and magnificent regions have been the haunts of majestic spirits, such as imbodied themselves with mist, and shaped them from the clouds, so as to be seen of heroes and bards of other days? Our tall, dense forests are fitter for the mysterious abodes of the shadowy powers, and our hills lead farther into the sky;—our mountains present a firmer pathway through the clouds, for the descent of the rushing hosts that deign a concern for the affairs of mortals. In every place, wherever we rest or walk, we may feel, in fancy, the animating spirit, declared by ancient philosophers and poets to pervade the stupendous frame of nature;—we may feel its life-breathing motions, perceive its immortal complacency in the gleamings which break from out the hill-side and the plain; and listen to its supernatural promptings.

[1818]

The choice of American subject was not enough to ensure a healthy native art. In this review of two poems by John Neal, Edward Tyrell Channing indicts the falseness and superficiality of manner which attends unreflecting imitation of popular foreign authors.

33

This volume is small, has good parts, gives promise of still better things, and yet is fatiguing. We shall begin with what appear to be its defects.— From the title page, we thought that these must be narrative poems, but they consist chiefly of description; and this is of a singular character, as it is rather telling what things are like, than what they are. And where a man has but an indistinct perception of what should be the prominent object, and introduces a string of similitudes for illustration, they generally become substitutes instead of auxiliaries,—a remark which is perfectly verified in the present work, where few distinct pictures are received from the description, but the fancy is perpetually drawn off and, for a time, amused by sparkling collateral beauties, to the almost entire desertion of the matter in hand. There is more brilliancy than there are objects to shine upon.—In the next place, a visionary, uncertain character is given to every thing,—to waters, shores, woods and hills, to men and their concerns, but with nothing of considerable value in place of the simple reality. There is strange music every where, whether of the air or earth, whether in the ear or fancy, it is not easy to determine. One knows not whether he is to regard himself as upon the ground or in the skies. This is not meant for praise, and as a proof of the author's power,—for he creates no illusion, but only an unfortunate doubt as to his purpose; he does not transport us beyond the world, but only confounds us by his mysterious representations of it. If he merely meant to show how a poetical spirit, in the contemplation of God's works, hears sounds that seem not earthly, and communicates to every object, forms, characters and uses, borrowed wholly from the imagination and suited to its own aspirations, his theory would not be questioned by any man of feeling who had lived long in the presence of nature;—but he does not appear to write from his experience of all this, nor to address our sympathies;—when he makes things cloudy and spiritual, and gives them secret virtues and powers, he is too often conjecturing, instead of feeling what he says.—Then, his poetry is of a singularly evasive cast. He eludes his subject whenever it comes to him in any definite shape,—he is not willing to have a certain topic. Besides this, we often find ourselves on the brink of something extraordinary,—it may be of something very fine,—and yet fail of it, and thus great injustice, we believe, is done to the author's conceptions, and certainly to our expectations.—Once more, there is a prevailing unwillingness to call things by their own or indeed by any names. The men and women (four or five glorious and shadowy beings) are always spoken of with affected emphasis and parade—'*that* youthful rider,'—'*that* wild one,'—'*that* young mother,'—'the brown-cheeked youth,'—and he, whose 'brow was always bare,' &c. This is not the way to make us acquainted with them, or much interested in their fortunes. For readers of this world, they should be more tangible, more accessible and defined, with less of glare at one time and dimness at another. A little more plain humanity and earthly scenery would have been of incalculable service to the book. But the armies are as indistinct and nameless as the individuals,—they are generally indicated by their banners; 'the red-cross flings a radiant challenge to its starry foe,' and 'the eagle breed flap over the star troops,'—and sometimes, even these faint designations are wholly omitted. After all,—"on, on, you noble English,"—could not be improved by the daintiest circumlocution in the language.

There are signs of poverty in the frequent recurrence of the same expressions, combinations, and we may almost say of whole passages. The author has selected a few favourites and loves to exhibit them every where. Objects appear in nearly the same light. Similitudes are poured upon us with almost eastern prodigality, but they are very closely allied. They are, indeed, enumerated with some rapidity,—the author might even have persuaded himself that he was kindled by new and crowding fancies;—but we miss that natural sprightliness which shews that the mind is at play rather than at work; more intent upon uttering thoughts than finding them; delighted with observing the natural relations of things rather than forcing them into artificial ones.—The book is much too uniform in its tone. The author seems to have resolved poetry into swell and dignity of verse, a strained and unusual way of telling every thing, a whimsical and often inscrutable refinement upon what is most common and entirely depending for its effect upon the perfect simplicity with which it is presented.

The author avows that his object, in the first poem, was 'to do justice to American scenery, and American character; not to versify the minutiæ of battles—not to give names, titles, or geographical references for his authority, for all these may be found in the *newspapers* of the day.' So the subject was too fresh and vulgar to be treated with plainness and particularity,—it would not bear out the poet, but needed to be sustained and countenanced and set off to advantage by him. For our parts, we are much better satisfied with the subject than the treatment. What justice is here done to American character, when, more than half the time, one is in doubt whether the persons are his countrymen or the enemy; and when the only distinction between them is in their banners or feathers, in something outward, and not the least in feeling or character?—As for American scenery, it is sufficiently various, magnificent and peculiar to inspire poetry, and bear honest, unaffected description; and none of our bards will do it justice, till they are willing to paint it as it is. It will not do to talk of it in general terms, and apply to it merely grand and swelling phrases, the common-places of poetry, which may be found every where, which always sound well, and now and then may be appropriate. Such is the favourite language of men whose poetical conceptions are merely conjectural, who undertake to describe what they never saw, to put words in order, rather than things. They 'never go to particulars, but stick to generals, and are safe,'—remembering Mr. Falconer's excellent advice to the ignorant.—Could the author, in his long and eloquent appeals to the Ontario, suppose that he was making any one better acquainted with that lake? He expresses, no doubt, many feelings which the scene would call up,—a wish that it might be ever dark and wild and free, that art might never intrude upon nature, and that the lake's rude children, (if we can make out the meaning of a strangely mixed passage,) should be always unsubdued, always possessed of their native vigour. There are indeed poetical combinations, and passages that have beauty; but American scenery is no more familiar, no more our own, by having a better place in our imagination and affections, than it was before.

If the author had only proposed to himself something definite, and used a less pretending and fallacious, but more significant phraseology,—if he had written more from impulse and personal notice of things, and appealed more directly to our experience and sympathy,—if he would not mistake vagueness for grandeur, and venture every thing which sounds violent or strange,—his good parts would appear less accidental, and his failures less alarming. It is but fair to say, that with much effort there is here some strength, and in the midst of show there are yet simple beauties;—still, these and the defects are so generally in company, that we can scarcely make extracts on the author's account, without doing some justice at the same time to ourselves. We cannot undertake to decide what he might accomplish, if he were to abandon affectation entirely and an imitation of two or three modern poets, of very unequal merit, indeed, but

equally popular and dangerous as examples:—and, probably, his pretensions are not so humble, as to make him very solicitous about the rank he
is to hold among American bards. So, all that remains is to give some
passages, which we shall take from both poems without much regard to
the order in which they stand, for their apparent or avowed subjects are
the least important things in them, and would baffle any attempt at a
narrative detail. They are devoted to things in general, such as an ambitious fancy easily accumulates, when a regard to facts or plan is wholly
out of the question, and when the writer is persuaded that the fainter the
analogy, the greater, of course, must be his own ingenuity and nicety of
perception. . . .

   It will be perceived, that we have spoken more of the defects than
beauties of this work, as if we thought that the former threatened more
than the latter promised. The truth is, that the faults of this writer do not
appear to be the consequences of an overheated mind, such as work their
own cure,—but of a perverted taste, a bad system, a mistaken adoption of
other men's peculiarities. Where he has done well, he is mostly indebted,
we think, to his own powers. He is one, whom men censure in the
hope,—too generally a vain one,—of seeing him grow better. It gives us no
small pleasure to cite so many good passages from the work of a native
poet, and we trust that the author will not allow this to be our only
opportunity.

   It will be time enough, by and by, to shew the disadvantages which our
poetry may suffer from its growing up under the eye of critics. Their chief
business at present is to save it from being a bad imitation of popular
authors abroad;—they will do no harm by insisting upon originality.—It
is some consolation to think, that a true poet will never consult critics to
ascertain the extent or proper direction of his powers. It is enough, if he
can learn from them his mistakes, their source and correction, and especially if he can find that he is surrounded by men who understand him
thoroughly.—Nor will a true poet consult his readers too often;—he is
more concerned with his thoughts than his success; and if he thinks of the
subject at all, he will feel that to humour men is not the way to be
permanently in favour with them. If there were any serious danger that
the censures of critics or even public opinion might repress literary enterprise in a great mind, it would be time now to urge upon authors and
readers the very wholesome remark of Bishop Hall;—'Certainly, look
what weather it would be, if every almanac should be verified,—much
what like poems, if every fancy should be suited.'

[1818]

Edward Tyrell Channing's discussion of Charles Brockden Brown is an important anticipation of the theoretical statements of Hawthorne and James. This remarkable essay recognizes the difficulties facing the novelist of broad social observation and suggests that American class structure is not well enough defined for this kind of fiction. Brown, however, solved or evaded many American literary problems by turning to romance, and especially to what we would now call psychological fiction.

34

. . . Brown died in 1809 at the age of thirty nine. For ten years before his death he had been an indefatigable author by profession, at first in New York and afterwards in Philadelphia, his native city. During this period he conducted and was principal contributor to three periodical works, of which we have seen at least fifteen volumes. To these we must add his political pamphlets, his unpublished manuscripts and his six novels. Wieland, Ormond, Arthur Mervyn, and Edgar Huntly are the earliest and best known, and to these we shall confine our remarks. Clara Howard and Jane Talbot, his two latest tales, are so very inferior to and unlike the others, that they require no particular notice.

Brown owes his reputation to his novels. He wrote them indeed principally for his amusement, and preferred publishing them when unfinished to labouring upon them after they had lost their interest to himself: they are proofs or signs of power rather than the result of its complete and steady exertion; but they shew the character of his mind and will justify our curiosity to examine it. In attempting this, we do not feel as if we were bringing forward a deserving but neglected author; he has received honourable notice from distinguished men abroad, and his countrymen discerned his merits without waiting till a foreign glory had shone on and revealed them. Still he is very far from being a popular writer. There is no call, as far as we know, for a second edition of any of his works. He is rarely spoken of but by those who have an habitual curiosity about every thing literary, and a becoming pride in all good writing which appears amongst ourselves. They have not met with the usual success of leaders in matters of taste, since, with all their admiration, they have not been able to extend his celebrity much beyond themselves. Some will explain this by saying that he wrote too rapidly, or that his subjects are too monstrous or at least too extraordinary for common sympathy. But the thoughts of great minds, when earnestly at work, are rarely improved by deliberation and change, and a powerful imagination can imprison us with any thing that is not spiritless, or incapable of suggesting something like reality to the mind. No reader would leave Wieland unfinished notwithstanding its self-combustion and ventriloquism, nor Edgar Huntly because of its sleep-walking. If we do not return to them, it is to avoid suffering, and not that they want fascination, and a terrible one, if we are willing to encounter it more than once.

Some have ascribed his want of popularity to his placing the scenes of his novels in our own country. What are the embarrassments from this cause, which the American novelist must be prepared for, and how far has Brown overcome or avoided them?—Our busy streets, and the commodious apartments of our unromantic dwellings are, it is thought, very unsuitable for the wonders and adventures which we have been accustomed to associate exclusively with the mouldering castles and unfrequented regions of older countries. Our cities are large, but new, and they constantly suggest to us the gainful habits and the secure homes of a recent and flourishing population; the labouring and happy are seen every where and not a corner or recess is secret. The deserted street at midnight produces no awful sense of solitude or danger, and the throng that passes us by day would scarcely suggest the thought that any one was alone in the crowd, buried in contemplation and perhaps brooding over mischief in darkness. We hear of crimes, but they usually appear so vulgar and selfish, so mean or cruel, that the imagination almost sleeps under abhorrence or disgust; we regard them as public evils, and think it enough to leave them to the benevolent reformer and the laws of the land. We hear of conspiracies and circumvention, but they are directed at our gains or good name and put us upon our guard; we think of the injury and its prevention, more than of the terrible power, dark purposes and inextricable toils of the contriver. The actions we esteem great, or are prepared to witness and encourage, are the useful rather than the heroic, such as tend to make society happier, not such as disturb or darken it. Our pride, good sense and warmest wishes are satisfied, but the imagination is not kindled, nor could it lend any lustre to what we approve. The writer then who frames a story to call forth extraordinary and violent interest, and lays the scene amongst ourselves, must encounter the difficulty of creating an illusion, where his events and characters are broad exceptions to all we witness or should expect, and where our imaginations are kept from wandering, and from deceiving us into a faint conviction of reality, by the mention of some place or circumstance which is too stubbornly familiar and unpoetical for any thing but common incidents and feelings. We are speaking of that kind of tale-writing in which Brown delights, the romantic; and we have ascribed the difficulty of succeeding in it here, not to the entire absence of romantic incident, situation and characters, but, which is just as unfortunate for the writer, to the want in his readers of romantic associations with the scenes and persons he must set before us, if he makes a strictly domestic story.

But there is another and an extremely popular kind of fictitious writing, which makes the fable subservient to the developing of national character, or of the manners, usages, prejudices and condition of particular classes. Besides truth, spirit and a nice discrimination of peculiarities in the sketches of individuals, a single picture is widely applicable, and gives us much knowledge of the state of society at the time, and what is still higher, an increased and nearer knowledge of mankind. These sketches are not caricatures, merely grotesque delineations of strange individuals, such as amuse or distress us chiefly for their total separation from the crowd to which we belong. They represent classes; they shew us some peculiar operation of familiar principles, in men who received their natures from our common author, and their distinctive characters from limited external influences. A source of sympathy is thus opened between the remotest nations; we read with delight of those who are separated from us by their institutions and manners as well as climate, not that they are represented as beings formed of another mould and with different capacities from ourselves, but because they resemble us in every thing except that distinguishing character and those prevailing tastes which are ascribable to the peculiar circumstances in which they are placed. We love to see the common world moulding the mind a thousand ways, and multiplying our studies and pleasures without lessening our sympathy and attachments.

How far may this kind of fictitious writing be expected to succeed among us? This cannot depend upon the genius only of authors; at least, mere invention is out of the question. The object is to present what exists, to appeal to men's observation and daily experience. We might possibly be more delighted with a merely poetical creation, than with a history of living men and a sketch of ordinary society, but these would lose all their attraction and value, when they profess to describe realities, while in fact they are occupied principally with an imaginary world.—Our state of society at present offers very imperfect materials for a novel, of the kind which has just been alluded to. If we admit that there is here a *lower class*, its peculiarity would not be found in character so much as in vulgarity of manners and narrowness of opinion; and a foreigner would be as little delighted as ourselves with the most lively record of corrupt speech, of coarse or indelicate customs, of sturdy insolence towards the rich, and indifference or contempt for those who consented to be poor, where competency was so easy and so privileged. If such a sketch should be true, it would be so only of individuals, whose influence is scarcely felt amongst ourselves, and whose peculiarities would give strangers very little knowledge of the effect of our institutions or pursuits upon our opinions and character.

We come next to a large and invaluable order, composed of sensible, industrious, upright men, whose whole experience seems at war with adventure, and whose chief distinction is in their unmolested happiness, and perfectly independent modes of living. They are exactly fitted to make society secure and prosperous, and to teach us the importance of good habits and principles; with more firmness and efficiency than variety, sprightliness or vehemence in their characters; free from wild superstitions; not much in the habit of forming poetical associations with the objects they are most familiar with; using, occasionally, highly pic-turesque expressions, without betraying the feelings in which they origi-nated; affected by many sober and rooted prejudices, which are insepa-rable perhaps from strong, unpolished character and are even its protec-tion, but such as might appear to more advantage in a book that was only to make us wiser, than in one designed also for our diversion. With such a class of men, we should find more instruction than entertainment, more to gratify our kind feelings and good sense than to fill our imagina-tions. To visit them in their own homes would please us more than to read of them in a novel; they might offer little to call forth discrimination and acute remark, but a great deal of general happiness and virtue for a good mind to approve and imitate.

If we should look for what are called the higher classes of society, the wealthy, fashionable and ostentatious, whose manners, parade and in-trigues in the older countries have given birth to some of the finest modern tales; we might be in a great measure disappointed. We should, indeed, find splendor, luxury and refinement, and possibly an incomplete imitation of foreign fashions; but little of the exclusive spirit of an estab-lished order, which owed its existence to something peculiar in our state of society, and had secured respect for its claims from those who are most impatient of superiority and all separate pretensions. More years, practice

and affluence might be necessary to render the class more distinct, character more various, peculiarities more graceful and easy, vice and folly more
finished and creditable, and affectation less insupportable than uncouth
sincerity.

No doubt, it is impossible to give a just account of society, whatever be
its state, without affording some entertainment, or at least knowledge.
Man is always our best study, and our most fruitful subject whether we
hate or love him. If a writer would be a despot, with power never to be
shaken or questioned, let him become the fearless and exact historian or
painter of real life. If he would be the most efficient moral teacher, let him
tell men what they are and what is thought of them; let him take us from
the crowd where there is too much motion for thought, where each is
countenanced and sheltered by the other, with an example on all sides for
his follies or vices, and where the very sense of fault dies because there is
none to condemn; let him shew us our conduct in a silent picture, when
there is nothing to dim our perceptions, or mislead our judgments, when
the music has ceased which put us all in the same motion, attracted us to
one object, and made every man happy without a thought of the cause or
the manner. We may then learn the real spirit and business of society,
with much to laugh at and something to lament as well as approve. In
every class amongst ourselves there are fine subjects for the moral and
satirical observer, which have already called forth much grave and light
rebuke, and many short, lively sketches of domestic manners, national
customs and individual singularities. But our common every-day life
hardly offers materials as yet for a long story, which should be full of
interest for its strong and infinitely various characters, fine conversation
and striking incident, for conflicting pretensions and subtile intrigues in
private life, and which should all appear to be exactly in the ordinary
course of things, and what every one would feel to be perfectly true,
without being obliged to verify it by particular and limited applications.
And genius is not apt to employ itself upon subjects where it feels em-
barrassed by the want of materials. It does not indeed court novelties, as if
it thought nothing else would do, nor shun what common minds might
think unpromising or impossible. It follows its own wishes, and chooses
what it can manage to advantage; what provokes its energy and is yet
within its controul.

Brown had the courage to lay the scenes of his stories at home, but no
one will charge him with a disgusting familiarity. He has not even
attempted to draw a peculiar American character; he seeks for many of
his most important persons abroad, or among those who had lived and

been educated abroad, where the character had been formed and opinions decidedly fixed, under better influences perhaps for his purposes than existed or at present could be expected to exist here, while many things in our situation and prospects would offer a good field for a new and striking exhibition of his characters. The scene is rarely in common life or for ordinary events. Sometimes he begins with a simple, domestic narrative, as in Ormond, which has no very distinct reference to our state of society, but which exhibits merely, though with great spirit, the unwearied solicitude of a daughter for a weak, sinful and helpless father, the victim of a young impostor whom he had received to his confidence. We are constantly expecting something more important, though without an intimation what it will be. At length some terrific being—little less than omnipotent, of strong mind and feelings, utterly and deliberately perverted—is introduced, and thence forward rules the destinies of every one else, without exhibiting very definite purposes, or adopting any distinct plan of operations. His power is usually of a moral kind; he establishes an inquisition to put the mind to torture; looks, tones, persuasions, threats and dark insinuations are his instruments. Our chief interest is not in the events, nor at all dependent upon the conviction that we ever saw the place or the man. We are not thinking of accustomed modes of living or our ordinary experience, but are held captive by the force of character, the intensity of intellectual suffering, the unrelenting perseverance of a bad spirit disappointed. A spell is thrown over our imaginations, and our belief is at least strong enough for sympathy.

Sometimes the events are placed so far back, that they belong to a somewhat different race from ourselves, at least with different pursuits, pleasures and dangers; but we are not in a strange country; what was then a wilderness is now covered with our own flourishing settlements; the savage and beast of prey are scarcely heard of; the wild, adventurous character of the recent settler has become softened by regular and secure industry, and we feel as if we are reading of our antiquities.

Sometimes the author takes advantage of a recent event amongst ourselves, as in Wieland, which is too shocking to receive any aid from exaggeration, or to lose any interest from its notoriety. A father is tempted by apparent communications from above to murder his family. The rapture and exultation with which he contemplates his triumph over his fond weakness in obedience to heaven, very often reach the sublime. This is equalled perhaps by his utter prostration when he learns that he has been deceived. The author connects this event with just such beings as should be concerned in it; he makes it illustrative of character and dependent upon it; and though it might appear rare and monstrous enough for a lie instead of a wonder, he contrives by the earnestness and argumentative cast of reflection, the depth, sincerity and torture of feeling, the suitableness of every circumstance and the apparent inevitableness of all that occurs, to chain us to a more revolting narrative than perhaps ever before made the smallest pretensions to truth.

Sometimes his stories rest chiefly upon recent events of public concern. We refer particularly to the pestilence that has more than once wasted our principal cities; and here he is so willing to confine himself to mere truth, that he proposes to make his narrative of practical use, by preserving such incidents as appeared to him most instructive amongst those which fell under his own observation. He enters the city; the streets are still, the dwellings deserted or occupied by the sick. There is such terrible distinctness in his description of the calamity, so much of vulgar suffering which cannot be relieved, and of disgusting, selfish inhumanity in the timid, too rarely contrasted with a generous self-exposure, that we are sometimes oppressed and sickened; the reality seems too near. But in connexion with this, there is sufficient horror and wildness for the imagination. We feel that all this suffering is crowded into one spot, where the poor and wretched are almost alone amongst the deserted mansions of the wealthy and in the scenes of recent gayety. The victim is left in a dark, closed dwelling, as if to die in his tomb, with no one near but the safe plunderer. The day and night are equally still—there are no sounds but of the dying and the hearse. The fugitive, whom we thought secure, perishes in a purer air; and to make our sense of hopelessness and desolation still more complete, we see the sun shining as brightly and the grass-walks as fresh in the morning, as if the happy were there to enjoy them.

We can offer only these few remarks upon the course Brown has followed in the selection of his subjects and the use of his materials. Though his scenes lie at home, yet in his four principal tales, we can say with some confidence, that there is little which is too humble and familiar for interest, or so monstrous and unusual that he has not been able to recommend it sufficiently to our belief for all his purposes.

We have alluded to the singular or improbable character of his persons and incidents; and it is the first thing that presents itself on reading his four principal tales. He selects minds that are strangely gifted or influenced, as if for the pleasure of exploring some secret principles of our nature, disclosing new motives of conduct, or old ones operating in a new direction; and especially that he may have an opportunity, the necessity of which we are to admit, of accounting at large for every thing that is resolved upon or done; as if he had discovered springs of action which could not be understood in the usual way, by our observation of their effects, but only from a minute, philosophical discussion of impulses and motives by the parties concerned, after a cool, thorough self-inspection, and a detailed enumeration of rapid and subtle thoughts which incessantly gleamed across their minds in the storm. In the language of one of his characters, 'I cannot be satisfied with telling you that I am not well, but I must be searching with these careful eyes into causes and labouring to tell you of what nature my malady is. It has always been so. I have always found an unaccountable pleasure in dissecting, as it were, my heart, uncovering, one by one, its many folds, and laying it before you as a country is shown in a map.' This scrutiny into the feelings is given with such an air of probability and conclusiveness, or at least sincerity, that we are disposed to admit the existence of the most extraordinary beings, and then their opinions, purposes, conduct, and influence over others are quite satisfactorily explained, without supposing any other despotism over the will but that which is to be found in the power of involuntary thoughts.

But this accounting for every thing is often excessively irksome. A ludicrous importance is given to trifles; the vast mind is seen busied, amazed and anxious about incidents or intimations that are wholly inadequate to the concern they give or the effects which are traced to them, and which ordinary men would be ashamed to notice. What would be nothing elsewhere is every thing here. The feelings not only appear to obey the impulse they receive and tend unerringly to their object, but in a state of excitement and tumult, they are excellent philosophers; they shew the mind's perfect consciousness of all that is passing within; they appear to prescribe their own operations, pass through anticipated changes, and remember that they are afterwards to render an account of themselves. The reader would be better pleased if the mind's rapid conclusions were given, and an opportunity left for his own sagacity to account for them from observation of the whole character.

Brown's principal characters are designed chiefly for our imaginations and ingenuity. They study and delineate themselves with exemplary diligence and fidelity. This is not done that they may grow better, or give us a moral lesson; they are perfectly satisfied with the study, and succeed in engaging us to watch them. They are of a contemplative turn, forever hunting for materials of thought rather than motives to action, not so much from irresolution or speculative indolence, as from a love of thinking and feeling deeply at all times, and associating every thing around them with their own minds. They defer as far as possible the day when the deed shall be done which is to deprive them of something to brood over; they are anxious to operate upon the minds of others rather than upon their conduct, to keep them in suspense, and divert them from the purpose which they themselves have inspired, as soon as they see it ripening into action. They would envy no man the calm assurance and prompt determination, which spring from a general consciousness of good intentions and a quick insight into the subject of his thoughts. They have a perverse love of perplexity and doubt, and of needless though not vulgar difficulties; and to gratify this, a false and bewildering consequence is given to their own most common feelings and the most obvious conduct in others. They have not been enough exposed to the world to acquire a contempt for their singularities; they feel as if they were very peculiar and must attract as much attention as they bestow upon themselves, and especially that mischief must lurk in every thing which appears mysterious to them. Then they plunge into solitudes and heap conjectures upon conjectures about endless possibilities. 'Thought is first made a vehicle of pain,' and then life is not worth enduring; but they live on, for to die would be as fatal as torpor to the wild dreamer, and a disposition to make evils supportable would be just as bad.

But the time for action at last comes—we could not anticipate what would be done, nor comprehend why any thing should be done—there is all at once a rushing and thronging of incidents; the bright heavens are suddenly darkened; a strange accumulation of unforeseen ills falls upon a single deserted being. His innocent actions are most ingeniously misconceived or misrepresented; he is made the blind instrument of all the woe he suffers or inflicts; his sad delusions are made use of to draw him to the most atrocious deeds; the means of vindication to the injured or of correction to the erring are always near but never possessed. It is of no consequence to the author whether you were prepared by the early view of a doubtful character for his conduct afterwards; whether he fulfils his promise or breaks it. He chooses to make men as intense in action as they were before in reflection. He conjures up at once a terrible scene for mighty agents; if one perishes, he supplies the place by infusing new strength and other purposes into him who remains. And the attention is so much engrossed, the imagination is so filled by what is passing now, that we care not for its connexion, if there be any, with the past or future; we want no more, and least of all such explanations as are sometimes given. We seem to have had a disturbed dream; we suddenly reached the precipice, plunged, and awoke in falling, rejoiced that it was an illusion and that it has passed away.

A writer so engrossed with the character of men and the ways in which they may be influenced; chiefly occupied with the mind, turning every thing into thought, and refining upon it till it almost vanishes, might not be expected to give much time to descriptions of outward objects. But in all his tales he shews great closeness and minuteness of observation. He describes as if he told only what he had seen in a highly excited state of feeling, and in connexion with the events and characters. He discovers every where a strong sense of the presence of objects. Most of his descriptions are simple, and many might appear bald. He knew perhaps that some minds could be awakened by the mere mention of a water-fall, or of full orchards and cornfields, or of the peculiar sound of the wind among the pines.—We have alluded to the distinctness and particularity with which he describes the city visited with pestilence; the dwelling-house, the hospital, the dying, the healed, all appear before our eyes; the imagination has nothing to do but perceive, though it never fails to multiply and enlarge circumstances of horror, and to fasten us to the picture more strongly by increasing terror and sympathy till mere disgust ceases.—The most formal and protracted description is in Edgar Huntly, of a scene in our Western wilderness. We become acquainted with it by following the hero night and day, in a cold, drenching rain-storm, or under the clear sky, through its dark caverns, recesses and woods, along its ridges and the river side. It produces throughout the liveliest sense of danger, and oppresses the spirits with an almost inexplicable sadness. Connected with it are incidents of savage warfare, the disturbed life of the frontier settler, the attack of the half-famished panther, the hero's lonely pursuit of a sleep-walker, and his own adventures when suffering under the same calamity. The question is not how much of this has happened or is likely to happen; but is it felt; are we for the time at the disposal of the writer, and can we never lose the impression he leaves? Does it appear in its first freshness when any thing occurs which a busy fancy can associate with it? Does it go with us into other deserts, and quicken our feelings and observation till a familiar air is given to strange prospects? If so, the author is satisfied. To object that he is wild and improbable in his story is not enough, unless we can shew that his intention failed or was a bad one.

Brown delights in solitude of all kinds. He loves to represent the heart as desolate; to impress you with the self-dependence of characters, plotting, loving, suspecting evil, devising good, in perfect secrecy. Sometimes, when he would exhibit strength of mind and purpose to most advantage, he takes away all external succour, even the presence of a friend who might offer at least the support of his notice and sympathy. He surrounds a person with circumstances precisely fitted to weaken resolution by raising vague apprehensions of danger, but incapable of producing so strong an excitement as to inspire desperate and inflexible energy. The mind must then fortify itself, calmly estimate the evil that seems to be approaching, and contemplate it in its worst forms and consequences in order to counteract it effectually.—He is peculiarly successful in describing a deserted house, silent and dark in the day-time, while a faint ray streams through the crevices of the closed doors and shutters, discovering in a peculiar twilight that it had been once occupied, and that every thing remained undisturbed since its sudden desertion. The sentiment of fear and melancholy is perhaps never more lively, nor the disturbed fancy more active than in such a place, even when we are strangers to it; but how much more, if we have passed there through happiness and suffering, if the robber has alarmed our security, or if a friend has died there and been carried over its threshold to the grave. The solemnity of our minds is unlike that which we feel when walking alone on the sea-shore at night, or through dark forests by day, for here there is no decay, nothing that man had created and which seems to mourn his absence: there is rapture as well as awe in our contemplations, and more of devotion than alarm in our fear.

Brown's mind is distinguished for strong, intense conception. If his thoughts are vast, he is still always master of them. He works with the greatest ease, as if his mind were fully possessed of his subject, and could not but suggest thoughts with freedom and rapidity. In the most monstrous and shocking narrative, he writes with the utmost sincerity, as if he laboured under a delusion which acted with a mischievous but uncontrollable power. He never, indeed, shews a desire to complete a story, nor draws a character so much for what it is to effect in the end, as for the development of mind. The present incident is perhaps fine in itself, and answers the author's purpose, and gives room for the display of great strength; but it has little or no connexion with others. With the greatest solicitude to tell us every thing that passes in the mind before a purpose is formed, he is very careless as to any continuity or dependence in the events which lead to or flow from that purpose. He sometimes crowds more into one day than we should have expected in many, and at others leaps over so large an interval as to make the narrative improbable to all who are not in the secret. His characters cannot be relied upon: notwithstanding their strength and apparently stubborn singularities, they accommodate themselves readily to the author, sometimes losing all the importance with which they were at first invested, and at others accomplishing something beyond or opposite to what was expected, and almost what we can believe to be within the compass of human power in the agent or weakness in the sufferer. This incompleteness of views and inconsistency of characters is not owing to carelessness or haste in the writer; he had never determined how things should end, nor proposed to himself any prevailing object when he began, nor discovered one as he advanced. We generally close a story with a belief that as much more might be said. He was engrossed by single, separate scenes, such as invention suggested from time to time; and while we can account from this fact for our feeling little solicitude about the story as a whole, we must at the same time form a high estimate of an author's power, who can carry us through almost disconnected scenes without any considerable failure of interest. He seems fond of exciting and vexing curiosity, but when he fails of satisfying it, it is more, we believe, from forgetfulness than design.

There is very little variety in his writings; at least in those where his genius is most clearly discerned. He loves unusual, lawless characters, and extraordinary and tragic incident. There should not be a moment of calm brightness in the world, unless as it may serve to heighten the effect of approaching gloom and tempest. The innocent are doomed to suffer, as if virtue were best capable of enduring and shone most conspicuously in trial, or at least drew the largest sympathy. This suffering is of the mind; bodily pain and death appear but moderate and vulgar evils, and rather a refuge than punishment for the triumphant criminal, who has rioted in mischief till he is weary, and willing to die for repose since his work is ended. In these sad views of life, which make society worse than the wilderness and men's sympathy and promises little better than a mockery, there is no apparent design to mislead the world, or covertly condemn its opinions and awards, but merely to take a firm hold of the heart, by appeals to its pity, terror, indignation or wonder. He wants the universality and justice of a fair observer of the world. He thinks too much in one way, and that a narrow one. His views are of one kind, and shew that he thought more than he observed.

His style is clear, simple and nervous, with very little peculiarity, and not the slightest affectation or even consciousness of manner; rarely varying to suit the subject, or to distinguish conversation from narrative or description. It uniformly bears marks of a serious, thoughtful mind, remembering its excitement and suffering rather than experiencing them. There are, now and then, some attempts at playfulness and humour, but they are wholly unsuccessful, and sometimes ludicrous and offensive. There are few striking sentences which the reader would unconsciously retain for the beauty of their structure, or any peculiar terms; we have the thought without the expression. We should not pronounce Brown a man of genius, nor deny him that distinction, from his style. It might have been acquired by care and study, but it is the result only and never betrays the process. There is no attempt at what is too vaguely called fine writing; no needless ornament, no sacrifice of spirit and energy from a weak ambition of harmony or finish, no use of a strictly poetical term to excite the imagination, when another and a simpler one will convey the meaning more definitely. He uses words merely to express his own thoughts, and not to multiply our associations. He never allows them to outstrip, or, which is nearly the same thing, to take the place of feeling and truth. He appears to be above the common temptation to exhibit tokens of more passion than is felt, merely on account of 'the imaginary gracefulness of passion,' or to decorate scenes with borrowed beauties till they have lost every thing which could distinguish them, or even persuade us that we were in our own world.

It has been our object in these remarks, to point out some of Brown's prominent defects and excellences. We never intended to make an abstract of his stories; and such extracts as we could admit would do little justice to the author.—His readers will observe every where that he was an ardent admirer of Godwin, though not his slave. Godwin himself has pronounced him a writer of distinguished genius and acknowledged himself in his debt.—The uses and evils of criticism can no longer be felt by him; the dead are beyond our judgment. It is for the living that their opinions and genius should be inquired into; and it is hardly less dishonourable to let the grave bury their worth than consecrate their errors.

[1819]

Washington Irving was determined to cast the spell of folklore over the familiar glades of the Hudson River Valley. James Kirke Paulding, however, insisted that "Fairies, giants, and goblins are not indigenous here, and with the exception of a few witches that were soon exterminated, our worthy ancestors brought over with them not a single specimen of Gothic or Grecian mythology." Paulding's long poem, The Backwoodsman, *suggests his hopes for the national letters. Unlike Channing, Paulding urged a national literature of "Rational Fictions." The history of the nineteenth century does not seem to have borne him out, but it is interesting to see him launch his tradition with the same author Channing chose to illustrate the strength of American Romance, Charles Brockden Brown.*

35 ✍

     Neglected Muse of this our Western clime,
How long in servile, imitative rhyme,
Wilt thou thy stifled energies enchain,
And tread the worn-out path still o'er again!
How long repress the brave decisive flight!
How long be blind to all thy native light!
Does not the story of our early days
Teem with the spirit of eternal lays?
Can not those glorious exiles who first sought
The untracked forest world, and with them brought
Unconquered and unconquerable mind,
That cast no weak and wistful look behind,
Scorned every danger in their high career
And planted every future blessing here,
Prompt some undying genius to engage,
With all a poet's strong yet tempered rage,
Above their tombs that laurel wreath to wave
'Tis true they need not, and they still should have?
Can grey tradition, or historic page,
Can every legend of each parted age,
Present a theme so fraught with patriot fire,

The dull to stir, the eager to inspire,
As that immortal struggle which here gave
To Freedom life, to Tyranny a grave?
Does Greece or Rome display a nobler field,
Or any nation's utmost records yield
A richer harvest, than our native land,
To him who'd reap it with a master's hand?
Or Nature in her generous zeal bestow
More splendid scenes to make his bosom glow,
Than here with mild exuberance she strews,
To rouse the dozing spirit of the Muse?

The Past, the Present, Future, all combine
To waken inspiration in each line;
And yet we turn to Europe's old Rag-fair,
To deck ourselves in cast-off finery there,
And, like the wretched prodigal of old
Whose plaintive story is in Scripture told,
The plenty of our Father's house resign,
To starve on offal, and to herd with swine.

[1818]

36 🖎

It has been often observed by such as have attempted to account for the
scarcity of romantic fiction among our native writers, that the history of
the country affords few materials for such works, and offers little in its
traditionary lore to warm the heart or elevate the imagination. The remark has been so often repeated that it is now pretty generally received
with perfect docility as an incontrovertible truth, though it seems to me
without the shadow of a foundation. It is in fact an observation that never
did nor ever will apply to any nation, ancient or modern.

Wherever there are men, there will be materials for romantic adventure.
In the misfortunes that befall them; in the sufferings and vicissitudes
which are everywhere the lot of human beings; in the struggles to
counteract fortune, and in the conflicts of the passions, in every situation
of life, he who studies nature and draws his pictures from her rich and
inexhaustible sources of variety, will always find enough of those charac-

ters and incidents which give a relish to works of fancy. The aid of superstition, the agency of ghosts, fairies, goblins, and all that antiquated machinery which till lately was confined to the nursery, is not necessary to excite our wonder or interest our feelings; although it is not the least of incongruities that in an age which boasts of having by its scientific discoveries dissipated almost all the materials of superstition, some of the most popular fictions should be founded upon a superstition which is now become entirely ridiculous, even among the ignorant.

The best and most perfect works of imagination appear to me to be those which are founded upon a combination of such characters as every generation of men exhibits, and such events as have often taken place in the world and will again. Such works are only fictions because the tissue of events which they record never perhaps happened in precisely the same train and to the same number of persons as are exhibited and associated in the relation. Real life is fraught with adventures to which the wildest fictions scarcely afford a parallel; and it has this special advantage over its rival, that these events, however extraordinary, can always be traced to motives, actions, and passions arising out of circumstances no way unnatural and partaking of no impossible or supernatural agency.

Hence it is that the judgment and the fancy are both equally gratified in the perusal of this class of fictions if they are skilfully conducted; while in those which have nothing to recommend them but appeals to the agency of beings in whose existence nobody believes and whose actions of course can have no alliance either with nature or probability, it is the imagination alone that is satisfied, and that only by the total subjection of every other faculty of the mind.

It must be acknowledged, however, that these probable and consistent fictions are by far the most difficult to manage. It is easy enough to bring about the most improbable, not to say impossible catastrophe by the aid of beings whose power is without limit and whose motives are inscrutable, though in my opinion it is always a proof of want of power in the writer when he is thus compelled to call upon Hercules to do what he cannot perform himself. It is either an indication that his judgment is inadequate to the arrangement of his materials and the adjustment of his plans, or that he is deficient in the invention of rational means to extricate himself from his difficulties.

On the contrary, nothing is more easy than the management of this machinery of ghosts, goblins, and fairies, who are subject neither to Longinus, Quintilian, or Dryden (whom I look upon as the best critic of modern times); who are always within call and can be made active or passive without the trouble of putting them or the author to the inconvenience of being governed by any rational motive whatever. Events that would be extraordinary, if they were not impossible, are thus brought about in a trice without any preparatory and laborious arrangements of causes and effects, and the fiction becomes thus complete in its kind by being equally elevated beyond our comprehension and belief.

The rare and happy combination of invention, judgment, and experience, requisite to produce such a work as *Tom Jones,* is seldom twice found in the same country while thousands of mere romance-writers flourish and are forgotten in every age.

In the raw material for the latter species of fiction, it must be acknowledged this country is quite deficient. Fairies, giants, and goblins are not indigenous here, and with the exception of a few witches that were soon exterminated, our worthy ancestors brought over with them not a single specimen of Gothic or Grecian mythology.

The only second-sight they possessed was founded on the solid basis of a keen recollection of the past, a rational anticipation of the future. They acknowledged no agency above that of the physical and intellectual man, except that of the Being that created him; and they relied for protection and support on their own resolute perseverance, aided by the blessings of God. But if I mistake not, there is that in the peculiarities of their character; in the motives which produced the resolution to emigrate to the wilderness; in the courage and perseverance with which they consummated this gallant enterprise; and in the wild and terrible peculiarities of their intercourse, their adventures, and their contests with the savages, amply sufficient for all the purposes of those higher works of imagination which may be called Rational Fictions.

That these materials have as yet been little more than partially interwoven into the few fictions which this country has given birth to is not owing to their being inapplicable to that purpose, but to another cause entirely. We have been misled by bad models or the suffrages of docile critics who have bowed to the influence of rank and fashion and given testimony in favour of works which their better judgment must have condemned. We have cherished a habit of looking to other nations for examples of every kind, and debased the genius of this new world by making it the ape and the tributary of that of the old. We have imitated where we might often have excelled; we have overlooked our own rich resources, and sponged upon the exhausted treasury of our empoverished neighbours; we were born rich, and yet have all our lives subsisted by borrowing. Hence it has continually occurred that those who might have gone before had they chosen a new path, have been content to come last, merely by following the old track. Many a genius that could and would have attained an equal height in some new and unexplored region of fancy has dwindled into insignificance and contempt by stooping to track some inferior spirit to whom fashion had assigned a temporary elevation. They ought to be told that though fashion may give a momentary popularity to works that neither appeal to national attachments, domestic habits, or those feelings which are the same yesterday, to-day, for ever, and everywhere, still it is not by imitation they can hope to equal any thing great. It appears to me that the young candidate for the prize of genius in the regions of invention and fancy has but one path open to fame. He cannot hope to wing his way above those immortal works that have stood the test of ages and are now with one consent recognised as specimens beyond which the intellect of man is not permitted to soar. But a noble prize is yet within his grasp, and worthy of the most aspiring ambition.

By freeing himself from a habit of servile imitation; by daring to think and feel, and express his feelings; by dwelling on scenes and events connected with our pride and our affections; by indulging in those little peculiarities of thought, feeling, and expression which belong to every nation; by borrowing from nature and not from those who disfigure or burlesque her—he may and will in time destroy the ascendency of foreign taste and opinions and elevate his own in the place of them. These causes lead to the final establishment of a national literature, and give that air and character of originality which it is sure to acquire, unless it is debased and expatriated by a habit of servile imitation.

The favourite yet almost hopeless object of my old age is to see this attempt consummated. For this purpose, it is my delight to furnish occasionally such hints as may turn the attention of those who have leisure, health, youth, genius, and opportunities, to domestic subjects on which to exercise their powers. Let them not be disheartened, even should they sink into a temporary oblivion in the outset. This country is not destined to be always behind in the race of literary glory. The time will assuredly come when that same freedom of thought and action which has given such a spur to our genius in other respects will achieve similar wonders in literature. It is then that our early specimens will be sought after with avidity, and that those who led the way in the rugged discouraging path will be honoured as we begin to honour the adventurous spirits who first sought, explored, and cleared this western wilderness.

These remarks will, we think, most especially apply to the fictions of the late Mr. Charles Brockden Brown, which are among the most vigorous and original efforts of our native literature. Indeed, it appears to us that few if any writers of the present day exceed or even approach him in richness of imagination, depth of feeling, command of language, and the faculty of exciting a powerful and permanent interest in the reader. They constitute a class of fictions standing alone by themselves; they are the product of our soil, the efforts of one of our most blameless and esteemed fellow-citizens, and they would do honour to any country. Yet they want the stamp of fashion and notoriety; they have never been consecrated by the approbation of foreign criticism; and, in all probability, a large portion of our readers are ignorant that they were ever written.

Yet we hazard little in predicting that the period is not far distant when they will be rescued from oblivion by the hand of some kindred spirit, and the people of the United States become sufficiently independent to dare to admire and to express their admiration of a writer who will leave many followers, but few equals; and whose future fame will furnish a bright contrast to the darkness in which he is now enveloped.

[1819–1820]

William Cullen Bryant's brief essay on the use of trisyllabic feet in iambic verse is not directly concerned with the theory of American literature. But it is interesting in its own right, and when seen against the background of American poetry's studied imitation of Pope, it suggests both theoretical independence and the growing flexibility of romantic prosody.

37 &

The only feet of three syllables which can be employed in English Iambics, are either those which have the two first short, and the third long, or those which have all three short—the anapest, and the tribrachys. A certain use of these feet, in that kind of verse, has been allowed from the very beginnings of English poetry. This takes place either when the two first syllables in these feet are vowels or diphthongs, as in the following instance—

> To scorn | delights | and live | labo | rĭŏŭs dāys.

or when the letter *r*, only, is interposed between the vowels, as in the following—

> and ev- | ery flower | that sad | embroid- | ĕrў̆ wēar.

or when the consonant *n* comes between the vowels, and the vowel preceding this letter is so obscurely or rapidly pronounced, as to leave it doubtful whether it may be considered as forming a distinct syllable, as in this instance.

> Under | the op- | ĕnĭng eȳe- | lids of | the morn.

Sometimes the letter *l*, in a like position, gives the poet a like liberty, as in the following example.

> Wafted | the trav- | ĕllĕr tŏ | the beau- | tious west.

In all these cases, the three syllables were, until lately, written with a contraction which shortened them into two, and it came at length to be regarded as a rule, by most critics and authors, that no trisyllabic feet should be admitted in Iambic measure, where such a contraction was not allowed, or where the two first syllables might not, by some dexterity of pronunciation, be blended into one. This was, in effect, excluding all trisyllabic feet whatever; but they are now generally written without the contraction, and in reading poetry it is not, I believe, usually observed.

There is a freer use of trisyllabic feet in Iambic verse, of equal antiquity with the former, but which was afterwards proscribed as irregular and inharmonious, and particularly avoided by those who wrote in rhyme. I allude to all those cases where the two first syllables will not admit of a contraction, or which is nearly the same thing, refuse to coalesce in the pronunciation. These may be called pure trisyllabic feet, and the following is an example of this kind.

Impos- | tor, do | not charge | most in- | nŏcĕnt nāture.

In excluding liberties of this description, it is difficult to tell what has been gained, but it is easy to see what has been lost—the rule has been observed to the frequent sacrifice of beauty of expression, and variety and vivacity of numbers.

I think that I can show, by examples drawn from some of our best poets, that the admission of pure trisyllabic feet into Iambic verse is agreeable to the genius of that kind of measure, as well as to the habits of our language. I begin with those who have written in blank verse. The sweetest passages of Shakspeare—those which appear to have been struck out in the ecstacy of genius, and flow with that natural melody which is peculiar to him, are generally sprinkled with freedoms of this kind. Take the following specimen among a thousand others—part of the eloquent apostrophe of Timon to gold.

> Thou ever young, fresh, loved and *delicate wooer*
> Whose blush doth thaw the consecrated snow
> That lies in Dian's lap! thou *visible god*
> That solderest close impossibilities
> And mak'st them kiss!

Most of the older dramatists have done the same thing,—some more frequently than others,—but none appear to have avoided it with much care. I will next point to the most perfect master of poetic modulation perhaps in our language—a man to whom nature had given an exquisite ear, whose taste had been improved and exalted by a close study of the best models in the most harmonious tongues we know, and who emulated, in their own languages, the sweetness of the Latin and Italian poets. The heroic verse of Milton abounds with instances of pure trisyllabic feet. The following passage is certainly not deficient in harmony.

> And where the *river of bliss,* through midst of heaven,
> Rolls o'er Elysian flowers her amber stream,

> With these, that never fade, the *spirits elect*
> Bind their resplendent locks inwreathed with beams.

Dryden sometimes admits feet of this kind in his tragedies in blank verse, and many other dramatic poets, his contemporaries and successors, have taken the same liberty. In the celebrated work of Young, I find no instance of this sort, and it is not hard to tell the reason. Young was a profound and blind admirer of Pope, nor is it to be wondered at that he, who, at the recommendation of his friend, gave his days and nights to the study of Thomas Aquinas, as a system of divinity, should take that friend for a model in poetry. Young, in his Night Thoughts, endeavoured to do that for which, of all things, his genius least fitted him—to imitate the manner of Pope; and the consequence was that he injured the fine flow of his own imagination by violent attempts at point and an awkward sententiousness. It was like sitting the Mississippi to spout little *jets d'eau* and turn children's water-wheels. He was probably afraid to use feet of three syllables, because he did not find them in the work of his master. About this time, and for some years afterwards, the exclusion of pure trisyllabic feet from blank verse seems to have been complete. I find no traces of them in Thompson and Dyer, nor in the heavy writings of Glover and Cumberland. Akenside's Pleasures of Imagination has been highly esteemed for the art with which the numbers are modulated, and the pauses adjusted. In this poem, as it was first written, I find no instances of the sort of which I am speaking—but when, in the maturity of his faculties, he revised, and partly wrote over the work, he seems to have been, in some measure dissatisfied with that versification which the world had praised so much. In looking over this second draught of his work, I have noted the following deviations from his former practice.

> Furies which curse the earth, and make the blows,
> The heaviest blows, of nature's *innocent hand*
> Seem sport—
> I checked my prow and thence with eager steps,
> The *city of Minos* entered—
> > But the chief
> Are poets, *eloquent men,* who dwell on earth.

Armstrong has given us some examples of a similar license in versification, Cowper's Task abounds with them, and they may be frequently found in the blank verse of some of our latest poets.

In accompanying me in the little retrospect which I have taken of the usage of our poets who have written in blank verse, I think the reader must be convinced, that there is something not incompatible with the principles of English versification, nor displeasing to an unperverted taste, in a practice, that in spite of rules and prejudices, is continually showing itself in the works of most of our sweetest and most valued poets, which prevailed in the best age of English poetry, and has now returned to us endeared by its associations with that venerable period. I will not here multiply examples to show how much it may sometimes improve the beauty of the numbers. I will only refer the reader to those already laid before him. I do not believe that he would be contented to exchange any of the words marked in the quotations which I have made, for tame Iambics, could it ever be done by the use of phrases equally proper and expressive. For my part, when I meet with such passages, amidst a dead waste of dissyllabic feet, their spirited irregularity refreshes and relieves me, like the sight of eminences and forests breaking the uniformity of a landscape.

If pure trisyllabic feet are allowed in blank verse, it would seem difficult to give any good reason why they should not be employed in rhyme. If they have any beauty in blank verse they cannot lose it merely because the ends of the lines happen to coincide in sound. The distinction between prose and verse is more strongly marked in rhymes than in blank verse, and the former therefore stands less in need than the latter, of extreme regularity of quantity, to make the distinction more obvious. Besides, the restraint which rhyme imposes on the diction is a good reason why it should be freed from any embarrassments which cannot contribute to its excellence. But whatever may be the reasons for admitting trisyllabic feet into Iambic rhyme, it is certain that most of our rhyming poets, from the time of Dryden, have carefully excluded them.

Spenser's verse is harmonious—but its harmony is of a peculiar kind. It is a long-drawn, diffuse, redundant volume of music, sometimes, indeed, sinking into languor, but generally filling the ear agreeably. His peculiar dialect has been called the Doric of the English language. I would rather call it the Ionic. It delights in adding vowels and resolving contractions, and instead of shortening two syllables into one, it often dilates one syllable into two. It is not in Spenser, therefore, that we are to look for frequent examples of pure trisyllabic feet in Iambic verse. They have an air of compression not well suited to the loose and liquid flow of his numbers. Yet he has occasionally admitted them, and without any apparent apprehension that he was sinning against propriety, for by a little variation of phrase he might have avoided them. In turning over his Fairy Queen, I meet, without any very laborious search, the following instances.

Unweeting of the *perĭloŭs* wăndering ways.
The sight whereof so *thoroŭghlў hĭm* dismayed.
That still it breathed forth sweet *spirĭt ănd* whōlesome smell.
When oblique Saturn sate *ĭn thĕ hoūse* of agonies.

That Milton did not think the use of these feet in rhyme, incompatible with correct versification, is evident from the following passages in his Lycidas—no unworthy or hasty effort of his genius.

Fame is the spur that the clear *spirĭt dŏth răise,*
Oh, fountain *Arĕthŭse! ănd* thou, honoured flood,
Smooth-sliding Mincius—
To all that wander in that *perĭloŭs flōod.*

Cowley employed pure trisyllabic feet in Iambics without scruple. Waller and Denham sometimes admitted them, but Dryden and his successors rigidly excluded them; or when in too great haste to do this, disguised them by some barbarous and almost unpronouncable elision. Pope, in one of his earlier poems, has an instance of this sort.

The courtier's learning, policy o' th' gown.

Who, at this day, would attempt to pronounce this line as it is written? I have observed some instances of pure trisyllabic feet in Garth's Dispensary; and a few even occur, at remote distances, to break the detestable monotony of Darwin's Iambics.

Some of our latest modern poets in rhyme have restored the old practice, and, as I think, with a good effect. Will the reader forgive me for setting before him an example of this kind, from one of those authors—an admirable specimen of representative versification?

Alone Mokanna, midst the general flight,
Stands, like the red moon in some stormy night,
Among the *fugitive clouds* that hurrying by
Leave only her unshaken in the sky.

Here the anapest in the third line quickens the numbers, and gives additional liveliness to the image which we receive of the rapid flight of the clouds over the face of heaven.

The liberty for which I have been contending, has often been censured and ridiculed. The utmost favour which it has, at any time, to my knowledge, received from the critics, is to have been silently allowed—no one has openly defended it. It has not been my aim to mark its limits or to look for its rules. I have only attempted to show that it is an ancient birthright of the poets, and ought not to be given up.

[1819

⤜ *The American author was often charged to imitate the classics, both ancient and British, but few critics were as specific as Theophilus Parsons in the* North American Review *in describing how and to what definite purpose such models should be emulated.*

38 ⤚

. . . It is necessary not only that the best models should be proposed, but that it should be known how they may be used to most advantage. A wide distinction should be made, and constantly kept in view between study and imitation. The best authors, they whose effect upon the mind would be to give it strength and elevation, may be and should be *studied,* with assiduity; but no writer, however excellent, however perfect in his own style, or however good that style may be, should be *imitated;* for imitation always tends to destroy originality and independence of mind, and cannot substitute in their place any thing half so valuable. It was once a very popular receipt for making a good writer, to take one of Addison's Spectators, read it carefully, and remember as much as possible of the thoughts and arguments, lay the book aside, until the phraseology and expressions were forgotten, and then reclothe what you remembered of the sentiments in language, as similar as possible to that of the original, and so one would learn to write like Addison! A shorter and equally effectual way would have been to commit the paper to memory, and then one might make sure of writing once at least like Addison. We will venture to say that such a plan has been rarely adopted and acted upon without lessening the little intellect, which could submit to it. We have not forgotten that Franklin says, that he formed his style in this way; and they who can think like Franklin and fill every period, phrase, and word with meaning, may pursue with safety this or almost any plan.

It is somewhat difficult to give precise and definite rules of study; they who are conversant with the great efforts of great minds may be benefited in two ways; in the first place immediate contact with a superior mind is directly beneficial; it gives an elevated tone to our thoughts and feelings, we catch some of the emanations of their pervading spirit, and a process of assimilation is constantly going on. But the principal advantage is that by following, or rather accompanying the march of powerful minds, we get something of their speed and impetus, which continues when we are left to ourselves—the strong action of their minds imparts a degree of sympathetic velocity to less active faculties—we form habits of thinking as they thought and reasoning as they reasoned—we learn what they have learnt, and we get what is far more valuable, the power of acquiring more. But these are effects, and most important effects, which cannot be caused by the study of Queen Anne's writers; the general character of their books; the tone of thought, which pervades and is manifested, both by the choice of subjects and the manner of treating them, is feeble and contracted, and but little adapted to rouse, or invigorate, or fill the mind, which dwells upon their pages. They can afford the intellect neither aliment nor *stimulus*.

A national literature uniting all the requisites of excellence, and each in its due proportion, has not perhaps as yet existed; it may be impossible to create such a one, but it is not therefore idle to aim at it. The natural progress of society must before long, and may soon, create in this country a national literature; and they, in whose hands are placed our literary destinies, should see that no endeavours are wanting, on their part, to ensure the existence of one which shall be at once honourable and useful. The inquiry how this great work may be achieved is of infinite importance, and if in making it we guard against prejudice and habit on one side, and the love of singularity on the other, the result will be, we think, a conviction, that the most effectual, if not the only means of attaining the great object will be to encourage and promote with earnestness the study of the classics, in the first place, and next, of the English writers of the middle of the 17th century. With regard to the classics, we shall not make a laboured defence of them, as we hope that a future number of this Journal may afford opportunity for a full discussion of the subject. The notion that the classics have done and are doing harm is, we know, entertained by some, and there never was a wild and chimerical opinion which had not its advocates; but there are men considered as belonging to this party, whose names should carry with them influence and authority, but who, we believe, hold very different opinions. A man may dread the introduction of German scholarship into our country, and wish that the ocean may continue to roll between us and our lexicographers and philologists, and still think an acquaintance with the classics an essential part of the education of a gentleman or a scholar; he may still be willing that they should be read, and studied, and loved. And they ever will be studied and loved, for their beauties are general and universal, and therefore imperishable; they have stood the test of time, their fashion cannot pass away.

While we are thinking of the old English writers, it is difficult to refrain

from believing that we have degenerated from our fathers, that our intellectual stature is less than theirs, that the mind of man has either lost its
strength, or refuses to put it forth. It is the usual, and perhaps a sufficient
answer to this, that the mind seems to act now with less energy and effect,
only because it acts in a different direction, and upon different objects.
However this may be, it is certain that the eminent men of the seven-
teenth century stood forth from the mass of mankind with a more decided
and marked superiority, than we are disposed to acknowledge in any men
in these days. They were animated by the consciousness of an intellectual
supremacy, which all would reverence, and none could shake, and they
felt the responsibility attaching to their high gifts and attainments.
Whatever they wrote was marked by a prodigal expenditure of thought
and fancy, which does not belong to this age or the last, and which could
only arise from a consciousness of inexhaustible resources of boundless
affluence. Not satisfied with the applause of their own age, with the
admiration of contemporaries, they strove, to use the noble language of
Milton, for 'that lasting fame and perpetuity of praise, which God and
good men have consented, shall be the reward of those whose published
labours advance the good of mankind.' An early and intimate acquaintance with these authors will give, as far as example can give, what we
think of the first importance to him who would be a great writer,—boldness, independence, and self-reliance; with these qualities, folly may make
itself more ridiculous, but without them genius can do nothing.

We have recommended these two classes of writers, not only because
they are in themselves excellent, but because each is, we think, calculated
to correct the evil which might arise from an exclusive study of the other.
The Greek and Roman languages are far more perfect, better contrived
vehicles for thought and feeling than any modern tongue. No writer can,
therefore, now equal the classic authors in mere style, and if he strives too
much to resemble them, he would perhaps form a tame, monotonous, and
artificial style; he might substitute excessive delicacy for purity of language. Now this evil would be less likely to befal him, if he were accustomed to the copiousness, variety, and force of the old English writers. On
the other hand, an excessive and indiscriminate admiration of these last
might make him careless, diffuse, and declamatory; but this could hardly
happen, if he had learned to appreciate aright the simple majesty, the lofty
and sustained, but disciplined energy of the mighty masters of the Grecian
and Roman school. It is apprehended by some that a style, formed by the
study of English authors, who flourished when our language was, as they
say, in its infancy, would be quaint, affected, and full of obsolete expres-

sions. He, who is much acquainted with those writers, with Jeremy Taylor particularly, cannot but discover that our language is very much impoverished since their day; he will perhaps feel strongly the contrast between their rich and varied expression, and the lifeless monotony of more modern writers; he may sometimes be tempted to use a word or idiom that has gone out of fashion; but this will be the extent of his offence, for the classics will teach him to hate every thing like affectation.

In this country, it should be the business and the object of literary men, not to reform and purify, but to create a national literature. We have never yet had one, and it is time the want should be supplied. So much has been said, and unskilfully said, about the peculiar advantages of our free and popular institutions, and the beneficial effects they might be expected to have upon our literature, that it has become a wearisome theme to many ears, and we almost fear to touch upon it; but the fact is, that while some of our countrymen are vain enough, they scarce know of what, the great body of the nation, the literary and the wealthy, of those who have influence in the community are not at all too proud of our peculiar and glorious advantages; and what is worse, they are not apt to be proud in the right place. Much yet remains to be said upon the subject, for which this is not the place or occasion. We would however remark, that if there be any truth, which reason and experience concur to teach, it is, that genius and liberty go hand in hand; and it is equally true, that we live under institutions whose very essence is freedom, and which must cease to exist when they are no longer animated by the spirit of freedom which called them into being.

[1820]

The year 1820 marks a significant watershed in the development of our national literature, for Irving's Sketch Book *was the first American work to be widely accepted both at home and abroad. Bryant's retrospective survey of American poetry and the summary statements from the* Edinburgh Review *are consequently useful points from which to measure the remarkable impact of the* Sketch Book *and the later popularity of Cooper. The best known of the pieces which follow is of course the Reverend Sydney Smith's. He asked his famous question, "In the four quarters of the globe, who reads an American book?" in the January* Edinburgh Review; *the August number carried praise of the volumes everyone was to read.*

39

Of the poetry of the United States different opinions have been entertained, and prejudice on the one side and partiality on the other have equally prevented a just and rational estimate of its merits. Abroad, our literature has fallen under unmerited contumely from those who were but slenderly acquainted with the subject on which they professed to decide; and at home, it must be confessed that the swaggering and pompous pretensions of many have done not a little to provoke and excuse the ridicule of foreigners. Either of these extremes exerts an injurious influence on the cause of letters in our country. To encourage exertion and embolden merit to come forward, it is necessary that they should be acknowledged and rewarded—few will have the confidence to solicit what has been withheld from claims as strong as theirs or the courage to tread a path which presents no prospect but the melancholy wrecks of those who have gone before them. National gratitude—national pride—every high and generous feeling that attaches us to the land of our birth or that exalts our characters as individuals, ask of us that we should foster the infant literature of our country, and that genius and industry, employing their efforts to hasten its perfection, should receive from our hands that celebrity which reflects as much honour on the nation which confers it as on those to whom it is extended. On the other hand, it is not necessary for these purposes—it is even detrimental to bestow on mediocrity the praise due to excellence, and still more so is the attempt to persuade ourselves and others into an admiration of the faults of favourite writers. We make but a contemptible figure in the eyes of the world and set ourselves up as objects of pity to our posterity when we affect to rank the poets of our own country with those mighty masters of song who have flourished in Greece, Italy and Britain. Such extravagant admiration may spring from a praise-worthy and patriotic motive, but it seems to us that it defeats its own object of encouraging our literature by seducing those who would aspire to the favour of the public into an imitation of imperfect models, and leading them to rely too much on the partiality of their countrymen to overlook their deficiencies. Were our rewards to be bestowed only on what is intrinsically meritorious, merit alone would have any apology for appearing before the public. The poetical adventurer should be taught that it is only the productions of genius, taste, and diligence that can find favour at the bar of criticism—that his writings are not to be applauded merely because they are written by an American, and are not decidedly bad; and that he must produce some more satisfactory evidence of his claim to celebrity than an extract from the parish register. To show him what we expect of him, it is as necessary to point out the faults of his predecessors as to commend their excellencies. He must be taught as well what to avoid as what to imitate. This is the only way of diffusing and preserving a pure taste, both among those who read and those who write and, in our opinion, the only way of affording merit a proper and effectual encouragement.

It must however be allowed that the poetry of the United States, though it has not reached that perfection to which some other countries have carried theirs, is yet even better than we could have been expected to produce, considering that our nation has scarcely seen two centuries since the first of its founders erected their cabins on its soil, that our literary institutions are yet in their infancy, and that our citizens are just beginning to find leisure to attend to intellectual refinement and indulge in intellectual luxury, and the means of rewarding intellectual excellence. For the first century after the settlement of this country, the few quaint and unskilful specimens of poetry which yet remain to us are looked upon merely as objects of curiosity, are preserved only in the cabinet of the antiquary, and give little pleasure if read without reference to the age and people which produced them. A purer taste began after this period to prevail—the poems of the Rev. John Adams, written in the early part of the eighteenth century, which have been considered as no bad specimen of the poetry of his time, are tolerably free from the faults of the generation that preceded him and show the dawnings of an ambition of correctness and elegance. The poetical writings of Joseph Green, Esq. who wrote about the middle of the same century, have been admired for their humour and the playful ease of their composition.

But, previous to the contest which terminated in the independence of the United States, we can hardly be said to have had any national poetry. Literary ambition was not then frequent amongst us—there was little motive for it and few rewards. We were contented with considering ourselves as participating in the literary fame of that nation of which we were a part and of which many of us were natives and aspired to no separate distinction. And indeed we might well lay an equal claim with those who remained on the British soil to whatever glory the genius and learning as well as the virtue and bravery of other times reflected on the British name. These were qualities which ennobled our common ancestors; and though their graves were not with us and we were at a distance from the scenes and haunts which were hallowed by their deeds, their studies, and their contemplations, yet we brought with us and preserved all the more valuable gifts which they left to their posterity and to mankind—their illumination—their piety—their spirit of liberty—reverence for their memory and example and all the proud tokens of a generous descent.

Yet here was no theatre for the display of literary talent—the worshippers of fame could find no altars erected to that divinity in America, and he who would live by his pen must seek patronage in the parent country. Some men of taste and learning amongst us might occasionally amuse their leisure with poetical trifles, but a country struggling with the difficulties of colonization and possessing no superfluous wealth wanted any other class of men rather than poets. Accordingly we find the specimens of American poetry before this period mostly desultory and occasional—rare and delicate exotics, cultivated only by the curious.

On our becoming an independent empire, a different spirit began to manifest itself and the general ambition to distinguish ourselves as a nation was not without its effect on our literature. It seems to us that it is from this time only that we can be said to have poets of our own, and from this period it is that we must date the origin of American poetry. About this time flourished Francis Hopkinson whose humorous ballad entitled the Battle of the Kegs is in most of our memories and some of whose attempts, though deficient in vigour, are not inelegant. The keen and forcible invectives of Dr. Church, which are still recollected by his contemporaries, received an additional edge and sharpness from the exasperated feelings of the times. A writer in verse of inferiour note was Philip Freneau whose pen seems to have been chiefly employed on political subjects and whose occasional productions, distinguished by a coarse strength of sarcasm and abounding with allusions to passing events, which is perhaps their greatest merit, attracted in their time considerable notice and in the year 1786 were collected into a volume. But the influence of that principle which awoke and animated the exertions of all who participated in the political enthusiasm of that time was still more strongly exemplified in the Connecticut poets—Trumbull, Dwight, Barlow, Humphreys and Hopkins—who began to write about this period. In all the productions of these authors there is a pervading spirit of *nationality* and patriotism—a desire to reflect credit on the country to which they belonged, which seems, as much as individual ambition, to have prompted their efforts and which at times gives a certain glow and interest to their manner.

McFingal, the most popular of the writings of the former of these poets, first appeared in the year 1782. This pleasant satire on the adherents of Britain in those times may be pronounced a tolerably successful imitation of the great work of Butler—though, like every other imitation of that author, it wants that varied and inexhaustible fertility of allusion which made all subjects of thought—the lightest and most abstruse parts of learning—every thing in the physical and moral world—in art or nature, the playthings of his wit. The work of Trumbull cannot be much praised for the purity of its diction. Yet perhaps great scrupulousness in this particular was not consistent with the plan of the author and to give the scenes of his poem their full effect it might have been thought necessary to adopt the familiar dialect of the country and the times. We think his Progress of Dulness a more pleasing poem as more finished and more perfect in its kind and though written in the same manner, more free from the constraint and servility of imitation. The graver poems of Trumbull contain some vigorous and animated declamation.

Of Dr. Dwight we would speak with all the respect due to talents, to learning, to piety, and a long life of virtuous usefulness—but we must be excused from feeling any high admiration of his poetry. It seems to us modelled upon a manner altogether too artificial and mechanical. There is something strained, violent, and out of nature in all his attempts. His Conquest of Canaan will not secure immortality to its author. In this work the author has been considered by some as by no means happy in the choice of his fable—however this may be, he has certainly failed to avail himself of the advantages it offered him—his epic wants the creations and colourings of an inventive and poetical fancy—the charm, which, in the hands of genius, communicates an interest to the simplest incidents and something of the illusion of reality to the most improbable fictions. The versification is remarkable for its unbroken monotony. Yet it contains splendid passages which, separated from the body of the work, might be admired, but a few pages pall both on the ear and the imagination. It has been urged in its favor that the writer was young—the poetry of his maturer years does not however seem to possess greater beauties or fewer faults. The late Mr. Dennie at one time exerted his ingenuity to render this poem popular with his countrymen; in the year 1800 he published in the Farmer's Museum, a paper printed at Walpole; of which he was the editor, a series of observations and criticisms on the Conquest of Canaan, after the manner of Addison in those numbers of the Spectator which made Milton a favourite with the English people. But this attempt did not meet with success—the work would not sell and loads of copies yet cumber the shelves of our booksellers. In the other poems of Dr. Dwight, which are generally obnoxious to the same criticisms, he sometimes endeavours to descend to a more familiar style and entertains his reader with laborious attempts at wit, and here he is still unsuccessful. Parts of his Greenfield Hill, and that most unfortunate of his productions, the Triumph of Infidelity, will confirm the truth of this remark.

Barlow when he began to write was a poet of no inconsiderable promise. His Hasty Pudding, one of his earliest productions, is a good specimen of mock-heroic poetry, and his Vision of Columbus at the time of its first appearance attracted much attention and was hailed as an earnest of better things. It is no small praise to say that when appointed by the General Assembly of Churches in Connecticut to revise Watts' Version of the Psalms and to versify such as were omitted in that work, he performed the task in a manner which made a near approach to the simplicity and ease of that poet who, according to Dr. Johnson, 'has done better than any body else what nobody has done well.' In his maturer years, Barlow became ambitious of distinguishing himself and doing honour to his country by some more splendid and important exertion of his talents and, for this purpose, projected a national epic in which was sung the Discovery of America, the successful struggle of the states in the defence of their liberties, and the exalted prospects which were opening before them. It is to be regretted that a design so honourable and so generously conceived should have failed. In 1807 appeared the Columbiad, which was his poem of the Vision of Columbus, much enlarged, and with such variations as the feelings and reflections of his riper age and judgment led him to make. The Columbiad is not, in our opinion, so pleasing a poem, in its present form, as in that in which it was originally written.

The plan of the work is utterly destitute of interest and that which was at first sufficiently wearisome has become doubly so by being drawn out to its present length. Nor are the additions of much value on account of the taste in which they are composed. Barlow in his later poetry attempted to invigorate his style, but instead of drawing strength and salubrity from the pure wells of ancient English, he corrupted and debased it with foreign infusions. The imposing but unchaste glitter which distinguished the manner of Darwin and his imitators appears likewise to have taken strong hold on his fancy, and he has not scrupled to bestow on his poem much of this meretricious decoration. But notwithstanding the bad taste in which his principal work is composed—notwithstanding he cannot be said to write with much pathos or many of the native felicities of fancy, there is yet enough in the poetry of Mr. Barlow to prove that, had he fixed his eye on purer models, he might have excelled, not indeed in epic or narrative poetry nor in the delineation of passion and feeling, but in that calm, lofty, sustained style which suits best with topics of morality and philosophy and for which the vigour and spirit of his natural manner, whenever he permits it to appear, shew him to have been well qualified.

Humphreys was a poet of humbler pretensions. His writings, which were first collected in 1790, are composed in a better taste than those of the two last, and if he has less genius, he has likewise fewer faults. Some of his lighter pieces are sufficiently pretty. He is most happy when he aims at nothing beyond an elegant mediocrity and to do him justice this is generally the extent of his ambition. On the whole, he may be considered as sustaining a respectable rank among the poets of our country.

A writer of a different cast from those we have mentioned and distinguished by a singular boldness of imagination, as well as great humour, was Dr. Samuel Hopkins, who, in 1786, and the year following, in conjunction with Trumbull, Barlow, and Humphreys, and other wits of that time, wrote the Anarchiad, a satire on a plan similar to that of the Rolliad, which appeared in the New Haven Gazette of those years and of which the mildest parts are attributed to him. He was likewise author of the Speech of Hesper, and some smaller poems which have been praised for their wit. There is a coarseness and want of polish in his style; and his imagination, daring and original but unrestrained by a correct judgment, often wanders into absurdities and extravagances. Still, if he had all the madness, he must be allowed to have possessed some of the inspiration of poetry.

One material error of taste pervades the graver productions of these authors, into which it should seem they were led by copying certain of the poets of England who flourished near the period in which they began to write. It was their highest ambition to attain a certain lofty, measured, declamatory manner—an artificial elevation of style from which it is impossible to rise or descend without abruptness and violence, and which allows just as much play and freedom to the faculties of the writer as a pair of stilts allows the body. The imagination is confined to one trodden circle, doomed to the chains of a perpetual mannerism, and condemned to tinkle the same eternal tune with its fetters. Their versification, though not equally exceptionable in all, is formed upon the same stately model of balanced and wearisome regularity. Another fault which arises naturally enough out of the peculiar style which we have imputed to these poets is the want of pathos and feeling in their writings—the heart is rarely addressed and never with much power or success. Amidst this coldness of manner, sameness of imagery and monotony of versification, the reader lays down his book dazzled and fatigued.

In 1800 appeared the poems of William Clifton who fell at the age of twenty seven a victim to that scourge of our climate which ceases not to waste when other diseases are sated—the pulmonary consumption. There is none of our American poetry on which we dwell with more pleasure, mingled indeed with regret at the untimely fate of the writer, than these charming remains. Amidst many of the immature effusions of his greener years and unfinished productions which were never meant to meet the eye of the world, there are to be found specimens of poetry not only more delicate, classical and polished, but more varied in imagery and possessing more of that flexibility of style of the want of which in others we have complained, and more faithful to nature and the feelings, than it has often been our lot to meet with in the works of our native poets. In his later and more finished productions, his diction is refined to an unusual degree of purity, and through this lucid medium the creations of his elegant fancy appear with nothing to obscure their loveliness.

Several respectable additions have been made to the mass of American poetry by Mr. Alsop. His monody on the death of Washington was admired at the time of its appearance. The public is likewise indebted to him for a version of the poem of Silius Italicus on the Punic war and another of the Second Canto of Berni's Orlando Inamorato. Often elegant, but occasionally relapsing into feebleness and languor, his poetry is that of a man of correct and cultivated taste but of no very fervid genius, nor bending the faculties of his mind with much intensity to the work in which he was engaged.

The posthumous works of St. John Honeywood, Esq. were published in the year 1801. These modest remains, the imperfect but vigorous productions of no common mind, have not been noticed as they deserved. They contain many polished and nervous lines.

We should not expect to be easily pardoned were we to pass by the writings of a poet who enjoyed, during his life time so extensive a popularity as the late Mr. Paine. The first glow of admiration which the splendid errors of his manner excited in the public is now over and we can calmly estimate his merits and defects. He must be allowed to have possessed an active and fertile fancy. Even in the misty obscurity which often shrouds his conceptions not only from the understanding of the reader but, it should seem, from that of the writer himself, there sometimes break out glimpses of greatness and majesty. Yet with a force and exuberance of imagination which, if soberly directed, might have gained him the praise of magnificence, he is perpetually wandering in search of conceits and extravagances. He is ambitious of the epigrammatic style and often bewilders himself with attempts to express pointedly what he does not conceive clearly. More instances of the false sublime might perhaps be selected from the writings of this poet than from those of any other of equal talents who lived in the same period. The brilliancy of Paine's poetry is like the brilliancy of frost-work—cold and fantastic. Who can point out the passage in his works in which he speaks to the heart in its own language? He was a fine but misguided genius.

With respect to the prevailing style of poetry at the present day in our country, we apprehend that it will be found, in too many instances, tinged with a sickly and affected imitation of the peculiar manner of some of the late popular poets of England. We speak not of a disposition to emulate whatever is beautiful and excellent in their writings,—still less would we be understood as intending to censure that sort of imitation which, exploring all the treasures of English poetry, culls from all a diction that shall form a natural and becoming dress for the conceptions of the writer,—this is a course of preparation which every one ought to go through before he appears before the public—but we desire to set a mark on that servile habit of copying which adopts the vocabulary of some favourite author and apes the fashion of his sentences and cramps and forces the ideas into a shape which they would not naturally have taken and of which the only recommendation is, not that it is most elegant or most striking, but that it bears some resemblance to the manner of him who is proposed as a model. This way of writing has an air of poverty and meanness—it seems to indicate a paucity of reading as well as perversion of taste—it might almost lead us to suspect that the writer had but one or two examples of poetical composition in his hands and was afraid of expressing himself except according to some formula which they might contain—and it ever has been, and ever will be, the resort of those who are sensible that their works need some factitious recommendation to give them even a temporary popularity.

We have now given a brief summary of what we conceived to be the characteristic merits and defects of our most celebrated American poets. Some names of which we are not at present aware, equally deserving of notice with those whom we have mentioned, may have been omitted—some we have passed over because we would not willingly disturb their passage to that oblivion towards which, to the honour of our country, they are hastening—and some elegant productions of later date we have not commented on because we were unwilling to tire our readers with a discussion which they may think already exhausted.

On the whole there seems to be more good taste among those who read than those who write poetry in our country. With respect to the poets whom we have enumerated, and whose merits we have discussed, we think the judgment pronounced on their works by the public will be found, generally speaking, just. They hold that station in our literature to which they are entitled and could hardly be admired more than they are without danger to the taste of the nation. We know of no instance in which great poetical merit has come forward and finding its claims unallowed, been obliged to retire to the shade from which it emerged. Whenever splendid talents of this description shall appear, we believe that there will be found a disposition to encourage and reward them. The fondness for literature is fast increasing in our country—and if this were not the case, the patrons of literature have multiplied, of course, and will continue to multiply with the mere growth of our population. The popular English works of the day are reprinted in our country—they are dispersed all over the union—they are to be found in every body's hands—they are made the subject of every body's conversation. What should hinder our native works, if equal in merit, from meeting an equally favourable reception? . . .

[1818]

40 ⚞

. . . Literature the Americans have none—no native literature, we mean. It is all imported. They had a Franklin, indeed; and may afford to live for half a century on his fame. There is, or was, a Mr Dwight, who wrote some poems; and his baptismal name was Timothy. There is also a small account of Virginia by Jefferson, and an Epic by Joel Barlow—and some pieces of pleasantry by Mr Irving. But why should the Americans write books, when a six weeks' passage brings them, in their own tongue, our sense, science and genius, in bales and hogsheads? Prairies, steam-boats, gristmills, are their natural objects for centuries to come. Then, when they have got to the Pacific Ocean—epic poems, plays, pleasures of memory, and all the elegant gratifications of an ancient people who have tamed the wild earth, and set down to amuse themselves.—This is the natural march of human affairs. . . .

[1818]

41

The Americans have no national literature, and no learned men. We say not, that there are no persons amongst them who make books, and exercise the other functions of the scribbling brotherhood. The work now before us [Bristed's *America*] for example, is completely American, in paper, printing, composition, and spirit; coarse, bombastic, and bitter. The talents of our transatlantic brethren shew themselves chiefly in political pamphlets, a species of production which the popular nature of their government cannot fail to multiply in peace and in war. They have an immense number of newspapers, too, federal and democratical; and they have repeatedly attempted, but without success, to support one or two Reviews. As yet they want both readers and writers. . . . .

The Americans are too young to rival in literature, the old nations of Europe, and they will never write with the simplicity and pathos, which have adorned the birth of learning among all indigenous people. The inhabitants of the United States will never have to boast of a native poetry, or a native music. . . . .

They have, therefore, neither history, nor romance, nor poetry, nor legends, on which to exercise their genius, and kindle their imagination. In truth, there is no room amongst them, for such men as an Alfred, a Chaucer, a Spencer [sic], a Bacon, a Newton, or a Locke; and, until their continent shall have been once more submerged in the waters of the ocean, there cannot possibly be such men in America; for the laws that immortalize the great monarch just mentioned, are not wanted there; the peculiar circumstances of society, which give charms to our early poets, can never be experienced there; and that singular condition of science, which called forth the astonishing powers of the philosophers, whose names we have recited, has gone by, not to return again, until the nations of the earth, if we may be permitted so to speak, shall have been visited once more with a renovation to liberty and knowledge, after another night of barbarism, servitude, and ignorance.

[1818]

42 🖋

. . . The Americans are a brave, industrious, and acute people; but they have hitherto given no indications of genius, and made no approaches to the heroic, either in their morality or character. They are but a recent offset indeed from England; and should make it their chief boast, for many generations to come, that they are sprung from the same race with Bacon and Shakespeare and Newton. Considering their numbers, indeed, and the favourable circumstances in which they have been placed, they have yet done marvellously little to assert the honour of such a descent, or to show that their English blood has been exalted or refined by their republican training and institutions. Their Franklins and Washingtons, and all the other sages and heroes of their revolution, were born and bred subjects of the King of England,—and not among the freest or most valued of his subjects: And, since the period of their separation, a far greater proportion of their statesmen and artists and political writers have been foreigners, than ever occurred before in the history of any civilized and educated people. During the thirty or forty years of their independence, they have done absolutely nothing for the Sciences, for the Arts, for Literature, or even for the statesman-like studies of Politics or Political Economy. Confining ourselves to our own country, and to the period that has elapsed since *they* had an independent existence, we would ask, Where are their Foxes, their Burkes, their Sheridans, their Windhams, their Horners, their Wilberforces?—where their Arkwrights, their Watts, their Davys?—their Robertsons, Blairs, Smiths, Stewarts, Paleys and Malthuses?—their Porsons, Parrs, Burneys, or Blomfields?—their Scotts, Campbells, Byrons, Moores, or Crabbes?—their Siddonses, Kembles, Keans, or O'Neils?—their Wilkies, Laurences, Chantrys?—or their parallels to the hundred other names that have spread themselves over the world from our little island in the course of the last thirty years, and blest or delighted mankind by their works, inventions, or examples? In so far as we know, there is no such parallel to be produced from the whole annals of this self-adulating race. In the four quarters of the globe, who reads an American book? or goes to an American play? or looks at an American picture or statue? What does the world yet owe to American physicians or surgeons? What new substances have their chemists discovered? or what old ones have they analyzed? What new constellations have been discovered by the telescopes of Americans?—what have they done in the mathematics? Who drinks out of American glasses? or eats from American plates? or wears American coats or gowns? or sleeps in American blankets?—Finally, under which of the old tyrannical governments of Europe is every sixth man a Slave, whom his fellow-creatures may buy and sell and torture?

When these questions are fairly and favourably answered, their laudatory epithets may be allowed: But, till that can be done, we would seriously advise them to keep clear of superlatives.

[1820]

43 🖎

Though this [*Sketch Book*] is a very pleasing book in itself, and displays no ordinary reach of thought and elegance of fancy, it is not exactly on that account that we are now tempted to notice it as a very remarkable publication,—and to predict that it will form an era in the literature of the nation to which it belongs. It is the work of an American, entirely bred and trained in that country—originally published within its territory— and, as we understand, very extensively circulated, and very much admired among its natives. Now, the most remarkable thing in a work so circumstanced certainly is, that it should be written throughout with the greatest care and accuracy, and worked up to great purity and beauty of diction, on the model of the most elegant and polished of our native writers. It is the first American work, we rather think, of any description, but certainly the first purely literary production, to which we could give this praise; and we hope and trust that we may hail it as the harbinger of a purer and juster taste—the foundation of a chaster and better school, for the writers of that great and intelligent country. Its genius, as we have frequently observed, has not hitherto been much turned to letters; and, what it has produced in that department, has been defective in taste certainly rather than in talent. The appearance of a few such works as the present will go far to wipe off this reproach also; and we cordially hope that this author's merited success, both at home and abroad, will stimulate his countrymen to copy the methods by which he has attained it; and that they will submit to receive, from the example of their ingenious compatriot, that lesson which the precepts of strangers do not seem hitherto to have very effectually inculcated.*

But though it is primarily for its style and composition that we are induced to notice this book, it would be quite unjust to the author not to add, that he deserves very high commendation for its more substantial qualities; and that we have seldom seen a work that gave us a more pleasing impression of the writer's character, or a more favourable one of his judgment and taste. There is a tone of fairness and indulgence—and of gentleness and philanthropy so unaffectedly diffused through the whole work, and tempering and harmonizing so gracefully, both with its pensive and its gayer humours, as to disarm all ordinarily good-natured critics of their asperity, and to secure to the author, from all worthy readers, the same candour and kindness of which he sets so laudable an example. The want is of force and originality in the reasoning, and speculative parts, and of boldness and incident in the inventive:—though the place of these more commanding qualities is not ill supplied by great liberality and sound sense, and by a very considerable vein of humour, and no ordinary grace and tenderness of fancy. The manner perhaps throughout is more attended to than the matter; and the care necessary to maintain the rythm and polish of the sentences, has sometimes interfered with the

* While we are upon the subject of American literature, we think ourselves called upon to state, that we have lately received two Numbers, being those for January and April last, of 'The North American Review, or Miscellaneous Journal,' published quarterly at Boston, which appears to us to be by far the best and most promising production of the press of that country that has ever come to our hands. It is written with great spirit, learning and ability, on a great variety of subjects; and abounds with profound and original discussions on the most interesting topics. Though abundantly patriotic, or rather national, there is nothing offensive or absolutely unreasonable in the tone of its politics; and no very reprehensible marks either of national partialities or antipathies. The style is generally good, though with considerable exceptions—and sins oftener from affectation than ignorance. But the work is of a powerful and masculine character, and is decidedly superior to any thing of the kind that existed in Europe twenty years ago.

It is a proud thing for *us* to see Quarterly Reviews propagating bold truths and original speculations in all quarters of the world; and, when we grow old and stupid ourselves, we hope still to be honoured in the talents and merits of those heirs of our principles, and children of our example.

force of the reasoning, or limited and impoverished the illustrations they might otherwise have supplied.

We have forgotten all this time to inform our readers, that the publication consists of a series or collection of detached essays and tales of various descriptions—originally published apart, in the form of a periodical miscellany, for the instruction and delight of America—and now collected into two volumes for the refreshment of the English public. The English writers whom the author has chiefly copied, are Addison and Goldsmith, in the humorous and discursive parts—and our own excellent Mackenzie, in the more soft and pathetic. In their highest and most characteristic merits, we do not mean to say that he has equalled any of his originals, or even to deny that he has occasionally caricatured their defects. But the resemblance is near enough to be highly creditable to any living author; and there is sometimes a compass of reasoning which his originals have but rarely attained. . . .

[1820]

Palfrey suggests that "Yamoyden" bases its treatment of King Philip on Irving's sketch. Irving had, in fact, recommended this tale of massacred Indians as a fit subject for epic poetry. Palfrey's essay is itself a remarkable anticipation of Hawthorne, who was seventeen when this appeared in the North American Review. *The prophecy is as uncanny as Emerson's later call to Whitman in "The Poet."*

44

We are gratified with the appearance of Yamoyden, for a reason distinct from that of its being an accession to the amount of good poetry. We are glad that somebody has at last found out the unequalled fitness of our early history for the purposes of a work of fiction. For ourselves, we know not the country or age which has such capacities in this view as N. England in its early day; nor do we suppose it easy to imagine any element of the sublime, the wonderful, the picturesque and the pathetic, which is not to be found here by him who shall hold the witch-hazel wand that can trace it. We had the same puritan character of stern, romantic enthusiasm of which, in the Scottish novels, such effective use is made, but impressed here on the whole face of society, and sublimed to a degree which it never elsewhere reached. The men who stayed by their comfortable homes to quarrel with the church and behead the king, were but an inferior race to those more indignant if not more aggrieved, who left behind them all that belongs to the recollections of infancy and the fortunes of maturer life,—institutions which they reverenced, and every association that clings to the names of home and country, to lay the foundations of a religious community in a region then far less known to them than the North Western Coast of our continent is now to us. Arrived at 'this outside of the world,' as they termed it, they seemed to themselves to have found a place, where the Governor of all things yet reigned alone. The solitude of their adopted land, so remote from the communities of kindred men that it appeared like another world,—a wide ocean before them, and an unexplored wilderness behind,—nourished the solemn deep-toned feelings. Man was of little account in a place, where the rude grandeur of nature bore as yet no trophies of his power. God in the midst of its stern magnificence seemed all in all; and with a warmer and devouter fancy than that which of old peopled the groves, the mountains and the streams, each with its tutelary tribe, they mused in the awful loneliness of their forests on the present deity, saw him directing the bolt of the lightning, and pouring out refreshment in the flood; throned on the cloud-girt hill, and smiling in the pomp of harvest. If ever the character of men has been seen more than any where else in powerful action of development, and operated on by the force of peculiar and strongly-moving causes, it was here. Nor, wrought on as all were by similar influences of place, fortune and opinion, was ever any thing produced like a lifeless, unpoetical monotony of character. Nothing could be more opposed to this than was the spirit of puritanism. Wrong or right, every thing about these men was at least prominent and high-toned. Excitement was their daily bread, as it is other men's occasional luxury; and the diversities of character in this community where, for the most part, people thought so much alike, were more strongly marked than they have often been in other places in the most violent conflicts of opinion. Here were consummate gentlemen and statesmen, like Winthrop,—dark unrelenting politicians, after the manner of Cromwell, like Sir Harry Vane; female heresiarchs of the stamp of Mrs. Hutchinson; scholars of the first name from the universities of Europe, captains from its fields, and courtiers from its capitals; soldiers, intrepid and adventurous like Standish and Church, the life guard of the state; or part religionist, part bravo, and part buffoon like Updike Underhill, who, in the relation of his experiences, professed to have first discerned the inward light, 'when taking a pipe of the good creature, tobacco;' or scrupulous as much as loyal, like Endicot, the first governor, who dreaded not the king's enemies half as much as the scandal of the red cross on his colours. Here were noble ladies 'coming from a paradise of plenty and pleasure in the family of nobles into a wilderness of wants,' like lady Arabella Johnson, and Earl Rivers' grand-daughter, the minister's wife of Watertown; and missionaries like Eliot, making the loftiest spirit of adventure, the most unwearied industry, the noblest talents, and the profoundest learning, subsidiary to an ambition, which held out no prize but that of treasures in heaven. Here were clergymen in the magistracy, and magistrates in the desk; devotees to the established faith, and hankerers after a new; persons, who thought a toleration of state 'a sconce built against the walls of heaven,' and others who were for having it go to the extent of letting people run naked through the streets and into the churches. Here were men, who with a late chief magistrate, thought non-intercourse the specific to keep liberty in health; like Blaxton, who could no more endure the neighbourhood of *the*

Lords Brethren, than the authority of *the Lords Bishops,* and Maverick, who lived in feudal state on Noddle's Island with his three *murtherers,* the fondling appellation he gave his cannon. Here were persons reputed to have a secret to keep, like Hugh Peters, said in the tattle of the day to have been the executioner of the king; and exiles like Goff and Whaley, his judges, who had made acquaintance with every hiding-place, whether friend's cellar or hollow tree, from Massachusetts Bay to the Connecticut, and from Hadley to the Sound. All these varieties of character and many more were brought together under a religious commonwealth. To a religious model, by force or accord, every thing,—even relating to the most private and secular concerns,—was made as far as might be to conform; for 'noe man,' saith Mr. Cotton, 'fashioneth his house to his hangings, but his hangings to his house.' Religion, politics, fashion and war never came elsewhere into so close companionship. The meeting-house and the armory were built side by side, as yet, by the force of old habit, they stand, the country through. A desperate courage and dexterity in arms were enjoined as religious duties. The old considered questions of polity at the meeting. The demure youth went from testifying with his mouth in the assembly to testify with his firelock in the field, and the muffled maiden lisped in biblical phrase her soft words of encouragement or welcome.— Mingled with these, in small proportion it is true, but enough to justify an author in using them at his convenience, were adventurers, thrown hither from the very vortex of transatlantc dissipation,—of every soil, purpose, character,—citizens of the world, as free of it as the winds that bore them wherever pleasure or danger was to be met, or fortunes to be made by the ready wit or the strong hand,—factious and dissolute, or loyal, staid and serviceable, as the case might be,—men like Morton, the author of New English Canaan, a cavalier as true as ever felt his heart dance to the rattling of spurs and broad sword; or in a higher style, like Smith, a pure abstraction of chivalry, a very knight-errant as ever perilled his life for a lady's smile,—brave to a fault, and high minded to a miracle,—'the soul of council, and the nerve of war,'—a man who was engaged in more adventures than other people have read of, tracing the Nile at one time, and coasting the Chesapeake at another,—now thrown for a heretic into the sea, now saved by an Indian woman from the block, and now challenging an Ottoman army;

> 'Exceedingly well read, and profited
> In strange concealments; valiant as a lion,
> And wondrous affable; and as bountiful
> As mines of India.'

To group with these characters, themselves strongly contrasted, developed in a situation entirely novel and splendidly romantic,—appealing to the mind by the force of all that is ridiculous or sublime in fanaticism, all that is interesting in danger, fascinating in the taste for adventure, elevating and touching in self devotion, or awing in the power of religious faith,—there are the Indians, a separate and strongly marked race of men,—with all the bold rough lines of nature yet uneffaced upon them,— phlegmatic but fierce, inconstant though unimpassioned, hard to excite and impossible to soothe, cold in friendship and insatiable in revenge, yet, though manifesting little sensibility to the wonders of art, alive to the impressions of natural grandeur and beauty, and speaking even in their common affairs the rich language of a sententious poetry; a nation so identified with the hard, cold soil where they were found, as to exemplify the idea of Lord Byron in his passionate apostrophe at the lake of Leman.

> 'Let me be
> A sharer in thy fierce and far delight
> A portion of the tempest and of thee.'

He who shall give them their just place in poetry, will differ from any delineator of artificial manners almost as much as a landscape of Salvator Rosa differs from an artist's draught of a modern house. Their superstitions furnish abundant food to an imagination inclined to the sombre and terrible, their primitive habits admit of pathos in the introduction of incidents of private life, and in public there occurred events enough to find place for the imposing qualities of heroism. The attitude of the Indian tribes, for nearly a century after the landing at Plymouth, was one of high poetical interest. The prince saw his followers half alienated, the priest his faith supplanted, the patriot his race declining towards political annihilation; and innumerable must have been the designs of valour, endlessly discordant the counsels of interest, deep the forebodings of despair, bitter the menaces of vengeance, sharp the contests of discordant policy throughout that anxious period. And as to the resources, which a poet might find for description of natural scenery, he whose mind recurs,—as whose does not when poetical description is named,—to the haunt of the northern muse,

> 'Stern and wild,
> Meet nurse for a poetic child,
> Land of brown heath and shaggy wood,
> Land of the mountain and the flood,'

must remember that compared with some of ours, Scottish rivers are but brooks, and Scottish forests mere thickets. And much more picturesque than even now was the land, when a line of thriving villages enclosed a space of Indian hunting ground, and rivers with banks all gay with vegetation, ran down into solitary lakes; when the cultivated farm was bounded with the boundless forests, when the wolf and red-deer found their way among the herds, and the Calvinist in his doublet and beaver crossed the path of the native in his peäg and plumes; when the little settlement read the fate of its twenty miles distant neighbour in the reddened sky, and men who had been honoured guests in the halls of nobles, slept without a tent to cover them in swamps, or nursed the sick Indian in his miserable hut.

Whoever in this country first attains the rank of a first rate writer of fiction, we venture to predict will lay his scene here. The wide field is ripe for the harvest, and scarce a sickle yet has touched it. . . .

[1821]

In the following few paragraphs Alexander Everett digresses from the subject of his review to offer advice—not to the American author but to the booksellers Everett feels must share the blame for "the paucity of good books published in this country." The next selection insists on the responsibilities of American teachers. It is part of Samuel Knapp's effort to supply the lack of adequate textbooks dealing with the national letters. Knapp's method is encyclopedic throughout; he hopes to demonstrate by sheer weight of citation that there has been a substantial body of significant writing and that his has indeed been "an age of poetry."

45

. . . Pankouke was a bookseller of the genuine, old-fashioned, open-hearted stamp, a legitimate successor of the Aldi, the Elzevirs, and the Stephens of former days. His press, his table, his purse, every thing was at the service of the learned. He printed their books, lent them money, fed them at his board, and gave them his sisters in marriage. No author left his house unrewarded. After concluding a treaty for a work, he has been known to advance a hundred thousand franks beyond the bargain. . . .

Such was the character of this exemplary and highly meritorious bookseller; an example truly worthy of imitation. What bookseller in the United States would advance twenty thousand dollars beyond his bargain? He that should do it would be laughed at for his simplicity, rather than extolled as a Mecenas. We go farther, and ask, what bookseller in the United States would offer twenty thousand dollars, for any book that could be written. In other countries when a gentleman has been at the trouble of writing a book, there is a competition among the booksellers to know who shall have the honour of printing it, and the author puts what price he pleases upon his manuscript. Here, on the contrary, it is not always that he can persuade the booksellers to print. We could name a most valuable treatise on the Revolutions of Empires, written by a President of one of our first literary institutions, which has been offered for years at all the booksellers' shops in New England, and has not yet seen the light nor probably ever will. As to the idea of receiving any money for the copyright, it would be thought the height of presumption in a writer to expect it. It is quite enough if the bookseller will do him the favor of printing his work, and will take the trouble of sending it about to his correspondents, with a proviso that he shall take the profits himself, if there be any, and leave the author the chance of a loss. It is compensation enough for the latter to see his name in the title page. We hear much of the paucity of good books published in this country, but we cannot help thinking that much of the blame if it is to be attributed to the booksellers. If these gentlemen, instead of investing their capital in republications of foreign works, from which they derive no honour and little profit, the sale being in general barely enough to cover the expense,—if, we say, instead of this, they would hold out a generous encouragement for the production of original compositions,—if they would offer twenty thousand dollars for a history,—ten thousand for a poem or a novel, and so in proportion; and would then, like the illustrious Pankouke, throw in a few thousand dollars above the bargain, to put the author in good spirits,—we should find the reproach of our literary poverty disappearing very fast. We should soon have a class of standard national works, that, after making the fortune of their writers, would become a lasting and valuable property to the booksellers that bought the copies; while the foreign books, which they now reprint, are all ephemeral, and, like fancy goods, are not worth a dollar to them after the first momentary demand is over. But we must leave this interesting subject, upon which we could say much more, and return to our immediate business. . . .

[1821]

46 🖋

Every book that is ushered into the world, is a mental experiment of the writer, to ascertain the taste, and to obtain the judgment of the community; and the author can only be certain of one thing, and that is, of his intentions in his publication. Of my intentions, I can only say, as, perhaps, I have a dozen times said in the course of my work, they were to exhibit to the rising generation something of the history of the thoughts and intellectual labours of our forefathers, as well as of their deeds. There is, however, an intimate connexion between thinking and acting, particularly among a free and an energetick people. My plan, when I commenced my researches, was an extensive one, and I gathered copious materials to carry it into effect. For several years past, I have had access to libraries rich in American literature; but when I sat down to work up the mass I had collected, the thought suggested itself to my mind, that no adequate compensation could ever be reasonably expected for my pains; and then the consciousness that I was in some measure trespassing upon my professional pursuits, went far to quench my zeal, and to chase away my visions of literary reputation. Still, I could not be persuaded to relinquish altogether my design, and I therefore set about abridging my outlines, dispensing with many of my remarks, and giving up numerous elaborate finishings I had promised myself to make in the course of my work. And another thought struck me most forcibly, that a heavy publication would not be readily within the reach of all classes of youth in our country, but that a single volume of common size, in a cheap edition, might find its way into some of our schools, and be of service in giving our children a wish to pursue the subject of our literary history, as they advanced in years and in knowledge. The instructors of our youth, when true to their trust, form a class in the community that I hold in respect and esteem, and they will pardon me for making a few remarks to them. Your calling is high, I had almost said holy. To your intelligence, patience, good temper, purity of life, and soundness of principles, parents look for the forming of healthy, vigorous minds, in their children. If you cannot create talents, you can do something better; you can guide the fiery, and wake up the dull; correct the mischievous, and encourage the timid. The temple of knowledge is committed to your care; the priesthood is a sacred one. Every inscription on the walls should be kept bright, that the dimmest eye may see, and the slowest comprehension may read and be taught to understand. Your task is great, and every member of the community, who is able to give you any assistance, should come to your aid in the great business of instruction. In this way much has been done;—much, however, remains to be done. The elements of learning have been simplified, and thousands of children have been beguiled along the pathway of knowledge, who never could have been driven onward. Geography has been made easy and fascinating, and the elements of natural philosophy very pleasant; and what was once difficult and harsh to young minds in many studies, has become attractive. History, both sacred and profane, has assumed new charms as it has been prepared for the school-room; I speak of the history of other countries, not of our own. We have very good histories—narrative, political, military, and constitutional; but I know none, as yet, that can be called literary—meaning by the term, a history of our literature, and of our literary men; and probably it will be a long time before we shall have such an one as we ought to have. Our Sismondis, D'Israelis, are yet to arise. You will struggle in vain to make American history well understood by your pupils, unless biographical sketches, anecdotes, and literary selections, are mingled with the mass of general facts. The heart must be affected, and the imagination seized, to make lasting impressions upon the memory.

One word to your pride:—you are aware that it has been said by foreigners, and often repeated, that there was no such thing as American literature; that it would be in vain for any one to seek for proofs of taste, mind, or information, worth possessing, in our early records; and some of our citizens, who have never examined these matters, have rested so quietly after these declarations, or so faintly denied them, that the bold asserters of these libels have gained confidence in tauntingly repeating them. The great epoch in our history—the revolution of 1775—seemed sufficient, alone, to many of the present generation, to give us, as a people, all the celebrity and rank, among the nations of the earth, we ought to aspire to, without taking the trouble to go back to the previous ages of heroick virtue and gigantick labours. Many of the present generation are willing to think that our ancestors were a pious and persevering race of men, who really did possess some strength of character, but, without further reflection, they are ready to allow that a few pages are "ample room and verge enough" to trace their character and their history to-gether. I have ventured to think differently, and also to flatter myself, that, at the present day, it would not be a thankless task to attempt to delineate some of the prominent features of our ancestors in justification of my opinion. This errour can only be eradicated by your assistance, and that by instilling into the minds of our children, in your every-day lessons, correct information upon these subjects;—and while you lead your pupils through the paths of miscellaneous and classical literature—and, at the present day, even the humblest education partakes of much that is of a classical nature—be it your duty, also, to make them acquainted with the minutest portions of their country's history. No people, who do not love themselves better than all others, can ever be prosperous and great. A sort of inferiority always hangs about him who unduly reverences another. If "*know thyself,*" be a sound maxim for individual consideration, "*think well of thyself,*" should be a national one. Patriotism and greatness begin at the maternal bosom, are seen in the nursery and primary school, and quicken into life in every advancing stage of knowledge. Guardians of a nation's morals, framers of intellectual greatness, show to your charge, in proper lights, the varied talent of your country, in every age of her history; and inscribe her glories of mind, and heart, and deed, as with a sun-beam, upon their memories.

[1829]

. . . It was fashionable in the latter days of Darwin, and in the early days of Southey, to speak lightly of the productions of Pope. The criticks found that he had sometimes indulged his resentments in the Dunciad, and doomed several characters to infamy who deserved a better fate. The small fry of authors who wished to hide their feebleness in the extravagancies of sentiment then becoming popular by the influence of the French Revolution, and the influx of German literature, which had not been well examined, nor the chaff separated from the wheat, supported by a few men of genius, who had taken up some erroneous impressions on the canons of poetry, did, for a while, obscure the fame of Pope; and it seemed, for a season, that he would at length be found in his own Dunciad. They attacked him as a writer wanting in variety and genius, and boldly called his morals in question. The clouds which obscured his brightness did not last long, but were soon dispersed, and his genius beamed in its ancient majesty. Byron would yield to no one in his reverence of Pope: and almost all the present poets of England, who are the arbiters of taste, have come into the opinion that Pope was a genius and a poet, such as it is seldom the good fortune of nations to produce.

This may be said to be an age of poetry. There are many living writers whose works have secured them wealth and fame, while they were able to enjoy it. Southey's muse has brought forth epicks as common songs; and Scott, before he commenced the Waverly novels, produced Marmion, the Lay of the Last Minstrel, Rokeby, the Lady of the Lake, and the Vision of Don Roderick, with other pieces, in quick succession. Byron from his boyhood never laid aside his pen until the wrongs of Greece seized his heart. Childe Harold, the Corsair, the Gaiour, the Bride of Abydos, Cain, and Don Juan, followed each other as rapidly as the French legions which crossed the Alps with Napoleon. Montgomery, Coleridge, Crabbe, and Moore, have been busy. The polished Campbell, and the Shakspearian Baillie, have not been idle.

The poets of our own country have had these fine models before them; and they have shown the world that they have profited by being in such a school. There is at present much talent, ambition, and information among our poets, and they are getting rid of the ridiculous impressions which have long been prevalent, that genius is every thing, and information nothing, in making a poet. The prophets of old had to build the altar, and lay on it the wood, before they called the fire from heaven to kindle the flame and burn the offering.

My intention, at first, was to have mentioned many of our living poets; two only have I named, Freneau and Trumbull, and these patriotick bards are so near, in the course of nature, to the confines of a better world, that I felt no reluctance to speak of them; but on mature reflection, I gave up the thought of bringing forward any more, fearing that it would be premature to discuss their merits in a work like this, as a fair criticism on these would be in a measure making comparisons between them. I have no hesitation in saying, that we abound in good poets, whose writings will remain to make up the literature of a future age; nor would I yield my admiration for their productions to others who are prodigal of praise whenever their works appear; but at this time I am not prepared to say whether Pierpont or Bryant be the greater poet, or whether Percival has higher claims to immortality than his brethren of the *"enchanted grounds and holy dreams;"* nor whether she of *"the banks of the Connecticut,"* whose strains of poetick thought are as pure and lovely as the adjacent wave touched by the sanctity of a Sabbath's morn, be equal to her tuneful sisters, Hemans and Landor, on the other side of the water, or superiour to her more sprightly rivals on this.

When all classes were busy in building up our national and state governments, the fine arts were neglected; and a few only knew how necessary the cultivation of them was to refine and polish a nation. Even in England, until within half a century, any devotion to them was considered inconsistent with weighty duties. Windham, Talbot, Murray, and Pulteney, "every muse gave o'er," before they entered the temple of justice, and assumed the causes of their clients; and Blackstone dropt a tear at parting with his muse at the vestibule of Westminster Hall. Parsons, of our own country, as great a name as either, who thought that he was made more decidedly for a poet than for any other calling, confined himself to writing a few occasional pieces, generally on some merry-making occurrence, not venturing to trust himself further; while he read with avidity every line that was published on this, or the other side of the Atlantick, in English, French, Italian, or Latin. It is not so now; it is thought quite possible to devote a few hours of relaxation from severe studies to the fine arts, without any fear of being seduced from graver duties. Opinions and taste are changed in many other respects. The good household dames of other days would have turned shuddering from the sight of Cupids, and Venuses, and Graces, which the maiden of the present day, pure as the stainless snow, will sit before whole hours, engaged in her innocent drawing lessons. The mind, properly disciplined, is capable of sustaining much; as the body in full health can support heat and cold. There are no sickly images while there is a sane mind in a sane body. Numerous instances of the facility of passing from severe labour to sportiveness, are now at hand. Sir Walter Scott wrote all his poetry, and many of his novels, in hours of relaxation from the dull details of a clerkship in a court of justice. Sir William Jones left Hafiz, and all the enchantments of Arabian poetry, to throw new light upon the black letter of the law, and to give a reason for a principle in Coke upon Littleton, when the two great luminaries of the science had only stated a decision. Some of the great dignitaries of the church have awakened their zeal by invoking the muse; and the great statesman of England, who has lately become a tenant of the tomb, found his poetry as effective as his eloquence in scattering and subduing his opposers, and in building up his systems, and supporting his policy. The poetry of the Anti-Jacobin did more than a thousand homilies to defend the cause of old fashioned honesty; and "the Loves of the Triangles," checked the false politicks and the bad taste of the Darwinian school. Like the eagle, Canning passed from watching the fish-hawks along the coast, to soaring and poising sublimely in the heavens, and to gazing with undazzled eye upon the sun.

We have, by the mistake or modesty of our own writers, been ranked among those nations which have lately become literary. But avoiding all further deception on that head, it is to be hoped that we have now arrived at that point in our literary history, when it is proper for us to assume some share of independence. Not only our mother country is pouring in her literature by the *bale* upon us, as usual, but other countries are also doing the same. The whole European continent is open to our researches, and yields her literary and scientifick treasures to our enterprise; and our missionaries, in conjunction with those of other countries, are throwing open the door to the immense storehouses of oriental learning, where the treasures of unnumbered ages have been lodged. Even a key to the mysteries of Egyptian wisdom has been found, and the veil of Isis is about to be removed. At the same time, all things have become well settled upon true principles among us, and the agitation and bustle of their establishment having passed away, some of the first minds will gratify their ambition by literary distinction; and claim their country's gratitude, by refining our taste, and raising our standard of literary eminence.

Here nature presents her beauties in as delicate forms, and her wonders in as bold relief, as she has in the birth place of the muses. She has laid the foundation of her mountains as broad, and raised their tops as high as in the old world. What are the Tibers and Scamanders, measured by the Missouri and the Amazon? Or what the loveliness of Illyssus or Avon, by the Connecticut or the Potomack? The waters of these American rivers are as pure and sweet, and their names would be as poetical, were they as familiar to us in song, as the others, which have been immortalized for ages. Whenever a nation wills it, prodigies are born. Admiration and patronage create myriads who struggle for the mastery, and for the olympick crown. Encourage the game, and the victors will come. In the smiles of publick favour, poets will arise, yea, have already arisen, whose rays of mental fire will burn out the foul stain upon our reputation, given at first by irritated and neglected genius, and continued by envy and malice—that this is the land

"Where fancy sickens, and where genius dies."

[1829]

*⤳ Discussion of the drama in nineteenth-century American peri-
odicals were rare. Robert Walsh, editor of the* American Quarterly
Review *and author of the celebrated* Appeal From the Judgments of
Great Britain, *probably wrote this essay. In it he discusses both the
purpose of a national drama and the resources available to nourish it.*

47 ⤳

It might perhaps be a question with some whether it be more indicative
of a want of genius in the dramatic writers or a want of taste in the
readers, of these United States that a large portion of the latter have, we
believe, remained to this day ignorant of the very existence of the former.
To the frequenters of the theatre, it is known that some such strange
monsters did once and perhaps do still inhabit this barren wilderness of
literature, unless perchance they have been starved to death or become
extinct like the mammoth and various other animals whose remains
sometimes rise up in judgment against them. But to a vast proportion of
our readers, they are as if they had never been—not forgotten, for that
would be something—but never known.

For this reason, it will no doubt surprise the reader to learn that we
have actually in our possession nearly sixty American dramas, consisting
of tragedies, comedies, operas, serious and comic, melo-dramas and farces,
besides others that baffle all our attempts at "codification." These last
cannot be called by any name, Christian or Pagan, with which we are
acquainted and, like certain equivocal substances which belong neither to
the animal nor vegetable kingdom, must be left to be defined when they
shall become sufficiently numerous to merit the distinction.

To those who have had occasion to observe and to regret the prevalence
of a certain colonial spirit which equally affects our legal and literary
tribunals, and, by a natural consequence, the opinions of the public, it will
probably occur that this total oblivion of our dramatic productions is
entirely owing to the accident of their not being worth remembering or
even meriting a passing notice. A perusal of the plays in our possession
has, however, satisfied us that this is not altogether the fact. Unless we are
greatly mistaken, there are some among them not entirely unworthy of
being read and which, if represented on our stage, with the advantage of
good scenery and good acting, would or at least ought to be successful.

They are, we really think, to say the least of them, quite equal to the productions of the present race of London playwrights, which are regularly brought out at our theatres and to which the certificate of having been performed a hundred nights with unbounded applause gives all the efficacy of a quack medicine.

Before, however, we proceed to notice some of these domestic wonders more particularly, it may perhaps be no uninteresting or useless task to glance at a few of the leading causes which have brought about that decline in the dignity and usefulness of the stage which is now acknowledged on all hands to be notorious in England, and as an almost inevitable consequence in this country. For ourselves, we cannot but lament it most deeply as one of those indications that point with unerring finger to the absence of that wholesome, manly and vigorous taste which may be said always to mark the best periods in the history of every civilized country. Notwithstanding all that has been said and written since the days of Jeremy Collier, we cannot but bear in our heads as well as our hearts a love and respect for an art which, in its purity, administers so delightfully to our taste as well as to our best feelings. Of all popular amusements ever devised, dramatic exhibitions are, when properly conducted, the most elegant and instructive. They address themselves both to the understanding and the senses, and carry with them the force of precept and example. In witnessing them, we are excited by the passions of others instead of our own, as is the case in the real transactions of life; and that stimulus which may be pronounced to be one of the actual wants of our nature is thus afforded to us without any of the evil consequences resulting from an indulgence of the passions in our own proper persons.

It is by this mode of giving play and excitement to the mind, by mimic representations, that the force of the operations of the passions in real life is unquestionably tempered and restrained; and hence it has always been held with justice that the stage, in its legitimate and proper state, is a most powerful agent in humanizing and refining mankind. It operates also in other ways in bringing about this salutary result. It allures the people from an attendance upon barbarous and brutifying spectacles—from brawls, boxing-matches, and bull-baitings;—it accustoms them, in a certain degree, to intellectual enjoyments and rational recreations and substitutes innocent amusement, if not actual instruction, in the place of those which afford neither one nor the other. A theatre where the price of admittance is within the means of the ordinary classes of people is a substitute, and a most salutary one, for tavern brawls and low debauchery. Those whose faculties are too obtuse to relish or comprehend the intrinsic excellence of a plot, the lofty morality or classic ease of the dialogue, are still instructed and amused through the medium of their eyes and actually see before them examples to imitate or avoid. If it be said that these examples are too far removed from the ordinary sphere of those who witness them to be of any use, still it may be replied that chastity, fortitude, patriotism, and magnanimity are virtues of all classes of mankind, and that all can feel and comprehend them, though they may be exercised in circumstances and situations in which they never expect to be placed. That the Drama may be, has been, and actually now is, in some degree diverted from its proper and most important purposes will hardly be denied by those who have the misfortune to like a good play; and though it cannot exactly be said of the infirmities of intellect as it is of the maladies of the body that when once the causes are known they are half cured; still it is certain, that a knowledge of the source of a defect is indispensable to the finding of an adequate remedy. For this reason, the ensuing remarks may not be entirely without utility.

It is generally, we believe, considered a sufficient apology in behalf of the persons who preside over this most delightful of all intellectual banquets that the degradation of the stage originated in the necessity of administering to a taste already vitiated. The public must be pleased that the manager may live. If the people require the attractions of a menagerie and a puppet-show combined, and will relish nothing living but horses, dogs, dromedaries, and elephants prancing in the midst of pasteboard pageantry, conflagrations, bombardments, springing of mines, blowing up of castles and such like accumulations of awful nursery horrors, it is alleged that there is no help for it. This taste must be gratified, like the appetites of other animals that chance to prefer raw meat and offals to the highest delicacies of the table. This may be true to a certain extent; but we are, notwithstanding, satisfied in our own judgment that it is very materially in the power of the managers of theatres, to give a better direction to the public taste; and that it would eventually lead to the most profitable results, were they to take equal pains and incur equal expense to cater for a good taste that they do to pamper a bad one.

We are quite sure, that a theatre, devoted to the exhibition of none but legitimate dramas, in the hands of competent actors, would prove permanently attractive, rally around it almost all the more enlightened portions of society and, by a natural consequence, all the inferior classes; and finally prove far more profitable to the manager than one devoted to expensive spectacles, one of which it costs more to get up than a dozen first-rate tragedies and comedies. If one-half of the sums laid out on pasteboard, tinsel, and trumpery were offered as a premium for good actors, a first-rate company might be collected, permanently, and fully adequate to give effect to the finest efforts of the dramatist. There would then be no necessity to depend upon perpetual novelty which supplies the place of good acting; and perpetual shows substituted for the beautiful creations of genius.

It is not attempted to be denied that a large portion of the attendants on the theatres, and on whom they are in a considerable degree dependent for its support, are of that order of people which, however worthy in other respects, is not distinguished either for a correct taste or a well disciplined judgment as to authors or actors. But still, there is always in every civilized country a sufficient number of persons better educated and of a more refined taste to give the tone to the others. Those who cannot feel like them or comprehend and relish the same beauties in literature and the arts are at first ashamed to dissent from their decisions, and at length partake in the enjoyment of the same beauties with an equal relish, since it is only necessary to become a little accustomed to what is good to be disgusted with what is bad. The example descends to those in the next degree below, until finally all will partake of its influence; and even the gods in the gallery will be ashamed not to be pleased with what they see applauded by their masters and mistresses in the pit and boxes.

We are therefore of opinion that no small portion of this bad taste which we deplore in relation to the stage may be fairly laid to the charge of the managers who, if we mistake not, have been at least accomplices in producing that very state of things which they now offer as an apology for presevering in the same course by which it was brought about. After having vitiated the public taste for more delicate viands by affording us nothing better, they make this an excuse for offering us still worse; like the bumpkin, who having fed his ass upon nothing but husks for a long while, took occasion afterwards to reproach him with his indifference to corn.

There certainly was a time when a sterling play, in the hands of sterling actors, was a sufficient attraction to ensure a good house. The public neither required the excitement of wild beasts nor the allurements of pasteboard mimicry of what nature every day presented to view in all the attractions of her own inimitable grace and beauty. Can it be pretended that it would not be so now, if the same motives were held out to the public? It is the boast of the present age that within the very period that has been marked by the decay of the stage, mankind have made greater advances in the general diffusion of knowledge and an improvement in taste than during any similar portion of time for many generations past. No one, it is presumed, will be disposed to deny that this improvement in almost every thing else would, if not counteracted by some cause peculiarly applicable to this art, have been accompanied by a similar advancement of theatrical taste and consequently in theatrical exhibitions, if not theatrical productions. That such "counteracting principles," as Mr. Owen calls them, have operated peculiarly against the stage is therefore, we think, undeniable. It may be worth while to advert to some of the most powerful of these.

The perpetual exhibition of shows possessing no other merit but that of imitating or rather caricaturing nature most vilely has by degrees rendered the more refined classes of society quite indifferent to the stage, which has of consequence fallen in a great measure into the occupation of those who relish "Tom and Jerry" better than Shakspeare or Sheridan. The fashionable people have, for this reason, decided the theatre to be unfashionable; and, one and all, prefer eating ice-cream and pickled oysters at parties to visiting a place which is not only not fashionable but where there is neither ice-cream nor pickled oysters. One of the first results of this abandonment or indifference to the stage is the deterioration of both plays and actors. There is no use in writing a good play to please people who have neither taste nor capacity to admire it; and no occasion for first-rate actors to please an audience whose keenest relish is for dogs, horses, and opera dancers. . . .

There are many other causes which have, without doubt, cooperated with the preceding to bring down the stage to its present dead level of degradation. Our limits will not permit us to enumerate them, and having thus far confined ourselves to those which equally apply to this country and England, we will now revert to such as peculiarly belong to the former.

The want of a National Drama is the first thing that strikes us in this inquiry. By a national drama, we mean, not merely a class of dramatic productions written by Americans, but one appealing directly to the national feelings; founded upon domestic incidents—illustrating or satirizing domestic manners—and, above all, displaying a generous chivalry in the maintenance and vindication of those great and illustrious peculiarities of situation and character by which we are distinguished from all other nations. We do not hesitate to say that, next to the interests of eternal truth, there is no object more worthy the exercise of the highest attributes of the mind than that of administering to the just pride of national character, inspiring a feeling for the national glory, and inculcating a love of country. It is this which we would call a national literature; and, unless we greatly err, it is these characteristics which must eventually constitute the principal materials of one. We have no peculiar language to create an identity of our own; and it must, in a great measure, be in its apt and peculiar application to ourselves, our situation, character, government and institutions that our literature would seem destined to become national.

We do not wish to be understood as making an appeal to the national feeling, an indispensable requisite in all American productions; but we do mean to say, that such appeals, when introduced with genuine sentiment and without affectation, are proper and praiseworthy. They are equally advantageous to the author and his readers. They give to the productions of the former all that peculiar and decisive interest derived from an association of the efforts of the mind with manners, incidents, and local affections; and they instil into the latter a more powerful feeling of patriotism. Every man contemplates his country with a greater degree of affection and pride when he sees its happiness, virtues, or glories commemorated by genius in a manner which evinces that he who thus celebrates them is himself worthy of admiration. There are so few writers of powerful creative imagination that it savours of a base desertion to withdraw their genius from the service of their country and devote those powers which were bestowed by Providence for higher purposes to themes and exploits having no connexion with her situation or history. The best and most permanent foundation for fame is our native soil; and a man who is admired or beloved by his own countrymen may almost dispense with the praises of the rest of the world.

There are two points essential to the existence and growth of this patriotic spirit of literature. The one is a proper degree of susceptibility on the part of the nation; the other, sufficient power in a writer to appeal to it successfully. It would be a hopeless attempt to appeal to a common feeling which had no existence, on the one hand, and on the other, the feeling would remain latent if there were no one to make the appeal. For many years subsequent to the establishment of our independence, an American writer laboured under the worst species of discouragement to an aspiring mind. There were comparatively but few general readers, and those were so accustomed to the productions of the mother country that they viewed the appearance of an American work pretty much in the light a Parisian coterie would the intrusion of a half-civilized Indian. A gentleman of that day would as soon have thought of wearing a homespun coat as of reading a book of home manufacture. The sense of inferiority in consequence kept down and discouraged the restless aspirations of actual or imagined genius; and if by chance a daring adventurer desperately invaded these barren regions of Parnassus, it was in the disguise of a foreigner or behind the leaden shield of abject imitation. He dared not attempt originality for fear of being stigmatized as a barbarian or select a purely native subject lest he should be laughed at by those who presided over the public taste as a dabbler in "Indian poetry,"—the favourite phrase of the day.

But times have changed and are daily changing for the better. Abroad, the public curiosity is excited towards the new world; and at home, there is a growing taste for historical truths and romantic fictions connected or associated with the progress of this nation. The public mind and taste have been and now are in a state to encourage and reward the successful efforts of genius employed on domestic subjects; and although it must be confessed that some considerable leaven of the old colonial vassalage still remains to embarrass and discourage, yet still it may be fairly asserted that no native writer can now justly plead the fact of the discouragements to which we have just alluded in extenuation of his indolence or in explanation of his ill success. By a proper choice of his subjects, and a tolerably happy mode of treating them he may reasonably calculate upon a moderate success. We do not say that he will actually add another to the wonders peculiar to the present times; to wit, rich authors—but he will bid fair to escape oblivion and a jail. We cannot offer a more apt and honourable example of the success attending such a course as we recommend than that of Mr. Cooper, the author of the Pioneers and other works, whose various and acknowledged excellence has received a peculiar and happy aid from the nature of the subjects which appeal directly to our early associations, local impressions, and sectional feelings. He displayed the same talent in his novel of "Precaution," but falling into the error of laying the *venue,* as the lawyers say, in the wrong place, his first work fell into oblivion and was only brought to light again by its connexion with the author of the Spy, and the Pioneers.

The remarks we made in relation generally to American literature may, we think, be specially applied to the drama which appeals most strongly to popular feelings. Were it not for the obstacles and discouragements we have previously noticed, among which are conspicuous a want of taste in the audience and a want of proper management in the conductors of theatres, we think there is little doubt that successful efforts could and would be made in this branch of literature. This land is full of materials—such as novelty of incident, character, and situation. Like the forests of our country which have never been cut down, those materials remain unemployed and unexhausted—fresh and novel, with all the bold features of primeval strength and vigour. It only requires a brave, original intellect, to convert them into the materials of excellence. It has been often imagined as one of the obstacles which stand in the way of a national drama that we lack variety in our national character. No idea, we think, can possibly be more erroneous than this. There is, probably, no country in the world which affords more numerous and distinct characters than the United States. Our cities are full of bipeds from every quarter of the old world, bringing with them all their peculiarities to be exhibited in a new sphere. From the city on the sea-side to the frontier settler—from him to the white hunter more than half savage—to the savage himself—there are continual gradations in the characters and situation of mankind; and every state in the Union is a little world by itself, exhibiting almost the same degrees of difference that we observe in the English, the Scotch, and the Irish. Their manners, habits, occupations, prejudices, and opinions, are equally various and dissimilar. For these reasons, we believe that there is no want of sufficient varieties of character in the United States, to afford ample materials for a diversified drama. We rather fear the obstacle has hitherto arisen from the habit of imitation we have noticed. The author perhaps did not catch any original characters because he did not think of looking for them and complained in consequence of the scarcity of what he never took the pains to find. But even conceding, for one moment only, that complaints of a want of variety of character are just, still no one will deny that there is an abundant field for novelty of situation, and novelty of situation is the best possible substitute for novelty of character if it does not in reality create it. . . .

Whatever talent there may be among us, it will unless encouraged lie inactive like those seeds which are buried in the forests perhaps for ages and which only vegetate into fruits and flowers when the warm rays of the sun awaken their dormant energy and vivify the chill bosom of the earth. The first requisite for producing a National Drama is national encouragement. We do not mean pensions and premiums—but liberal praise and rewards to success—and a liberal allowance for failures. The second is a little more taste and liberality in the managers of our theatres; and the third is the presence of competent performers, collected in companies of sufficient strength to give effectual support to a new piece and sufficient talent to personate an original character without resorting to some hacknied model which has descended from generation to generation and, like all copies, lost something of the original in the hands of each succeeding imitator.

Let not, however, our youthful aspirants after honest fame be discouraged by the obstacles we have placed before them. Genius has often a divinity within itself, a sort of prophetic consciousness, a daring insight into futurity, an irrepressible impulse, which animates and supports it in the midst of discouragements and neglect. But one man out of millions is a hero, a saint, or a sage. Yet this should be no obstacle to the pursuit of glory, virtue, or wisdom. If but one man out of millions attain the summit of Parnassus, let it be recollected that his reward is immortality.

[1827]

One of the more curious arguments to occupy students of literature was the purity of American English. The British complained of American barbarism, and most native commentators felt challenged to defend—as Noah Webster does here—the "pure" and "genuine" English employed by the best national writers. Webster's Preface to the important American Dictionary of the English Language *makes a striking contrast of Whitman, Twain, and the post–Civil War writers who gloried in the flavor of native diction, dialect, and usage.*

48

. . . There are many other considerations of a public nature, which serve to justify this attempt to furnish an American Work which shall be a guide to the youth of the United States. Most of these are too obvious to require illustration.

One consideration however which is dictated by my own feelings, but which I trust will meet with approbation in correspondent feelings in my fellow citizens, ought not to be passed in silence. It is this. "The chief glory of a nation," says Dr. Johnson, "arises from its authors." With this opinion deeply impressed on my mind, I have the same ambition which actuated that great man when he expressed a wish to give celebrity to Bacon, to Hooker, to Milton and to Boyle.

I do not indeed expect to add celebrity to the names of *Franklin, Washington, Adams, Jay, Madison, Marshall, Ramsay, Dwight, Smith, Trumbull, Hamilton, Belknap, Ames, Mason, Kent, Hare, Silliman, Cleaveland, Walsh, Irving,* and many other Americans distinguished by their writings or by their science; but it is with pride and satisfaction, that I can place them, as authorities, on the same page with those of *Boyle, Hooker, Milton, Dryden, Addison, Ray, Milner, Cowper, Davy, Thomson* and *Jameson.*

A life devoted to reading and to an investigation of the origin and principles of our vernacular language, and especially a particular examination of the best English writers, with a view to a comparison of their style and phraseology with those of the best American writers and with our colloquial usage, enables me to affirm with confidence that the genuine English idiom is as well preserved by the unmixed English of this country as it is by the best *English* writers. Examples to prove this fact will be

found in the Introduction to this work. It is true that many of our writers
have neglected to cultivate taste and the embellishments of style; but even
these have written the language in its genuine *idiom*. In this respect,
Franklin and Washington, whose language is their hereditary mother
tongue unsophisticated by modern grammar, present as pure models of
genuine English as Addison or Swift. But I may go farther and affirm,
with truth, that our country has produced some of the best models of
composition. The style of President Smith; of the authors of the Fed-
eralist; of Mr. Ames; of Dr. Mason; of Mr. Harper; of Chancellor Kent;
of Mr. Barlow; of the legal decisions of the Supreme Court of the United
States; of the reports of legal decisions in some of the particular states;
and many other writings; in purity, in elegance and in technical precision
is equaled only by that of the best British authors and surpassed by that of
no English compositions of a similar kind. . . .

[1828]

≫ Not every British critic saw The Sketch Book *as a final answer to the question of an American literature. The following brief samples suggest the kind of assessment our efforts continued to receive.*

49 ≰

. . . The literary attempts of the Americans are in every way interesting, and if they compel us to laugh at them the fault lies not with us. They are in their perfect infancy; their authors have at present neither experience enough to fall in with the taste of the nation, nor genius enough to direct it. Still the irresistible impulse of scribbling, and the encouragement which is offered to literary aspirants where the competition is so inconsiderable, produces books with tolerable rapidity. The authors, without models of their own, are often too proud to form themselves upon those of other countries which the sanction of ages has rendered classical, or they have not the skill to see the wisdom and the necessity of doing so. They have no foundation of their own to build on—nothing can come of nothing—and the consequence of their perverseness or blindness is, that all which they attempt of originality is an heterogeneous mass of unskilled plagiarism, while those of them who have drank from those deep wells of inspiration which are to be found in the labours of past ages, have attained success proportioned to their talent and exertions. . . .

[1823]

50 ≰

. . . The charges of borrowing from English literature are allowed, but with as little blame. From what other source has any American borrowed his ideas? From what other source can any American borrow? He has no native literature. He has even no material for the foundation of a native literature. What visions, what exalting ancestral recollections can the wand of poetry summon from the rude traffic of exiles with savages, from sectarian bickerings and Indian massacre, from the unhappy life of fugitives struggling with the difficulties of a strange and unpropitious land, or from the brutishness, squalidness, and ferocity of the wigwam. . . .

[1824]

51 🖋

. . . America has hitherto had little or no originality in her literature; or, to speak more properly, she had [sic] done nothing but copy. Unlike other nations, she had not worked up her way gradually from barbarism to civilization; she had no religion, no manners, and, above all, no language, essentially her own. Peopled chiefly by the fanatic, the adventurer, and the criminal, bringing with them the usages and tongue of their mother land—exposed alike to want, and danger—literally forced to live by the sweat of their brow—the farmer, the husbandman, and the woodsman, had little time, and less inclination, for literary pursuits.

The deluge [of the 1812 war] has passed, and, like most deluges, has probably left a rich and fertile soil, which needs only to be cultivated to yield a glorious harvest; but, as yet it is almost in a few of her novels alone, that America has shown anything like originality of talent. The one before us [*Brother Jonathan*] is what an American novel should be: American in its scene, actors, and plot; curious as a picture of language and manners; and interesting as a tale of deep passion, and belonging to a very striking period of the world's history. There is much of power and much of interest in these volumes. . . .

[1825]

⊱ The early pages of Gardiner's review of The Spy *attack the notion that America cannot offer social classes and variety of character sufficient for the novel. Romance of the Gothic type, at least, will never be at home here: "We have no particular longing after this species of American castle building." There is, however, abundant material for romance of another sort, and by recognizing it Cooper "has laid the foundations of American [historical] romance."*

52 ⊰

We have long been of opinion that our native country opens to the adventurous novel-writer a wide, untrodden field, replete with new matter admirably adapted to the purposes of fiction. Our views on this subject have already been partially developed, (N. A. Rev. No. 31.) and our conviction has not been staggered by any arguments we have heard opposed to them. That nothing of the kind has hitherto been accomplished, is but a poor argument at best—especially when taken in connexion with the fact, that nothing has as yet been attempted. We are told, it is true, that there is among us a cold uniformity and sobriety of character; a sad reality and utility in our manners and institutions; that our citizens are a downright, plain-dealing, inflexible, matter-of-fact sort of people; in short, that our country and its inhabitants are equally and utterly destitute of all sorts of romantic association. We are not so foolhardy as to deny the truth of the theory on which these objections rest. It is not enough that solitary exceptions may be found here and there, if there be in fact great general uniformity pervading the mass of the people. The characters of fiction should be descriptive of classes, and not of individuals, or they will seem to want the touch of nature, and fail in that dramatic interest which results from a familiarity with the feelings and passions portrayed, and a consciousness of their truth. Admitting then, that the power of creating interest in a work of fiction, so far as it arises from development of character, lies in this generalizing principle which substitutes classes for individuals, we are triumphantly asked whether that state of society is not best fitted to the end proposed, in which this system of classification is already carried to its greatest extent;—where order rises above order in the most distinct and uniform gradation,—each pinnacle standing aloof from its neighbor, each separated by its own impenetrable barrier. No—certainly not; if by these distinctions are meant the mere formal divisions of society into lords, gentlemen, and villains. It is not such artificial and arbitrary distinctions which give the greatest possible variety and scope to character, or effect that kind of classification which is best adapted to the wants of the author. On the contrary, they are so many impediments in his way, forcing character out of its natural development into constrained and formal fashions, if such principles were left to their own tendency, they would make all men so many flat-headed Indians; and when the causes of these unnatural distinctions in human character had ceased to exist, we should look round in vain for the model of the dull and uniform monsters they had created. Not so where men have sprung up in active and adventurous communities, unshackled by forms, unfashioned by governments, and left freely to work out their own way, pursuing their own objects, with nothing to interrupt or affect them, but that mutual attrition which has not always the effect of polishing in the moral, as in the physical world. When therefore we are told that the country whose society contains the most abundant distinction of classes is the chosen fairy land of poetry and romance, and that America can never be such because it contains none, we are instinctively brought to remember a certain forensic maxim, which may be of use before more than one species of tribunal, namely, where the law is against you, always deny the fact. Now we do most seriously deny, that there is any such fatal uniformity of character among us, as is herein above supposed;—we deny (bating the formidable division into king, lords, and commons,) that there is not in this country a distinction of classes precisely similar in kind, and of extent nearly equal to that which exists in Great Britain; nay, we boldly insist, that in no one country on the face of the globe can there be found a greater variety of specific character, than is at this moment developed in these United States of America. Do any of our readers look out of New England and doubt it? Did any one of them ever cross the Potomac, or even the Hudson, and not feel himself surrounded by a different race of men? Is there any assimilation of character between the highminded, vainglorious Virginian, living on his plantation in baronial state, an autocrat among his slaves, a nobleman among his peers, and the active, enterprizing, moneygetting merchant of the East, who spends his days in bustling activity among men and ships, and his nights in sober calculations over his ledger and day-book? Is the Connecticut pedlar, who travels over mountain and moor by the side of his little red wagon and half-starved pony, to the utmost bounds of civilization, vending his *'notions'* at the very ends of the earth, the same animal with the long shaggy boatman *'clear from Kentuck,'* who wafts him on his way over the Mississippi, or the Ohio? Is there nothing of the Dutch burgomaster yet sleeping in the blood of his descendants; no trace of the prim settler of Pennsylvania in her rectangular cities and trim farms? Are all the remnants of her ancient puritanism swept out of the corners of New England? Is there no bold peculiarity in the white savage who roams over the remote hunting tracts of the West; and none in the red native of the wilderness that crosses him in his path? It would be hard indeed out of such materials, so infinitely diversified, (not to descend to the minuter distinctions which exist in each section of the country) which, similar in kind but far less various, have in other countries been wrought successfully into every form of the popular and domestic tale, at once amusing and instructive, if nothing can be fabricated on this degenerate soil.

But where are your materials for the higher order of fictitious composition? What have you of the heroic and the magnificent? Here are no 'gorgeous palaces and cloud capped towers;' no monuments of Gothic pride, mouldering in solitary grandeur; no mysterious hiding places to cover deeds of darkness from the light of the broad sun; no cloistered walls, which the sound of woe can never pierce; no ravages of desolating conquests; no traces of the slow and wasteful hand of time. You look over the face of a fair country, and it tells you no tale of days that are gone by. You see cultivated farms, and neat villages, and populous towns, full of health, and labor, and happiness. You tread your streets without fear of the midnight assassin, and you perceive nothing in their quiet and orderly inhabitants, to remind you of misery and crime. How are you to get over this familiarity of things, yet fresh in their newest gloss? You go to your mighty lakes, your vast cataracts, your stupendous mountains, and your measureless forests. Here indeed you find nature in her wildest and most magnificent attire. But these boundless solitudes are not the haunts of fierce banditti; you have never peopled these woods and waters with imaginary beings; they are connected with no legendary tales of hoary antiquity;—but you cast your eye through the vista of two short centuries, and you see them as they now are, and you see nothing beyond. Where then are the romantic associations, which are to plunge your reader, in spite of reason and common sense, into the depths of imaginary woe and wonder?

If we are asked with reference to the good old fashioned romance, and are required to construct a second castle of Otranto, to amaze our reader with mysteries, like those of the far famed Udolpho, or harrow up his young blood with another Fatal Revenge, we answer, that in our humble judgment, it matters little in regard to these mere creations of the brain, in what earthly region the visionary agents are supposed to reside; the moon, for aught we know, it has been elsewhere said, may be as eligible a theatre of action, as any on this earth. Not that we would speak disparagingly of the wildest creations of romance, or have it thought that we are less affected than others, by those masterly efforts of a bold imagination, left to luxuriate in its own ideal world. But we are not ambitious that scenes so purely imaginary, should be *located* on this side of the Atlantic, when they cannot from their very nature, partake any thing of the character of the soil and climate which give them birth; although we are by no means sure that a first rate horror, of the most imaginative kind, might not be invented without the aid of Gothic architecture, or Italian scenery.— While for these reasons, which do not peculiarly affect ourselves, we have no particular longing after this species of American castle building, we do hope to see the day, when that more commodious structure, the modern historical romance, shall be erected in all its native elegance and strength on American soil, and of materials exclusively our own. The truth is, there never was a nation whose history, studied with that view, affords better or more abundant matter of romantic interest than ours. When you ask us how we are to get over the newness and quietude of every thing among us, your question points only at the present time—a thing in itself utterly destructive of romance in all quarters of the globe. What should we think of a historical romance, for instance, in which the duke of Wellington should win the battle of Waterloo, and the marquis of Londonderry be made the secretary of state for foreign affairs? And yet if their noble lordships should meet with any different fortune or fate, however excellent the plot, however spirited and well sustained the characters, who would not throw down the book with a *quodcunque ostendis mihi sic, incredulus odi?* Since then the præterperfect is our only romantic tense, we reply, a little paradoxically perhaps, go back to the days when things were newer—but not so quiet as they now are. It is no new principle in the laws of imagination, that remoteness in point of time attaches romantic associations to objects which have them not in themselves—and these, so soon as they are created, become heightened by contrast. A ruin is a romantic object, only because it carries you perforce into remote antiquity, and suggests on its very front the moated castle with all its battlements and towers standing in proud proportion, a stately pile that seemed to bid defiance to the ravages of time and storm. You look at an elegant modern edifice, with a stack of chimneys for its minarets, and a smiling cornfield for its court yard, and it suggests nothing of itself, but the unromantic notion of peace and comfort, which are reigning within. Go back then to the day when its walls were slumbering in their native quarry, and its timbers flourishing in the living oak; when the cultivated farm was a howling wilderness, the abode of savages and outlaws, and nothing was to be seen in its borders but rapine and bloodshed. Imagine some stern enthusiast, voluntarily flying the blandishments of more luxurious abodes—or some accomplished courtier, driven from the scene of his ambition and intrigues—or some gallant soldier wearied of the gay capital, and panting anew for adventure and renown, fearlessly marching with his chosen band into these dreary and dangerous solitudes; follow him through the perils and difficulties he surmounts, and witness the long struggle of civilization, encroaching on the dominion of barbarism; and you will then find that romantic associations may become attached even to this familiar spot. Neither need we revert to any very remote period of antiquity to rid us of this familiarity, which forever plays about present things with a mischievous tendency to convert the romantic into the ludicrous. It is astonishing what changes are effected in manners, customs, names, and outward appearances, in the course of a single human generation; and when we look at the days of the fathers of the oldest now living, how little do we see that we recognize, how much that we wonder at! Not the least pleasing, perhaps, of the many admirable productions of the great master of romance in modern times, refer to a period hardly so remote as that of which we speak; and yet no one, not even they who live on the very spot, which is represented as the theatre of great and romantic action, complains of the familiarity of those scenes.

There seem to be three great epochs in American history, which are peculiarly well fitted for historical romance;—the times just succeeding the first settlement—the æra of the Indian wars, which lie scattered along a considerable period—and the revolution. Each of these events, all pregnant with interest in themselves, will furnish the fictitious historian with every variety of character and incident, which the dullest imagination could desire or the most inventive desire. What is there for instance in the rebellions and wars of the Scotch covenanters, to compare with the fortunes of those sterner puritans, who did *not* rise in arms against their prince; but who, with a boldness of adventure, under which the spirit of chivalry itself would have quailed, leaving behind them all that is most dear to men on earth, the companions of their youth, the graves of their fathers, the home of their hearts, crossed a trackless ocean; fixed their habitations on an unknown and inhospitable shore; not for the visit of a day, not cherishing a latent hope of future return, when they should have amassed wealth, or acquired fame, to raise them in the estimation of their countrymen; but with the humble hope and firm resolve to expend their lives and their children's lives in the wilderness, for the sake of worshipping their God after the fashion of their own hearts. The situation and character of these men, who 'had they been as free from all sins as gluttony and drunkenness,' (so says one of their quaint historians) 'might have been canonized for saints,' are in the highest degree picturesque; and moreover afford a singular contrast to those of Raleigh's successors in the south, headed by that man of adventure, who had challenged a whole Ottaman army in his youth, carrying off the heads of three Turkish champions at his saddle-bow, and who was now solacing his riper years, amidst the cares of a colonial government, in the arms of the renowned Pocahontas. The gloomy but sustaining spirit of fanaticism in these, who had fled to the wilderness for conscience' sake; the disappointed avarice of those who had come to it for silver and gold; the stern ecclesiastical oligarchy first established in the east; the worldly time-serving despotism of Smith and the succeeding governors in the south; the one punishing with banishment and death 'that damnable heresie of affirming justification by works;' the other promulgating in the new world the laws of the old 'to prevent sectarie infection' from creeping into the pale of mother church; the former denouncing temporal punishment and eternal wrath, against 'all idlers, common coasters, unprofitable fowlers, and tobacco takers;' the latter formally enacting and literally executing that salutary law, that 'he who will not work shall not eat;' the Virginian colony importing into the country a cargo of negroes, to entail the curse of slavery on their remotest posterity, in the same year that our first fathers were founding the liberties of America on the Plymouth rock, and Winthrop with his company of sturdy Independents, extending along the shores of Massachusetts the work which had been so happily begun, while 'refiners, goldsmiths, and jewellers,' 'poor gentlemen, tradesmen, serving men, libertines, and *such like,* ten times more fit to spoil a commonwealth, than either to begin or maintain one,' as the old writers inform us, were still flocking over to the shores of Virginia. Such contrasts judiciously exhibited, as, notwithstanding the distance of the two colonies, they well might be, with no very unpardonable poetical license, especially by the link of the New Netherlands, while they supply at once an infinite variety of individual character to the author's hands, could not fail to confer on a work of fiction the additional value of developing the political history of the times, and the first beginnings, perhaps, of those conflicting sectional interests, which sometimes perplex us at the present day. Or if more rigid rules of composition require us to confine our views to the colony of Massachusetts Bay, for instance, what character could be more obsequious to the imagination than that of the moody and mysterious Blaxton? who was found by the colonists, the solitary lord of the little isthmus of Shawmut,* which he claimed and was allowed to hold against them, by the acknowledged right of established possession; of whom history only tells us that he had been a clergyman of the church of England, that he dissented equally from her canons, and those of his non-conforming brethren; but how or when he emigrated to America, and built his humble hut on a spot destined to become the seat of a populous and flourishing city, it tells us not. What shall we say to Sir Christopher, the knight of Jerusalem, a lineal descendant of the famous bishop of Winchester, who with the strange lady was travelling and revelling through the land, until he was stopped by the scandalized 'seekers of the Lord,' and arraigned on a charge of suspicion of bigamy, *et alia enormia contra pacem,* before such a judicial assembly as the politic Winthrop, the scholastic Cotton, the fiery and intolerant Dudley, with Underhill perhaps for a witness, and Miles Standish for captain of the guard? What would not the author of Waverly make of such materials? But we forebear to enlarge further on this prolific theme.

The Indian wars, of which the first occurred soon after the time of which we have just spoken, and the last of any note in New England, in the years 1722–25, are fruitful of incidents, which might, to great advantage, be interwoven with the materials before noticed; and it scarcely needs to be asserted, that the Indians themselves are a highly poetical people. Gradually receding before the tread of civilization, and taking from it only the principle of destruction, they seem to be fast wasting to utter dissolution; and we shall one day look upon their history, with such emotions of curiosity and wonder, as those with which we now survey the immense mounds and heaps of ruin in the interior of our continent, so extensive that they have hardly yet been measured, so ancient that they lie buried in their own dust and covered with the growth of a thousand years, forcing upon the imagination the appalling thought of some great and flourishing, perhaps civilized people, who have been so utterly swept from the face of the earth, that they have not left even a traditionary name behind them. At the present day, enough is known of our aborigines to afford the ground-work of invention, enough is concealed to leave full play for the warmest imagination; and we see not why those superstitions

* The Indian name of the peninsula on which Boston now stands.

of theirs, which have filled inanimate nature with a new order of spiritual beings, may not be successfully employed to supersede the worn out fables of Runic mythology, and light up a new train of glowing visions, at the touch of some future wizard of the West. At any rate we are confident that the savage warrior, who was not less beautiful and bold in his figurative diction, than in his attitude of death, the same who 'suffered not the grass to grow upon the warpath,' and hastened 'to extinguish the fire of his enemy with blood,' tracking his foe through the pathless forest, with instinctive sagacity, by the fallen leaf, the crushed moss, or the bent blade, patiently enduring cold, hunger, and watchfulness, while he crouched in the night-grass like the tiger expecting his prey, and finally springing on the unsuspicious victim with that war-whoop, which struck terror to the heart of the boldest planter of New England in her early day, is no mean instrument of the sublime and terrible of human agency. And if we may credit the flattering pictures of their best historian, the indefatigable Heckewelder, not a little of softer interest might be extracted from their domestic life.

Instead of wearying our reader with a formal disquisition on the characters and scenes of the third epoch, we beg leave to introduce him, without farther ceremony, if he has not already made the acquaintance, to Mr. Harvey Birch, better known by the name of the Spy of the Neutral Ground; whom we greet, as doubtless the reader does also, with the greater satisfaction, in that he has taken a world of trouble off our hands, doing away the painful necessity of establishing by syllogism and inference this part of our proposition, viz, that the American revolution is an admirable basis, on which to found fictions of the highest order of romantic interest. This trouble is taken off our hands, however, not because the work before us is a perfect model of its kind, but because, whatever other deficiencies or deformities may appertain to it, want of interest, the only unpardonable sin of romance, is not among them.

We do not propose, however, to give a minute analysis of a work, which has already been some months before the public, and has withal sufficient notoriety to have reached its third edition. We have a right to assume, that our readers are fashionable enough to have kept pace with their neighbors, and shall therefore tell no more of the story, than we find necessary for our purpose. . . .

But we must put a period to remarks which have already swelled our article to unlooked for dimensions. We have to thank our author for having demonstrated so entirely to our satisfaction, that an admirable topic for the romantic historian has grown out of the American Revolution; although we still think it a less prolific source than our earlier history. If he has not done all that man could do, he has at least exhibited powers from which we have every thing to hope. The Spy of the Neutral Ground is not the production of an ordinary mind, and we will not presume to set limits to that capacity of improvement, which the author of *Precaution* has evinced in this second attempt. He has the high praise, and will have, we may add, the future glory, of having struck into a new path—of having opened a mine of exhaustless wealth—in a word, he has laid the foundations of American romance, and is really the first who has deserved the appellation of a distinguished American novel writer. Brown, who is beginning to attain a merited distinction abroad as well as at home, although his scenes are laid in America, cannot be said with truth to have produced an American novel. So far from exhibiting any thing of our native character and manners, his agents are not beings of this world; but those dark monsters of the imagination, which the will of the master may conjure up with an equal horror in the shadows of an American forest, or amidst the gloom of long galleries and vaulted aisles. His works have nothing but American topography about them. We recognize the names of places that are familiar to us and nothing more. Not even his natural scenery, wild, romantic, sublime, possibly a true copy of the particular spots it represents, can be said to possess the peculiar characteristics of America; and with him the aboriginal savage moves to his fell purpose, not as the real warrior of the wilderness, but a mere fiendlike instrument of death.—The graceful and humorous author of Knickerbocker and the Sketch Book, we regret to say, has not yet permitted us to view him threading the mazes of romance; and when we have named these, we know not who else there is to enter into competition with our author for the palm as an American novelist. We hope to hear from him again—not too soon. We do not exactly

> 'drop in unwilling ears
> This saving counsel—keep your piece *nine years,*'

But we protest most seriously against modern rapidity of production; and really beg that he will be so good (for it is a virtue now-a-days,) as just to write his book before he prints it; and it would do no harm if he were to read it over once into the bargain.

[1822]

One British reader who preferred Cooper to Irving was William Hazlitt. The following remarks were made in conversation with Northcote.

53

. . . I asked if he had seen the American novels, in one of which (the Pilot) there was an excellent description of an American privateer expecting the approach of an English man-of-war in a thick fog, when some one saw what appeared to be a bright cloud rising over the fog, but it proved to be the topsail of a seventy-four. N———thought this was striking, but had not seen the book. 'Was it one of I———'s?' Oh! no, he is a mere trifler—a *filligree* man—an English *litterateur* at second-hand; but the *Pilot* gave a true and unvarnished picture of American character and manners. The storm, the fight, the whole account of the ship's crew, and in particular of an old boatswain were done to the life—everything

> Suffered a sea-change
> Into something new and strange.

On land he did not do so well. The fault of American literature (when not a mere vapid imitation of ours) was, that it ran too much into dry, minute, literal description; or if it made an effort to rise above this ground of matter-of-fact, it was forced and exaggerated "horrors accumulating on horror's head." They had *no natural imagination*. This was likely to be the case in a new country like America, where there were no dim traces of the past—no venerable monuments—no romantic associations; where all (except the physical) remained to be created, and where fiction, if they attempted it, would take as extravagant and preposterous a shape as their local descriptions were jejune and servile. Cooper's novels and Brown's romances (something on the manner of Godwin's) were the two extremes. . . .

[1826–1827]

Although there was often disagreement over what constituted a truly national literature, most critics were certain they could recognize what is was not. The ironic paragraphs indicate what W. H. Gardiner, one of the more lively contributors to the North American Review, *could do with an unsuccessful effort—in this case James McHenry's* The Wilderness.

54

It has been a question seriously agitated among our cisatlantic literati, even at so late a period as since the publication of this journal, whether America did or did not afford sufficient materials for a new and peculiar historical romance; yet now, so prolific are we in this species of production, that the reader who keeps pace with the outpourings of the press, and studies all the wonderful works, that are daily coming forth with the lofty pretensions of *American novels,* must have some industry and a great deal of patriotism. There are those among us, perhaps, who may be curious to know what constitutes the *Americanism* of an American novel. Many persons have doubtless been so far deluded as to imagine, that the peculiarities of such a work are mere *fac similes* of the peculiarities of the country, and consist in strong graphic delineations of its bold and beautiful scenery, and of its men and manners, as they really exist, or have at some time existed. They might look to see, perhaps, from the hand of a master, something of our lakes, rivers, and cataracts; something of our autumnal woods and skies, so beautiful and peculiar; something of our rich and rapid summer vegetation, outstripping the tardy growth of more equal climes; or the sudden desolation of our winter tempests. And in regard to the human beings who animate the soil, they would possibly expect to find the familiar manners, habits, and dialects of those immediately about them.

It is with the honest view of correcting such erroneous impressions, that we have taken leave to refer to the works named at the head of our article, as containing all the elements of an American novel, so far as we have been able to digest them from the mass of writings, (always making exceptions enough to prove the rule,) which have appeared under that lofty appellation. By casting an eye over these pages, it will be seen at a glance, that the art of writing an American novel, is neither more nor less, than the art of describing under American names such scenes as are in no respect American, peopling them with adventurers from all quarters of the globe, except America, with a native or two here and there, acting as no American ever acts, and talking a language which, on the other side of the water, may pass for American, simply because it is not English. Thus the chief *dramatis personæ* of the Wilderness are a Scotch Irishman, (by which we mean an Irishman who talks Scotch,) and his wife, with their sons and daughters; an American Irishman, (by which we mean an Irishman born in America,) with an Irish Irishman, (by which we mean Paddy himself,) for his servant; a sort of mad Indian, who turns out to be a Frenchified Scotchman; together with General Washington, and a few other mere nondescripts. The plot is carried on by means of the wars of the last century between the French and English settlers of our western wilderness, and the loves of General Washington, who plays the double part of Romeo among the ladies, and Alexander the Great among the Indians, with signal success.

That we may not be astonished at the Scotch Irishman, we are informed in the outset, that the Presbyterians of Ulster are little more or less than Lowlanders in manners and dialect. Of this class is Gilbert Frazier, who marries Miss Nelly M'Clean, and comforts her, as they are taking their last look at the promontory of Inishowen, on their way to America, 'by half whispering and half singing in her ear' the following exquisite specimen of Scotch Irish poetry, translated into what passes, we suppose, for *American* English.

> 'We need not grieve now, our friends to leave now,
>   For Erin's fields we again shall see,
> But first a lady in Pennsylvania,
>   My dear, remember thou art to be.'

Arrived in America, Gilbert sets himself down on the Juniata. Thence he is soon routed by the Indians, who make prisoners of the whole settlement. Some are burnt, and others run the gauntlet. Gilbert was selected for the latter exercise; a favor for which he found he was indebted to a French officer, who had enlisted in the Indian service, and who had taken a fancy to Mrs Nelly Frazier, as a fit attendant on his wife, then lying at the royal wigwam of Queen Aliquippa. This good lady dies in the act of giving birth to the heroine of the piece, and her husband thereupon runs mad into the woods.

Gilbert meanwhile had built him a log cabin, not far from the wigwam, at the junction of Turtle Creek with the Monongahela; and there brought up, or to speak more appropriately, *raised,* the Frenchman's daughter as his own, in company with Miss Nancy and Messieurs Paddy and Archy Frazier. In process of time Paddy providentially breaks a leg, by which means the reader is made acquainted with Tonnaleuka, a very remarkable Indian, supposed to be a prophet, and also somewhat of a chirurgeon. In this latter capacity he first introduces himself to the family, and afterwards, being conversant with all arts, sciences, and tongues, becomes the tutor of the little Maria, who is thus educated as a first rate heroine. . . .

[1824]

American unbelievers continued to have their counterparts abroad. By 1829 the Edinburgh Review *might admit awareness of several American books, but whenever the balance was struck faults seemed to outnumber virtues.*

55 ⚹

Of the later American writers, who, besides Dr Channing, have acquired some reputation in England, we can only recollect Mr Washington Irving, Mr Brown, and Mr Cooper. To the first of these we formerly paid an ample tribute of respect; nor do we wish to retract a tittle of what we said on that occasion, or of the praise due to him for brilliancy, ease, and a faultless equability of style. Throughout his polished pages, no thought shocks by its extravagance, no word offends by vulgarity or affectation. All is gay, but guarded,—heedless, but sensitive of the smallest blemish. We cannot deny it—nor can we conceal it from ourselves or the world, if we would—that he is, at the same time, deficient in nerve and originality. Almost all his sketches are like patterns taken in silk paper from our classic writers;—the traditional manners of the last age are still kept up (stuffed in glass cases) in Mr Irving's modern version of them. The only variation is in the transposition of dates; and herein the author is chargeable with a fond and amiable anachronism. He takes Old England for granted as he finds it described in our stock-books of a century ago—gives us a Sir Roger de Coverley in the year 1819, instead of the year 1709; and supposes old English hospitality and manners, relegated from the metropolis, to have taken refuge somewhere in Yorkshire, or the fens of Lincolnshire. In some sequestered spot or green savannah, we can conceive Mr Irving enchanted with the style of the wits of Queen Anne;—in the bare, broad, straight, mathematical streets of his native city, his busy fancy wandered through the blind alleys and huddled zig-zag sinuosities of London, and the signs of Lothbury and East-Cheap swung and creaked in his delighted ears. The air of his own country was too poor and thin to satisfy the pantings of youthful ambition; he gasped for British popularity,—he came, and found it. He was received, caressed, applauded, made giddy: the national politeness owed him some return, for he imitated, admired, deferred to us; and, if his notions were sometimes wrong, yet it was plain he thought of nothing else, and was ready to sacrifice every thing to obtain a smile or a look of approbation. It is true, he brought no new earth, no sprig of laurel gathered in the wilderness, no red bird's wing, no gleam from crystal lake or new-discovered fountain, (neither grace nor grandeur plucked from the bosom of this Eden-state like that which belongs to cradled infancy); but he brought us *rifaciméntos* of our own thoughts—copies of our favourite authors: we saw our self-admiration reflected in an accomplished stranger's eyes; and the lover received from his mistress, the British public, her most envied favours.

Mr Brown, who preceded him, and was the author of several novels which made some noise in this country, was a writer of a different stamp. Instead of hesitating before a scruple, and aspiring to avoid a fault, he braved criticism, and aimed only at effect. He was an inventor, but without materials. His strength and his efforts are convulsive throes—his works are a banquet of horrors. The hint of some of them is taken from Caleb Williams and St Leon, but infinitely exaggerated, and carried to disgust and outrage. They are full (to disease) of imagination,—but it is forced, violent, and shocking. This is to be expected, we apprehend, in attempts of this kind in a country like America, where there is, generally speaking, no *natural imagination*. The mind must be excited by over-straining, by pulleys and levers. Mr Brown was a man of genius, of strong passion, and active fancy; but his genius was not seconded by early habit, or by surrounding sympathy. His story and his interests are not wrought out, therefore, in the ordinary course of nature; but are, like the monster in Frankenstein, a man made by art and determined will. For instance, it may be said of him, as of Gawin Douglas, 'Of Brownies and Bogilis full is his Buik.' But no ghost, we will venture to say, was ever seen in North America. They do not walk in broad day; and the night of ignorance and superstition which favours their appearance, was long past before the United States lifted up their head beyond the Atlantic wave. The inspired poet's tongue must have an echo in the state of public feeling, or of involuntary belief, or it soon grows harsh or mute. In America, they are 'so well policied,' so exempt from the knowledge of fraud or force, so free from the assaults of *the flesh and the devil,* that in pure hardness of belief they hoot the *Beggar's Opera* from the stage: with them, poverty and crime, pickpockets and highwaymen, the lock-up-house and the gallows, are things incredible to sense! In this orderly and undramatic state of security and freedom from natural foes, Mr Brown has provided one of his heroes with a demon to torment him, and fixed him at his back;—but what is to keep him there? Not any prejudice or lurking superstition on the part of the American reader: for the lack of such, the writer is obliged to make up by incessant rodomontade, and face-making. The want of genuine imagination is always proved by caricature: monsters are the growth, not of passion, but of the attempt forcibly to stimulate it. In our own unrivalled Novelist, and the great exemplar of this kind of writing, we see how ease and strength are united. Tradition and invention meet half way; and nature scarce knows how to distinguish them. The reason is, there is here an old and solid ground in previous manners and opinion for imagination to rest upon. The air of this bleak northern clime is filled with legendary lore: Not a castle without the stain of blood upon its floor or winding steps: not a glen without its ambush or its feat of arms: not a lake without its Lady! But the map of America is not historical; and, therefore, works of fiction do not take root in it; for the fiction, to be good for any thing, must not be in the author's mind, but belong to the age or country in which he lives. The genius of America is essentially mechanical and modern.

Mr Cooper describes things to the life, but he puts no motion into them. While he is insisting on the minutest details, and explaining all the accompaniments of an incident, the story stands still. The elaborate accumulation of particulars serves not to embody his imagery, but to distract and impede the mind. He is not so much the master of his materials as their drudge: He labours under an epilepsy of the fancy. He thinks himself bound in his character of novelist to tell the truth, the whole truth, and nothing but the truth. Thus, if two men are struggling on the edge of a precipice for life or death, he goes not merely into the vicissitudes of action and passion as the chances of the combat vary; but stops to take an inventory of the geography of the place, the shape of the rock, the precise attitude and display of the limbs and muscles, with the eye and habits of a sculptor. Mr Cooper does not seem to be aware of the infinite divisibility of mind and matter; and that an 'abridgment' is all that is possible or desirable in the most individual representation. A person who is so determined, may write volumes on a grain of sand or an insect's wing. Why describe the dress and appearance of an Indian chief, down to his tobacco-stopper and button-holes? It is mistaking the province of the artist for that of the historian; and it is this very obligation of painting and statuary to fill up all the details, that renders them incapable of telling a story, or of expressing more than a single moment, group, or figure. Poetry or romance does not descend into the particulars, but atones for it by a more rapid march and an intuitive glance at the more striking results. By considering truth or matter-of-fact as the sole element of popular fiction, our author fails in massing and in impulse. In the midst of great vividness and fidelity of description, both of nature and manners, there is a sense of jejuneness,—for half of what is described is insignificant and indifferent; there is a hard outline,—a little manner; and his most striking situations do not tell as they might and ought, from his seeming more anxious about the mode and circumstances than the catastrophe. In short, he anatomizes his subjects; and his characters bear the same relation to living beings that the botanic specimens collected in a portfolio do to the living plant or tree. The sap does not circulate kindly; nor does the breath of heaven visit, or its dews moisten them. Or, if Mr Cooper gets hold of an appalling circumstance, he, from the same tenacity and thraldom to outward impressions, never lets it go: He repeats it without end. Thus, if he once hits upon the supposition of a wild Indian's eyes glaring through a thicket, every bush is from that time forward furnished with a pair; the page is studded with them, and you can no longer look about you at ease or in safety. The high finishing we have spoken of is particularly at variance with the rudeness of the materials. In Richardson it was excusable, where all was studied and artificial; but a few dashes of red ochre are sufficient to paint the body of a savage chieftain; nor should his sudden and frantic stride on his prey be treated with the precision and punctiliousness of a piece of *still life*. There are other American writers, (such as the historiographer of *Brother Jonathan*,) who carry this love of veracity to a pitch of the marvellous. They run riot in an account of the dishes at a boarding-house, as if it were a banquet of the Gods; and recount the overturning of a travelling stage-waggon with as much impetuosity, turbulence, and exaggerated enthusiasm, as if it were the fall of Phaeton. In the absence of subjects of real interest, men make themselves an interest out of nothing, and magnify mole-hills into mountains. This is not the fault of Mr Cooper: He is always true, though sometimes tedious; and correct, at the expense of being insipid. His *Pilot* is the best of his works; and truth to say, we think it a master-piece in its kind. It has great unity of purpose and feeling. Every thing in it may be said

> ——'To suffer a *sea-change*
> Into something new and strange.'

His Pilot never appears but when the occasion is worthy of him; and when he appears, the result is sure. The description of his guiding the vessel through the narrow strait left for her escape, the sea-fight, and the incident of the white topsail of the English man-of-war appearing above the fog, where it is first mistaken for a cloud, are of the first order of graphic composition; to say nothing of the admirable episode of Tom

Coffin, and his long figure coiled up like a rope in the bottom of the boat. The rest is *common-place;* but then it is American common-place. We thank Mr Cooper he does not take every thing from us, and therefore we can learn something from him. He has the saving grace of originality. We wish we could impress it, 'line upon line, and precept upon precept,' especially upon our American brethren, how precious, how invaluable *that* is. In art, in literature, in science, the least bit of nature is worth all the plagiarism in the world. The great secret of Sir Walter Scott's enviable, but unenvied success, lies in his transcribing from nature instead of transcribing from books. . . .

[1829]

As a historian, Jared Sparks realized that most American writers were hampered by their ignorance of the American past, especially the history of the Indians. When the Indian is well known, he argues, it will be realized how useless a subject he is for poetry: "The day is not to be expected, when the exploits of the Iroquois and Mohawks . . . shall be faithfully committed to the numbers of ever enduring song."

56 &

If an opinion may be formed by the experiments already tried, the character of the North American Indian affords but a barren theme for poetry. *Atala* is an Indian story, it is true, yet the fancy of the poet has made the grace and beauty of his picture consist more in adscititious ornaments, than in any strongly drawn lines peculiar to Indian life and manners. Campbell, in his *Gertrude of Wyoming,* has attempted the portraiture of an Indian, in the character of Outalissi the Oneyda warrior,

> 'Train'd from his tree rock'd cradle to his bier,
> The fierce extremes of good and ill to brook
> Impassive—fearing but the shame of fear—
> A stoic of the woods—a man without a tear.'

These characteristics are true to nature, but viewed in all his conduct, Outalissi is only half an Indian, partaking alike of the habitudes and feelings of the white and the red man. It cannot be denied, however, that the poet has succeeded better than the painter, who has thought to illustrate his conceptions by embodying them in a visible form. In one of Westall's designs for a beautiful edition of Campbell's poems, the Oneyda warrior is represented with curled hair, African features, and a white beard, three most extraordinary appendages to the head of a North American Indian.

Our own countrymen have begun recently to invoke the Muses in behalf of these ancient sons of the forest. A poem has appeared, the express object of which is to delineate *Traits of the Aborigines of America.* So unproductive was the theme, that the author has wandered in other climes and other ages to find materials for the work, and the Greeks and Romans, the warriors and sages of antiquity, figure nearly as much in the drama, as the Indians themselves. There is good poetry in this performance, but that is not the best which draws traits of the Indians. The author of *Ontwa* has been more successful in describing Indian character and scenery, than any writer whom we have read. As a descriptive poem this has much merit, but it descends little into the deep feelings of the human heart, and the strong movements of the passions. It tells of the wars between the Iroquois and the Eries, by which the latter race was exterminated; and the warlike propensities of the natives, their modes of going to battle, making peace, their treatment of captives, and other peculiarities relating to this subject, are well delineated. Many things the author describes from his own observation, and he applies to Ontwa the language, which Chateaubriand had before applied to Atala, 'that it was written in the desert, and under the huts of the savages.' This familiarity with the local condition of the Indians gave him advantages, which he has well employed in his descriptions of savage life; but after all, there is so little of the romantic and of the truly poetical in the native Indian character, that we doubt whether a poem of high order can ever be woven out of the materials it affords. The Indian has a lofty and commanding spirit, but its deeply marked traits are few, stern, and uniform, never running into those delicate and innumerable shades, which are spread over the surface of civilised society, giving the fullest scope to poetic invention, and opening a store of incidents inexhaustible, and obedient to the call of fancy. When you have told of generosity, contempt of danger, patience under suffering, revenge, and cruelty, you have gone through with the catalogue of the Indian's virtues and vices, and touched all the chords that move his feelings or affections. To analyse and combine these into a poem of high interest, without extensive aid from other sources than the real Indian character, is no easy task, and the day is not to be expected, when the exploits of the Iroquois and Mohawks, or the rough features of their social habits, shall be faithfully committed to the numbers of ever enduring song. The minstrel's harp would recoil at its own notes in hazarding such a strain, and the Muses would deny inspiration to a votary bent on so desperate an enterprise. . . .

[1825]

⋟ Like Sparks, this reviewer believed that the aborigines were not a fit subject for the American writer. The remarks which close this excerpt, moreover, define a position which many would view with alarm: "It is not necessary that the scene of an American work of imagination should be laid in America. . . . It is the author, not his theatre or his matter, that nationalizes his work." The point would find its proof, years later, in the work of Henry James.

57 ⋞

. . . It strikes us, that there is something a little peculiar in the history of novel-writing in this country. Starting with a principle, correct in itself, but like other correct principles requiring judicious application, that works of imagination should represent the character and manners of the country where they are written, our novel-writers, at least those of the second class, have made their works too purely of the soil. As though treason lay in too near an approach to the waters, or as though there were a fear that something transatlantic would there creep into their fancies, they have even avoided the lakes themselves, and make a dry-land story of it, among woods, and ravines, and wigwams, and tomahawks. The Indian chieftain is the first character upon the canvass or the carpet; in active scene or still one, he is the nucleus of the whole affair; and in almost every case is singularly blessed in some dark-eyed child, whose convenient complexion is made sufficiently light for the whitest hero. This bronze noble of nature, is then made to talk like Ossian for whole pages, and measure out hexameters, as though he had been practising for a poetic prize.

Now, though we may applaud the spirit which has led some of our novelists to place the scene of their stories invariably and pertinaciously somewhere between the Rocky Mountains and the Atlantic,—and the deeper in the forest the better,—still we must wonder at the taste that peoples them with such a mass of wild and copper men; and moreover question the necessity, on the whole, of going back, as a matter of course, to the precise time when the struggle was the fiercest between the colonists and these barbarians. We are aware that we are disputing the first principle which these writers set out upon; but it appears certain to us, that there is a barrenness of the novelist's peculiar circumstance in the life of a savage, which cannot be easily got over, when we set about a story of him in his hut and in his wanderings; and it must necessarily be a troublesome tax upon the ingenuity to throw a moderate share of interest round a narrative, founded upon events connected with these simple, silent creatures. This tax has rarely been paid to our satisfaction.

In fact, the species of writing, we believe, began in mistake; heretical as it may seem, it strikes us that there is not enough in the character and life of these poor natives to furnish the staple of a novel. The character of the Indian is a simple one, his destiny is a simple one, all around him is simple. We use the expression here in its most unpoetical sense. But mere simplicity is not all that is needed. There must be some event in the life of a hero, to keep us from growing weary of him. He must not lie upon our hands; the author must keep him in business, and he must have more business than is comprehended in the employment of the scalping-knife or the paddle, to become the subject of our refined sympathies, or to gratify a cultivated taste. He must be mentally engaged. The savage says but little; and after we have painted him in the vivid and prominent colors which seem necessary to represent him amidst his pines and waterfalls,—after we have set him before our readers with his gorgeous crown of feathers, his wampum, and his hunting-bow, it would seem that we have done as well as we could for him. Beyond this bare description, which indeed may be one of the most beautiful in the world, it is not easy to advance. Nature leaves us, as soon as we leave nature, in this case, and put our calm, taciturn son of the desert into the attitudes of civilized life. The Indians, as *a people,* offer little or nothing that can be reasonably expected to excite the novelist, formed as his taste must be on a foreign standard. View them in New Zealand or Otaheite, go through all Australasia, and then come to the wilderness of America, and the native will still be found nearly the same being on the continent as on the island. The cannibal or the rude hunter will alternately present himself; but neither, we apprehend, with much distinctness or individuality of character. Occasionally an individual will start forth from the herd, whom skill or strength may have raised to eminence among his brethren, and whose mind gives token of what it might have been and might have done under the hand of civilization. But the Indians exhibit little of that mixture of character in the same person, which arises from an acquaintance with the arts and artifices of life and the world, and which is the source of that adventure and interest, that must belong to a good novel.

Such seems to be the insuperable obstacle in the way of those, who venture into our early wilderness for a plot. They leave the abodes of

civilization, the places where incident grows out of the nature of circumstances, and where it is probable we may realize many of those pictures
and variations of life that give interest and grace to the works of fancy,—
all these they leave for the reeking hut of the Indian, to hurry a hero
through the ordeal of Indian cruelties and Indian mummery, through a
series of scenes that have been a thousand times presented to us, and
which admit of no change.

Apart from the impossibility of remaining true to his subject, and still
making the native a being of true interest in the bustling and social parts
of his book, the Indian novelist has to contend with the spirit of the age,
which demands, for the most part, descriptions of real life, and the display
of characters who talk and act like ourselves or our acquaintance, and
who have not cast off allegiance to common sense. Many by no means
grey-haired among us, can remember reading the works of Mrs Radcliffe,
and of Lewis, with all due reverence for their secret passages, their
murtherous castles, their spectres, trap-doors, and dungeons. We can ourselves recollect, with what supreme horror we read the 'Mysteries of
Udolpho' in broad daylight. But how does our terrible respect for
Ambrosio diminish before the dignity of Father Eustace, and Udolpho
lose its glory beside the Tolbooth of Auld Reekie. The reign of terror is
over. Eidolon has but waved his wand, and the castles of romance, those
formidable piles of mystery and mischief, have vanished before its flourish, as monks and monasteries vanished before the heretical hands of the
'defender of the faith.' But the public taste has undergone a change.
Manners, as peculiar to some chosen period, and associated with certain
events of importance that have become matter of history, must now fill up
the descriptive department of works that aspire even to the title of
romances. Dialogue has superseded narration; and in the true spirit of the
drama, into which many of the best tales of the day may be resolved,
characters are made to act their parts. This change of taste subjects the
Indian novelist to an arduous task. He will feel the necessity of going
wide of nature, in any attempt to make a varied and imposing story out of
such materials as the situation of the colonies, considered in their isolated
state, or in their relation to the Indians, would probably afford. Hardly,
indeed, from our young annals could a tale be woven, that should meet
the prevailing feeling of propriety and interest in relation to this subject.

Moreover the elements of society, considered *implicitly* as the society
among the early settlements of this country, offer little in the shape of
sects or classes, that is calculated to meet and satisfy the popular taste. Our
retrospection affords us no privileged and important tribes of *togati,* full

of lore and prophecy; no bands of merry archers whose very thievery is full of romantic adventure; and no minstrels overflowing with chivalry and song. We have no Robin Hoods, or Blue Gowns, no Vidals nor Cadwallons, and no gypsies to lend just mystery enough to our stories, and preside over the destinies of our heroes and ladies. We have none of these dim and ancient things to season our fiction withal. But it will be said, if we have anything like legendary lore, we must seek for it among the children of the forest, for the good reason that it is nowhere else to be found. But there is a fallacy in this. We belong as a people to the English school of civilization. It is not necessary that the scene of an American work of imagination should be laid in America. It is enough that it represent our character and manners either at home or abroad. Whatever of romance, or tradition, or historical fact England may boast, as material for her novelists and poets, rightfully belongs as well to us as to herself. Neither would we be understood to say, that a stirring novel may not be drawn out from Indian life and character. It can be, and it has been done. But we hold, that once done, it is, comparatively, done for ever; and our complaint is, that we are overdoing the matter, or have been overdoing it. It is a mistaken idea also, that to constitute an American novel, either the scene must be laid in the early wilderness of this country, or that events of so recent date as those connected with our revolution, must occupy a prominent portion of its pages. It is the author, not his theatre or his matter, that nationalizes his work. Our accomplished countryman Geoffrey Crayon in his beautiful Sketches of Old England, has given us a book as essentially American as it is possible for any book to be, which is written in good taste, by a person belonging to the English school of civilization. An American work of taste *cannot* differ from an English, as a tragedy of Racine differs from one of Shakspeare. . . .

[1828]

⊰ This review of Catherine Maria Sedgwick's Clarence *concludes with advice on future topics and themes: American society is new enough to offer "vigorous and fantastic shoots of character," but it is "too coarse to bear the embroidery of romance."*

58 ⊱

. . . We close our imperfect notice by cordially recommending this novel to the reading public, and we would even beg those who, as a general rule, avoid works of modern fiction, to make an exception in this instance. We are proud of our distinguished countrywoman, and regard her works as an honor to our land; and the reason that we have spoken so much of the faults of Clarence and dwelt so sparingly upon its beauties, is, that the latter bear so large a proportion to the former, and are in themselves so striking, that no reader of common apprehension can help finding them out and admiring them for himself. We are grateful to her for the pleasure she has afforded us, and would beg her to continue her labors in the neglected vineyard of American fiction; to paint the glorious scenery of her own native land and the virtues of its children, to tell us of the nobleness of its sons, and the beauty of its daughters, and 'to hold the mirror up to every shape of life and every hue of opinion.' Let her not attempt to give a highly romantic coloring to her plots, for the web of life in our Western world is too coarse to bear the embroidery of romance. Nor let her attempt to give a highly dramatic effect to detached scenes and particular situations, for the power of doing this is a gift bestowed upon very few, and much as we admire the author of Clarence, we are constrained to say that she is not one of them. Her excellence consists in her strong sense, her feminine feeling, her powers of description, her vigorous and beautiful English, the touching eloquence with which she pleads the cause of humanity, and above all, the keenness of her observation and her skill in delineating the lights and shadows of character. She has but to look around her to find an ample field for the exercise of her talents;—she may find abundant food for speculation in the Protean forms which society assumes in our wide continent,—in the gay throngs that chase amusement from one watering-place to another, and in the lowly virtues that cluster round our farm-house hearths, and, like flowers that twine around the living rock, give beauty and fragrance to the hardest and coarsest forms of life. To the writer of fiction, whose *forte* is character-drawing, we know of no land like ours, whether we regard the extent of our territory, the variety of the stocks from which we sprung, the youthful and electric vigor with which the veins of our world are filled, and the unchecked freedom with which it is our unvalued privilege to act and think. The face of society has not by long attention been ground down to one uniform level, and vigorous and fantastic shoots of character are not nipped by the frost of hoary convention. The mountain-wind is not more free to blow, than is each man to indulge his wildest whims. And as the harvest is plenty, so are the laborers few;—the materials of romance in the old world are waxing threadbare, but the charm of unworn freshness is here like morning-dew. We would call upon all the sons and daughters of genius to be up and doing, and we would entreat the author of Clarence in particular, to persevere in the course she has so successfully entered upon, for her own sake and her country's sake.

[1831]

≥ *Bryant prefaced his review of Mrs. Sedgwick's* Redwood *with a thorough investigation of the native resources available to the American writer and a list of universal motifs with which they might be combined. (Walter Scott has by now become the touchstone of fictional excellence, with Cooper often seen as our impressive version of the master.) Bryant's essay confronts the questions of historical and realistic fiction in sufficient detail to make it an important document in the theory of American literature.*

59 ⚞

This is a story of domestic life, the portraiture of what passes by our firesides and in our streets, in the calm of the country, and amidst a prosperous and well ordered community. The writer, who, we understand, is the same lady to whom the public is already indebted for another beautiful little work of a similar character, has not availed herself of the more obvious and abundant sources of interest, which would naturally suggest themselves to the author of a fictitious history, the scene of which should be laid in the United States. She has not gone back to the infancy of our country, to set before us the fearless and hardy men, who made the first lodgment in its vast forests, men in whose characters is to be found the favorite material of the novelist, great virtues mingled with many errors, the strange land to which they had come, and its unknown dangers, and the savage tribes by whom they were surrounded, to whose kindness they owed so much, and from whose enmity they suffered so severely. Nor does the thread of her narrative lead us through those early feuds between the different colonies of North America, who brought with them and kept alive, in their settlements, the animosities of the nations from whom they proceeded, and, in the midst of all their hardships and sufferings, contended about the division of the wilderness, with a fierceness and an obstinacy exasperated by the difference in the characters of those who composed them. Nor has the writer made any use of the incidents of our great national struggle for independence, at once so calamitous and so glorious, the time of splendid virtues and great sufferings, the war which separated friends, and divided families, and revived the half laid spirit of bloodshed in the uncivilised races about us, and called to our shores so many military adventurers to fight under the standard of Britain, and so many generous volunteers in the cause of humanity and liberty to combat under ours. She has passed by all these periods and situations, so tempting to the writer of fictitious history, so pregnant with interest and teeming with adventure, to make a more hazardous experiment of her powers. She has come down to the very days in which we live, to quiet times and familiar manners, and has laid the scene of her narrative in the most ancient and tranquil parts of the country; presenting us not merely with the picture of what she has imagined, but with the copy of what she has observed.

We have called this a comparatively hazardous experiment, and this, because it seems to us far more difficult to deal successfully with the materials which the author has chosen, than with those which she has neglected. There is a strong love of romance inherent in the human mind. We all remember how our childhood was captivated with stories of sorcerers and giants. We do not, in our riper age, forget with what a fearful and thrilling interest we hung over tales of the interpositions of supernatural beings, of acts of desperate heroism, followed by incredible successes, of impossible dangers, and equally impossible deliverances. And when our maturer judgment has caused us to turn with disgust, from the relation of what is contrary to the known laws of nature, we transfer the same intense attention to narratives that keep within the bounds of possibility. We love to read of imminent perils, and hairbreadth escapes, of adventures in strange lands and among strange races of men, or in times of great public commotion or unusual public calamity. Something of this taste exists in every mind, though variously modified and diversified, and contented with a greater or less degree of verisimilitude, according as the imagination is more or less inflammable. Some preserve a fondness for fictions almost as wild as those, which amused their earlier years, while others can be pleased only with the recital of what is strictly probable. Some will listen with interest to stories of 'antres vast and deserts idle,' and the adventures of the intrepid voyager who traverses them, while others delight to have their blood curdle at being told of

> The Anthropophagi, and men whose heads
> Do grow beneath their shoulders.

In reading narratives of the romantic kind, our curiosity comes in aid of the author. We are eager to learn the issue of adventures so new to us. The imagination of the reader is also ready with its favorable offices. This faculty, always busiest when we are told of scenes and events out of the range of men's ordinary experience, expatiates at large upon the suggestions of the author, and, as we read, rapidly fills up the outline he gives with bright colors and deep shades of its own. From all these causes it may happen, that by the mere fortunate invention and happy arrangement of striking incidents, a work of fiction shall succeed in gaining the public favor, without any considerable proportion of the higher merits of that kind of writing, without any uncommon beauty of style, or any unusual degree either of pathos or humor, or splendor of imagination, or vivacity of description, or powerful delineation of character.

But with a novel founded on domestic incidents, supposed to happen in our own time and country, the case is different. We have seen the original, and require that there be no false coloring or distortion in the copy. We want to be delighted with the development of traits, that had escaped our observation, or of which, if observed, we had never felt the peculiar significance. It will not do to trust to the imagination of the reader to heighten the interest of such a narrative; if it ever attempts to fill up the sketch given by the writer, it is not often in a way calculated to increase its effect, for it is done with the plain and sober hues, that color the tissue of our own lives. We are too familiar with the sort of life described, we are too well acquainted with the situations in which the characters are placed, we have stood too long in the very relations out of which grows the interest of the narrative, to be much interested by reading about them, unless they are vividly and strikingly set before us. These are things which have so often moved the heart in their reality, that it refuses to be strongly affected by them in a fictitious narrative, unless they are brought home to it and pressed upon it, with more than ordinary power. They are chords that will not yield their music to the passing wind, they must be touched by the hand of a master. The mere description of ordinary, everyday scenes and events, is too plain a banquet to be relished without some condiment to make it palatable. Readers require not only the exclusion of those tame scenes and incidents, without connexion or consequence, that make up so much of real life, but that the incidents set down be related with pathos, or at least with spirit or humor; they look for natural and sprightly dialogue, and well drawn characters.

On more than one occasion, we have already given somewhat at large our opinion of the fertility of our country, and its history, in the materials of romance. If our reasonings needed any support from successful examples of that kind of writing, as a single fact is worth a volume of ingenious theorising, we have had the triumph of seeing them confirmed beyond all controversy, by the works of a popular American author, who has shown the literary world into what beautiful creations those materials may be wrought. In like manner, we look upon the specimen before us as a conclusive argument, that the writers of works of fiction, of which the scene is laid in familiar and domestic life, have a rich and varied field before them in the United States. Indeed, the opinion on this subject, which, till lately, prevailed pretty extensively among us, that works of this kind, descriptive of the manners of our countrymen, could not succeed, never seemed to us to rest on a very solid foundation. It was rather a sweeping inference drawn from the fact, that no highly meritorious work of the kind had appeared, and the most satisfactory and comfortable way of accounting for this, was to assert, that no such could be written. But it is not always safe to predict what a writer of genius will make of a given subject. Twenty years ago, what possible conception could an English critic have had of the admirable productions of the author of Waverley, and of the wonderful improvement his example has effected in that kind of composition? Had the idea of one of those captivating works, destined to take such strong hold on all minds, been laid before him by the future author, he would probably only have wondered at his vanity.

There is nothing paradoxical in the opinion, which maintains that all civilised countries, we had almost said all countries whatever, furnish matter for copies of real life, embodied in works of fiction, which shall be of lasting and general interest. Wherever there are human nature and society, there are subjects for the novelist. The passions and affections, virtue and vice, are of no country. Everywhere love comes to touch the hearts of the young, and everywhere scorn and jealousy, the obstacles of fortune and the prudence of the aged, are at hand to disturb the course of love. Everywhere there exists the desire of wealth, the love of power, and the wish to be admired, courage braving real dangers, and cowardice shrinking from imaginary ones, friendship and hatred, and all the train of motives and impulses, which affect the minds and influence the conduct of men. They not only exist everywhere, but they exist infinitely diversified and compounded, in various degrees of suppression and restraint, or fostered into unnatural growth and activity, modified by political institutions and laws, by national religions and subdivisions of those religions, by different degrees of refinement and civilisation, of poverty or of abundance, by arbitrary usages handed down from indefinite antiquity, and even by local situation and climate. Nor is there a single one of all these innumerable modifications of human character and human emotion which is not, in some degree, an object of curiosity and interest. Over all the world is human sagacity laying its plans, and chance and the malice of others are thwarting them, and fortune is raising up one man and throwing down another. In none of the places of human habitation are the accesses barred against joy or grief; the kindness of the good carries gladness into families, and the treachery of the false friend brings sorrow and ruin; in all countries are tears shed over the graves of the excellent, the brave, and the beautiful, and the oppressed breathe freer when the oppressor has gone to his account. Everywhere has nature her features of grandeur and of beauty, and these features receive a moral expression from the remembrances of the past, and the interests of the present. On her face, as on an immense theatre, the passions and pursuits of men are performing the great drama of human existence. At every moment, and in every corner of the world, these mighty and restless agents are perpetually busy, under an infinity of forms and disguises, and the great representation goes on with that majestic continuity and uninterrupted regularity, which mark all the courses of nature. Who then will undertake to say, that the hand of genius may not pencil off a few scenes, acted in our own vast country, and amidst our large population, that shall interest and delight the world?

It is a native writer only that must or can do this. It is he that must show how the infinite diversities of human character are yet further varied, by causes that exist in our own country, exhibit our peculiar modes of thinking and action, and mark the effect of these upon individual fortunes and happiness. A foreigner is manifestly incompetent to the task; his observation would rest only upon the more general and obvious traits of our national character, a thousand delicate shades of manner would escape his notice, many interesting peculiarities would never come to his knowledge, and many more he would misapprehend. It is only on his native soil, that the author of such works can feel himself on safe and firm ground, that he can move confidently and fearlessly, and put forth the whole strength of his powers without risk of failure. His delineations of character and action, if executed with ability, will have a raciness and freshness about them, which will attest their fidelity, the secret charm, which belongs to truth and nature, and with which even the finest genius cannot invest a system of adscititious and imaginary manners. It is this quality, which recommends them powerfully to the sympathy and interest even of those, who are unacquainted with the original from which they are drawn, and makes such pictures from such hands so delightful and captivating to the foreigner. By superadding, to the novelty of the manners described, the interest of a narrative, they create a sort of illusion, which places him in the midst of the country where the action of the piece is going on. He beholds the scenery of a distant land, hears its inhabitants conversing about their own concerns in their own dialect, finds himself in the bosom of its families, is made the depository of their secrets, and the observer of their fortunes, and becomes an inmate of their firesides without stirring from his own. Thus it is that American novels are eagerly read in Great Britain, and novels descriptive of English and Scottish manners as eagerly read in America.

It has been objected, that the habits of our countrymen are too active and practical; that they are too universally and continually engrossed by the cares and occupations of business to have leisure for that intrigue, those plottings and counterplottings, which are necessary to give a suffi-cient degree of action and eventfulness to the novel of real life. It is said that we need for this purpose a class of men, whose condition in life places them above the necessity of active exertion, and who are driven to the practice of intrigue, because they have nothing else to do. It remains, however, to be proved that any considerable portion of this ingredient is necessary in the composition of a successful novel. To require that it should be made up of nothing better than the manœuvres of those, whose only employment is to glitter at places of public resort, to follow a per-petual round of amusements, and to form plans to outshine, thwart, and vex each other, is confining the writer to a narrow and most barren circle. It is requiring an undue proportion of heartlessness, selfishness, and vice in his pictures of society. It is compelling him to go out of the wholesome atmosphere of those classes, where the passions and affections have their most salutary and natural play, and employ his observations on that where they are most perverted, sophisticated, and corrupt. But will it be seriously contended, that he can have no other resource but the rivalries and machinations of the idle, the frivolous, and the dissolute, to keep the reader from yawning over his pictures? Will it be urged that no striking and interesting incidents can come to pass without their miserable aid? If our country be not the country of intrigue, it is at least the country of enterprise; and nowhere are the great objects that worthily interest the passions, and call forth the exertions of men, pursued with more devotion and perseverance. The agency of chance too is not confined to the shores of Europe; our countrymen have not attained a sufficient degree of cer-tainty in their calculations to exclude it from ours. It would really seem to us, that these two sources, along with that proportion of the blessed quality of intrigue, which even the least favorable view of our society will allow us, are abundantly fertile in interesting occurrences, for all the purposes of the novelist. Besides, it should be recollected, that it is not in any case the dull diary of ordinary occupations, or amusements, that forms the groundwork of his plot. On the contrary, it is some event, or at least a series of events, of unusual importance, standing out in strong relief from the rest of the biography of his principal characters, and to which the daily habits of their lives, whatever may be their rank or condition, are only a kind of accompaniment.

But the truth is, that the distinctions of rank, and the amusements of elegant idleness, are but the surface of society, and only so many splendid disguises put upon the reality of things. They are trappings which the writer of real genius, the anatomist of the human heart, strips away when he would exhibit his characters as they are, and engage our interest for them as beings of our own species. He reduces them to the same great level where distinctions of rank are nothing, and difference of character everything. It is here that James First, and Charles Second, and Louis Ninth, and Rob Roy, and Jeanie Deans, and Meg Merrilies are, by the great author of the Waverley novels, made to meet. The monarch must come down from the dim elevation of his throne, he must lay aside the assumed and conventional manners of his station, and unbend and unbosom himself with his confidants, before that illustrious master will condescend to describe him. In the artificial sphere in which the great move, they are only puppets and pageants, but here they are men. A narrative, the scene of which is laid at the magnificent levees of princes, in the drawing rooms of nobles, and the bright assemblies of fashion, may be a very pretty, showy sort of thing, and so may a story of the glittering dances and pranks of fairies. But we soon grow weary of all this, and ask for objects of sympathy and regard, for something, the recollection of which shall dwell on the heart, and to which it will love to recur; for something, in short, which is natural, the uneffaced traits of strength and weakness, of the tender and the comic, all which the pride of rank either removes from observation or obliterates.

If these things have any value, we hesitate not to say, that they are to be found abundantly in the characters of our countrymen, formed as they are under the influence of our free institutions, and shooting into a large and vigorous, though sometimes irregular luxuriance. They exist most abundantly in our more ancient settlements, and amidst the more homogeneous races of our large population, where the causes that produce them have operated longest and with most activity. It is there that the human mind has learned best to enjoy our fortunate and equal institutions, and to profit by them. In the countries of Europe the laws chain men down to the condition in which they were born. This observation, of course, is not equally true of all those countries, but when they are brought into comparison with ours, it is in some degree applicable to them all. Men spring up, and vegetate, and die, without thinking of passing from the sphere in which they find themselves, any more than the plants they cultivate think of removing from the places where they are rooted. It is the tendency of this rigid and melancholy destiny to contract and stint the intellectual faculties, to prevent the development of character, and to make the subjects of it timid, irresolute, and imbecile. With us, on the contrary, where the proudest honors in the state, and the highest deference in society, are set equally before all our citizens, a wholesome and quickening impulse is communicated to all parts of the social system. All are possessed with a spirit of ambition and a love of adventure, an intense competition calls forth and exalts the passions and faculties of men, their characters become strongly defined, their minds acquire a hardihood and activity, which can be gained by no other discipline, and the community, throughout all its conditions, is full of bustle, and change, and action.

Whoever will take the pains to pursue this subject a little into its particulars, will be surprised at the infinite variety of forms of character, which spring up under the institutions of our country. Religion is admitted on all hands to be a mighty agent in moulding the human character; and accordingly, with the perfect allowance and toleration of all religions, we see among us their innumerable and diverse influences upon the manners and temper of our people. Whatever may be his religious opinions, no one is restrained by fear of consequences from avowing them, but is left to nurse his peculiarities of doctrine into what importance he pleases. The Quaker is absolved from submission to the laws in those particulars, which offend his conscience, the Moravian finds no barriers in the way of his work of proselytism and charity, the Roman Catholic is subjected to no penalty for pleasing himself with the magnificent ceremonial of his religion, and the Jew worships unmolested in his synagogue. In many parts of our country we see communities of that strange denomination, the Shakers, distinguished from their neighbors by a garb, a dialect, an architecture, a way of worship, of thinking, and of living, as different, as if they were in fact of a different origin, instead of being collected from the families around them. In other parts we see small neighborhoods of the Seventh Day Baptists, retaining the simplicity of manners and quaintness of language delivered down from their fathers. Here we find the austerities of puritanism preserved to this day, there the rites and doctrines of the Church of England are shown in their effect on the manners of the people, and in yet another part of the country springs up a new and numerous sect, who wash one another's feet, and profess to revive the primitive habits of the apostolic times.

It is in our country also, that these differences of character, which grow naturally out of geographical situation, are least tampered with and re-pressed by political regulations. The adventurous and roving natives of our seacoasts, and islands, are a different race of men from those who till the interior, and the hardy dwellers of our mountainous districts are not like the inhabitants of the rich plains, that skirt our mighty lakes and rivers. The manners of the northern states are said to be characterised by the keenness and importunity of their climate, and those of the southern to partake of the softness of theirs. In our cities you will see the polished manners of the European capitals, but pass into the more quiet and unvisited parts of the country, and you will find men, whom you might take for the first planters of our colonies. The descendants of the Hollanders have not forgotten the traditions of their fathers, and the legends of Germany are still recited, and the ballads of Scotland still sung, in settlements whose inhabitants derive their origin from those countries. It is hardly possible that the rapid and continual growth and improvement of our country, a circumstance wonderfully exciting to the imagination, and altogether unlike anything witnessed in other countries, should not have some influence in forming our national character. At all events, it is a most fertile source of incident. It does for us in a few short years, what, in Europe, is the work of centuries. The hardy and sagacious native of the eastern states, settles himself in the wilderness by the side of the emigrant from the British isles; the pestilence of the marshes is braved and over-come; the bear, and wolf, and catamount are chased from their haunts; and then you see cornfields, and roads, and towns springing up as if by enchantment. In the mean time pleasant Indian villages, situated on the skirts of their hunting grounds, with their beautiful green plats for dances and martial exercises, are taken into the bosom of our extending popula-tion, while new states are settled and cities founded far beyond them. Thus a great deal of history is crowded into a brief space. Each little hamlet, in a few seasons, has more events and changes to tell of, than a European village can furnish in a course of ages.

But, if the writer of fictitious history does not find all the variety he wishes in the various kinds of our population, descended, in different parts of our country, from ancestors of different nations, and yet preserv-ing innumerable and indubitable tokens of their origin, if the freedom with which every man is suffered to take his own way, in all things not affecting the peace and good order of society, does not furnish him with a sufficient diversity of characters, employments, and modes of life, he has yet other resources. He may bring into his plots men, whose characters and manners were formed by the institutions and modes of society in the nations beyond the Atlantic, and he may describe them faithfully, as things which he has observed and studied. If he is not satisfied with indigenous virtue, he may take for the model of his characters men of whom the old world is not worthy, and whom it has cast out from its bosom. If domestic villany be not dark enough for his pictures, here are fugitives from the justice of Europe come to prowl in America. If the coxcombs of our own country are not sufficiently exquisite, affected, and absurd, here are plenty of silken fops from the capitals of foreign king-doms. If he finds himself in need of a class of men more stupid and degraded, than are to be found among the natives of the United States, here are crowds of the wretched peasantry of Great Britain and Germany, flying for refuge from intolerable suffering, in every vessel that comes to our shores. Hither also resort numbers of that order of men who, in foreign countries, are called the middling class, the most valuable part of the communities they leave, to enjoy a moderate affluence, where the abuses and exactions of a distempered system of government cannot reach them, to degrade them to the condition of the peasantry. Our country is the asylum of the persecuted preachers of new religions, and the teachers of political doctrines, which Europe will not endure; a sanctuary for dethroned princes, and the consorts of slain emperors. When we consider all these innumerable differences of character, native and foreign, this infinite variety of pursuits and objects, this endless diversity and change of fortunes, and behold them gathered and grouped into one vast assem-blage in our own country, we shall feel little pride in the sagacity or the skill of that native author, who asks for a richer or wider field of observation. . . .

[1825]

⅄ "I have never seen a nation so much alike in my life, as the people of the United States," Cooper remarks. "And what is more, they are not only like each other, but they are remarkably like that which common sense tells them they ought to resemble." (Alexis de Tocqueville would soon reach the same conclusion.) This is only one of the problems Cooper found facing the native writer: he extends what was to become the familiar litany, thus adding his considerable authority to the complaint and ensuring its influence on several generations of American authors.

60 ⅄

. . . As respects authorship, there is not much to be said. Compared to the books that are printed and read, those of native origin are few indeed. The principal reason of this poverty of original writers, is owing to the circumstance that men are not yet driven to their wits for bread. The United States are the first nation that possessed institutions, and, of course, distinctive opinions of its own, that was ever dependent on a foreign people for its literature. Speaking the same language as the English, and long in the habit of importing their books from the mother country, the revolution effected no immediate change in the nature of their studies, or mental amusements. The works were re-printed, it is true, for the purposes of economy, but they still continued English. Had the latter nation used this powerful engine with tolerable address, I think they would have secured such an ally in this country as would have rendered their own decline not only more secure, but as illustrious as had been their rise. There are many theories entertained as to the effect produced in this country by the falsehoods and jealous calumnies which have been undeniably uttered in the mother country, by means of the press, concerning her republican descendant. It is my own opinion that, like all other ridiculous absurdities, they have defeated themselves, and that they are now more laughed at and derided, even here, than resented. By all that I can learn, twenty years ago, the Americans were, perhaps, far too much disposed to receive the opinions and to adopt the prejudices of their relatives; whereas, I think it is very apparent that they are now beginning to receive them with singular distrust. It is not worth our while to enter further into this subject, except at it has had, or is likely to have, an influence on the national literature.*

It is quite obvious, that, so far as taste and forms alone are concerned, the literature of England and that of America must be fashioned after the same models. The authors, previously to the revolution, are common property, and it is quite idle to say that the American has not just as good a right to claim Milton, and Shakespeare, and all the old masters of the language, for his countrymen, as an Englishman. The Americans having continued to cultivate, and to cultivate extensively, an acquaintance with the writers of the mother country, since the separation, it is evident they must have kept pace with the trifling changes of the day. The only peculiarity that can, or ought to be expected in their literature, is that which is connected with the promulgation of their distinctive political opinions. They have not been remiss in this duty, as any one may see, who chooses to examine their books. But we will devote a few minutes to a more minute account of the actual condition of American literature. . . .

The literature of the United States has, indeed, too [two] powerful obstacles to conquer before (to use a mercantile expression) it can ever enter the markets of its own country on terms of perfect equality with that of England. Solitary and individual works of genius may, indeed, be occasionally brought to light, under the impulses of the high feeling which has conceived them; but, I fear, a good, wholesome, profitable and continued pecuniary support, is the applause that talent most craves. The fact, that an American publisher can get an English work without money, must, for a few years longer, (unless legislative protection shall be extended to their own authors,) have a tendency to repress a national literature. No man will pay a writer for an epic, a tragedy, a sonnet, a history, or a romance, when he can get a work of equal merit for nothing. I have conversed with those who are conversant on the subject, and, I confess, I have been astonished at the information they imparted.

A capital American publisher has assured me that there are not a dozen writers in this country, whose works he should feel confidence in publishing at all, while he re-prints hundreds of English books without the least hesitation. This preference is by no means so much owing to any differ-

* The writer might give, in proof of this opinion, one fact. He is led to believe that, so lately as within ten years, several English periodical works were re-printed, and much read in the United States, and that now they patronize their own, while the former are far less sought, though the demand, by means of the increased population, should have been nearly doubled. Some of the works are no longer even re-printed.

ence in merit, as to the fact that, when the price of the original author is to be added to the uniform hazard which accompanies all literary speculations, the risk becomes too great. The general taste of the reading world in this country is better than that of England.* The fact is both proved and explained by the circumstance that thousands of works that are printed and read in the mother country, are not printed and read here. The publisher on this side of the Atlantic has the advantage of seeing the reviews of every book he wishes to print, and, what is of far more importance, he knows, with the exception of books that he is sure of selling, by means of a name, the decision of the English critics before he makes his choice. Nine times in ten, popularity, which is all he looks for, is a sufficient test of general merit. Thus, while you find every English work of character, or notoriety, on the shelves of an American book-store, you may ask in vain for most of the trash that is so greedily devoured in the circulating libraries of the mother country, and which would be just as eagerly devoured here, had not a better taste been created by a compelled abstinence. That taste must now be overcome before such works could be sold at all.

When I say that books are not rejected here, from any want of talent in the writers, perhaps I ought to explain. I wish to express something a little different. Talent is sure of too many avenues to wealth and honours, in America, to seek, unnecessarily, an unknown and hazardous path. It is better paid in the ordinary pursuits of life, than it would be likely to be paid by an adventure in which an extraordinary and skilful, because practised, foreign competition is certain. Perhaps high talent does not often make the trial with the American bookseller; but it is precisely for the reason I have named.

The second obstacle against which American literature has to contend, is in the poverty of materials. There is scarcely an ore which contributes to the wealth of the author, that is found, here, in veins as rich as in Europe. There are no annals for the historian; no follies (beyond the most vulgar and commonplace) for the satirist; no manners for the dramatist; no obscure fictions for the writer of romance; no gross and hardy offences against decorum for the moralist; not any of the rich artificial auxiliaries of poetry. The weakest hand can extract a spark from the flint, but it would baffle the strength of a giant to attempt kindling a flame with a

---

* The writer does not mean the best taste of America is better than that of England; perhaps it is not quite so good; but, as a whole, the American reading world requires better books than the whole of the English reading world.

pudding-stone. I very well know there are theorists who assume that the society and institutions of this country are, or ought to be, particularly favourable to novelties and variety. But the experience of one month, in these States, is sufficient to show any observant man the falsity of their position. The effect of a promiscuous assemblage any where, is to create a standard of deportment; and great liberty permits every one to aim at its attainment. I have never seen a nation so much alike in my life, as the people of the United States, and what is more, they are not only like each other, but they are remarkably like that which common sense tells them they ought to resemble. No doubt, traits of character that are a little peculiar, without, however, being either very poetical, or very rich, are to be found in remote districts; but they are rare, and not always happy exceptions. In short, it is not possible to conceive a state of society in which more of the attributes of plain good sense, or fewer of the artificial absurdities of life, are to be found, than here. There is no costume for the peasant, (there is scarcely a peasant at all,) no wig for the judge, no baton for the general, no diadem for the chief magistrate. The darkest ages of their history are illuminated by the light of truth; the utmost efforts of their chivalry are limited by the laws of God; and even the deeds of their sages and heroes are to be sung in a language that would differ but little from a version of the ten commandments. However useful and respectable all this may be in actual life, it indicates but one direction to the man of genius.

It is very true there are a few young poets now living in this country, who have known how to extract sweets from even these wholesome, but scentless native plants. They have, however, been compelled to seek their inspiration in the universal laws of nature, and they have succeeded, precisely in proportion as they have been most general in their application. Among these gifted young men, there is one (Halleck) who is remarkable for an exquisite vein of ironical wit, mingled with a fine, poetical, and, frequently, a lofty expression. This gentleman commenced his career as a satirist in one of the journals of New-York. Heaven knows, his materials were none of the richest; and yet the melody of his verse, the quaintness and force of his comparisons, and the exceeding humour of his strong points, brought him instantly into notice. He then attempted a general satire, by giving the history of the early days of a *belle*. He was again successful, though every body, at least every body of any talent, felt that he wrote in leading-strings. But he happened, shortly after the appearance of the little volume just named, (Fanny,) to visit England. Here his spirit was properly excited, and probably on a rainy day he was induced to try his hand at a *jeu d'esprit,* in the mother country. The result was one of the finest semi-heroic ironical descriptions to be found in the English language.* This simple fact, in itself, proves the truth of a great deal of what I have just been writing, since it shows the effect a superiority of material can produce on the efforts of a man of true genius.

Notwithstanding the difficulties of the subject, talent has even done more than in the instance of Mr. Halleck. I could mention several other young poets of this country of rare merit. By mentioning Bryant, Percival, and Sprague, I shall direct your attention to the names of those whose works would be most likely to give you pleasure. . . .

The next, though certainly an inferior branch of imaginative writing, is fictitious composition. From the facts just named, you cannot expect that the novelists, or romance writers of the United States, should be very successful. The same reason will be likely, for a long time to come, to repress the ardour of dramatic genius. Still, tales and plays are no novelties in the literature of this country. Of the former, there are many as old as soon after the revolution; and a vast number have been published within the last five years. One of their authors of romance, who curbed his talents by as few allusions as possible to actual society, is distinguished for power and comprehensiveness of thought. I remember to have read one of his books (Wieland) when a boy, and I take it to be a never-failing evidence of genius, that, amid a thousand similar pictures which have succeeded, the images it has left, still stand distinct and prominent in my recollection. This author (Mr. Brockden Brown) enjoys a high reputation among his countrymen, whose opinions are sufficiently impartial, since he flattered no particular prejudice of the nation in any of his works.

The reputation of Irving is well known to you. He is an author distinguished for a quality (humour) that has been denied his countrymen; and his merit is the more rare, that it has been shown in a state of society so cold and so restrained. Besides these writers, there are many others of a similar character, who enjoy a greater or less degree of favour in their own country. The works of two or three have even been translated (into French) in Europe, and a great many are reprinted in England. Though every writer of fiction in America has to contend against the difficulties I have named, there is a certain interest in the novelty of the subject, which is not without its charm. I think, however, it will be found that they have all been successful, or the reverse, just as they have drawn warily, or freely, on the distinctive habits of their own country. I now speak of their

---

* This little *morceau* of pleasant irony is called Alnwick Castle.

success purely as writers of romance. It certainly would be possible for an American to give a description of the manners of his own country, in a book that he might choose to call a romance, which should be read, because the world is curious on the subject, but which would certainly never be read for that nearly indefinable poetical interest which attaches itself to a description of manners less bald and uniform. All the attempts to blend history with romance in America, have been comparatively failures, (and perhaps fortunately,) since the subjects are too familiar to be treated with the freedom that the imagination absolutely requires. Some of the descriptions of the progress of society on the borders, have had a rather better success, since there is a positive, though no very poetical, novelty in the subject; but, on the whole, the books which have been best received, are those in which the authors have trusted most to their own conceptions of character, and to qualities that are common to the rest of the world and to human nature. This fact, if its truth be admitted, will serve to prove that the American writer must seek his renown in the exhibition of qualities that are general, while he is confessedly compelled to limit his observations to a state of society that has a wonderful tendency not only to repress passion, but to equalize humours. . . .

Of dramatic writers there are none, or next to none. The remarks I have made in respect to novels apply with double force to this species of composition. A witty and successful American comedy could only proceed from extraordinary talent. There would be less difficulty, certainly, with a tragedy; but still, there is rather too much foreign competition, and too much domestic employment in other pursuits, to invite genius to so doubtful an enterprise. The very baldness of ordinary American life is in deadly hostility to scenic representation. The character must be supported solely by its intrinsic power. The judge, the footman, the clown, the lawyer, the belle, or the beau, can receive no great assistance from dress. Melo-dramas, except the scene should be laid in the woods, are out of the question. It would be necessary to seek the great clock, which is to strike the portentous twelve blows, in the nearest church; a vaulted passage would degenerate into a cellar; and, as for ghosts, the country was discovered, since their visitations have ceased. The smallest departure from the incidents of ordinary life would do violence to every man's experience; and, as already mentioned, the passions which belong to human nature must be delineated, in America, subject to the influence of that despot— common sense.

Notwithstanding the overwhelming influence of British publications, and all the difficulties I have named, original books are getting to be numerous in the United States. The impulses of talent and intelligence are bearing down a thousand obstacles. I think the new works will increase rapidly, and that they are destined to produce a powerful influence on the world. . . .

Although there are so many reasons why an imaginative literature should not be speedily created in this country, there is none, but that general activity of employment which is not favourable to study, why science and all the useful arts should not be cultivated here, perhaps, more than any where else. Great attention is already paid to the latter. Though there is scarce such a thing as a capital picture in this whole country, I have seen more beautiful, graceful, and convenient ploughs in positive use here, than are probably to be found in the whole of Europe united. In this single fact may be traced the history of the character of the people, and the germ of their future greatness. Their axe is admirable for form, for neatness, and precision of weight, and it is wielded with a skill that is next to incredible. . . .

The purely intellectual day of America is yet in its dawn. But its sun will not arise from darkness, like those of nations with whose experience we are familiar; nor is the approach of its meridian to be calculated by the known progress of any other people. The learned professions are now full to overflowing, not so much with learning as with incumbents, certainly, but so much so, as to begin to give a new direction to education and talents. Writers are already getting to be numerous, for literature is beginning to be profitable. Those authors who are successful, receive prices for their labours, which exceed those paid to the authors of any country, England alone excepted; and which exceed even the prices paid to the most distinguished authors of the mother country, if the difference in the relative value of money in the two countries, and in the luxury of the press, be computed. The same work which is sold in England for six dollars, is sold in the United States for two. The profit to the publisher is obtained out of a common rate of per centage. Now, as thirty-three and a third per cent. on six thousand dollars, is two thousand,* and on two thousand dollars, only six hundred and sixty-six, it is quite evident, that if both parties sell one thousand copies of a work, the English publisher pockets three times the most profit. And yet, with one or two exceptions,

---

* This calculation supposes one-third of the price to go to the trade in discount, one-third to the expenses, and the other third to constitute the joint profit of the author and publisher.

and notwithstanding the great difference in the population of the two countries, the English bookseller rarely sells more, if he does as many, copies of a book, than the American. It is the extraordinary demand which enables the American publisher to pay so well, and which, provided there was no English competition, would enable him to pay still better, or rather still more generally, than he does at present.

The literature of the United States is a subject of the highest interest to the civilized world; for when it does begin to be felt, it will be felt with a force, a directness, and a common sense in its application, that has never yet been known. If there were no other points of difference between this country and other nations, those of its political and religious freedom, alone, would give a colour of the highest importance to the writings of a people so thoroughly imbued with their distinctive principles, and so keenly alive to their advantages. The example of America has been silently operating on Europe for half a century; but its doctrines and its experience, exhibited with the understanding of those familiar with both, have never yet been pressed on our attention. I think the time for the experiment is getting near. . . .

[1828]

61 ✑

. . . This country, in its ordinary aspects, probably presents as barren a field to the writer of fiction, and to the dramatist, as any other on earth; we are not certain that we might not say the most barren. We believe that no attempt to delineate ordinary American life, either on the stage or in the pages of a novel, has been rewarded with success. Even those works in which the desire to illustrate a principle has been the aim, when the picture has been brought within this homely frame, have had to contend with disadvantages that have been commonly found insurmountable. The latter being the intention of this book, the task has been undertaken with a perfect consciousness of all its difficulties, and with scarcely a hope of success. It would be indeed a desperate undertaking, to think of making anything interesting in the way of a *Roman de Société* in this country; still, useful glances may possibly be made even in that direction, and we trust that the fidelity of one or two of our portraits will be recognized by the looker-on, although they will very likely be denied by the sitters themselves.

There seems to be a pervading principle in things, which gives an accumulating energy to any active property that may happen to be in the ascendant at the time being: money produces money; knowledge is the parent of knowledge; and ignorance fortifies ignorance. In a word, like begets like. The governing social evil of America is provincialism; a misfortune that is perhaps inseparable from her situation. Without a social capital, with twenty or more communities divided by distance and political barriers, her people, who are really more homogeneous than any other of the same numbers in the world perhaps, possess no standard for opinion, manners, social maxims, or even language. Every man, as a matter of course, refers to his own particular experience, and praises or condemns agreeably to notions contracted in the circle of his own habits, however narrow, provincial, or erroneous they may happen to be. As a consequence, no useful stage can exist; for the dramatist who should endeavor to delineate the faults of society, would find a formidable party arrayed against him, in a moment, with no party to defend. As another consequence, we see individuals constantly assailed with a wolf-like ferocity, while society is everywhere permitted to pass unscathed.

That the American nation is a great nation, in some particulars the greatest the world ever saw, we hold to be true, and are as ready to maintain as any one can be; but we are also equally ready to concede, that it is very far behind most polished nations in various essentials, and chiefly that it is lamentably in arrears to its own avowed principles. Perhaps this truth will be found to be the predominant thought, throughout the pages of "Home as Found."

[1838]

If we can trust W. B. O. Peabody, what the American poet most lacked was conscientious industry. Peabody appears to have found no shortage of versification, at any rate, but only a reluctance to accept the discipline that significant writing demands.

62

If we may believe certain high authorities, it was once thought that poetry required peculiar natural powers; such as are not given to all men, at least in the same measure. The poet, in order to pass muster, was required to possess the highest attributes of mind and the best affections of the heart; to have an eye wide and searching, quick to discern the magnificence and glory of nature, and able to look down into the depths of the soul. Beside the delicate sensibility which voluntary retirement could give him, he was expected to have an acquaintance with all the principles of human action, from the power which lifted and swayed the stormy passions of the multitude, to the hair-spring which set in motion the wayward ambition of kings. But not to dwell on these easy generalities, it is enough to say, that the poet was the favorite creation of the imagination of the ancients. Their deities were hardly respectable in their character and pretensions; they were nothing more than human agents, exalted to the power and dignity of evil spirits; with more capacity of doing evil, and even less disposition to do good. The poet made the hero; so that he had no rival in the admiration of men; and this may account for the number and greatness of the qualifications required in those who aspired to the sacred name.

For many years this imaginary being has ceased to be found, and grave men have doubted, whether any such ever existed. Certainly, the impression that any peculiar powers are required for the production of poetry is completely done away. The time which Johnson prophesied, in no good humor, is come in this country, if not in his own, when 'the cook warbles lyrics in the kitchen, and the thresher vociferates his dithyrambics in the barn.' One of the first efforts of our forefathers was to destroy the monopoly of genius, and to impress upon their children the valuable truth, that man could do again whatever man had done. They entered the sacred ground of poetry without putting off their shoes, and made sure of success beforehand, by establishing the principle, that praise was due to well-meant exertion. If an epitaph, an elegy, or even a hymn-book was called for, they considered it not a matter of choice, but of duty, to supply the demand. Even the great epics of our country, in more modern times, were written with the same intrepidity. The writers saw that all other great nations had their distinguished poetical works, and they resolved that their own land should not be without them; if no one else would write them, they would; though they had little leisure for the labor, and for the art itself neither propensity nor vocation.

From their time to the present, Mr Kettell will bear us witness, vast quantities of good merchantable poetry, of which his three volumes are only specimens, have been thrown into the market every year; or rather, we should say, have been produced; for some of the worthies of that collection little dreamed of being translated from the dark corner of a newspaper to a place among the northern stars. The result of making this business so common has been a great developement of mechanical skill. Very tolerable verse may now be made with very little expense of time and labor; though there is reason to fear, that, in many cases, the workmanship covers the want of material. It is not long since an individual in one of our cities offered to supply the public with good verse, suited to any occasion, and at low prices; but the domestic manufacture had become so common, that he found no encouragement in his profession. We are evidently approaching a state of independence, even beyond that contemplated by the American system; when not only our nation shall cease to be indebted to others, but every individual shall furnish his own supply; and as all are pretty well satisfied with their exploits in verse, we rejoice in believing that every one will be supplied to his mind with poetry, which, if none of the best, is good enough for him.

But it must not be denied, that those who are inclined to look upon the dark side, represent this as a sign of the temporary decline of the art. For they say, and, it must be confessed, with some show of reason, that the gods have made excellence the prize of labor; and if the public are disposed to favor productions of the lighter kind, the fact, that excellence is no longer required, proves that the public taste is also declining. Neither is the success of the great poets of the present day any objection to this statement, because the labor spoken of is not required for single efforts, but in the preparation for great exertions. Thus it was by slow degrees, that Scott prepared himself for those works, which are now the wonder of the world; it was not at once, that Moore became master of his miraculous versification and imagery; and it was long before Mrs Hemans acquired that beautiful power, which now appears, however lightly her hand passes over the strings. With all their fine natural talent, they evidently felt and acted upon the conviction, that labor was essential to excellence and permanent success. Such is the opinion of sundry poetical skeptics; and whether it is a sound and sensible doctrine, or only an antiquated prejudice, time will show, when the momentary fashion is passed away. One thing, however, is clear; that those, who believe that no industry is required, fall into direct and servile imitation, and that not of the best models. For even to become sensible of the excellences of the great masters of the art, requires thought and study; no man is struck, at the first glance, with the greatness of the Paradise Lost, any more than the power of one of Raffaelle's pictures; we do not choose such works for the entertainment of our leisure hours, till we have become familiar with their beauties; and as such works are not so popular as those which are less admired, the judicious race of imitators choose a nearer way to applause, and copy the marvels of the hour. But the peculiarities, which are pleasing in original writers, will not bear imitation by the ablest hand, and such are not the hands which usually engage in this employment; so that the imitation, like Gothic architecture in our country, is more desperately Gothic than its original, and at last model and imitation are brought alike into contempt; a fate, of which we have abundant illustration. We must not judge of excellence in this way. No man chooses the noblest sciences, the sublimest scenes, nor the greatest men, for the companions of leisure hours; and it is but a mistaken gratitude to pronounce those who have best entertained us the greatest masters of the lyre.

A great proportion of the poetry in our country is of this imitative kind. There is evidence enough, that it is not owing to want of genius, and we are inclined to ascribe it to a want of correct and strong ambition. No man here makes poetry a serious and engrossing pursuit; and those who treat it merely as a graceful accomplishment, naturally imitate the manner of the writers they are most familiar with; and as, for the reason just given, the writers most admired are not always most read, it has come to pass, as once in Israel, that they 'go in by-paths,' and the highways are deserted. Still we are confident, that the way of Milton and Pope, by which we mean the way of thoughtfulness, care, and labor, will triumph at last; for we are convinced that there is a large body of cultivated men in our country, who, though no lovers of what bears the name of poetry at present, do yet take pleasure in reading our older writers and the truly excellent of the day; who know that genius is as much a matter of cultivation as of nature; who know that a taste for the beauty and grandeur of the visible world is formed by meditation, that acquaintance with the heart is not intuitive, and that power over hearts and souls is not to be acquired in an hour; who therefore have no patience with those, who rest their claims upon immediate inspiration, and will neither read nor hear without first having some assurance, that the writer, who invites their attention, instead of relying on charms and spells, has deliberately prepared himself for one of the highest and most difficult, and, when successful, most glorious enterprises of the mind. . . .

[1830]

➤ *Cooper might well predict a brighter day to dawn—as Emerson and Whitman would do in turn. For those who looked abroad for reassurance, there continued to be very little encouragement. "To talk of the literature of America," remarked* Coluburn's New Monthly Magazine,

63 ➤

. . . is to talk of that which has no existence. Nor is it in the nature of things that this should be otherwise. . . . and it may be reasonably doubted whether, in a much more extended period, the people of the United States will be able to take rank with the nations of Europe most distinguished for literature.

[1827]

64 ➤

The *Athenæum* concludes an article on *America and American Writers* with the statement: "We do not believe that America has a literature; we do not see that it has the germs of one; we do not believe that it can have one till its institutions are fundamentally changed."

[1829]

Two years later the Athenæum *returned to the subject:*

65 ➤

The literary independence of the Americans is far from being so complete as their political, for as yet they possess no national literature, and invariably regard ours as appertaining also to them. By national literature we do not merely mean works written by Americans; but a literature that appeals directly to the national feelings—is founded on domestic incidents, illustrates or satirizes domestic manners, and, above all, administers to the just pride of a nation, inspires a feeling for the national glory, and inculcates a love of country—a literature which foreigners may admire, but none can feel, in the deep sanctuary of the heart, but a native. Of course this is said generally, and all that we wish to be understood by it is, that the Americans possess no body of authors whose *esprit de corps* is national. . . .

This want of originality in American literature is, we think, likely long to continue . . . at least it will continue until a dozen or two minds such as the authors of Knickerbocker and the Pioneers, shall shed the radiance of their genius over the infant literature of America—giving confidence to the admiring millions of their countrymen, by winning golden opinions from Europe. . . .

[1831]

⤜ *Longfellow was a student at Bowdoin College when he dedicated himself to winning a place of leadership in his country's literary world. He became the best-known poet ever to write in America. In his Graduation Address, he admits that the national literature is yet in its infancy, but he insists that "a rich development of poetic feeling . . . shall break forth in song." Seven years later, in reviewing a new printing of Sidney's essay, Longfellow wrote his own defense of poetry. Only the latter half deals directly with the subject of this anthology, but the essay is not widely available and so there seems good reason to include it all. It is worth noting that Longfellow's call for intellectual independence preceded Emerson's "American Scholar Address" by five years.*

66 ⤛

To an American there is something endearing in the very sounds—Our Native Writers. Like the music of our native tongue when heard in a foreign land, they have power to kindle up within him the tender memory of his home and fireside;—and more than this, they foretell that whatever is noble and attractive in our national character will one day be associated with the sweet magic of Poetry. Is then our land to be indeed the land of song? Will it one day be rich in romantic associations? Will poetry, that hallows every scene, that renders every spot classical, and pours out on all things the soul of its enthusiasm, breathe over it that enchantment which lives in the isles of Greece, and is more than life amid the "woods, that wave o'er Delphi's steep." Yes!—and palms are to be won by our native writers!—by those that have been nursed and brought up with us in the civil and religious freedom of our country. Already has a voice been lifted up in this land, already a spirit and a love of literature are springing up in the shadow of our free political institutions.

But as yet we can boast of nothing farther than a first beginning of a national literature: a literature associated and linked in with the grand and beautiful scenery of our country—with our institutions, our manners, our customs, in a word, with all that has helped to form whatever there is peculiar to us and to the land in which we live. We cannot yet throw off our literary allegiance to Old England, we cannot yet remove from our shelves every book which is not strictly and truly American. English Literature is a great and glorious monument, built up by those master-spirits of old time that had no peers, and rising bright and beautiful until its summit is hid in the mists of antiquity.

Of the many causes which have hitherto retarded the growth of polite literature in our country, I have not time to say much. The greatest which now exists is doubtless the want of that exclusive attention which eminence in any profession so imperiously demands. Ours is an age and a country of great minds, though perhaps not of great endeavors. Poetry with us has never yet been anything but a pastime. The fault however is not so much that of our writers as of the prevalent modes of thinking which characterize our country and our times. We are a plain people that have had nothing to do with the mere pleasures and luxuries of life: and hence there has sprung up within us a quick-sightedness to the failings of literary men, and an aversion to everything that is not practical, operative, and thorough-going. But if we would ever have a national literature, our native writers must be patronized. Whatever there may be in letters, over which time shall have no power, must be "born of great endeavors," and those endeavors are the offspring of a liberal patronage. Putting off, then, what Shakspeare calls "the visage of the times," we must become hearty well-wishers to our native authors: and with them there must be a deep and thorough conviction of the glory of their calling, an utter abandonment of everything else, and a noble self-devotion to the cause of literature. We have indeed much to hope from these things: for our hearts are already growing warm towards literary adventures, and a generous spirit has gone abroad in our land, which shall liberalize and enlighten.

In the vanity of scholarship, England has reproached us that we have no finished scholars. But there is reason for believing that men of mere learning, men of sober research and studied correctness, do not give to a nation its great name. Our very poverty in this respect will have a tendency to give a national character to our literature. Our writers will not be constantly toiling and panting after classical allusions to the vale of Tempe and the Etrurian river, nor to the Roman fountains shall

> "The emulous nations of the West repair
> To kindle their quenched urns, and drink fresh
>   spirit there."

We are thus thrown upon ourselves: and thus shall our native hills become renowned in song, like those of Greece and Italy. Every rock shall become a chronicle of storied allusions: and the tomb of the Indian prophet be as hallowed as the sepulchres of ancient kings, or the damp vault and perpetual lamp of the Saracen monarch.

Having briefly mentioned one circumstance which is retarding us in the way of our literary prosperity, I shall now mention one from which we may hope a happy and glorious issue: It is the influence of national scenery in forming the poetical character. Genius, to be sure, must be born with a man; and it is its high prerogative to be free, limitless, irrepressible. Yet how is it moulded by the plastic hand of Nature! how are its attributes shaped and modulated, when a genius like Canova's failed in the bust of the Corsican, and amid the splendor of the French metropolis languished for the sunny skies and vine-clad hills of Italy? Men may talk of sitting down in the calm and quiet of their libraries and of forgetting, in the eloquent companionship of books, all the vain cares that beset them in the crowded thoroughfares of life: but, after all, there is nothing which so frees us from the turbulent ambition and bustle of the world, nothing which so fills the mind with great and glowing conceptions and at the same time so warms the heart with love and tenderness, as a frequent and close communion with natural scenery. The scenery of our own country, too, so rich as it is in everything beautiful and magnificent, and so full of quiet loveliness or of sublime and solitary awe, has for our eyes enchantment, for our ears an impressive and unutterable eloquence. Its language is in the high mountains, and in the pleasant valleys scooped out between them, in the garniture which the fields put on, and in the blue lake asleep in the hollow of the hills. There is an inspiration, too, in the rich sky that "brightens and purples" o'er our earth when lighted up with the splendor of morning, or when the garment of the clouds comes over the setting sun.

Our poetry is not in books alone. It is in the hearts of those men whose love for the world's gain, for its business and its holiday has grown cold within them, and who have gone into the retirements of nature, and have found there that sweet sentiment, and pure devotion of feeling can spring up and live in the shadow of a low and quiet life, and amid those that have no splendor in their joys, and no parade in their griefs.

Thus shall the mind take color from things around us: from them shall there be a genuine birth of enthusiasm, a rich development of poetic feeling that shall break forth in song. Though the works of art must grow old and perish away from earth, the forms of nature shall keep forever their power over the human mind, and have their influence upon the literature of a people.

We may rejoice, then, in the hope of beauty and sublimity in our national literature, for no people are richer than we are in the treasures of nature. And well may each of us feel a glorious and high-minded pride in saying, as he looks on the hills and vales, on the woods and waters of New England,

"This is my own, my native land."

[1825]

67 🖎

'Gentle Sir Philip Sidney, thou knewest what belonged to a scholar; thou knewest what pains, what toil, what travel, conduct to perfection; well couldest thou give every virtue his encouragement, every art his due, every writer his desert, 'cause none more virtuous, witty or learned than thyself.'* This eulogium was bestowed upon one of the most learned and illustrious men, that adorned the last half of the sixteenth century. Literary hisory is full of his praises. He is spoken of as the ripe scholar, the able states-man,—'the soldier's, scholar's, courtier's eye, tongue, sword,'—the man 'whose whole life was poetry put into action.' He and the Chevalier Bayard were the connecting links between the ages of chivalry and our own.

Sir Philip Sidney was born at Penshurst in West Kent, on the 29th of November, 1554, and died on the 16th day of October, 1586, from the wound of a musket-shot, received under the walls of Zutphen, a town in Guelderland, on the banks of the Issel. When he was retiring from the field of battle, an incident occurred, which well illustrates his chivalrous spirit, and that goodness of heart which gained him the appellation of the 'Gentle Sir Philip Sidney.' The circumstance has been made the subject of an historical painting by West. It is thus related by Lord Brooke.

> 'The horse he rode upon was rather furiously choleric than bravely proud, and so forced him to forsake the field, but not his back, as the noblest and fittest bier to carry a martial commander to his grave. In which sad progress, passing along by the rest of the army where his uncle the General was, and being thirsty with excess of bleeding, he called for drink, which was presently brought him; but, as he was putting the bottle to his mouth, he saw a poor soldier carried along, who had eaten his last at the same feast, ghastly casting up his eyes at the bottle. Which Sir Philip perceiving, took it from his head, before he drank, and delivered it to the poor man, with these words, "Thy necessity is yet greater than mine." '

* Nash's Pierce Penniless.

The most celebrated productions of Sidney's pen are the Arcadia and the Defence of Poetry. The former was written during the author's retirement at Wilton, the residence of his sister, the Countess of Pembroke. Though so much celebrated in its day,* it is now little known, and still less read. Its very subject prevents it from being popular at present; for now the pastoral reed seems entirely thrown aside. The muses no longer haunt the groves of Arcadia. The shepherd's song,—the sound of oaten pipe, and the scenes of pastoral loves and jealousies, are no becoming themes for the spirit of the age. Few at present take for their motto, '*flumina amo, silvasque inglorius,*' and, consequently, few read the Arcadia.

The Defence of Poetry is a work of rare merit. It is a golden little volume, which the scholar may lay beneath his pillow, as Chrysostom did the works of Aristophanes. We do not, however, mean to analyze it in this place; but recommend to our readers to purchase this 'sweet food of sweetly uttered knowledge.' It will be read with delight by all who have a taste for the true beauties of poetry; and may go far to remove the prejudices of those who have not. To this latter class, we address the concluding remarks of the author.

'So that since the ever praiseworthy poesy is full of virtue, breeding delightfulness, and void of no gift that ought to be in the noble name of learning; since the blames laid against it are either false or feeble; since the cause why it is not esteemed in England is the fault of poet-apes, not poets; since, lastly, our tongue is most fit to honor poesy, and to be honored by poesy; I conjure you all that have had the evil luck to read this ink-wasting toy of mine, even in the name of the nine muses, no more to scorn the sacred mysteries of poesy; no more to laugh at the name of poets, as though they were next inheritors to fools; no more to jest at the reverend title of "a rhymer;" but to believe, with Aristotle, that they were the ancient treasurers of the Grecians' divinity; to believe, with Bembus, that they were the first bringers in of all civility; to believe, with Scaliger, that no philosopher's precepts can sooner make you an honest man, than the reading of Virgil; to believe, with Clauserus, the translator of Cornutus,

* Many of our readers will recollect the high-wrought eulogium of Harvey Pierce, when he consigned the work to immortality. 'Live ever sweete, sweete booke: the simple image of his gentle witt; and the golden pillar of his noble courage; and ever notify unto the world, that thy writer was the secretary of eloquence, the breath of the muses, the honey-bee of the daintyest flowers of witt and arte; the pith of morale and intellectual virtues, the arme of Bellona in the field, the tongue of Suada in the chamber, the sprite of Practice in *esse,* and the paragon of excellency in print.'

that it pleased the heavenly Deity by Hesiod and Homer, under the veil of fables, to give us all knowledge, logic, rhetoric, philosophy, natural and moral, and "quid non?" to believe, with me, that there are many mysteries contained in poetry, which of purpose were written darkly, lest by profane wits it should be abused; to believe, with Landin, that they are so beloved of the gods, that whatsoever they write proceeds of a divine fury; lastly, to believe themselves, when they tell you, they will make you immortal by their verses.

'Thus doing, your names shall flourish in the printers' shops; thus doing, you shall be of kin to many a poetical preface; thus doing, you shall be most fair, most rich, most wise, most all; you shall dwell upon superlatives; thus doing, though you be "libertino patre natus," you shall suddenly grow "Herculea proles,"

"Si quid mea carmina possunt:"

thus doing, your soul shall be placed with Dante's Beatrix, or Virgil's Anchises.

'But if (fie of such a but!) you be born so near the dull-making cataract of Nilus, that you cannot hear the planet-like music of poetry; if you have so earth-creeping a mind, that it cannot lift itself up to look to the sky of poetry, or rather, by a certain rustical disdain, will become such a mome, as to be a Momus of poetry; then, though I will not wish unto you the ass's ears of Midas, nor to be driven by a poet's verses, as Bubonax was, to hang himself; nor to be rhymed to death, as is said to be done in Ireland; yet thus much curse I must send you in the behalf of all poets; that while you live, you live in love, and never get favor, for lacking skill of a sonnet; and when you die, your memory die from the earth, for want of an epitaph.'

As no 'Apologie for Poetrie' has appeared among us, we hope that Sir Philip Sidney's Defence will be widely read and long remembered. O that in our country, it might be the harbinger of as bright an intellectual day as it was in his own!—With us, the spirit of the age is clamorous for utility,—for visible, tangible utility,—for bare, brawny, muscular utility. We would be roused to action by the voice of the populace, and the sounds of the crowded mart, and not 'lulled asleep in shady idleness with poet's pastimes.' We are swallowed up in schemes for gain, and engrossed with contrivances for bodily enjoyments, as if this particle of dust were immortal,—as if the soul needed no aliment, and the mind no raiment. We glory in the extent of our territory, in our rapidly increasing population, in our agricultural privileges, and our commercial advantages. We boast of the magnificence and beauty of our natural scenery,—of the various climates of our sky,—the summers of our Northern regions,—the salubrious winters of the South, and of the various products of our soil, from the pines of our Northern highlands to the palm-tree and aloes of our Southern frontier. We boast of the increase and extent of our physical strength, the sound of populous cities, breaking the silence and solitude of our Western territories,—plantations conquered from the forest, and gardens springing up in the wilderness. Yet the true glory of a nation consists not in the extent of its territory, the pomp of its forests, the majesty of its rivers, the height of its mountains, and the beauty of its sky; but in the extent of its mental power,—the majesty of its intellect,—the height and depth and purity of its moral nature. It consists not in what nature has given to the body, but in what nature and education have given to the mind:—not in the world around us, but in the world within us:—not in the circumstances of fortune, but in the attributes of the soul:—not in the corruptible, transitory, and perishable forms of matter, but in the incorruptible, the permanent, the imperishable mind. True greatness is the greatness of the mind;—the true glory of a nation is moral and intellectual pre-eminence.

But still the main current of education runs in the wide and not well defined channel of immediate and practical utility. The main point is, how to make the greatest progress in worldly prosperity,—how to advance most rapidly in the career of gain. This, perhaps, is necessarily the case to a certain extent in a country, where every man is taught to rely upon his own exertions for a livelihood, and is the artificer of his own fortune and estate. But it ought not to be exclusively so. We ought not, in the pursuit of wealth and worldly honor, to forget those embellishments of the mind and the heart, which sweeten social intercourse and improve the condition of society. And yet, in the language of Dr. Paley, 'Many of us are brought up with this world set before us, and nothing else. Whatever promotes this world's prosperity is praised; whatever hurts and obstructs this world's prosperity is blamed; and there all praise and censure end. We see mankind about us in motion and action, but all these motions and actions directed to worldly objects. We hear their conversation, but it is all the same way. And this is what we see and hear from the first. The views, which are continually placed before our eyes, regard this life alone and its interests. Can it then be wondered at, that an early worldly-mindedness is bred in our hearts so strong, as to shut out heavenly-mindedness en- tirely!'—And this, though not in so many words, yet in fact and in its practical tendency, is the popular doctrine of utility.

Now, under correction be it said, we are much led astray by this word utility. There is hardly a word in our language whose meaning is so vague, and so often misunderstood and misapplied. We too often limit its application to those acquisitions and pursuits, which are of immediate and visible profit to ourselves and the community; regarding as comparatively or utterly useless many others, which, though more remote in their effects and more imperceptible in their operation, are, notwithstanding, higher in their aim, wider in their influence, more certain in their results, and more intimately connected with the common weal. We are too apt to think that nothing can be useful, but what is done with a noise, at noonday, and at the corners of the streets; as if action and utility were synonymous, and were not as useless to act without thinking, as it is to think without acting. But the truth is, the word utility has a wider signification than this. It embraces in its proper definition whatever contributes to our happiness; and thus includes many of those arts and sciences, many of those secret studies and solitary avocations, which are generally regarded either as useless, or as absolutely injurious to society. Not he alone does service to the State, whose wisdom guides her councils at home, nor he whose voice asserts her dignity abroad. A thousand little rills, springing up in the retired walks of life, go to swell the rushing tide of national glory and prosperity; and whoever in the solitude of his chamber, and by even a single effort of his mind, has added to the intellectual pre-eminence of his country, has not lived in vain, nor to himself alone. Does not the pen of the historian perpetuate the fame of the hero and the statesman? Do not their names live in the song of the bard? Do not the pencil and the chisel touch the soul while they delight the eye? Does not the spirit of the patriot and the sage, looking from the painted canvass, or eloquent from the marble lip, fill our hearts with veneration for all that is great in intellect, and godlike in virtue?

If this be true, then are the ornamental arts of life not merely ornamental, but at the same time highly useful; and Poetry and the Fine Arts become the instruction, as well as the amusement of mankind. They will not till our lands, nor freight our ships, nor fill our granaries and our coffers; but they will enrich the heart, freight the understanding, and make up the garnered fulness of the mind. And this we hold to be the true use of the subject.

Among the barbarous nations, which, in the early centuries of our era, overran the South of Europe, the most contumelious epithet which could be applied to a man, was to call him a Roman. All the corruption and degeneracy of the Western Empire were associated, in the minds of the Gothic tribes, with a love of letters and the fine arts. So far did this belief influence their practice, that they could not suffer their children to be instructed in the learning of the South. 'Instruction in the sciences,' said they, 'tends to corrupt, enervate, and depress the mind; and he who has been accustomed to tremble under the rod of a pedagogue, will never look on a sword or a spear with an undaunted eye.'* We apprehend that there are some, and indeed not a few of our active community, who hold the appellation of scholar and man of letters in as little repute, as did our Gothic ancestors that of Roman; associating with it about the same ideas of effeminacy and inefficiency. They think, that the learning of books is not wisdom; that study unfits a man for action; that poetry and nonsense are convertible terms; that literature begets an effeminate and craven spirit; in a word, that the dust and cobwebs of a library are a kind of armor, which will not stand long against the hard knocks of 'the bone and muscle of the State,' and the 'huge two-fisted sway' of the stump orator. Whenever intellect is called into action, they would have the mind display a rough and natural energy,—strength, straight-forward strength, untutored in the rules of art, and unadorned by elegant and courtly erudition. They want the stirring voice of Demosthenes, accustomed to the roar of the tempest, and the dashing of the sea upon its hollow-sounding shore; rather than the winning eloquence of Phalereus, coming into the sun and dust of the battle, not from the martial tent of the soldier, but from the philosophic shades of Theophrastus.

But against no branch of scholarship is the cry so loud as against poetry, 'the quintessence, or rather the luxury of all learning.' Its enemies pretend, that it is injurious both to the mind and the heart; that it incapacitates us for the severer discipline of professional study; and that, by exciting the feelings and misdirecting the imagination, it unfits us for the common duties of life, and the intercourse of this matter-of-fact world. And yet such men have lived, as Homer, and Dante, and Milton;—poets and scholars, whose minds were bathed in song, and yet not weakened; men who severally carried forward the spirit of their age, who soared upward on the wings of poetry, and yet were not unfitted to penetrate the deepest recesses of the human soul, and search out the hidden treasures of wisdom, and the secret springs of thought, feeling, and action. None fought more bravely at Marathon, Salamis, and Platæa, than did the poet Æschylus. Richard Cœur-de-Lion was a poet; but his boast was in his very song:

> 'Bon guerrier à l'estendart
> Trouvaretz le Roi Richard.'

* Procop. de bello Gothor. ap. Robertson, Hist. Charles V. Vol. I. p. 234.

Ercilla and Garcilasso were poets; but the great epic of Spain was written in the soldier's tent and on the field of battle, and the descendant of the Incas was slain in the assault of a castle in the South of France. Cervantes lost an arm at the battle of Lepanto, and Sir Philip Sidney was the breathing reality of the poet's dream, a living and glorious proof, that poetry neither enervates the mind nor unfits us for the practical duties of life.

Nor is it less true, that the legitimate tendency of poetry is to exalt, rather than to debase,—to purify, rather than to corrupt. Read the inspired pages of the Hebrew prophets; the eloquent aspirations of the Psalmist! Where did ever the spirit of devotion bear up the soul more steadily and loftily, than in the language of their poetry? And where has poetry been more exalted, more spirit-stirring, more admirable, or more beautiful, than when thus soaring upward on the wings of sublime devotion, the darkness and shadows of earth beneath it, and from above the brightness of an opened heaven pouring around it? It is true, the poetic talent may be, for it has been, most lamentably perverted. But when poetry is thus perverted,—when it thus forgets its native sky to grovel in what is base, sensual, and depraved,—though it may not have lost all its original brightness, nor appear less than 'the excess of glory obscured,' yet its birthright has been sold, its strength has been blasted, and its spirit wears 'deep scars of thunder.'

It does not, then, appear to be the necessary nor the natural tendency of poetry to enervate the mind, corrupt the heart, or incapacitate us for performing the private and public duties of life. On the contrary, it may be made, and should be made, an instrument for improving the condition of society, and advancing the great purpose of human happiness. Man must have his hours of meditation as well as of action. The unities of time are not so well preserved in the great drama, but that moments will occur, when the stage must be left vacant, and even the busiest actors pass behind the scenes. There will be eddies in the stream of life, though the main current sweeps steadily onward, till 'it pours in full cataract over the grave.' There are times, when both mind and body are worn down by the severity of daily toil; when the grasshopper is a burden; and thirsty with the heat of labor, the spirit longs for the waters of Shiloah, that go softly. At such seasons, both mind and body should unbend themselves; they should be set free from the yoke of their customary service, and thought take some other direction, than that of the beaten, dusty thoroughfare of business. And there are times, too, when the divinity stirs within us; when the soul abstracts herself from the world, and the slow and regular motions of earthly business do not keep pace with the Heaven-directed mind. Then earth lets go her hold; the soul feels herself more akin to Heaven; and soaring upward, the denizen of her native sky, she 'begins to reason like herself, and to discourse in a strain above mortality.' Call, if you will, such thoughts and feelings the dreams of the imagination; yet they are no unprofitable dreams. Such moments of silence and meditation are often those of the greatest utility to ourselves and others. Yes, we would dream awhile, that the spirit is not always the bondman of the flesh; that there is something immortal in us, something, which amid the din of life, urges us to aspire after the attributes of a more spiritual nature. Let the cares and business of the world sometimes sleep, for this sleep is the awakening of the soul.

To fill up these interludes of life with a song, that shall soothe our worldly passions and inspire us with a love of Heaven and virtue, seems to be the peculiar province of poetry. On this moral influence of the poetic art, there is a beautifully written passage in the 'Defence of Poesy.'

'The philosopher showeth you the way, he informeth you of the particularities, as well of the tediousness of the way and of the pleasant lodging you shall have when your journey is ended, as of the many by-turnings that may divert you from your way; but this is to no man, but to him that will read him, and read him with attentive, studious painfulness; which constant desire whosoever hath in him, hath already passed half the hardness of the way, and therefore is beholden to the philosopher but for the other half. Nay, truly, learned men have learnedly thought, that where once reason hath so much over-mastered passion, as that the mind hath a free desire to do well, the inward light each mind hath in itself is as good as a philosopher's book; since in nature we know it is well to do well, and what is well and what is evil, although not in the words of art which philosophers bestow upon us; for out of natural conceit the philosophers drew it; but to be moved to do that which we know, or to be moved with desire to know, "hoc opus, hic labor est."

'Now, therein, of all sciences (I speak still of human, and according to the human conceit,) is our poet the monarch. For he doth not only show the way, but giveth so sweet a prospect into the way, as will entice any man to enter into it; nay, he doth, as if your journey should lie through a fair vineyard, at the very first give you a cluster of grapes, that full of that taste you may long to pass farther. He beginneth not with obscure definitions, which must blur the margin with interpretations, and load the memory with doubtfulness, but he cometh to you with words set in delightful proportion, either accompanied with, or prepared for, the well-enchanting skill of music; and with a tale, forsooth, he cometh unto you, with a tale which holdeth children from play, and old men from the chimney-corner; and, pretending no more, doth intend the winning of the mind from wickedness to virtue.'

In fine, we think that all the popular objections against poetry may be, not only satisfactorily, but triumphantly answered. They are all founded upon its abuse, and not upon its natural and legitimate tendencies. Indeed, popular judgment has seldom fallen into a greater error, than that of supposing that poetry must necessarily, and from its very nature, convey false and therefore injurious impressions. The error lies in not discriminating between what is true to nature, and what is true to fact. From the very nature of things, neither poetry nor any one of the imitative arts, can in itself be false. They can be false no farther than, by the imperfection of human skill, they convey to our minds imperfect and garbled views of what they represent. Hence a painting, or poetical description, may be true to nature, and yet false in point of fact. The canvass before you may represent a scene, in which every individual feature of the landscape shall be true to nature;—the tree, the water-fall, the distant mountain,—every object there shall be an exact copy of an original, that has a real existence, and yet the scene itself may be absolutely false in point of fact. Such a scene, with the features of the landscape combined precisely in the way represented, may exist nowhere but in the imagination of the artist. The statue of the Venus de' Medici is the perfection of female beauty; and every individual feature had its living original. Still the statue itself had no living archetype. It is true to nature, but it is not true to fact. So with the stage. The scene represented, the characters introduced, the plot of the piece, and the action of the performers may all be conformable to nature, and yet not be conformable to any pre-existing reality. The characters there personified may never have existed; the events represented may never have transpired. And so, too, with poetry. The scenes and events it describes; the characters and passions it portrays, may all be natural though not real. Thus, in a certain sense, fiction itself may be true,—true to the nature of things, and consequently true in the impressions it conveys. And hence the reason, why fiction has always been made so subservient to the cause of truth.

Allowing, then, that poetry is nothing but fiction; that all it describes is false in point of fact; still its elements have a real existence, and the impressions we receive can be erroneous so far only, as the views presented to the mind are garbled and false to nature. And this is a fault incident to the artist, and not inherent in the art itself. So that we may fairly conclude, from these considerations, that the natural tendency of poetry is to give us correct moral impressions, and thereby advance the cause of truth and the improvement of society.

There is another very important view of the subject, arising out of the origin and nature of poetry, and its intimate connexion with individual character and the character of society.

The origin of poetry loses itself in the shades of a remote and fabulous age, of which we have only vague and uncertain traditions. Its foundation, like that of the river of the desert, springs up in a distant and unknown region, the theme of visionary story, and the subject of curious life, and in the quiet and repose of a golden age. There is something in the soft melancholy of the groves, which pervades the heart, and kindles the imagination. Their retirement is favorable to the musings of the poetic mind. The trees that waved their leafy branches to the summer wind, or heaved and groaned beneath the passing storm,—the shadow moving on the grass,—the bubbling brook,—the insect skimming on its surface,—the receding valley and the distant mountain,—these would be some of the elements of pastoral song. Its subject would naturally be the complaint of a shepherd and the charms of some gentle shepherdess,

> 'A happy soul, that all the way
> To Heaven, hath a summer's day.'

It is natural, too, that the imagination, familiar with the outward world, and connecting the idea of the changing seasons and the spontaneous fruits of the earth with the agency of some unknown power, that regulated and produced them, should suggest the thought of presiding deities, propitious in the smiling sky, and adverse in the storm. The fountain that gushed up as if to meet the thirsty lip, was made the dwelling of a nymph; the grove that lent its shelter and repose from the heat of noon, became the abode of dryads; a god presided over shepherds and their flocks, and a goddess shook the yellow harvest from her lap. These deities were propitiated by songs and festive rites. And thus poetry added new charms to the simplicity and repose of bucolic life, and the poet mingled in his verse the delights of rural ease, and the praise of the rural deities which bestowed them.

Such was poetry in those happy ages, when, camps and courts unknown, life was itself an eclogue. But in later days it sang the achievements of Grecian and Roman heroes, and pealed in the war-song of the Gothic Scald. These early essays were rude and unpolished. As nations advanced in civilization and refinement, poetry advanced with them. In each successive age, it became the image of their thoughts and feelings, of their manners, customs, and characters; for poetry is but the warm expression of the thoughts and feelings of a people, and we speak of it as being national, when the character of a nation shines visibly and distinctly through it.

Thus, for example, Castilian poetry is characterized by sounding expressions, and that pomp and majesty, so peculiar to Spanish manners and character. On the other hand, English poetry possesses in a high degree the charms of rural and moral feeling; it flows onward like a woodland stream, in which we see the reflection of the sylvan landscape and of the heaven above us.

It is from this intimate connexion of poetry with the manners, customs, and characters of nations, that one of its highest uses is drawn. The impressions produced by poetry upon national character at any period, are again re-produced, and give a more pronounced and individual character to the poetry of a subsequent period. And hence it is, that the poetry of a nation sometimes throws so strong a light upon the page of its history, and renders luminous those obscure passages, which often baffle the long-searching eye of studious erudition. In this view, poetry assumes new importance with all who search for historic truth. Besides, the view of the various fluctuations of the human mind, as exhibited, not in history, but in the poetry of successive epochs, is more interesting, and less liable to convey erroneous impressions, than any record of mere events. The great advantage drawn from the study of history is not to treasure up in the mind a multitude of disconnected facts, but from these facts to derive some conclusions, tending to illustrate the movements of the general mind, the progress of society, the manners, customs, and institutions, the moral and intellectual character of mankind in different nations, at different times, and under the operation of different circumstances. Historic facts are chiefly valuable, as exhibiting intellectual phenomena. And so far as poetry exhibits these phenomena more perfectly and distinctly than history does, so far is it superior to history. The history of a nation is the external symbol of its character; from it, we reason back to the spirit of the age that fashioned its shadowy outline. But poetry is the spirit of the age itself,—embodied in the forms of language, and speaking in a voice that is audible to the external as well as the internal sense. The one makes known the impulses of the popular mind, through certain events resulting from them; the other displays the more immediate presence of that mind, visible in its action, and presaging those events. The one is like the marks left by the thunder-storm,—the blasted tree,—the purified atmosphere; the other like the flash from the bosom of the cloud, or the voice of the tempest, announcing its approach. The one is the track of the ocean on its shore; the other the continual movement and murmur of the sea.

Besides, there are epochs, which have no contemporaneous history; but have left in their popular poetry pretty ample materials for estimating the character of the times. The events, indeed, therein recorded, may be exaggerated facts, or vague traditions, or inventions entirely apocryphal; yet they faithfully represent the spirit of the ages which produced them; they contain indirect allusions and incidental circumstances, too insignificant in themselves to have been fictitious, and yet on that very account the most important parts of the poem, in a historical point of view. Such, for example, are the *Nibelungen Lied* in Germany; the *Poema del Cid* in Spain; and the *Songs of the Troubadours* in France. Hence poetry comes in for a large share in that high eulogy, which, in the true spirit of the scholar, a celebrated German critic has bestowed upon letters: 'If we consider literature in its widest sense, as the voice which gives expression to human intellect,—as the aggregate mass of symbols, in which the spirit of an age or the character of a nation is shadowed forth, then indeed a great and various literature is, without doubt, the most valuable possession of which any nation can boast.*

From all these considerations, we are forced to the conclusion, that poetry is a subject of far greater importance in itself, and in its bearing upon the condition of society, than the majority of mankind would be willing to allow. We heartily regret, that this opinion is not a more prevailing one in our land. We give too little encouragement to works of imagination and taste. The vocation of the poet does not stand high enough in our esteem; we are too cold in admiration, too timid in praise. The poetic lute and the high-sounding lyre are much too often and too generally looked upon as the baubles of effeminate minds, or bells and rattles to please the ears of children. The prospect, however, brightens. But a short time ago, not a poet 'moved the wing, or opened the mouth, or peeped;' and now we have a host of them,—three or four good ones, and three or four hundred poor ones. This, however, we will not stop to cavil about at present. To those of them, who may honor us by reading our article, we would whisper this request,—that they should be more original, and withal more national. It seems every way important, that now, whilst we are forming our literature, we should make it as original, characteristic, and national as possible. To effect this, it is not necessary

* Schlegel. Lectures on the History of Literature, Vol. I. Lec. VII.

that the war-whoop should ring in every line, and every page be rife with scalps, tomahawks and wampum. Shade of Tecumseh forbid!—The whole secret lies in Sidney's maxim,—'Look in thy heart and write.' For

'Cantars non pot gaire valer,
Si d'inz del cor no mov lo chang.'*

Of this anon. We will first make a few remarks upon the word *national,* as applied to the literature of a country; for when we speak of a national poetry, we do not employ the term in that vague and indefinite way, in which many writers use it.

A national literature, then, in the widest signification of the words, embraces every mental effort made by the inhabitants of a country through the medium of the press. Every book written by a citizen of a country belongs to its national literature. But the term has also a more peculiar and appropriate definition; for when we say that the literature of a country is *national,* we mean that it bears upon it the stamp of national character. We refer to those distinguishing features, which literature receives from the spirit of a nation,—from its scenery and climate, its historic recollections, its Government, its various institutions,—from all those national peculiarities, which are the result of no positive institutions, and, in a word, from the thousand external circumstances, which either directly or indirectly exert an influence upon the literature of a nation, and give it a marked and individual character, distinct from that of the literature of other nations.

In order to be more definite and more easily understood in those remarks, we will here offer a few illustrations of the influence of external causes upon the character of the mind, the peculiar habits of thought and feeling, and, consequently, the general complexion of literary performances. From the causes enumerated above, we select natural scenery and climate, as being among the most obvious, in their influence upon the prevailing tenor of poetic composition. Every one who is acquainted with the works of the English Poets, must have noted, that a moral feeling and a certain rural quiet and repose are among their most prominent characteristics. The features of their native landscape are transferred to the printed page, and as we read we hear the warble of the sky-lark,—the 'hollow murmuring wind, or silver rain.' The shadow of the woodland scene lends a pensive shadow to the ideal world of poetry.

'Why lure me from these pale retreats?
Why rob me of these pensive sweets?

* 'The poet's song is little worth,
If it moveth not from within the heart.'

> Can Music's voice, can Beauty's eye,
> Can Painting's glowing hand supply,
> A charm so suited to my mind,
> As blows this hollow gust of wind,
> As drops this little weeping rill
> Soft tinkling down the moss-grown hill,
> While through the west, where sinks the crimson day,
> Meek twilight slowly sails, and waves her banners grey?'*

In the same richly poetic vein are the following lines from Collins's Ode to Evening.

> 'Or if chill blustering winds, or driving rain,
> Prevent my willing feet, be mine the hut,
> That from the mountain's side,
> Views wilds and swelling floods,

> 'And hamlets brown, and dim-discover'd spires,
> And hears their simple bell, and marks o'er all
> Thy dewy fingers draw
> The gradual dusky veil.'

In connexion with the concluding lines of these two extracts, and as an illustration of the influence of climate on the character of poetry, it is worthy of remark, that the English Poets excel those of the South of Europe in their descriptions of morning and evening. They dwell with long delight and frequent repetition upon the brightening glory of the hour, when 'the northern wagoner has set his sevenfold teme behind the stedfast starre;' and upon the milder beauty of departing day, when 'the bright-hair'd sun sits in yon western tent.' What, for example, can be more descriptive of the vernal freshness of a morning in May, than the often quoted song in Cymbeline?

> 'Hark! hark! the lark at heaven's gate sings,
> And Phœbus 'gins arise
> His steeds to water at those springs
> On chalic'd flowers that *lies:*
> And winking Mary-buds begin
> To ope their golden eyes;
> With every thing that pretty bin;
> My lady sweet, arise;
> Arise, arise!'

---

* Mason's Ode to a Friend.

How full of poetic feeling and imagery is the following description of the dawn of day, taken from Fletcher's Faithful Shepherdess!

> 'See, the day begins to break,
> And the light shoots like a streak
> Of subtle fire, the wind blows cold,
> While the morning doth unfold;
> Now the birds begin to rouse,
> And the squirrel from the boughs
> Leaps, to get him nuts and fruit;
> The early lark, that erst was mute,
> Carols to the rising day
> Many a note and many a lay.'

Still more remarkable than either of these extracts, as a graphic description of morning, is the following from Beattie's Minstrel.

> 'But who the melodies of morn can tell?
> The wild brook babbling down the mountain's side;
> The lowing herd; the sheepfold's simple bell;
> The pipe of early shepherd dim descried
> In the lone valley; echoing far and wide
> The clamorous horn along the cliffs above;
> The hollow murmur of the ocean tide;
> The hum of bees, and linnet's lay of love,
> And the full choir that wakes the universal grove.

> 'The cottage curs at early pilgrim bark;
> Crown'd with her pail, the tripping milk-maid sings;
> The whistling ploughman stalks afield; and hark!
> Down the rough slope the ponderous wagon rings;
> Through rustling corn the hare astonish'd springs;
> Slow tolls the village clock the drowsy hour;
> The partridge bursts away on whirring wings;
> Deep mourns the turtle in sequester'd bower;
> And shrill lark carols clear from her aerial tower.'

Extracts of this kind we might multiply almost without number. The same may be said of similar ones, descriptive of the gradual approach of evening and the close of day. But we have already quoted enough for our present purpose. Now, to what peculiarities of natural scenery and climate may we trace these manifold and beautiful descriptions, which in their truth, delicacy and poetic coloring, surpass all the pictures of the kind in Tasso, Guarini, Boscan, Garcilasso, and, in a word, all the most celebrated poets of the South of Europe? Doubtless, to the rural beauty which pervades the English landscape, and to the long morning and evening twilight of a northern climate.

Still, with all this taste for the charms of rural descripion and sylvan song, pastoral poetry has never been much cultivated, nor much admired in England. The Arcadia of Sir Philip Sidney, it is true, enjoyed a temporary celebrity, but this was, doubtless, owing in a great measure to the rank of its author; and though the pastorals of Pope are still read and praised, their reputation belongs in part to their author's youth at the time of their composition. Nor is this remarkable. For though the love of rural ease is characteristic of the English, yet the rigors of their climate render their habits of pastoral life any thing but delightful. In the mind of an Englishman, the snowy fleece is more intimately associated with the weaver's shuttle, than with the shepherd's crook. Horace Walpole has a humorous passage in one of his letters, on the affectation of pastoral habits in England. 'In short,' says he, 'every summer one lives in a state of mutiny and murmur, and I have found the reason; it is because we will affect to have a summer, and we have no title to any such thing. Our poets learnt their trade of the Romans, and so adopted the terms of their masters. They talk of shady groves, purling streams, and cooling breezes, and we get sore throats and agues by attempting to realize these visions. Master Damon writes a song, and invites Miss Chloe to enjoy the cool of the evening, and the deuce a bit have we of any such thing as a *cool* evening. Zephyr is a north-east wind, that makes Damon button up to the chin, and pinches Chloe's nose till it is red and blue; and they cry, *This is a bad Summer;* as if we ever had any other. The best sun we have is made of Newcastle coal, and I am determined never to reckon upon any other.' On the contrary, the poetry of the Italians, the Spanish, and the Portuguese, is redolent of the charms of pastoral indolence and enjoyment; for they inhabit countries in which pastoral life is a reality and not a fiction, where the winter's sun will almost make you seek the shade, and the summer nights are mild and beautiful in the open air. The babbling brook and cooling breeze are luxuries in a Southern clime, where you

> 'See the sun set, sure he'll rise tomorrow,
> Not through a misty morning twinkling, weak as
> A drunken man's dead eye, in maudlin sorrow,
> But with all heaven t' himself.'

A love of indolence and a warm imagination are characteristic of the inhabitants of the South. These are natural effects of a soft voluptuous climate. It is there a luxury to let the body lie at ease, stretched by a fountain in the lazy stillness of a summer noon, and suffer the dreamy fancy to lose itself in idle reverie, and give a form to the wind, and a spirit to the shadow and the leaf. Hence the prevalence of personification and the exaggerations of figurative language, so characteristic of the poetry of Southern nations. As an illustration, take the following beautiful sonnet from the Spanish. It is addressed to a mountain brook.

> 'Laugh of the mountain!—lyre of bird and tree!
> Mirror of morn, and garniture of fields!
> The soul of April, that so gently yields
> The rose and jasmin bloom, leaps wild in thee!
>
> 'Although, where'er thy devious current strays,
> The lap of earth with gold and silver teems,
> To me thy clear proceeding brighter seems
> Than golden sands, that charm each shepherd's gaze.
>
> 'How without guile thy bosom all transparent
> As the pure crystal, lets the curious eye
> Thy secrets scan, thy smooth round pebbles count!
> How, without malice murmuring, glides thy current!
> O sweet simplicity of days gone by!
> Thou shunnest the haunts of man, to dwell in limpid fount!'*

We will pursue these considerations no longer, for fear of digressing too far. What we have already said will illustrate, perhaps superficially, but sufficiently for our present purpose, the influence of natural scenery and climate upon the character of poetical composition. It will at least show, that in speaking of this influence, we did not speak at random and with-

---

> * 'Risa del monte, de las aves lira!
> pompa del prado, espejo de la aurora!
> alma de Abril, espíritu de Flora
> por quien la rosa y el jazmin espira!
>   'Aunque tu curso en cuantos pasos gira
> tanta jurisdiccion argenta y dora,
> tu claro proceder mas me enamora
> que lo que en tí todo pastor admira.
>   'Cuan sin engaño tus entrañas puras
> dejan por transparente vidriera
> las guijuelas al número patentes!
>   'Cuan sin malicia cándida murmuras!
> O sencillez de aquella edad primera,
> huyes del hombre y vives en las fuentes.'

out a distinct meaning. Similar, and much more copious illustrations of
the influence of various other external circumstances on national literature, might here be given. But it is not our intention to go into details.
They will naturally suggest themselves to the mind of every reflecting
reader.

We repeat, then, that we wish our native poets would give a more
national character to their writings. In order to effect this, they have only
to write more naturally, to write from their own feelings and impressions,
from the influence of what they see around them, and not from any pre-
conceived notions of what poetry ought to be, caught by reading many
books, and imitating many models. This is peculiarly true in descriptions
of natural scenery. In these, let us have no more sky-larks and nightin-
gales. For us they only warble in books. A painter might as well introduce
an elephant or a rhinoceros into a New England landscape. We would
not restrict our poets in the choice of their subjects, or the scenes of their
story; but when they sing under an American sky, and describe a native
landscape, let the description be graphic, as if it had been seen and not
imagined. We wish too, to see the figures and imagery of poetry a little
more characteristic, as if drawn from nature and not from books. Of this
we have constantly recurring examples in the language of our North
American Indians. Our readers will all recollect the last words of Pushmataha, the Choctaw Chief, who died at Washington in the year 1824.
'I shall die, but you will return to your brethren. As you go along the
paths, you will see the flowers, and hear the birds; but Pushmataha will
see them and hear them no more. When you come to your home, they
will ask you, where is Pushmataha? and you will say to them, He is no
more. They will hear the tidings *like the sound of the fall of a mighty oak
in the stillness of the wood.*' More attention on the part of our writers, to
these particulars, would give a new and delightful expression to the face of
our poetry. But the difficulty is, that instead of coming forward as bold,
original thinkers, they have imbibed the degenerate spirit of modern
English poetry. They have hitherto been imitators either of decidedly bad,
or of, at best, very indifferent models. It has been the fashion to write
strong lines,—to aim at point and antithesis. This has made writers turgid
and extravagant. Instead of ideas, they give us merely the signs of ideas.
They erect a great bridge of words, pompous and imposing, where there
is hardly a drop of thought to trickle beneath. Is not he, who thus
apostrophizes the clouds, 'Ye posters of the wakeless air!'—quite as extravagant as the Spanish poet, who calls a star, a 'burning doublon of the
celestial bank?' *Doblon ardiente del celeste banco!*

This spirit of imitation has spread far and wide. But a few years ago, what an aping of Lord Byron exhibited itself throughout the country! It was not an imitation of the brighter characteristics of his intellect, but a mimicry of his sullen misanthropy and irreligious gloom. We do not wish to make a bugbear of Lord Byron's name, nor figuratively to disturb his bones; still we cannot but express our belief, that no writer has done half so much to corrupt the literary taste as well as the moral principle of our country, as the author of Childe Harold.* Minds that could not understand his beauties, could imitate his great and glaring defects. Souls that could not fathom his depths, could grasp the straw and bubbles that floated upon the agitated surface, until at length every city, town, and village had its little Byron, its self-tormenting scoffer at morality, its gloomy misanthropist in song. Happily, this noxious influence has been in some measure checked and counteracted by the writings of Wordsworth, whose pure and gentle philosophy has been gradually gaining the ascendency over the bold and visionary speculations of an unhealthy imagination. The sobriety, and, if we may use the expression, the republican simplicity of his poetry, are in unison with our moral and political doctrines. But even Wordsworth, with all his simplicity of diction and exquisite moral feeling, is a very unsafe model for imitation; and it is worth while to observe, how invariably those who have imitated him have fallen into tedious mannerism. As the human mind is so constituted, that all men receive to a greater or less degree a complexion from those with whom they are conversant, the writer who means to school himself to poetic composition,—we mean so far as regards style and diction,—should be very careful what authors he studies. He should leave the present age, and go back to the olden time. He should make, not the writings of an individual, but the whole body of English classical literature, his study.

* We here subjoin Lord Byron's own opinion of the poetical taste of the present age. It is from a letter in the second volume of Moore's Life of Byron. 'With regard to poetry in general, I am convinced, the more I think of it, that he and *all* of us,— Scott, Southey, Wordsworth, Moore, Campbell, I,—are all in the wrong, one as much as another; that we are upon a wrong revolutionary poetical system, or systems, and from which none but Rogers and Crabbe are free; and that the present and next generations will finally be of this opinion. I am the more confirmed in this, by having lately gone over some of our classics, particularly *Pope,* whom I tried in this way;—I took Moore's poems and my own and some others, and went over them side by side with Pope's, and I was really astonished (I ought not to have been so) and mortified at the ineffable distance in point of sense, learning, effect and even *imagination,* passion, and *invention,* between the Queen Anne's man, and us of the Lower Empire. Depend upon it, it is all Horace then, and Claudian now, among us; and if I had to begin again, I would mould myself accordingly.'

There is a strength of expression, a clearness, and force and raciness of thought in the elder English poets, which we may look for in vain among those who flourish in these days of verbiage. Truly the degeneracy of modern poetry is no school-boy declamation! The stream, whose fabled fountain gushes from the Grecian mount, flowed brightly through those ages, when the souls of men stood forth in the rugged freedom of nature, and gave a wild and romantic character to the ideal landscape. But in these practical days, whose spirit has so unsparingly levelled to the even surface of utility the bold irregularities of human genius, and lopped off the luxuriance of poetic feeling, which once lent its grateful shade to the haunts of song, that stream has spread itself into stagnant pools, which exhale an unhealthy atmosphere, whilst the parti-colored bubbles that glitter on its surface, show the corruption from which they spring.

Another circumstance which tends to give an effeminate and unmanly character of our literature, is the precocity of our writers. Premature exhibitions of talent are an unstable foundation to build a national literature upon. Roger Ascham, the school-master of princes, and for the sake of antithesis, we suppose, called the Prince of School-masters, has well said of precocious minds; 'They be like trees that showe forth faire blossoms and broad leaves in spring-time, but bring out small and not long-lasting fruit in harvest-time; and that only such as fall and rott before they be ripe, and so never, or seldome come to any good at all.' It is natural that the young should be enticed by the wreaths of literary fame, whose hues are so passing beautiful even to the more sober-sighted, and whose flowers breathe around them such exquisite perfumes. Many are deceived into a misconception of their talents by the indiscreet and indiscriminate praise of friends. They think themselves destined to redeem the glory of their age and country; to shine as 'bright particular stars;' but in reality their genius

> 'Is like the glow-worm's light the apes so wonder'd at,
> Which, when they gather'd sticks and laid upon 't,
> And blew,—and blew,—turn'd tail and went out presently.'

We have set forth the portrait of modern poetry in rather gloomy colors; for we really think, that the greater part of what is published in this book-writing age, ought in justice to suffer the fate of the children of Thetis, whose immortality was tried by fire. We hope, however, that ere long, some one of our most gifted bards will throw his fetters off, and relying on himself alone, fathom the recesses of his own mind, and bring up rich pearls from the secret depths of thought.

We will conclude these suggestions to our native poets, by quoting Ben

Johnson's 'Ode to Himself,' which we address to each of them individually.

'Where do'st thou careless lie
Buried in ease and sloth?
Knowledge, that sleeps, doth die;
And this securitie
It is the common moth
That eats on wits, and arts, and quite destroyes them both.

'Are all th' Aonian springs
Dri'd up? lies Thespia waste?
Doth Clarius' harp want strings,
That not a nymph now sings!
Or droop they as disgrac't,
To see their seats and bowers by chatt'ring pies defac't?

'If hence thy silence be,
As 'tis too just a cause,
Let this thought quicken thee,
Minds that are great and free
Should not on fortune pause;
T''is crowne enough to virtue still, her owne applause.

'What though the greedy frie
Be taken with false baytes
Of worded balladrie,
And thinke it poesie?
They die with their conceits,
And only pitious scorne upon their folly waites.'

[1832]

W. J. Snelling did not think Bryant a "first-rate poet," but he praised him for avoiding the two major pitfalls of American writers: he developed his craft with slow deliberation, and he dared to resist imitation and seek originality.

68

... On the whole, we may pronounce the book before us, the best volume of American poetry that has yet appeared.

The publication of such a volume is an important event in our literature. We have been too much in the habit of looking abroad for examples and models; and our poets, generally, have had the usual fortune of imitators,—their copies have fallen short of the originals. In many, perhaps the majority of instances, the originals themselves have been ill selected. We have had no standard of excellence of our own. It seems to be universally admitted, that while we have cultivated the arts of life and the fine arts with success, we have no reason to boast of our progress in the art of poetry. We are so sensible of our deficiency in this respect, that we hardly dare to judge favorably of an American work, till it has received the approbation of the British critics. We always resent their censure, it is true; but we confirm it, by suffering its objects to sink into oblivion. While this is the case, it is of no avail to flatter ourselves that it is undeserved. Mr. Bryant has taken the only proper way to answer the sneers of foreigners. Such works as his say more in favor of our country, than all the appeals that were ever uttered by wounded national pride.

We could almost wish, that no such brilliant anomalies in the order of nature, as Burns, had ever appeared. We do not add Shakspeare and Walter Scott, because it is by no means clear that Shakspeare did not study; and if Scott be the most rapid of writers, no author ever gave more time to preparation. Burns, and some others, have made the opinion common, that genius can atone for all defects. Hence the carelessness of the authors of the present day; hence the flood of mediocrity, with which the reading world is overwhelmed. First thoughts are indeed commonly the most vigorous; and occasional pieces have been thrown off, at a heat, which art could not improve. But such things are accidents, not examples for imitation. Fame is, in general, not to be attained without effort.

This pernicious error has had the most injurious effect on American authors. The materials of poetry lie scattered about us in boundless profusion. The Alleghanies and the White Mountains ought to suggest as many ideas, to say the least, to an American, as Benan and Benvenue can to an Englishman. The Mississippi and Missouri are as much superior to Cam and Isis, as Erie and Ontario are to the meres of Cumberland. An Indian is as poetical a personage, as a Turk or a Highlander. But we put these materials together in a hurry. We cultivate our literature as we do our soil, with the greatest possible economy of labor. A poem is made, like a shoe, to answer the present demand. Sooth to say, our poets do not meet with much encouragement. The hope of distinction may be a sufficient stimulus to those who, like Byron, are born to fortunes; but there are few, if any, American poets, who can afford to write for fame. Those who write for money are so paid, that starvation would be their reward, for any extraordinary care bestowed on their productions. . . .

[1832]

Edward Everett's lengthy review of A Tour on the Prairies serves to recall for us what Irving meant to an earlier America: he was "a national matter." Irving is here taken not only as a model of style but also as witness to the wide availability of material; Everett did not admit our need of "feudal castles . . . traditions of chivalry . . . moss-clad ruins."

69

We regard Washington Irving as the best living writer of English prose. Let those who doubt the correctness of this opinion name his superior. Let our brethren in England name the writer, whom they place before Washington Irving. He unites the various qualities of a perfect manner of writing; and so happily adjusted and balanced are they, that their separate marked existence disappears in their harmonious blending. His style is sprightly, pointed, easy, correct, and expressive, without being too studiously guarded against the opposite faults. It is without affectation, parade, or labor. If we were to characterize a manner, which owes much of its merit to the absence of any glaring characteristic, we should perhaps say, that it is, above the style of all other writers of the day, marked with an expressive elegance. Washington Irving never buries up the clearness and force of the meaning, under a heap of fine words; nor on the other hand does he think it necessary to be coarse, slovenly, or uncouth, in order to be emphatic.

At the present day, mere ordinary good writing is no great affair. The daily newspapers are filled with it. Every election brings out compositions, we will not say equal to those of Junius, but such as if, by any accident, they could be shuffled in, among the letters of the 'shadow of a great name,' with the requisite change of topics and dates, would furnish no easy means of detection, from internal evidence. For this reason, it is certainly no great praise, at the present day, to say of an author, that he writes well. But to accord to him, with any shew of justice, the praise of being the best writer of the time, is, for the same reason, a far higher tribute, than would be paid, in the same judgment, bestowed at any other period in the history of our language.

Did Mr. Irving's merit in this respect rest in the mere point of criticism, we should deem it a matter of less import, though by no means insignificant; for of all the fine arts, which is more admirable than fine writing? But we desire to make a national matter of our countryman's merit in this respect. Mr. Irving, before his long residence in Europe, was a popular and successful writer; and the style of his earliest productions has all the essential merits of those recently published. We do not say, that there has been no improvement; for what kind of a mind would it be, that should make no progress, in the art of its choice, during seventeen years of successful cultivation? But all the elements of Washington Irving's style are as visible in his contributions to the Salmagundi, and in Knickerbocker, as they are in his last work. We commend this to the worshipful company of tourists and critics in England, as a phenomenon worthy of consideration; not the ordinary rabble of tourists and critics, but your philosophical Captain Halls, and your Quarterly Reviewers of high education and high breeding. Captain Hall, who has been wrecked on the Loo-choo islands, where they speak a terribly corrupt Chinese, found the Americans harder to understand, than *any* people he had ever fallen in with! We pity the poor captain the fagging it will cost him, to work his way through this first number of the Crayon Sketches. If we had a spare copy of one of the miscellaneous tracts of Confucius, we would get it forwarded to the captain, as his *délassement,* from the labor of puzzling out this last specimen of Jonathan's *patois.* If, however, he has prepared himself, by a pretty diligent study of the Sketch Book and the Life of Columbus, he may, in the course of the summer, master all but the hard places and the more outrageous Americanisms, which none but a native, fresh caught, could be expected to grapple with. The whole would furnish a pretty introduction to the study of Channing, Cooper, and Bryant, should the captain form the adventurous purpose of going to the bottom of the American language;—a purpose, however, which would need to be pursued with some caution, lest he should be betrayed, meantime, into forgetfulness of his mother tongue. We remember to have heard of an unfortunate professor at Leyden, who had actually studied himself out of the possession of any vernacular dialect. A native of Pomerania, he had been early transplanted to Holland. Being there wholly occupied with lecturing in the Latin language, he lost his German, without acquiring Dutch. At the end of thirty years, he could have held a very tolerable conversation with a Greek scholiast, and he spoke a Latin more exquisitely Ciceronian than that of Cicero himself, but could not have asked for a piece of bread and butter from the mother who bore him. Should Captain Hall take us at our word, and devote himself too exclusively to the American dialect, he might end in wholly dispossessing himself of that English undefiled, which forms the glory of the native citizen of Westmoreland and Yorkshire, the land of Cockayne and the land of cakes.

In bestowing upon Mr. Irving the praise of a perfect style of writing, it must not be understood, that we commend him, in a point of mere manner. To write as Mr. Irving writes, is not an affair, which rests in a dexterous use of words alone; at least not if we admit the popular, but unphilosophical distinction, between words and ideas. Mr. Irving writes well, because he thinks well; because his ideas are just, clear, and definite. He knows what he wants to say, and expresses it distinctly and intelligibly, because he so apprehends it. There is also no affectation in the writer, because there is none in the man. There is no pomp in his sentences, because there is no arrogance in his temper. There is no overloading with ornament, because with the eye of an artist, he sees when he has got enough; and he is sprightly and animated, because he catches his tints from nature, and dips his pencil in truth, which is always fresh and racy. No man contemplates, with greater tenderness than we do, the frailties of Dr. Johnson; none respects more the sound parts of his moral system; or admires more the vigor of the elephantine step, with which he sometimes tramples down insolent error and presumptuous sophistry. But let no young man, who wishes to learn to write well, study his style. Let him rather obey the precept, than follow the example of the venerable sage, whose vigorous judgment often broke out into candor, and give his days and nights, not to the volumes of the Rambler, but of the Spectator. And if he wishes to study a style, which possesses the characteristic beauties of Addison's, its ease, simplicity, and elegance, with greater accuracy, point, and spirit, let him give his days and nights to the volumes of Irving.

Washington Irving has been much and justly commended in England and America, but full justice has not yet been done him. Compare him with any of the distinguished writers of his class of this generation, excepting Sir Walter Scott, and with almost any of what are called the English classics of any age. Compare him with Goldsmith, one of the canonized names of the British pantheon of letters; who touched every kind of writing, and adorned every kind, that he touched. In one or two departments, it is true, that of poetry and the drama, departments which Mr. Irving has not attempted and in which much of Goldsmith's merit lies, the comparison partly fails; but place their pretensions, in every other respect, side by side. Who would think of giving the miscellaneous writings of Goldsmith a preference over those of Irving, and who would name his historical compositions with the life of Columbus? If in the drama and in poetry Goldsmith should seem to have extended his province, greatly beyond that of Irving, the life of Columbus is a *chef d'œuvre* in a department, which Goldsmith can scarcely be said to have touched; for the trifles on Grecian and Roman history, which his poverty extorted from him, deserve to enter into comparison with Mr. Irving's great work, about as much as Eutropius deserves to be compared with Livy. Then how much wider Irving's range in that department, common to both, the painting of manners and character! From Mr. Irving we have the humors of contemporary politics and every-day life in America,—the traditionary peculiarities of the Dutch founders of New-York,—the nicest shades of the school of English manners of the last century,—the chivalry of the middle ages in Spain,—the glittering visions of Moorish Romance,—a large cycle of sentimental creations founded on the invariable experience,—the pathetic sameness,—of the human heart,—and lastly, the whole unhackneyed freshness of the West,—life beyond the border,—a camp outside the frontier,—a hunt on buffalo ground, beyond which neither white nor Pawnee, man nor muse, can go. This is Mr. Irving's range, and in every part of it he is equally at home. When he writes the history of Columbus, you see him weighing doubtful facts, in the scales of a golden criticism. You behold him, laden with the manuscript treasures of well-searched archives, and disposing the heterogeneous materials, into a well-digested and instructive narration. Take down another of his volumes, and you find him in the parlor of an English country inn, of a rainy day, and you look out of the window with him upon the dripping, dreary desolation of the back-yard. Anon, he takes you into the ancestral hall of a baronet of the old school, and instructs you in the family traditions, of which the memorials adorn the walls and depend from the rafters. Before you are wearied with the curious lore, you are on the pursuit of Kidd the pirate, in the recesses of Long-Island; and by the next touch of the enchanter's wand, you are rapt into an enthusiastic reverie of the mystic East, within the crumbling walls of the Alhambra. You sigh to think you were not born six hundred years ago, that you could not have beheld those now deserted halls, as they once blazed in triumph, and rang with the mingled voices of oriental chivalry and song, when you find yourself once more borne across the Atlantic, whirled into the western wilderness, with a prairie wide as the ocean before you, and a dusky herd of buffaloes, like a crowded convoy of fleeing merchantmen, looming in the horizon and inviting you to the chace. This is literally *nullum fere genus scribendi non tigit nullum quod tetigit non ornviit.* Whether any thing like an equal range is to be found in the works of him, on whom the splendid compliment was first bestowed, it is not difficult to say. . . .

. . . Irving possesses, in the highest degree, the gift of the poet, *the maker*. And delightful it is to reflect, as in a case like this, how little it imports to the man, to whom this divine gift is imparted, what materials he shall take in hand to employ it upon, or where he shall lay the scene of his creations. The time has been, when, baited and persecuted by the whole body of British critics, on the poverty of our national literature, (at a period too, when the people of America were diffusing the English civilization over the continent with a rapidity, absolutely unexampled in the annals of mankind;—doing, in two hundred years, more to extend the empire of mind, than had been done in the mother country, in two thousand,) we were all at our wits' ends, to assign causes for the want of that particular form of polite literature, which cannot subsist, but in the bosom of a dense and wealthy population, and in a highly artificial state of society. Among the causes, to which we were driven, it was one, that works of imagination could not be expected in a country, where there are no feudal castles;—no traditions of chivalry;—no moss-clad ruins: a sufficient reason, perhaps, why the imagination in America should not habitually dwell on pictures of this class; but no more. Many things in the state of society are necessary to form a flourishing school of polite literature; but the want of any one class of subjects, elsewhere existing, is never, we believe, one of them. We have great doubts whether, in the present state of things in Greenland, there could, by possibility, be any Coopers or Irvings, but it is not for want of topics. Either of these masters, if it were possible that he should be found there, would create a world upon the eternal glaciers, that encompass its shores, as gorgeous, as various, as full of action, as ever moved and acted in courts or castles. The power of the poet, (and these men, and those like them are all poets,) as the name imports, is that of creating; and, we may venture to subjoin, out of nothing: for there is no irreverence in comparing with the operations of the Great All-powerful Intelligence, the action of those finite spirits, which he has pronounced himself to be his own image. They *create* the scene, which they set before us. It comes from within. It springs from beneath the wand of their genius. No matter how cold, and barren, and desolate the scene;—they fill it with life and motion; with interest and passion. They strike the desert rock and it flows with the full tide of fancy. A blasted oak in the wilderness, filled with a swarm of bees, drops with a honey of sweet imagery more delicious than that, which nature's little chemists have elaborated. They people a bare and blasted heath with men, with phantoms, with the visions of kingdoms grasped, and won, and lost. The barren surface of the sea, ploughed by the solitary pirate, who knows his fellow beings, but as objects to be alternately shunned and assailed, is made the theatre of the most deep and stirring interest. The dens of trivial iniquity in crowded cities,—the awful crags of the desert, where the hermit has fixed his cell,—the modern or the ancient battle-field,—the heart of man, with or without tradition,—and lastly, as in the present case, the fresh, uninhabited, unexplored desert,—the hunting ground of the wild Indian, who slays the primeval beast of the forest, with an arrow, the primeval weapon,—these all, and we believe *equally,* serve the purpose of the man of genius. No matter how remote the region. With one bound of the imagination, he is there, and his reader with him, at once familiarized and at home. No matter how novel and uncouth the scenery, in a single chapter, it is like the village, where we are born. If the subject is low, it is raised into importance, by a magic infusion of mind; and though it belong to the dull routine of business, one touch of the creative wand invests it with significance and curiosity. The colloquy of Saxon swineherds is as full of poetry, as the headstrong chivalry of Richard, or the mysterious and lordly heroism of Saladin. This is the characteristic of the great masters,—of Shakspeare and Scott,—shared in greater or less degree, by every man of genius and taste. Subject, incident, character are all next to nothing except in their treatment:—or as they are the creation of the poet himself. Sir Walter confesses that he did not know, at the beginning of his stories, how he was to come out at the end. And how should he? Does the man who possesses the talent of enchain-ing the delighted circle, with the fascinations of his conversation, know, at the beginning of the evening, all,—any thing,—that he is to say during its continuance, to its close?—Does the gifted speaker foretell the happy flashes, that are to break in upon him, as he warms and rises with his subject? To suppose that the creative mind of man, cultivated to the skilful use of its capacities, and called into action by the strong sympathy of surrounding intellects looking to him for excitement, is to rest torpid in America, for want of ruined castles and crumbling abbeys, on which it may pour forth its eloquent meditations, is to confound the understand-ing, with a single one of the occasions, on which its powers are to be exercised. For ourselves, we wish for nothing so ardently, as that the literature of the country should be the indigenous growth of the soil; indigenous in its topics, associations and spirit,—not for patriotic reasons merely, but on principles of art and taste. For though it is the prerogative of genius to give novelty to the tritest theme, to make the character of Julius Cæsar or Achilles as fresh as that of Napoleon, yet the thousand causes, which naturally guide the mind to the choice of a subject, (since subject there must be), point the American writer to his native land; and it is matter of study or conscious effort, if he goes elsewhere for his themes. We are proud of Mr. Irving's sketches of English life, proud of the gorgeous canvass upon which he has gathered in so much of the glowing imagery of Moorish times. We behold with delight his easy and triumphant march over these beaten fields; but we glow with rapture as we see him coming back from the Prairies, laden with the poetical treasures of the primitive wilderness,—rich with spoil from the uninhabited desert. We thank him for turning these poor barbarous *steppes* into classical land;—and joining his inspiration to that of Cooper, in breathing life and fire into a circle of imagery, which was not known before to exist, for the purposes of the imagination. . . .

And now we take leave of our countryman for the present, bidding him pursue the happy path of his popularity, and enjoy his fame. Let him chase every cloud from his spirits, if a cloud still hovers over them. Let him repose in the pure sunshine of a well earned and unenvied renown. Europe admires, and America admires and loves him. Let him write on; he can write nothing which will not be eagerly anticipated and cordially welcomed; and we trust we may add, well paid. If it be not, it is a scandal to the country. If, in these times of overflowing prosperity; when princely fortunes are daily built up in the country; when, under our happy institutions, an energy and enterprise, elsewhere unexampled, are in a state of the intensest action, and are daily reaping a golden harvest, in all the fields of prosperous industry, if there is not, on all hands, the disposition,—the resolute and affectionate purpose,—to make the talents and accomplishments of a man, like Washington Irving,—who is an honor to his country,—the source of fortune to himself, then we shall deserve, that he once again leave us and forever. But we indulge no such sinister anticipation. We believe a better day is dawning on American letters; that our republican princes are beginning to understand, that of all sordid things sordid affluence is the meanest; and that the portion of their riches, which will bring in the most exuberant return of pleasure to their possessors, is the portion devoted to a generous and discriminating patronage. The American father, who can afford it, and does not buy a copy of Mr. Irving's book, does not deserve that his sons should prefer his fireside to the bar-room;—the pure and chaste pleasures of a cultivated taste, to the gross indulgences of sense. He does not deserve that his daughters should prefer to pass their leisure hours in maidenly seclusion and the improvement of their minds, rather than to flaunt on the side-walks by day, and pursue by night an eternal round of tasteless dissipation.

[1835]

"We are now the literary vassals of England, and continue to do homage to the mother country. Our literature is tame and servile, wanting in freshness, freedom, and originality. We write as Englishmen, not as Americans." By 1838 this charge was common enough; the nationalistic confidence which followed the War of 1812 came under increasing pressure from the obvious fact of artistic imitation. Brownson used the publication of Ripley's Specimens to introduce a fresh, sociopolitical argument into the debate. Americans should eschew British models because their aristocratic values might tempt us toward monarchy. The writings of the French and Germans, on the other hand, *"breathe altogether more of a democratic spirit than do those of the English."*

70

These two volumes are the first of a series of translations, Mr. Ripley proposes to bring out, from time to time, under the general title of Specimens of Foreign Standard Literature. The works he proposes to translate, or to cause to be translated, are the works in highest repute in France and Germany, the best works of the ablest scholars and most distinguished authors of the two nations in the departments of Philosophy, Theology, History, and General Literature. He will be assisted in this undertaking by some of our first scholars and most eminent literary men, and will, if he realizes his plan, give us not only specimens of foreign standard literature, but also specimens of correct and elegant translation.

Mr. Ripley's undertaking is a noble one, and one in which our whole country is deeply interested. The importance of reproducing in our own language the standard literature of other nations cannot easily be overrated. Every nation has its peculiar idea, its special manner of viewing things in general, and gives a prominence, a development to some one element of universal truth, which is given by no other nation. The literature of one nation has therefore always something peculiar to itself; something of value, which can be found in the literature of no other. The study of the literatures of different nations will necessarily tend, therefore, to liberalize our minds, to enlarge our ideas, and augment our sum of truth. Very few among us have the leisure or the opportunity to make ourselves sufficiently acquainted with foreign languages, to be able to relish the works of foreigners save in translations. It is always on translations that the great mass of the people must depend for all the direct benefit they are to receive from the labors and researches of foreign scholars; and it is the direct benefit of the great mass of the people, that the American scholar is bound always to consult.

If translations are to be made at all, they ought to be well made, and to be of the best works, the standard works of the languages from which they are made. We have many translations from the French and German, but in a majority of cases, perhaps, we may say of works that were hardly worth the translating. This may be said especially in reference to the German. The American public study Germany not in the mature productions of her ripest scholars. Second and third rate authors, and second and third rate performances, at best, are those most generally translated. This is a grievous wrong to Germany, for it compels us to judge her for altogether less than she is; it is also a grievous wrong to ourselves, for it deprives us of a good we might receive, and which we need. Translations too are in general miserably executed, by persons who are in no sense whatever qualified to be translators. This perhaps is more especially the case in England than in this country. They are made too often by literary hacks, who must make them or starve, and who have no adequate knowledge of either the foreign language or their own, and not the faintest conception of the thought they undertake to reproduce. In consequence of want of taste and judgment in selecting the works to be translated, and of proper qualifications on the part of translators, translations in general, unless of purely scientific works, serve little other end than to encumber our book-shelves, corrupt the language, and overload it with foreign idioms and barbarous words and phrases. Both these evils are sought to be avoided by Mr. Ripley's plan, and will be, if his plan be realized, as we doubt not it must. His plan ensures us a French or German classic reproduced in English, and constituting ever after an English classic, whereby the intellectual and literary treasures within reach of the mere English student will be greatly augmented, the language itself enriched and perfected, the national taste refined and purified, and the national character elevated.

We are also much in want of the works Mr. Ripley proposes to reproduce. We have much to learn in the departments of Philosophy, Theology, and History, from the literatures of France and Germany. We are comparatively a young people. We have had a savage world to subdue, primitive forests to clear away, material interests to provide for. Our hands have necessarily and rightly been employed, and our thoughts busy, in procuring the means of subsistence and in preparing the theatre of our future glory; and we have not had the leisure to pore over the records of the past, to push our inquiries into surrounding nature, to sit down and patiently watch the fleeting phenomena which rapidly pass and repass over the field of consciousness, or to engage with spirit and ardor in high and extensive literary pursuits. It is not our fault, then, if we are in some respects behind the cultivated nations of the Old World. We shall not be behind them long. There is a literature in the American soul, waiting but a favorable moment to burst forth, before which the most admired literatures of the Old World will shrink into insignificance, and be forgotten. This nation is destined to excel in every department of human activity. It now takes the lead in commercial and industrial activity; it will take the lead in the sciences and the arts. From us is, one day, light to radiate, as from the central sun, to illumine the moral and intellectual universe. To us shall come, from all lands, the statesman, the philosopher, the artist, to gain instruction and inspiration, as from the God-appointed prophets of Humanity. We need not blush, then, to avail ourselves for the moment of foreign resources. The capital we borrow from abroad we shall profitably invest, and be able soon to repay, and with usury too.

This is not all. We are now the literary vassals of England, and continue to do homage to the mother country. Our literature is tame and servile, wanting in freshness, freedom, and originality. We write as Englishmen, not as Americans. We are afraid to think our own thoughts, to speak our own words, or to give utterance to the rich and gushing sentiments of our own hearts. And so must it be so long as we rely on England's literature as exclusively as we have hitherto done. Not indeed so much because that literature is not a good one. English literature, so long as it boasts a Shakspeare and a Milton, cannot suffer in comparison with the literature of any other nation. For ourselves we reverence it, and would on no account speak lightly of it. But it cramps our national genius, and exercises a tyrannical sway over the American mind. We cannot become independent and original, till we have in some degree weakened its empire. This will be best done by the study of the fresher, and in some respects superior literatures of continental Europe. We must bring in France and Germany to combat or neutralize England, so that our national spirit may gain the freedom to manifest itself.

Moreover, excellent as is the English literature, it is not exactly the literature for young republicans. England is the most aristocratic country in the world. Its literature is, with some noble exceptions, aristocratic. It is deficient in true reverence for man as man, wholly unconscious of the fact that man is everywhere equal to man. It is full of reverence for that mass of incongruities, the British Constitution, which contains more of the character of the institutions of the Middle Age, than any other constitution or form of government to be found in Europe. It bristles from beginning to end with Dukes and Duchesses, Lords and Ladies, and overflows with servility to the great, and with contempt, or what is worse, condescension for the little. The constant and exclusive study of a literature like this cannot fail to be deeply prejudicial to republican simplicity of thought and taste, to create a sort of disgust for republican manners and institutions, and to make us sigh to reproduce, on American soil, the aristocratic manners and institutions of England. Things seen at a distance are always more enchanting than when seen close by. Did we live in England we should spurn her institutions; but seeing them only at a distance and through the idealizing medium of poetry and works of fiction, they appear unto us beautiful and exceedingly desirable. We think it would be a fine thing to be Dukes and Duchesses, Lords and Ladies, to wear titles, ribbons, stars, and coronets, and to be elevated above the vulgar herd. We grow aweary of our democratic institutions, submit to them with an ill grace, and do what in us lies to hinder their free and beneficial working. It does not occur to us that those of us, who sigh to reproduce English institutions, might, were the thing done, possibly be at the foot instead of the summit of the new social hierarchy; nor do we reflect that a nobility is elevated to its height only by making the immense majority of the people serve as its pedestal. It may be pleasant to be one of the nobility, to stand with one's head far above one's fellows; but it is not very pleasant to be the pedestal on which another stands. We wish no brother man to appear tall because his feet stand on our head; and rather than be obliged to run the risk of having some vain, fat, ignorant, proud, titled mortal stand on our head, we choose to forego the pleasure of standing on another man's head.

The corrupting tendency of English literature in this respect, on our young men and young women too, is easy to be seen, and threatens to be disastrous. Patriotism dies out; love for democracy becomes extinct; and our own government, in proportion to its fidelity to American principles, becomes the object of the severest censure, the most uncompromising hostility, or the most withering ridicule. Our own writers cannot arrest the tendency; because a considerable portion of them, formed by the study of English literature, are themselves carried away by it; and because the remainder are too few in number, and their voices, though clear and strong, are lost in the universal din of English voices, which we are

continually importing. In other words, English works reprinted and circulated here are so much more numerous, and owing to the fact that they
can be furnished much cheaper, are so much more extensively circulated
than the works of native authors, that they overpower them, and almost
wholly counteract their influence.

Now in this situation nothing can be more suitable or more succoring
for us, than large importations of French and German literature. France
and Germany are monarchical, it is true, but not aristocratic. Monarchy
has been, in Europe in general, popular rather than aristocratic in its
tendency. The people have in most countries less to dread from the
monarch than from the noble. Monarchy raises one man indeed above, far
above the people, but in doing this, it lessens or neutralizes to some extent
the distinctions which obtain below it. The writings of French or even
German scholars breathe altogether more of a democratic spirit than do
those of the English. Those of the French are altogether more democratic
than the writings of American scholars themselves. Then, again, we have
in this country not much to fear from the monarchical tendency. There is
nothing monarchical in the genius or temper of the American people. We
remember yet the struggles our fathers had with the king, and that we are
the descendants of those who dethroned Mary Stuart, and brought
Charles Stuart to the scaffold. Then we have no powerful families as yet
that could make interest for a throne, no individual influential enough,
universally popular enough, or far enough elevated above his brethren, to
be thought of in connexion with a crown. We have too long been accustomed to govern ourselves, too large a portion of our citizens have taken a
direct share in the affairs of government, and may always hope to take a
direct share in them, to think of abandoning them to any one man. We
can arrive at monarchy in this country only through aristocracy. We do
not apprehend that this will ever be the case. The aristocratic tendency is
the only tendency we have to apprehend serious danger from; but even
this tendency will, we trust, be arrested before it shall have done any
lasting injury to our institutions. The study of French and German literature will arrest this tendency. It will break the dominion of England; and,
without excluding English literature, will furnish us new elements, and a
broader and more democratic basis for our own.

We are also anxious that French and German literature should be
cultivated among us, because it will correct in some measure the faults of
our own democracy. One extreme always begets another. The tendency on
the one hand to adore England, and approach English manners and
institutions, begets on the other hand a tendency to a rabid radicalism,

from which danger may be apprehended, but from which good is not to be looked for. If the wealthy, the cultivated, and literary, as is and has been too much the case, approach England, the democracy of the country becomes to a great degree deprived of the helps of refinement, cultivation, literature, and the conservative element which always goes with them. True democracy has always a conservative element, and is no less wedded to order than to liberty. It unites the two; and is always normal in its proceedings. It is broad enough to take in all Humanity, and free enough to allow all the elements of human nature to develope themselves fully and harmoniously. Now in English literature this is never the case. The element of order and its adherents are separated from the element of liberty and its adherents. The exclusive study of that literature has to a considerable extent produced the same result here. Hence our democracy becomes in some measure partial, exclusive, and able to enlist on its side only at best a small majority of the nation. This is a serious evil, and it is that from which we have more to dread than from anything else whatever. Democracy so long as it is broad and comprehensive, so long as it is true to itself, and to all the elements of human nature, is invincible, and able to go forth "conquering and to conquer."

Now in the master-pieces of French and German literature we shall find the two great elements, of which we have spoken, always united and working in harmony. There is nothing rash, nothing violent, destructive. Progress, the perfectibility of man and society is admitted and contended for, at the same time peaceable and orderly means by which to effect it are pointed out. The tree has its natural growth, and by natural growth attains its height. It is not made higher by being plucked up by the roots, and held up by artificial means. Erudition, science, philosophy, religion, art, refinement, are all combined with the spirit of progress, and made subservient to the elevation of the people. The cultivation of French and German literature must have a similar effect here, and this is what we want, and what, if Mr. Ripley's plan succeeds, we shall have.

This too is the country in which the noble ideas of man and society, which French and German scholars strike out in their speculations, are to be first applied to practice, realized in institutions. There the scholar may study; there the philosopher may investigate man; there the politician may explore the city, and ascertain how the state should be organized; and there they all may deposite the result of their speculations, their researches, their inspirations in books; but, alas, in books only; for to them is wanting the theatre on which to act them out, the practical world in which to realize them. They have old institutions to combat; old prejudices to overcome; old castles and old churches to clear away; an old people to re-youth, before they can proceed to embody their ideas, or to reduce them to practice. More than all this, they want the freedom to do it. Authority is against them, and armed soldiery are ready to repulse them. But here is a virgin soil, an open field, a new people, full of the future, with unbounded faith in ideas, and the most ample freedom. Here, if any where on earth, may the philosopher experiment on human nature, and demonstrate what man has it in him to be when and where he has the freedom and the means to be himself. Let Germany then explore the mines, and bring out the ore, let France smelt it, extract the pure metal, determine its weight and fineness, and we will work it up into vessels of ornament or utility, apply it to the practical purposes of life. . . .

[1838]

When Brownson was invited to address the literary society at Brown University, he chose "American Literature" as his subject. The occasion led him to repeat the assumptions of his Ripley review, but when he turned to the impulse which would drive American letters to greatness, he gave one of the most explicit accounts of impending class struggle to appear in nineteenth-century America.

71 &

The anniversary of a literary society composed of young men, who are prosecuting, or who have just closed their academical studies, can never be without its interest. It is a season of pleasant recollection, and joyful hope. Literature, in the progress of events, has become a power, and one of the mightiest powers of our times; and whatever, therefore, pertains to it, or to those who cultivate it, must have a deep interest for all who have not yet to learn, that their own lot is bound up with that of their kind.

The influence of literature on the destiny of nations, its power to develop the energies of the soul, to purify the taste, exalt the sentiment, enlarge the views, and advance the civilization of mankind, were, perhaps, an appropriate subject to be discussed on an occasion like the one which now calls us together; but I have thought that I should best consult my own powers and your wishes, by choosing a more limited, but I hope not a less interesting subject. I have therefore, selected the hackneyed, but important subject of American Literature. This is a subject which must be uppermost in your thoughts, as scholars and as patriots. Every young man who engages in literary pursuits, doubtless hopes to be able one day to do somewhat to advance the literature of his country, and to exalt her intellectual character in the eyes of the world.

In considering American literature, it will not be my object to point out its various characteristics, or to dwell on what it has already achieved. When the question is between us and foreigners, who reproach us for not having accomplished more for the literature of the world, it may become us to assume as proud an air, and to speak in as lofty tones as we can; but when the question is merely a domestic one, and we are discussing it in our own family circle, it behooves us rather to inquire why our literature has not attained to a larger and healthier growth, and by what means it may become worthy of ourselves and of our country. This inquiry is the subject to which I respectfully invite your attention.

Of American literature as it has been, and even as it now is, not much is to be said flattering to our national vanity. We have produced some works respectable for their practical aims and utility; we have brought forth much which passes for poetry, but there is no great poem of American origin, unless we call Barlow's *Columbiad* such,—our only national epic,—and we could make up but a meagre collection of national songs. Latterly, we have given birth to some tolerable novels, and made a good beginning in history. But, aside from the newspaper press, which we are somewhat prone to underrate, we have produced nothing in the literary way whereof to boast. We have no literature that can begin to compare with the literature of England, the literature of Germany, or that of France.

To what are we to ascribe this? Many are somewhat prone to ascribe it to the fact that we are a young people, and have not lived long enough to create a literature. They may not be wholly wrong in this. In a political sense, and in relation to the long future before us, we are undoubtedly a young people. But there is a sense in which we are an old people. We did not begin in this country as savages, or as barbarians. Our fathers were of a civilized race. They brought with them to these western wilds, the polity, arts, and refinements of civilized life. They could boast one of the richest literatures of the world. Chaucer, Shakspeare, Spenser, Bacon, Milton, were among our ancestors; and the literatures of the Old World have ever been open to us. The Bible and the classics have been in our possession, and these lie at the bottom of all modern literature. I have, therefore, not much confidence in this plea of minority, on which our countrymen are so much disposed to rely. We must seek the cause of the meagreness of our literature elsewhere.

This cause is sometimes looked for in the democratic institutions which we have adopted. We have, it is said, no court, the centre of fashion and elegance, to exalt the imagination, and give laws to taste; no long line of titled nobility, raised far above the people, and presenting us models of excellence. We see, it is said, nothing great among us, no elevated rank to which we may aspire, and therefore can have no lofty ambition; and having no ambition to be great we can produce nothing great. Our minds and deeds of necessity sink down to the level of our condition. This is the tory version of the matter, repeated with sickening frequency in the *Quarterly Review,* and kindred prints in the Old World and the New. But there is nothing in democratic institutions to hinder the expansion of mind, to check the play of fancy and imagination, or to impede free thought and free utterance. It is true that we democrats have little room for the display of that ambition which craves to be raised to the baronet-age, or to be called my Lord; but we have in revenge ample room for the workings of the somewhat loftier ambition to be a man amongst men, and to devote ourselves to the service of our God, our country, or our race. That democratic institutions are not unfavorable to the creation of a free, rich, and living literature, the sacred remains of Athenian literature are amply sufficient to prove.

One of the real causes of the meagreness of our literature is to be looked for, I apprehend, in the fact, that we were for a long time dependent as colonies on England. The condition of colonists, which so long continued, generated a feeling of dependence, a habit of looking to England for direction in nearly all cases, which we have not yet wholly surmounted. Colonists almost invariably regard the mother country as their moral and intellectual superior. It is their native land; their home, to which they look back as exiles, with deep yearning and tender recollection. In it are the objects with which they are most familiar, which are dear to the heart, and around which cluster all the hallowed associations of childhood and youth. They borrow its language, its laws, its customs, fashions, senti-ments, and opinions. Through these the mother country exerts an almost absolute spiritual dominion over the colonies, which may be continued long after events shall have severed the political ties which bind them together.

This is especially true, if the mother country be herself really a noble nation, ranking among the foremost nations of the civilized world, advanced in its literary and scientific culture, and filled with the monu-ments of renowned ancestry. England, we all know, has her faults; her political constitution is a medley of jarring and discordant principles, and her administration is selfish, and rarely moral; but, nevertheless, her people are among the most remarkable recorded in history. They want the sprightliness, the versatility, the clear perception and the keen relish of the beautiful, so characteristic of the ancient Athenians; the warm household feelings, the strong religious faith, original and profound metaphysical thought of the modern Germans; the wit, the delicate taste, the expansive-ness and sociability of their neighbors, the French; but they are brave, enterprising, energetic, practical,—the Romans of modern history, and a no inconsiderable advance on the Romans of antiquity. At the epoch of the colonization of this country, in their political institutions, and social arrangements, in literature and science, they were foremost among the leading nations of Europe. They were to the colonists, and not without some show of truth, to say the least, the first nation of the world.

Possessing this character, and held in this estimation by the colonists, England's dominion over their minds and hearts is nothing wonderful. The loyalty natural to the human heart, and especially to the English heart, which leads us to reverence and obey what we regard as above us, very naturally induced homage to England, and made us receive her word as law. There was little for us to reverence and obey in our wilderness homes. The colonists were few in number, strangers to one another, at best companions in exile. They were equals in rank, and very nearly equals in wealth, and intellectual attainments. All that *they had been accustomed* to regard as superior to themselves, was in the mother country. Where else, then, were they to look for their spiritual sovereign?

The colonists, we know, did in fact regard the mother country with the greatest deference, and with child-like affection. This is seen in the institutions they adopted, the laws they enacted, the usages they perpetuated, and the names they gave to their towns and villages. All these speak of home, of fatherland. Everywhere did they seek to reproduce England, or to erect monuments to her memory. They gloried in calling themselves Englishmen; and whatever was English, was right in their eyes,—unless it conflicted with some immediate interest, or with their interpretation of the Jewish and Christian codes. On these latter points, our fathers showed no want of independence. From England they imported all their articles of luxury, and most of those of use; from England, also, they received their fashions, usages, and most of their sentiments and opinions.

The revolution, which converted the colonies into independent states, and sundered the political ties which bound us to Great Britain, changed but little of all this. After the temporary animosity generated by the struggle for independence had subsided, the affection of the people for England revived in nearly all its former force. England was still the mother country. She was still in our estimation, if not in fact, our moral and intellectual superior. She continued to manufacture our cottons and woollens, our knives and forks, our fashions, our literature, our sentiments and opinions. We regarded her, after the revolution, in all but political matters, as the superior and ruling nation. We wished for her approbation; we sought her sanction for what we had done and were doing; and were anxious that she should own that we had not been naughty children in running away from our mother and setting up for ourselves.

Here, if I mistake not, is a chief cause why we have made no greater advances in literature. With this feeling towards England, we must needs regard her literature as the model of excellence, and anxious to commend ourselves to her grace, we must needs conclude that, in order to do it, we

must write as much like Englishmen as possible. Feeling ourselves inferior, we could have no confidence in our own taste or judgment, and
therefore could not think and speak freely. We could not be ourselves. We
could not trust the workings of our own minds. We were safe only when
we thought as the English thought, wrote as the English wrote, or sang as
the English sang. But how the English thought, wrote, or sang, we could,
at the distance we were placed, and the little intercourse we had with
good English society, know but imperfectly. When, therefore, we attempted to write, we were like those who write in a foreign language,
which they have studied only late in life, and which they have but imperfectly acquired. The energy of mind, due to the subject we proposed to
treat, was wasted in avoiding Americanisms, and in trying to conceal the
place of our birth and education. We sank of necessity into servile imitators, into mere copyists; and in seeking to write as Englishmen, abdi-
cated our power to write as Americans, and as men.

Whoever would attain to excellence in any thing, must repose a
generous confidence in himself. He must feel that he is equal to what he
undertakes. He must proceed calmly, and with a conscious strength, to his
task. If he doubts himself, if he feels that he must make an effort, he
must strain, he will do nothing but betray his weakness. We Americans,
in literary matters, have had no self-confidence. There is no repose in our
literature. There is ever a straining after effect, a labor to be eloquent,
striking, or profound. This proceeds in a great measure from the fact,
that we have found our model of excellence, not in our own minds
and hearts, nor in human nature generally, but in the literature of that
land from which our forefathers came. Instead of studying man, we have
studied English literature; instead of drawing our inspirations from the
universal reason, which glows within and agitates the American heart,
not less than the English heart, we have sought them in the productions
of the English muse. We have written and sung, or at least aimed to write
and sing, for Englishmen, and to gain the applause, or escape the censure
of the English critic. Hence our minds have been crippled, and our literature has been tame and servile.

But so long as we retain the memory of our colonial dependence on
England, we shall not attain to literary excellence. We shall attain to
freedom and originality, and produce works worthy of admiration for
their freshness and power, not till we dare set up for ourselves; till we
come to feel that American human nature is as rich as English human
nature; that the emotions and the forms of speech, natural to an American, are as proper in themselves, as conformable to the laws of universal

human nature, as those natural to an Englishman; and that Boston, New York, or Providence, has as much right to decide authoritatively on matters of taste and composition, as London.

Another cause of the meagreness of our literature, nearly akin to the one just mentioned, if not growing out of it, is to be found in the fact that our literary men have been but slow to accept our democratic institutions, and conform to the order of things which our fathers established. Educated in schools modelled after the English, early accustomed by the literature they study, and the lessons of their professors, to distrust the people, to look upon democratic institutions as unfavorable to the development of genius, and to regard the institutions of their own country as a doubtful experiment, they have failed to imbibe the national spirit, and have therefore been able to fetch but a feeble echo from the national heart. Till quite recently, the literary men of our country have not sympathized with the people, and have had in their hearts no deep and abiding love, as they have had in their minds no clear conceptions of the great doctrine of equal rights, and social equality, to which this nation stands pledged. They may have had a tender concern for the people; they may have been willing to labor to enlighten them; they may even have preferred a republican form of government, but they have not been true democrats in their hearts. There has been a great gulf between them and the American people.

Now nothing is more certain than that the men, who create a national literature, must be filled with the spirit of their nation, be the impersonations of its wishes, hopes, fears, sentiments. The American people are democratic,—I use the word in its etymological and philosophical sense,—and consequently the creators of American literature must be democrats. It is not I that says this; it is truth, it is philosophy, and therefore if you dislike it, blame not me. No man, who studies attentively the American people, can doubt that their souls, however defective their utterance, or crude their notions, are wedded to democracy. No party, not believed to be democratic, can rise in the nation to even a respectable minority; and no measure, believed to be anti-democratic, can stand any chance of success. We may deny this, we may quarrel with it, and declare it altogether wrong; but so it is; and it is only they who conform to it, not from policy, but from the heart, from the real love of democracy, and a full understanding of what it is, that can do much to advance American literature. The fact, that the majority of our literary men have been distrustful of the majority, or opposed to it, is one reason why our literature has not attained to a larger growth, and become more honorable to the country.

Another cause why our literature has continued so meagre, is to be found in the circumstances of our country, which have made no great literary demands, and which have turned our mental energies almost altogether in another direction. Literature is not a nation's first want, any more than reading and writing is the first want of the individual. We are not, properly speaking, as I have said, a young people, but ours is a young country. We received it at a comparatively recent period, fresh from the hands of nature. We have had the primitive forests to clear away, the virgin soil to cultivate, commerce and manufactures to call into existence and encourage, cities and villages to erect, roads, canals, and railways to construct, in a word our whole material interests to provide for, and the field of our future glory to prepare. Here was our first work, and in this work we have shown our creative powers, displayed our skill and energy, and done that whereof it is permitted us to boast. While engaged in this work, we could not turn our attention to the cultivation of a national literature. Moreover, while engaged in this work, while clearing away the forest, planting the rose in the wilderness, and erecting cities and villages where lately prowled the beast of prey, or curled the smoke of the wigwam, literature adequate to our wants was furnished by the mother country, of a better quality, and at a cheaper rate, than we could furnish it for ourselves. Here is, after all, the chief cause of the deficiency of our literature, and the main reason why we have remained so long the literary vassals of England.

The truth is, there has been, as yet, no great demand for literature among us. We have been engaged in no great work for the successful prosecution of which literature was necessary, and the activity of our minds, and the sentiments of our hearts, have found thus far their utterance in deeds rather than in words. This remark, to those who have not reflected, may seem of little importance. It may be thought that literature, like virtue, is independent on time and place, and may spring up wherever it is the will of scholars that it should. But literature is no arbitrary creation. It is dependent on higher laws than those of human enactment. It comes only when it is needed, and comes always in a shape and of a quality, in commercial phrase, to suit the market. No matter what your schools are, or what is the number and excellence of your scholars, you cannot force its growth, or introduce it before its time.

Literature springs up only in those epochs when there is some great work to be performed for the human race, when there are great moral, philosophical, or social problems up for solution, and when all minds and hearts are busy with them. It never amounts to any thing in a nation or in an epoch, where all is settled. China is full of schools and literary men; and what is more, holds literature in the highest honor, and finds her aristocracy in her scholars; yet has China no literature worth naming. In that land of immovability, of routine, where all is prescribed, where all change is prohibited, and every thing must be to-day what it was yesterday, what can literature be but an empty form, or an endless repetition? No new thought is there permitted, no new problem ever comes up for solution, and what can literature find there to do?

If you consult literary history, you will find that there is no literature, ancient or modern, which is not indebted for its existence to some social fermentation, to some social change or revolution, which has brought along a new class of sentiments to be uttered, or raised up new problems to be solved. The men who contribute to its existence or growth are always men affected by the movement spirit. They are dissatisfied with what is. Weary of the present, they look back and yearn for what appears to them the serene past; or they look forward to the future, see in their mind's eye an unrealized good, which they must strive to obtain. In this they do but represent their age. The spirit, the hope, or the regret which agitates them, agitates the mass. It is on this condition that they become popular, and it is on the condition of becoming popular that their works form a part of the literature of their epoch.

This fact will appear evident, if we glance at a few of the more renowned literatures of the world. . . .

But why proceed further in the attempt to establish what perhaps nobody will deny, that literature comes not when it is bidden, but at those epochs when there is work to be done for the human race? In all the instances I have referred to, as well as in the many I have passed over, there were great questions at issue, grave problems up for solution, with which the minds and the hearts of the multitude were busy; and the men who contributed to the literature were also busy with these questions, these problems; felt a deep and thrilling interest in them; were men who saw work to be done, and came forth with what skill and energy were in them to do it.

This rapid survey, which I have taken of a few points in literary history, may teach us that we must not rely on our schools nor on our scholars. If we have not already created a literature, of which we need not be ashamed, it is because we have not had a work for humanity to perform which demanded a literature; and if we are to have a literature, we must have some great work to do which will need it.

The great questions which have agitated Europe since the middle of the last century, have never but partially agitated us; and so far as they have agitated us at all, they were settled by our political revolution. We secured then all that the Old World has as yet contended for. We established then a republican government, which was already established in our convictions and in our habits, and we fancied that we had solved the social problem for ever. The wild commotion of the Old World has scarcely affected us. We have listened to the distant roar of her contending hosts with unmoved hearts and serene brows. We have stood upon the mountain, with our heads bathed in clear sunshine, and beheld the cloud below, seen the lightning flash and heard the thunder roll at our feet, with a tranquil pulse. Had we felt the same agitation that Germany felt, doubtless we should have contributed our share to the literature of the epoch. But in that fearful war we were not enlisted. We had served our campaign and were honorably discharged.

But have we solved the problem for ever—finished the work humanity gave us to do? and is there henceforth nothing for us but to rest from our labors and repose beneath the laurels won by our fathers? As we answer this question, so must we answer the question whether there is to be an American literature. You may demand an American literature, you may give yourselves up to its creation with the generous enthusiasm of youth, and labor for it through life with unflagging zeal; but it shall be in vain, unless your country be called to perform a great and glorious work for the human race, and a work too for the successful accomplishment of which a free, rich, and living literature shall be indispensable. This is the law of Providence, and you cannot withdraw yourselves from its action. Have we then done our work? Is there nothing more for us to do?

Done our work? What mean we? Has the world fulfilled its mission, and is the human race about to be annihilated? One generation cometh and another goeth, but the earth abideth for ever; individuals die, but the race is immortal. When an individual has fulfilled its work it dies; all beings die, when they have nothing more to do, and the human race itself is immortal only on the condition that there is for it an eternal task-work. But we are yet in the infancy of the race; we have but just begun our work; why then talk of its being ended? As well might the infant that has achieved its first step, and ascertained that it can walk without assistance, lie down and say there is nothing more for it to do. Eternity is before us, and the progress of the race is illimitable. Let thought stretch its pinions, soar to the highest point it can reach, and man in his upward career shall rise above it.

But I need not resort to general principles to make out my case.

Whoever has eyes to see or ears to hear, cannot fail to perceive that grave questions, problems of immense magnitude, are coming up among us, and demanding a solution in tones which it is not in man to resist. The Old World is still engaged in the old war between the plebeians and the patricians. The great struggle going on there need not indeed alarm us, for it cannot come here. That struggle has for its object, on the part of the people, not republicanism in the state, nor equal wealth among the members of society, but the abolition of rank, founded on birth. It has never existed with us, and, as I have said, never can; for here birth confers no distinction. The struggle which is coming up here is not between the high-born and the low-born, between the gentlemen and the simplemen; for, thank God, we have learned that all who are born at all are well born. It is to be a struggle between the accumulator of wealth and the simple laborer who actually produces it; briefly, a struggle between man and money. This struggle has not yet fairly commenced in the Old World, but it must come there and ultimately make the tour of the globe.

In the Old World, the interests of labor are, to a great extent, lost in the interests of the rich commoner, and will be, so long as the rich commoner finds an hereditary nobility above him. But here we have no hereditary nobility, no titled rank, no privileges of birth. We have established political equality, declared the lists open to all, and the prize to the swiftest runner. But we have not obtained in practice the equality we have established in theory. There are distinctions amongst us, inequalities, not without a long train of grievous evils, which an increasing party will hold to be compatible neither with the principles of our institutions, nor with the true interests of humanity. The question has already been asked, What are the boasted advantages of a democratic government, if the people under it are to be in point of fact cursed with all the evils of social inequality? What avails it that I am declared equal to my neighbor, when in fact I am regarded by him, and by myself, and by all others, as his social inferior, when he may task my labor almost at will, and fix himself the wages he shall pay me? when, in fact, he may live in ease and luxury without labor, and I, an able-bodied man, and well skilled in all kinds of labor, can by my simple labor but barely keep myself and family from starving? The question has been asked, too, Can a rich man, a man who has accumulated and possesses great wealth, be a good Christian? There are those among us who begin to suspect that Jesus meant something when he said, "It is easier for a camel to go through the eye of a needle, than for a rich man to enter the kingdom of heaven." There are those who ask themselves, when they see the extremes of wealth and poverty which meet us in our cities, bloated luxury and pining want side by side, if this be a Christian order of things, if indeed this order of things is to last for ever. As a Christian, am I not bound to love my fellow-men, even the lowest and most polluted, well enough, if need be, to die for them, as Jesus died on the cross for me? Am I then permitted to avail myself of the labors of others, so as to accumulate an immense estate; am I then permitted to live in luxury, to feast on the rarities of every clime which commerce procures me, while my brother languishes in poverty, while the poor mother at my next door is watching, pale and emaciated, over her starving boy, and the poor sempstress is prostituting herself so as not to die of famine? You will see at once that these are fearful and searching questions, such as cannot be put in a tone of solemn earnest, without shaking society to its centre.

Questions like these are coming up amongst us. We may deny it, may seek to suppress them, or to hush the matter up; but come they will, and come they must. It is not in my power nor in yours to suppress these questions. We may regret as much as we will that they must come, but nothing remains for us but to meet them. The whole matter of wealth and labor, of the means by which wealth is accumulated, of the relations between capitalists and laborers, of wages, which a French nobleman has pronounced "a prolonged slavery," must come up, be discussed and disposed of.* To my view, questions relating to this matter, are the most fearful questions which can be asked, and they seem to me to involve a revolution to which all preceding revolutions were but mere child's play. Questions of equal magnitude have never come up for the discussion of humanity, none which go so deep, or extend so far. It is not for me to say what is to be the issue of this struggle between wealth and labor, and this is neither the place nor the occasion on which to decide the part the philosopher, the Christian, the philanthropist, ought to take. I have not put the questions I have for the purpose of answering them. I merely point you to a war of two great social elements, describe to you its dominant traits, and say, in that war, on one side or the other, we are all to enlist, and do battle as best we may.

In the struggle of these two elements, true American literature will be born. This struggle, which has already commenced, presents the conditions of its birth and its growth. We have now to solve, not the question of political equality, but the problem of social equality. This problem, if I

* Brownson discusses the matter further himself in his remarkable, "The Laboring Classes," *The Boston Quarterly Review* III (July 1840), 358–395. [Ed.]

have not wholly misconceived its magnitude and bearing, will present work for whosoever has a hand, a head, or a heart; and in the effort to finish this work, a literature will be born before which all the literatures now extant may, perhaps, shrink into insignificance.

I confess, Brothers, that notwithstanding the fearful nature of the social contest I see coming on, I am not alarmed. I even behold it with the joy with which the war-horse snuffs the battle from afar. I behold it, and feel that I have not been born too early, nor too late; that there is work for me also, if I have but the skill and the courage to undertake it. And as to the result, I apprehend nothing. I have faith in principle; I have faith in humanity; above all, I have faith in God. The right side in the long run always comes up, and the cause is ultimately victorious which ought to be victorious. Truth is never vanquished; right cannot be defeated; nor humanity successfully betrayed. Onward through the ages humanity pursues its course. Kings, castes, nobles may attempt to block up its path, but it pushes aside their feeble barriers, sweeps away their bastilles, and passes on unobstructed through the marshalled ranks of their armed soldiery.

Whoso would contribute to American literature, ought indeed to reflect deeply on the nature and wants of his own soul; ought to store his mind with the riches of ancient and modern literature and science; but he must engage in this great work, live and labor with no thought of creating a literature, but give himself up wholly to the work of solving some great problem, or of making some great moral, religious, philosophical, or social principle prevail. If in his efforts to make what he believes the right cause triumphant, he utter a true word, humanity shall catch it up and echo it through eternity. He must be an active, living man, living for his race and striving to do its work. The discipline he needs is that which fits him to sympathize with humanity, and strengthens him to do battle in her cause. The American poet must sing for the human race; draw his inspiration, not from Castaly, or Helicon, but from the human heart; and the orator must not study to turn and polish his periods, but to kindle up his countrymen, to compel them to arm and march against the enemies of freedom, truth, justice, and love.

Rest easy, Brothers, as to literature. Regard literature always as a means, never as an end. Early seek out a noble end to be gained; early wed yourselves to great principles; early convince yourselves that you live for man, for truth, for God, and you shall speak, write, or sing words that shall not die, but which shall be life, and life-giving.

What will be the destiny of American literature, I know not, and pretend not to foretell. But this much you will permit me to say in conclusion, that God in his providence has given the American people a great problem to work out. He has given it us in charge to prove what man may be, when and where he has free and full scope to act out the almightiness that slumbers within him. Here, for the first time since history began, man has obtained an open field and fair play. Everywhere else, up to the present moment, he has been borne down by kings, priests, and nobles; the loftier aspirations of his nature have been suppressed, and the fire of his genius smothered, by unhallowed tyranny. Long, long ages has he struggled under every disadvantage; and under every disadvantage, though oft defeated, he has never despaired, or bated a jot of heart or hope, but always rallied himself anew with fresh courage and strength to the combat. Here, at length, he has gained the vantage ground. No longer must he struggle for very existence; no longer must he make a wall of his dead body to protect his wife and little ones. His domestic hearth is sacred, his fields are safe from the invader, and his flocks and herds may graze unmolested. He can now choose his ground. He may now abandon the attitude of defence and assume that of attack. He has no longer to defend his right to free thought and free speech, to the possession and use of himself. Here, thank God, we have no apologies to offer for speaking out for man, for truth, for justice, for freedom, for equality. We carry the war into the enemy's country. We summon the oppressor to judgment; the adherents to arbitrary governments and heavy abuses to stand forth and show cause, if they can, why sentence shall not be pronounced against them.

Such is the position we now occupy, such the progress we have made in working out the problem committed to us. Shall we stop here? I do not believe we shall, I do not believe that we shall prove false to our trust, or slight our work. I seem to myself to see many proofs around me, that we are beginning to comprehend more fully our mission, and to prepare ourselves to engage in earnest for its execution. I see this in the wide and deep agitation of the public mind; I see it in the new parties and associations which every day is forming; I see it in the weighty problems, moral, religious, social, political, economical, which both the learned and the unlearned are discussing; I feel it in the new spirit which has of late been breathed into American publications; and I recognize it in the increasing depth and earnestness of American writers. No; I cannot be mistaken. America will not be false to her mission. She will be true to that cause which landed our fathers on Plymouth Rock, which sustained the free mind and warm heart of Roger Williams, in which Warren fell, for which Washington fought, to which Jefferson and Franklin gave their lives.

In prosecuting the work committed to us, there will arise poets, philosophers, theologians, politicians, whose wide and deep experience will find utterance in a living literature. When they will arise, how soon or how late, I know not, ask not. And, Brothers, do not ye ask. But seek ye out the work God has given your country to perform for the human race; woo it as a bride; wed yourselves to it for better or for worse; be true to it in good report and in evil, in life and in death; and though you may not write books, compose poems, or construct theories, your lives shall be books, poems, theories, which will not die, but live,—live for ever in the memory of your race, and, what is better, in the ever improving condition of all coming generations.

[1839]

⚐ *The noisiest proponents of American literary nationalism be-*
longed to the Young America group of New York. When the Boston
Morning Post *took the publication of Simms's* Views and Reviews
as an occasion for ridiculing Cornelius Mathews, the most outspoken
and persistent nationalist of them all, the stolid Knickerbocker
supported the attack with evident relish.

72 ⚐

. . . The *'Boston Morning Post,'* one of the liveliest and pleasantest
journals of the country, thus 'hits the nail on the head' in a notice of Mr.
SIMMS' pen-and-ink *'Views and Reviews of American Literature:* 'If we
understand Mr. SIMMS and his colleagues,' ('Puffer-Hopkins'-MATHEWS
and the rest), it is necessary that our writers should choose American subjects, in order that their productions, however good, should constitute a
real 'American literature;' and that they should fill their books with a
certain mysterious 'American spirit,' very difficult to describe and exceedingly hard to imagine. Hence SHAKSPEARE's 'Romeo and Juliet' is scarcely
English literature, because its subject and its spirit are Italian. At least,
this is all we can make of the argument of Mr. SIMMS and his brethren. It
is a pity that some one of these gentlemen should not *produce a work*
which would serve to show what this singular 'American literature' really
is. One look at such a *model* would be more convincing than the perusal
of scores of essays.' It was thought for some time that we could have no
'American literature' unless our writers infused a large proportion of
Indian character into all their works; so that we came to have aboriginal
ingredients in all our indigenous intellectual food; Indian bread, Indian
hoe-cake, Indian Johnny-cake, Indian Hasty-pudding, (*very* hasty, much
of it,) and Indian baked-pudding, by 'half-baked' authorlings, until the
public became utterly surfeited with these *'made-dishes.'* . . .

[1847]

The many essays of Cornelius Mathews deal more with the need for a national literature than with the principles which will support it, but it is only fitting that some sample of his work appear here. The anonymity of this selection enables the supernationalist to quote himself; in the sequel he was to use several pages to defend and praise his own novels and poems and to scorn before the fact any effort to label him an American Dickens.

73

"Behold, now, this vast city: a city of refuge, the mansion-house of liberty, encompassed and surrounded with God's protection; the shop of war hath not there more anvils and hammers waking, to fashion out the plates and instruments of armed justice in defence of beleaguered truth, than there be pens and heads there sitting by their studious lamps, musing, searching, revolving new notions and ideas, wherewith to present, as with their homage and their fealty, the approaching reformation; others, as fast reading, trying all things, assenting to the force of reason and convincement. What could a man require more—from a nation so pliant and so prone to seek after knowledge? What wants there to such a towardly and pregnant soil, but wise and faithful laborers, to make a knowing people, a nation of prophets, of sages, and of worthies?"— MILTON'S AREOPAGITICA.

We are a nation of readers, thirty millions strong; but what are our books, and who are our writers?

There are many persons who have not yet tasted of death, who were living when Edmund Burke, on the floor of the British Parliament, described America as having been, within the life-time of the then Lord Bathurst, "a little speck, scarce visible in the mass of the national interest; a small seminal principle, rather than a formed body." That infant people, then "but in the gristle, and not yet hardened into the bone of manhood,"—struggling with the vicissitudes of life in a new country, and subduing the wilderness and the savage tribes who peopled it,—thirteen feeble colonies, "growing by the neglect of their parent state,—have, within the threescore years and ten which have since elapsed, achieved their National Independence, through the fiery ordeal of a long and bloody war,—erected new institutions of government, a new civil polity and social condition,—become the first political power in the Western hemisphere, and the second commercial power in the world,—and is beginning to exert an influence upon human affairs, which, if wisely directed, seems likely to change the destinies of our race, through all future time, and over the entire surface of the globe. Our Republic occupies a land, suited to the grand part which seems to be alloted to it on the great stage of time. Its shores washed by two oceans,—its interior penetrated by noble rivers, and dotted over with vast lakes and inland seas,—its mountains rich with the most useful and valuable minerals,—its fertile soil teeming with all the productions of the temperate zone, and thickly studded with broad prairies and nobly-timbered forests,—a domain equal in extent to the whole of Southern and Western Europe, adequate to the government of fifty independent states, and the maintenance of the hundreds of millions, who are advancing from the future to occupy it,—present elements of growth, of strength, and of greatness, which give assurance of the most splendid career to be traced in the annals of the human race.

The writer of the article "America," in the ENCYCLOPAEDIA BRITANNICA, (a foreign writer, and a foreign work of high authority,) after stating the then (in 1830) population of the United States, and the ratio of its increase to be such as to double itself every twenty-five years; and, after making a proper allowance for the diminished ratio of increase after it has reached a specified limit, makes an estimate of the population of the country at several remote periods of time. In 1880, he computes it at eighty-four millions; in 1905, at one hundred and sixty-eight millions; in 1966, at six hundred and seventy-two millions; in 2002, at one billion three hundred and forty-four millions; and in 2030, at two billions six hundred and eighty-eight millions; thus, in less than two centuries,—less than the period which has elapsed since the weary feet of the Pilgrims first pressed the rock at Plymouth,—the population of the United States will be about three times as great as the whole population now on the face of the globe. And the same writer, in the same authoritative work, remarking, that "History shows that wealth, power, science, and literature, all follow in the train of numbers, general intelligence and freedom," expresses the opinion, that "The same causes which transferred the sceptre of civilization from the banks of the Euphrates and the Nile to Western Europe, must, in the course of no long period, carry it from the latter to the plains of the Mississippi and the Amazon."

Although based on sober calculation, and, apparently, a strict induction from well-ascertained data, these stupendous results almost exceed our power of belief. As, in contemplating the immense distances and vast magnitude of the planets, the almost inconceivable speed and complexity, yet harmony, of their motions, and the brilliancy of the myriad lights, which, from their high and distant orbs, flame upon us out of our cold, northern, midnight sky, our minds are overpowered by the greatness of the works of the All-Creating hand,—so these visions of the rising glory of our country overwhelm us with their brightness. Cold, indeed, must be the heart, which does not feel a quickened throb; sluggish the blood, which does not course with a fiercer current through the veins; dead the faith, which does not rise into rapture, in contemplating the destiny which seems to await the land of our birth, and in which those who bear our name and inherit our blood are to share, after we have done our appointed work, and passed away.

And yet this great country that is—this greater country that is to be; this nation of churches and school-houses, as well as canals and railroads—"pliant and prone to seek after knowledge," has no native literature, but is, in letters, in a state of colonial and provincial dependency upon the old world.

It is not difficult to point out the causes which have retarded the literary growth of this country. The settlers of a new country have neither the leisure to enjoy, nor the wealth to procure the means of enjoying the delights of literature. An inhospitable climate, a rude wilderness, savage enemies, privation and sickness, all had to be borne or overcome by the founders of the American States. And as if these were not sufficient to crush those who here planted the seeds of our civilization and freedom, the despotic hand of the parent government was laid heavily upon them. They gave what time they could to religious worship, to the instruction of the young, in the necessary rudiments of knowledge—to brief household endearments; to the government and order of the settlements; to necessary repose, and the rest was painfully devoted to toil. The forest had to be cleared, the crop sown and harvested—the hut, the dwelling, and the log-fort reared and defended from the fierce onslaught of savage foes, and the despotic authority of England to be watched and resisted. It can excite no surprise that letters were not cultivated under such adverse circumstances. Again, the loyalty of the colonists to the parent government operated in the same direction. They resisted exaction and oppression as infractions of the British Constitution, but they loved their country, and submitted cheerfully to the exercise of legitimate authority over themselves and their property. They were Englishmen, and English literature was the common heritage of Englishmen wherever their lot might be cast. Speaking the English tongue, deeply imbued with English tastes and prejudices, reared in the admiration of English writers, and acknowledging nothing as superior to English models, nothing is more natural than that whatever was attempted in composition in this country, should be a close imitation of, and bear a marked resemblance to, the literature of the old country.

And when the colonies finally asserted their independence, it was only against the political power of the mother-country. They retained her language, her letters, and the fame of her great writers, as their birth-right as Englishmen, or the descendants of Englishmen; their young career in letters was commenced under all the influences of old habits, old associations, and old prejudices in favor of English models, and the mind of the country has not yet cast off this old literary domination.

This intellectual servitude produced the same effects upon the writings of this country, which was produced upon the literature of Germany by the despotic influence of the writers of France over those of Germany. Abounding in institutions of learning, in profound scholars, in all the elements of a national literature, Germany had no rank in letters, and was merely a French province. Her writers servilely imitated the writers of France, and, as is usually the case with mere imitators, imitated the worst of the French writers, and the worst parts of their worst writings. It was not till Goethe came, that Germany was delivered from this degrading intellectual bondage. Sir James Mackintosh, in his review of Madame De Stael's "De l'Allemagne," in the Edinburgh Review, says, that

> "Till the middle of the eighteenth cenutry, Germany was, in one important respect, singular among the great nations of Christendom. She had attained a high rank in Europe by discoveries and inventions, by science, by abstract speculation as well as positive knowledge, by the genius of the art of war, and above all, by the theological revolution, which unfettered the understanding in one part of Europe, and loosened its chains in the other; but she was without a national literature. The country of Guttenberg, of Copernicus, of Luther, of Kepler, and of Leibnitz, had no writer in her own language whose name was known in the neighboring nations. German captains and statesmen, philosophers and scholars, were celebrated, but German writers were unknown. Germany had, therefore, no exclusive mental possession; for poetry and eloquence may, and in some measure *must be, national*. A great revolution, however, at length began, which in the course of half a century terminated in bestowing on Germany a literature, perhaps *the most characteristic possessed by any European nation*. It had the important peculiarity of being the first which had its birth in an enlightened age."

Overmastered by the literature of England, we have consented to remain in a state of pupilage, instead of aspiring to be masters in the vocation of letters. "The parents have eaten sour grapes, and the children's teeth are set on edge." We have gone on from generation to generation, imitating old English authors, and working by old critical rules. "The imitation of our own antiquities," says Sir James Mackintosh, "may be as artificial as the copy of a foreign literature." In every department of literary composition, we have come to consider that which is but one mode of writing to be *the* mode, and the only permissible one. Instead of regarding the drama as comprehending an unlimited range of passion and of modes of manifestation, Shakspeare's plays are received by us as bounding the horizon of dramatic composition. So Milton is accepted as the only standard of sublimity, and Addison as the perfect measure of ease and grace. We are to make the metals, torn from the virgin soil of a new country, flow into these old moulds, and harden into these antique forms. We must take these shapes, or not be at all.

If Shakspeare or Milton had grown up in such a state of vassalage to a previous age, or to old writers, the boon of the Paradise Lost, of Lear, Macbeth and Hamlet, had been denied to the world. We shall emulate these examples of intellectual power and literary success in vain, unless we also emulate that intellectual intrepidity which dares to search for and walk in new paths, and which enabled Milton and Shakspeare to reach the highest eminences of English literature.

Something will be gained for the cause of an indigenous literature by a clear development of the idea and the necessity of nationality. First and foremost, nationality involves the idea of home writers. Secondly, the choice of a due proportion of home themes, affording opportunity for descriptions of our scenery, for the illustration of passing events, and the preservation of what tradition has rescued from the past, and for the exhibition of the manners of the people, and the circumstances which give form and pressure to the time and the spirit of the country; and all these penetrated and vivified by an intense and enlightened patriotism. The literature of a country should, as from a faithful mirror, reflect the physical, moral and intellectual aspects of the nation. Other nations and later ages should look to the writers of the land for the lineaments of its people, and to trace the influence of institutions, of civil and religious polity, upon the condition, the manners and the happiness of individuals, and upon the strength, the power and the permanency of the state. The Scriptures represent man as speaking "out of the abundance of the heart." The literature of a people should be its written thought, uttered "out of the abundance of its heart," and exhibiting its interior as well as exterior life. Madame De Stael's great work on the influence of literature upon society, was written, says that Aristarchus of modern criticism, Jeffrey, "to show that all the peculiarities in the literature of different ages and countries may be explained by a reference to the condition of society, and the political and religious institutions of each; and at the same time to point out in what way the progress of letters has, in its turn, modified and affected the government and religion of those nations among whom they have flourished." In the execution of her task, that distinguished authoress took a survey of literature and philosophy from Homer to the tenth year of the French revolution, and after characterising the literature of Greece and of Rome, and briefly sketching the dark ages, "she enters upon a more detailed examination of the peculiarities of all the different aspects of national taste and genius that characterise the literature of Italy, Spain, England, Germany and France, entering, as to each, into a pretty minute exposition of its general merits and defects; and not only of the circumstances in the situation of the country that have produced those characteristics, but even of the authors and productions in which they are chiefly exemplified." And as the result of her profound and elaborate investigation, she concludes, that the form of government, the laws, the private manners and pursuits, and the religion of a people, are reflected by, and characterize their literature; and that these circumstances, in their turn, react upon the form of the government, the spirit of the laws, and the temper and condition of the people.

What cultivated mind fails to distinguish between the literature of Greece and that of Rome; of Italy and that of Spain; of Germany and that of France and England? Undoubtedly, there are many things common to them all; but these are strongly marked and characteristic differences, which constitute the individuality of each. The dissimilarity of Homer and Virgil; of Camoens, Dante, and Milton; of Goethe, Racine, and Shakspeare, is not more sharply cut and strongly defined, than that between the general literature of the countries to which they respectively belonged. Referring to Madame De Stael's brilliant observations on the Greek Drama, and the prodigious effects produced by the representation of the Greek Tragedies, Jeffrey says: "A great part of the effect of these representations must have depended on *the exclusive nationality of their subjects, and the extreme nationality of their auditors."* And the same eminent critic expresses the opinion, that Shakspeare could not have written his great dramas,—could not have been Shakspeare,—if he had been born in any other country than England. Indeed, Shakspeare, notwithstanding his infinite variety, and those "touches of nature which make the whole world kin," is a thorough Briton, and his writings are surcharged with the spirit of nationality. Could Milton have written the Iliad, or Homer the Paradise Lost? Could Goethe have wrought the

Heart of Mid-Lothian, or Scott the Tragedy of Faust? Are not those works instinct with the characteristics of the country and age in which they were produced? What but a heroic age could have produced a Homer? What but Puritanical times a Milton? What age, but an age of unbelief; what country, except one given over for the time to irreligious opinions and social profligacy, could have produced the character of Mephistophiles? What Lord Bacon, in his Advancement of Learning, says of laws, is equally true, in its spirit, of literature: "For there are," says Bacon, "in nature certain fountains of justice, whence all civil laws are derived, but as streams; and like as waters do take tinctures and tastes from the soils through which they run, so do civil laws vary according to the regions and governments where they are planted, though they proceed from the same fountains." And Montesquieu,—who of all writers had most profoundly studied the causes which influence national character, and the manifestation of that character in the laws and institutions of a country,—in his celebrated work on the Spirit of Laws, has an analogous passage, which forcibly illustrates the view we are inculcating:

"Law in general," says he, (in Book I. chap. 3,) "is human reason, inasmuch as it governs all the inhabitants of the earth; the political and civil laws of each nation ought to be the only particular cases in which this human reason is applied. They should be adapted in such a manner to the people for whom they are framed, *as to render it very unlikely for those of one nation to be proper for another.* * * * * They should be adapted to the climate of each country, to the quality of the soil, to its situation and extent, to the manner of living of the natives, whether husbandmen, huntsmen, or shepherds; they should have a relation to the degree of liberty which the constitution will bear; to the religion of the inhabitants; to their inclinations, riches, numbers, commerce, manners, customs. These relations form what I call the Spirit of laws."

Do not these relations just as essentially enter into, and characterize, the spirit of a national literature?

It will thus be seen that our view of nationality is conceived in no narrow spirit. Illiberality and exclusiveness have no part in our creed. We would burn no books, banish no authors, shut our hearts against no appeal which speaks to them in the voice of nature. We would not narrow, but enlarge, the horizon of letters; we would not restrict the empire of thought, but annex our noble domain to it. A writer in the last Oct. number of the North American Review, says, that "an intense national self-consciousness, though the shallow may name it patriotism, is the worst foe to the true and generous unfolding of national genius." Against the opinion of this learned Theban, we set the high authorities we have already cited; we set the fact, that Greece, Rome and England, the nations which have possessed the most intense self-consciousness, whose writers have been most penetrated by the sense of nationality, and with whose people patriotism has risen almost into a religious senti-ment,—have excelled all the other states of the world in their literature, no less than in their physical prowess. And this intense nationality, instead of narrowing the domain of their great writers, has made their chief works the peerless gifts and priceless treasures of the whole intellectual world. We would ask, especially, under what reigns was the national spirit of England, pervading alike the cot, the castle, and the palace, raised to a loftier tone, than during the reign of Elizabeth, and the period of the Commonwealth, under Cromwell,—a period to which the noblest names of English literature, Bacon, Shakspeare, and Milton, belong? We incline to the opinion that Homer must have possessed a burning, intense national self-consciousness; and that Burns was not less deficient in the same sentiment. And Scott, fired with the generous ardor of patriotism, ("an intense national self-consciousness,") rises into Homeric strains, in his "Lay of the Last Minstrel:"

> "Breathes there a man, with soul so dead,
> Who never to himself hath said,
> This is my own, my native land!
> Whose heart hath ne'er within him burned,
> As home his foosteps he hath turn'd
> From wandering on a foreign strand?
> If such there breathe, go, mark him well;
> For him no minstrel raptures swell;
> High though his titles, proud his name,
> Boundless his wealth, as wish can claim—
> Despite those titles, power and pelf,
> The wretch, concentrated all in self,
> Living, shall forfeit all renown,
> And doubly dying, shall go down
> To the vile dust from whence he sprung,
> Unwept, unhonored, and unsung."

The writer of the article on "Scotch Nationality," in the last number of the North British Review, states, that on lately passing through the Liddisdale district, where Scott collected many of the materials for his Border Minstrelsy, he was assured,

"That the old border traditions of Liddisdale are rapidly disappearing before the romantic fictions of Scott himself; and the glens and streams formerly remembered for the scene of some actual moss-trooping foray, are now associated with the 'Lay of the Last Minstrel,' or the adventures of Dandie Dinmount and Meg Merrilies. All who have visited Loch Katrine,—and who has not? know that it is the same there, and that the boatmen on the lake, instead of chanting a Highland legend, show you the scene of the stag hunt—the place where died the 'gallant grey,' and the path by which Fitz James climbed into sight of the lake; while the beautiful islet that once rejoiced in a hard Gaelic name, is now known only as 'Ellen's Isle.' These are the witcheries of genius, but it is a genius *national in its essence, and heightening and spreading its nationality;* it comprehends all classes; it makes itself felt by the most unimpressible; it affords a common ground for the most worldly and the most imaginative—for the utilitarian politician, and the poet in his finest frenzy. Harry Dundas and Robert Burns might meet there, and feel for once alike."

These memorials which the mighty "Wizard of the North" has left of himself in highland and lowland, and in the hearts of the highest no less than of the humblest of Scotchmen, are prouder monuments of his genius than that which art or the pride of his countrymen have reared to his memory in the metropolis of the land which gave him birth, and which enjoys an immortality in his world-wide renown.

Schlegel, in his Lectures on the History of Literature, says of Shakspeare,

"The feeling by which he seems to have been most connected with ordinary men, is that of nationality. He has represented the heroic and glorious period of English history, during the conquests in France, in a series of dramatic pieces, which possess all the simplicity and liveliness of the ancient chronicles, but approach in their ruling spirit of patriotism and glory to the most dignified and effected productions of the epic muse."

And the same eminent critic in another place says, that *"a single work, such as the Cid, is of more real value to a nation, than a whole library of books, however abounding in wit or intellect, which are destitute of the spirit of nationality."*

Our apology for thus accumulating authorities in support of a proposition which is nearly or quite self-evident, is that it has been denied in a quarter of respectability. We find a warrant for its truth in every drop of blood which bounds through our veins; in every pulsation of life that throbs at our heart; in every glimpse of the sky which beams upon our native land. Nationality in literature is only one of the many forms of patriotism. The instinct which prompts the eagle to shelter its young on the high cliffs, or the lions to guard their whelps in the wide forest, or human kind to love and cherish their offspring, is not more universal, and is scarcely more powerful, than the sentiment of love for country, and pride in whatever enhances her greatness or perpetuates her renown. The "spot where we were born"—where the ashes of our progenitors repose, and where our ashes and those of our offspring to the remotest posterity will mingle with the ashes of the forefathers; earth, river and skies; institutions of government and civil polity; neighborhood, kindred, household ties and household joys; the desire of honorable station and name, and of a worthy posterity; victorious fields, great works of art, and proud achievements in letters—all enter into the form a part of the sentiment of patriotism. More than towering battlements, more than serried ranks of steel, more than the most destructive enginery of war, does this sentiment of love for, and pride in country—an intense sense of nationality—guard the soil and preserve the sacred independence of nations.

The North American reviewer before referred to, says, that "the advocates of nationality seem to think that American authors ought to limit themselves to American subjects, and hear none but American criticism." This is erroneous. They have nowhere intimated such an opinion. We say that Shakspeare, Milton, Dante, Goethe and Racine, were all writers who wrote in a truly national spirit, and yet they did not limit themselves to subjects belonging exclusively to their own country or times. As we are men, whatever is common to humanity, falls fairly within the range of the American author; but as we are Americans, whatever is peculiar to our country and characteristic of our countrymen, is especially deserving of his regard. Is there any lack of home themes that our authors should lack home thoughts? Is there not the same variety in the play of human passions in the new world as in the old—in the present as in the past ages—under free as under despotic institutions? We would set no limits to the subjects on which our authors should write. We would leave to them the whole range of nature and humanity. We would wish them to strike every key in the grand scale of human passion. But we would have them true to their country. If there is anything peculiar in our institutions and condition, we would have some native bard to sing, some native historian to record it. We would have those who are born upon our soil; who have faith in republican governments; who cherish noble hopes and aspirations for our country; whose hearts beat in unison with our countrymen, to manifest their faith, their hopes, their sympathies, in some suitable manner. What we complain of is, the unnational spirit of our writers; that they slavishly adhere to old and foreign models; that alike in their subjects, and in their method of handling them, they are British, or German, or something else than American. We are not ungrateful for what some of our writers have done; but we ask, if the American people were suddenly destroyed by some great convulsion of nature, what fitting memorial of our national existence would be left, to instruct and delight, centuries hence, the nations which are yet in the womb of time?

The American writer who seems most deeply to have felt the want of, and who has most ably and earnestly, as well as earliest, insisted upon, nationality in our literature, is Mr. Cornelius Mathews. In an address before one of the Literary Societies of the New-York University, on "Home Writers, Home Writings, and Home Criticism," he thus alludes to some of the characteristics of a literature suited to the wants of the country:

> "I, therefore, in behalf of this young America of ours, insist on nation-ality and true Americanism in the books this country furnishes to itself and to the world; nationality in its purest, highest, broadest sense. Not such as is declaimed in taverns, ranted off in Congress, or made the occa-sion of boasting and self-laudation on public anniversaries. It need not (though it may) speak of the Revolution, nor Washington, nor the Dec-laration of Independence, nor Plymouth Rock, nor Bunker Hill, nor Bunker Hill Monument. And yet it may be instinct with the life of the country, full of a hearty, spontaneous, genuine home feeling; relishing of the soil and of the spirit of the people. * * * The writings of a great country should sound of the great voices of nature, of which she is full. The march of a great people in literature should be majestic and assured as the action of their institutions is calm and secure."

It poorly comports with our lofty assertion of national superiority, or with even an ordinary and just sense of self-respect, to be dependent for the intellectual aliment of the people, for those things which most adorn and ennoble a nation, and which are the highest boast and pride of civilized states, upon foreign writers, who write upon impulses not im-parted by us, who primarily, if not exclusively, aim to please a different reading community, to whose standards of opinion, feeling and taste, they subject their productions, and who often, in obedience to the influences which surround them, write in a spirit not only alien, but positively hostile to our people, our institutions and national character.

Having thus attempted to develope the idea of nationality, we shall, in another number, state some of the higher uses of a national literature, and point out the American writers and writings most deeply imbued with a national spirit.

[1847]

≥ *In the following excerpt from* Kavanagh, *Longfellow—as Mr. Churchill—takes his turn in having fun at the expense of Mathews (Mr. Hathaway) and his extreme nationalism. (Hathaway's magazine is to be named* The Niagara, *but it never appears.)*

74 ½

. . . One evening, as he was sitting down to begin, for at least the hundredth time, the great Romance,—subject of so many resolves and so much remorse, so often determined upon but never begun,—a loud knock at the street-door, which stood wide open, announced a visitor. Unluckily, the study-door was likewise open; and consequently, being in full view, he found it impossible to refuse himself; nor, in fact, would he have done so, had all the doors been shut and bolted,—the art of refusing one's self being at that time but imperfectly understood in Fairmeadow. Accordingly, the visitor was shown in.

He announced himself as Mr. Hathaway. Passing through the village, he could not deny himself the pleasure of calling on Mr. Churchill, whom he knew by his writings in the periodicals, though not personally. He wished, moreover, to secure the coöperation of one, already so favorably known to the literary world, in a new Magazine he was about to establish, in order to raise the character of American literature, which, in his opinion, the existing reviews and magazines had entirely failed to accomplish. A daily increasing want of something better was felt by the public, and the time had come for the establishment of such a periodical as he proposed. After explaining, in rather a florid and exuberant manner, his plan and prospects, he entered more at large into the subject of American literature, which it was his design to foster and patronize.

"I think, Mr. Churchill," said he, "that we want a national literature commensurate with our mountains and rivers,—commensurate with Niagara, and the Alleghanies, and the Great Lakes!"

"Oh!"

"We want a national epic that shall correspond to the size of the country; that shall be to all other epics what Banvard's Panorama of the Mississippi is to all other paintings,—the largest in the world!"

"Ah!"

"We want a national drama in which scope enough shall be given to our gigantic ideas, and to the unparalleled activity and progress of our people!"

"Of course."

"In a word, we want a national literature altogether shaggy and unshorn, that shall shake the earth, like a herd of buffaloes thundering over the prairies!"

"Precisely," interrupted Mr. Churchill; "but excuse me!—are you not confounding things that have no analogy? Great has a very different meaning when applied to a river, and when applied to a literature. Large and shallow may perhaps be applied to both. Literature is rather an image of the spiritual world, than of the physical, is it not?—of the internal, rather than the external. Mountains, lakes, and rivers are, after all, only its scenery and decorations, not its substance and essence. A man will not necessarily be a great poet because he lives near a great mountain. Nor, being a poet, will he necessarily write better poems than another, because he lives nearer Niagara."

"But, Mr. Churchill, you do not certainly mean to deny the influence of scenery on the mind?"

"No, only to deny that it can create genius. At best, it can only develop it. Switzerland has produced no extraordinary poet; nor, as far as I know, have the Andes, or the Himalaya mountains, or the Mountains of the Moon in Africa."

"But, at all events," urged Mr. Hathaway, "let us have our literature national. If it is not national, it is nothing."

"On the contrary, it may be a great deal. Nationality is a good thing to a certain extent, but universality is better. All that is best in the great poets of all countries is not what is national in them, but what is universal. Their roots are in their native soil; but their branches wave in the unpatriotic air, that speaks the same language unto all men, and their leaves shine with the illimitable light that pervades all lands. Let us throw all the windows open; let us admit the light and air on all sides; that we may look towards the four corners of the heavens, and not always in the same direction."

"But you admit nationality to be a good thing?"

"Yes, if not carried too far; still, I confess, it rather limits one's views of truth. I prefer what is natural. Mere nationality is often ridiculous. Every one smiles when he hears the Icelandic proverb, 'Iceland is the best land the sun shines upon.' Let us be natural, and we shall be national enough. Besides, our literature can be strictly national only so far as our character and modes of thought differ from those of other nations. Now, as we are very like the English,—are, in fact, English under a different sky,—I do not see how our literature can be very different from theirs. Westward from hand to hand we pass the lighted torch, but it was lighted at the old domestic fireside of England."

"Then you think our literature is never to be anything but an imitation of the English?"

"Not at all. It is not an imitation, but, as some one has said, a continuation."

"It seems to me that you take a very narrow view of the subject."

"On the contrary, a very broad one. No literature is complete until the language in which it is written is dead. We may well be proud of our task and of our position. Let us see if we can build in any way worthy of our forefathers."

"But I insist upon originality."

"Yes; but without spasms and convulsions. Authors must not, like Chinese soldiers, expect to win victories by turning somersets in the air."

"Well, really, the prospect from your point of view is not very brilliant. Pray, what do you think of our national literature?"

"Simply, that a national literature is not the growth of a day. Centuries must contribute their dew and sunshine to it. Our own is growing slowly but surely, striking its roots downward, and its branches upward, as is natural; and I do not wish, for the sake of what some people call originality, to invert it, and try to make it grow with its roots in the air. And as for having it so savage and wild as you want it, I have only to say, that all literature, as well as all art, is the result of culture and intellectual refinement."

"Ah! we do not want art and refinement; we want genius,—untutored, wild, original, free."

"But, if this genius is to find any expression, it must employ art, for art is the external expression of our thoughts. Many have genius, but, wanting art, are forever dumb. The two must go together to form the great poet, painter, or sculptor."

"In that sense, very well."

"I was about to say also that I thought our literature would finally not be wanting in a kind of universality. As the blood of all nations is mingling with our own, so will their thoughts and feelings finally mingle in our literature. We shall draw from the Germans, tenderness; from the Spaniards, passion; from the French, vivacity,—to mingle more and more with our English solid sense. And this will give us universality, so much to be desired."

"If that is your way of thinking," interrupted the visitor, "you will like the work I am now engaged upon."

"What is it?"

"A great national drama, the scene of which is laid in New Mexico. It is entitled Don Serafin, or the Marquis of the Seven Churches. The principal characters are Don Serafin, an old Spanish hidalgo, his daughter Deseada, and Fra Serapion, the Curate. The play opens with Fra Serapion at breakfast; on the table a game-cock, tied by the leg, sharing his master's meal. Then follows a scene at the cockpit, where the Marquis stakes the remnant of his fortune—his herds and hacienda—on a favorite cock, and loses."

"But what do you know about cock-fighting?" demanded, rather than asked, the astonished and half-laughing schoolmaster.

"I am not very well informed on that subject, and I was going to ask you if you could not recommend some work."

"The only work I am acquainted with," replied Mr. Churchill, "is the Reverend Mr. Pegge's Essay on Cock-fighting among the Ancients, and I hardly see how you could apply that to the Mexicans."

"Why, they are a kind of ancients, you know. I certainly will hunt up the essay you mention, and see what I can do with it."

"And all I know about the matter itself," continued Mr. Churchill, "is, that Mark Antony was a patron of the pit, and that his cocks were always beaten by Cæsar's; and that, when Themistocles the Athenian general was marching against the Persians, he halted his army to see a cock-fight, and made a speech to his soldiery, to the effect, that those animals fought, not for the gods of their country, nor for the monuments of their ancestors, nor for glory, nor for freedom, nor for their children, but only for the sake of victory. On his return to Athens, he established cock-fights in that capital. But how this is to help you in Mexico I do not see, unless you introduce Santa Anna, and compare him to Cæsar and Themistocles."

"That is it; I will do so. It will give historic interest to the play. I thank you for the suggestion."

"The subject is certainly very original, but it does not strike me as particularly national."

"Prospective, you see!" said Mr. Hathaway, with a penetrating look.

"Ah, yes; I perceive you fish with a heavy sinker,—down, far down in the future,—among posterity, as it were."

"You have seized the idea. Besides, I obviate your objection, by introducing an American circus company from the United States, which enables me to bring horses on the stage and produce great scenic effect. . . ."

[1849]

Longfellow's Kavanagh *drew from James Russell Lowell an urbane and penetrating development of Mr. Churchill's universalist position. Lowell praises some of Mathews' verse, but his entire argument seeks to replace superficial nationalism with the common denominator of universal human nature. Lowell's distinction became more and more significant as the century wore on: there is a difference, he insists, between "truth to nature" and the "fidelity of local coloring. . . . Literature survives, not because of its nationality, but in spite of it." Equally noteworthy is Lowell's method. In denying a narrowly national character to British or any other great literature, he tries to destroy the analogies on which most nationalist arguments were based. The erudition, balance, and reasonableness of his statement seems to imply that the problem of American literature is actually no problem at all.*

75

Time is figured with scythe, hour-glass, wallet, and slippery forelock. He is allegorized as the devourer of his own offspring. But there is yet one of his functions, and that not the least important, which wants its representative among his emblems. To complete his symbolical outfit, a sieve should be hung at his back. Busy as he must be at his mowing, he has leisure on his hands, scents out the treacherous saltpetre in the columns of Thebes, and throws a handful of dust over Nineveh, that the mighty hunter Nimrod may not, wanting due rites of sepulture, wander, a terrible shadow, on this side the irrepassable river. A figurative personage, one would say, with quite enough to do already, without imposing any other duty upon him. Yet it is clear that he finds opportunity also thoroughly to sift men and their deeds, winnowing away with the untired motion of his wings, monuments, cities, empires, families, generations, races, as chaff.

We must go to the middle of a child's bunch of cherries to be sure of finding perfect fruit. The outer circles will show unripened halves, stabs of the robin's bill, and rain-cracks, so soon does the ambition of quantity deaden the nice conscience of quality. Indeed, with all of us, men as well as children, amount passes for something of intrinsic value. But Time is more choice, and makes his sieve only the coarser from age to age. One book, one man, one action, shall often be all of a generation busy with sword, pen, and trowel, that has not slipped irrevocably through the ever-widening meshes.

We are apt to forget this. In looking at the literature of a nation, we take note only of such names as Dante, Shakspeare, Goethe, not remembering what new acres have been added to the wide chaff-desert of Oblivion, that we may have these great kernels free from hull and husk. We overlook the fact that contemporary literature has not yet been put into the sieve, and quite gratuitously blush for the literary shortcomings of a whole continent. For ourselves, we have long ago got rid of this national (we might call it hemispherical) sensitiveness, as if there were any thing in our western half-world which stimulated it to produce great rivers, lakes, and mountains, mammoth pumpkins, Kentucky giants, two-headed calves, and what not, yet at the same time rendered it irremediably barren of great poets, painters, sculptors, musicians, and men generally. If there be any such system of natural compensations, whereby geological is balanced against human development, we may, at least, console ourselves with the anticipation, that America can never (from scientifically demonstrable inability) incur the odium of mothering the greatest fool.

There is, nevertheless, something agreeable in being able to shift the responsibility from our own shoulders to the broader ones of a continent. When anxious European friends inquire after our Art and our Literature, we have nothing to do but to refer them to Mount Washington or Lake Superior. It is their concern, not ours. We yield them without scruple to the mercies of foreign reviewers. Let those generously solicitous persons lay on and spare not. There are no such traitors as the natural features of a country which betray their sacred trusts. They should be held strictly to their responsibilities, as, in truth, what spectacle more shameful than that of a huge, lubberly mountain, hiding its talent under a napkin, or a repudiating river? Our geographers should look to it, and instil proper notions on this head. In stating the heights of our mountains and the lengths of our rivers, they should take care to graduate the scale of reproach with a scrupulous regard to every additional foot and mile. They should say, for example, that such a peak is six thousand three hundred feet high, and has never yet produced a poet; that the river so-and-so is a thousand miles long, and has wasted its energies in the manufacture of alligators and flatboatmen. On the other hand, they should remember to the credit of the Mississippi, that, being the longest river in the world, it has very properly produced the longest painter, whose single work would overlap by a mile or two the pictures of all the old masters stitched together. We can only hope that it will never give birth to a poet long in proportion.

Since it seems to be so generally conceded, that the form of an author's work is entirely determined by the shape of his skull, and that in turn by the peculiar configuration of his native territory, perhaps a new system of criticism should be framed in accordance with these new developments of science. Want of sublimity would be inexcusable in a native of the mountains, and sameness in one from a diversified region, while flatness could not fairly be objected to a dweller on the praries, nor could eminent originality be demanded of a writer bred where the surface of the country was only hilly or moderately uneven. Authors, instead of putting upon their title-pages the names of previous works, or of learned societies to which they chance to belong, should supply us with an exact topographical survey of their native districts. The Himalaya mountains are, we believe, the highest yet discovered, and possibly society would find its account in sending the greater part of our poets thither, as to a university, either by subscription or by a tax laid for the purpose. How our literature is likely to be affected by the acquisition of the mountain ranges of California, remains to be seen. Legislators should certainly take such matters into consideration in settling boundary lines, and the General Court of Massachusetts should weigh well the responsibility it may incur to posterity, before transferring to New York the lofty nook of Boston Corner with its potential Homers and Miltons.

But perhaps we have too hastily taken the delinquency of our physical developments for granted. Nothing has hitherto been demanded of rivers and lakes in other parts of the world, except fish and mill privileges, or, at most, a fine waterfall or a pretty island. The received treatises on mountainous obstetrics give no hint of any parturition to be expected, except of mice. So monstrous a conception as that of a poet is nowhere on record; and what chloroform can we suggest to the practitioner who should be taken unawares by such a phenomenon?

At least, before definitive sentence be passed against us, the period of gestation which a country must go through, ere it bring forth a great poet, should be ascertained with scientific exactness. Let us not be in any hurry to resort to a Cæsarian operation. Poets, however valuable in their own esteem, are not, after all, the most important productions of a nation. If we can frame a commonwealth in which it shall not be a misfortune to be born, in which there shall never be a pair of hands nor a mouth too much, we shall be as usefully employed as if we should flower with a Dante or so, and remain a bony stalk forever after. We can, in the meantime, borrow a great poet when we want one, unless the pleasure and profit which we derive from the works of a great master, depend upon the proprietary right in him secured to us by compatriotism. For ourselves, we should be strongly inclined to question any exclusive claim to Shakspeare on the part of our respected relative, John Bull, who could do nothing better than look foolish when the great dramatist was called *bizarre,* and who has never had either the taste or the courage to see a single one of his most characteristic plays acted as he wrote it.

The feeling that it was absolutely necessary to our respectability that we should have a literature, has been a material injury to such as we have had. Our criticism has oscillated between the two extremes of depreciation and overpraise. On the one hand, it has not allowed for the variations of the magnetic needle of taste, and on the other, it has estimated merit by the number of degrees west from Greenwich. It seems never to have occurred to either sect of critics, that there were such things as principles of judgment immutable as those of mathematics. One party has been afraid to commend lest an English Reviewer might afterward laugh; the other has eulogized because it considered so terrible a catastrophe probable. The Stamp Act and the Boston Port Bill scarcely produced a greater excitement in America than the appalling question, *Who reads an American book?* It is perfectly true, that the amount of enlightenment which a reader will receive from a book depends upon the breadth of surface which he brings within its influence, for we never get *something* for *nothing;* but we would deferentially suggest for the relief of many a still trembling soul, repeating to itself the *quid sum miser tunc dicturus* to that awful question from the Edinburgh judgment-seat, that it is barely possible that the *power* of a book resides in the book itself, and that real books somehow compel an audience without extraneous intervention. From the first, it was impossible that Art should show here the successive stages of growth which have characterized it in the Old World. It is only geographically that we can call ourselves a new nation. However else our literature may avoid the payment of its liabilities, it can surely never be by a plea of infancy. Intellectually, we were full-grown at the start. Shakspeare had been dead five years, and Milton was eleven years old, when Mary Chilton leaped ashore on Plymouth Rock.

In looking backward or forward mentally, we seem to be infected with a Chinese incapacity of perspective. We forget the natural foreshortening, taking objects as they are reflected upon our retina, and neglecting to supply the proper interstices of time. This is equally true whether we are haruspicating the growth of desired opinions and arts, or are contemplating those which are already historical. Thus, we know statistically the amount which any race or nation has stored in its intellectual granaries, but make no account of the years of scarcity, of downright famine even, which have intervened between every full harvest. There is an analogy between the successive stages of a literature and those of a plant. There is, first of all, the seed, then the stalk, and then the seed again. What a length of stalk between Chaucer and Spenser, and again between Milton and Wordsworth! Except in India, perhaps, it would be impossible to affirm confidently an indigenous literature. The seed has been imported, accidentally or otherwise, as the white-weed and Hessian fly into America. Difference of soil, climate, and exposure will have their legitimate influence, but characteristics enough ordinarily remain for the tracing of the pedigree. The locality of its original production is as disputable as that of the garden of Eden. Only this is certain, that our search carries us farther and farther eastward.

No literature, of which we have authentic record or remains, can be called national in this limited and strict sense. Nor, if one could be found, would the calling it so be commendation. The best parts of the best authors in all languages can be translated; but, had they this element of exclusive nationality, the idea would demand a lexicon as well as the language which enveloped it. This shell within a shell would give more trouble in the cracking than any author can safely demand of his readers. Only a Dante can compel us to take an interest in the petty local politics of his day. No grubs were ever preserved in such amber. No Smiths and Browns were ever elevated upon so sublime and time-defying pinnacles of love, horror, and pity. The key by which we unlock the great galleries of Art is their common human interest. Nature supplies us with lexicon, commentary, and glossary to the great poems of all ages.

It would be hard to estimate the immediate indebtedness of Grecian literature; easier to reckon how much must have been due to the indirect influence of a religion and philosophy, whose esoteric ideas were of Egyptian derivation. Aristophanes is perhaps the only Grecian poet who is characterized by that quality of nationality of which we are speaking. Nay, it is something intenser than mere nationality in which his comedy is steeped. It is not the spirit of Greece, not even of Attica, but of Athens. It is cockneyism, not nationality. But his humor is more than Athenian. Were it not so, it would be dreary work enough deciphering jokes, as it were, in a mummypit, by the dim light of the scholiast's taper, too choked with dust and smoke to do any thing but cough when we are solemnly assured that we have come to the point.

There is a confusion in men's minds upon this subject. Nationality and locality are not distinguished from one another; and, were this jumble fairly cleared up, it would appear that there was a still farther confounding of truth to nature with fidelity of local coloring. Mere nationality is no more nor less than so much provincialism, and will be found but a treacherous antiseptic for any poem. It is because they are men and women, that we are interested in the characters of Homer. The squabbles of a score of petty barbarian chiefs, and the siege of a city which never existed, would have been as barren and fruitless to us as a Welsh genealogy, had the foundations of the Iliad been laid no wider and deeper than the Troad. In truth, the only literature which can be called purely national is the Egyptian. What poetry, what philosophy, the torch of the Arab has fruitlessly lighted up for European eyes, we as yet know not; but that any ideas valuable to mankind are buried there, we do not believe. These are not at the mercy of sand, or earthquake, or overflow. No race perishes without intellectual heirs, but whatever was locally peculiar in their literature, their art, or their religious symbols, becomes in time hieroglyphical to the rest of the world, to be, perhaps, painfully deciphered for the verification of useless history, but incapable of giving an impulse to productive thought. Literature survives, not because of its nationality, but in spite of it.

After the United States had achieved their independence, it was forthwith decided that they could not properly be a nation without a literature of their own. As if we had been without one! As if Shakspeare, sprung from the race and the class which colonized New England, had not been also ours! As if we had no share in the puritan and republican Milton, who had cherished in secret for more than a century the idea of the great puritan effort, and at last embodied it in a living commonwealth! But this ownership in common was not enough for us, and, as partition was out of the question, we must have a drama and an epos of our own. It must be national, too; we must have it all to ourselves. Other nations kept their poets, and so must we. We were to set up a literature as people set up a carriage, in order to be as good as our neighbors. It was even seriously proposed to have a new language. Why not, since we could afford it? Beside, the existing ones were all too small to contain our literature whenever we should get it. One enthusiast suggested the ancient Hebrew, another a firenew tongue of his own invention. Meanwhile, we were busy growing a literature. We watered so freely, and sheltered so carefully, as to make a soil too damp and shaded for any thing but mushrooms; wondered a little why no oaks came up, and ended by voting the mushroom an oak, an American variety. Joel Barlow made the lowest bid for the construction of our epos, got the contract, and delivered in due season the Columbiad, concerning which we can only regret that it had not been entitled to a still higher praise of nationality by being written in one of the proposed new languages.

One would think that the Barlow experiment should have been enough. But we are still requested by critics, both native and foreign, to produce a national literature, as if it were some school exercise in composition to be handed in by a certain day. The sharp struggle of a day or a year may settle the question of a nation's political independence, but even for that, there must be a long moral preparation. The first furrow drawn by an English plough in the thin soil of Plymouth was truly the first line in our Declaration of Independence. Jefferson was not the prophet looking forth into the future, but the scribe sitting at the feet of the past. But nationality is not a thing to be won by the sword. We may safely trust to the influence of our institutions to produce all of it that is valuable. Let us be content that, if we have been to blame for a Columbiad, we have also given form, life, and the opportunity of entire development to social ideas ever reacting with more and more force upon the thought and the literature of the Old World.

The poetry and romance of other nations are assumed to be national, inasmuch as they occupy themselves about local traditions or objects. But we, who never had any proper youth as a nation, never had our mythic period either. We had no cradle and no nursery to be haunted with such bugaboos. One great element of external and immediate influence is therefore wanting to our poets. They cannot, as did Goethe in his Faust, imbue an old legend, which already has a hold upon the fancy and early associations of their countrymen, with a modern and philosophical meaning which shall make it interesting to their mature understandings and cultivated imaginations. Whatever be the cause, no race into whose composition so large a Teutonic element has entered, is divided by such an impassable chasm of oblivion and unbelief from the ancestral mythology as the English. Their poets accordingly are not popular in any true sense of the word, and have influenced the thought and action of their countrymen less than those of any other nation except those of ancient Rome. Poets in other countries have mainly contributed to the creating and keeping alive of national sentiment; but the English owe theirs wholly to the sea which islands them. Chaucer and Spenser are Normans, and their minds open most fairly southward. Skelton, the Swift of his day, a purely English poet, is forgotten. Shakspeare, thoroughly English as he is, has chosen foreign subjects for the greatest of his dramas, as if to show that genius is cosmopolitan. The first thorough study, criticism, and consequent appreciation of him we owe to the Germans; and he can in no sense be called national except by accident of birth. Even if we grant that he drew his fairy mythology from any then living faith among his countrymen, this formed no bond of union between him and them, and was even regarded as an uncouthness and barbarism till long after every vestige of such faith was obliterated. If we concede any nationality to Milton's great poem, we must at the same time allow to the English an exclusive title to the localities where the scene is laid, a title which they would hardly be anxious to put forward in respect, at least, to one of them. When he was meditating a national poem, it was, he tells us, on the legend of Arthur, who, if he had ever existed at all, would have been English only in the same sense that Tecumseh is American. Coleridge, among his thousand reveries, hovered over the same theme, but settled at last upon the siege of Jerusalem by Titus as the best epical subject remaining. Byron, in his greatest poem, alludes only to England in a rather contemptuous farewell. Those strains of Wordsworth, which have entitled his name to a place on the selecter list of English poets, are precisely the ones in which England has only a common property with the rest of mankind. He could never have swum over Lethe with the sonnets to the river Duddon in his pocket. Whether we look for the cause in the origin of the people, or in their insular position, the English mind has always been characterized by an emigrating tendency. Their most truly national epic was the colonizing of America.

If we admit that it is meritorious in an author to seek for a subject in the superstitions, legends, and historical events of his own peculiar country or district, yet these (unless delocalized by their own intrinsic meaning) are by nature ephemeral, and a wide tract of intervening years makes them as truly foreign as oceans, mountains, or deserts could. Distance of time passes its silent statute of outlawry and alienage against them, as effectually as distance of space. Indeed, in that strictness with which the martinets of nationality use the term, it would be a hard thing for any people to prove an exclusive title to its myths and legends. Take, for example, the story of Wayland the Smith, curious as furnishing the undoubted original of the incident of Tell and the apple, and for its analogies with the Grecian fable of Dædalus. This, after being tracked through the *folklore* of nearly all the nations of Northern Europe, was at last, to the great relief of the archæologic mind, supposed to be *treed* in Scandinavia, because the word *voelund* was found to mean smith among the Icelanders. Yet even here we cannot rest secure that this piece of mythical property has been restored to its rightful owners. As usual in such cases, investigation points Asia-ward, and the same word is found with the same signification in Ceylon. However unsatisfying in other respects, the search has at least turned up a euphonious synonym for the name Smith, which might be assumed by any member of that numerous patronymic guild desirous of attaining a nearer approach to individuality.

But even the most indisputable proof of original ownership is of no great account in these matters. These tools of fancy cannot be branded with the name of any exclusive proprietor. They are his who can use them. Poor Peter Claus cries out in vain that he has been robbed of himself by the native of a country undiscovered when he took his half-century's nap on the Kypphauser mountains. *Caret vate sacro,* and nobody gives him the least heed. He has become the shadow, and Rip Van Winkle the substance. Perhaps he has made up his mind to it by this time, and contrives to turn an honest penny among the shades by exhibiting himself as the *Original* Rip Van Winkle. We trust, for the honor of our country, that Rip brazens it out there, and denounces the foreign impostor in the purest—American, we were going to say; but here another nationality interposes its claim, and we must put up with Low Dutch.

The only element of permanence which belongs to myth, legend, or history, is exactly so much of each as refuses to be circumscribed by provincial boundaries. When once superstitions, customs, and historic personages are dead and buried in antiquarian treatises or county annals, there is no such thing as resurrection for them. The poet who encumbers himself with them takes just that amount of unnecessary burthen upon his shoulders. He is an antiquary, not a creator, and is writing what posterity will read as a catalogue rather than a poem. There is a homeliness about great genius which leads it to glorify the place of its "kindly engendure," (as Chaucer calls it,) either by a tender allusion, or by images and descriptions drawn from that fairest landscape in the gallery of memory. But it is a strange confusion of thought to attribute to a spot of earth the inspiration whose source is in a universal sentiment. It is the fine humanity, the muscular sense, and the generous humor of Burns which save him from being merely Scotch, like a score of rhymesters as national as he. The Homers of Little Pedlington die, as their works died before them, and are forgotten; but let a genius get born there, and one touch of his nature shall establish even for Little Pedlington an immortal consanguinity which the whole world shall be eager to claim. The field-mouse and the mountain-daisy are not Scotch, and Tam O'Shanter died the other day within a mile of where we are writing. Measuring Burns by that which is best in him, and which ensures to him a length of life coincident with that of the human heart, he is as little national as Shak-speare, and no more an alien in Iowa than in Ayrshire. There is a vast difference between truth to nature and truth to fact; an impassable gulf between genius, which deals only with the true, and that imitative faculty which patiently and exactly reproduces the actual. This makes the distinction between the works of Fielding, which delight and instruct forever, and those of Smollett, which are of value as affording a clear insight into contemporaneous modes of life, but neither warm the heart nor impregnate the imagination. It is this higher and nobler kind of truth which is said to characterize the portraits of Titian, which gives an indefinable attraction to those of Page, and which inspires the busts of Powers. This excuses meagreness of color and incorrectness of drawing in Hogarth, who was truly rather a great dramatist than a great painter, and gives them that something which even indifferent engraving cannot destroy, any more than bad printing can extinguish Shakspeare.

This demand for a nationality bounded historically and geographically by the independent existence and territory of a particular race or fraction of a race, would debar us of our rightful share in the past and the ideal. It was happily illustrated by that parochially national Gascon, who would have been edified by the sermon had it been his good fortune to belong to the parish. Let us be thankful that there is no court by which we can be excluded from our share in the inheritance of the great poets of all ages and countries, to which our simple humanity entitles us. No great poet has ever sung but the whole human race has been, sooner or later, the wiser and better for it. Above all, let us not tolerate in our criticism a principle which would operate as a prohibitory tariff of ideas. The intellect is a diœcious plant, and books are the bees which carry the quickening pollen from one to another mind. It detracts nothing from Chaucer that we can trace in him the influences of Dante and Boccaccio; nothing from Spenser that he calls Chaucer master; nothing from Shakspeare that he acknowledges how dear Spenser was to him; nothing from Milton that he brought fire from Hebrew and Greek altars. There is no degradation in such indebtedness. Venerable rather is this apostolic succession, and inspiring to see the *vitai lampada* passed thus from consecrated hand to hand.

Nationality, then, is only a less narrow form of provincialism, a sublimer sort of clownishness and ill-manners. It deals in jokes, anecdotes, and allusions of such purely local character that a majority of the company are shut out from all approach to an understanding of them. Yet so universal a demand must have for its basis a more or less solid substratum of truth. There are undoubtedly national, as truly as family, idiosyncrasies, though we think that these will get displayed without any special schooling for that end. The substances with which a nation is compelled to work will modify its results, as well intellectual as material. The still renewing struggle with the unstable desert sands gave to the idea of durability in the Egyptian imagination a preponderance still further increased by the necessity of using granite, whose toughness of fibre and vagueness of coloring yielded unwillingly to fineness of outline, but seemed the natural helpmates of massiveness and repose. The out-of-door life of the Greeks, conducing at once to health and an unconscious education of the eye, and the perfection of physical development resulting from their palæstral exercises and constantly displayed in them, made the Greeks the first to perceive the noble symmetry of the human figure, for embodying the highest types of which Pentelicus supplied the fittest material. Corporeal beauty and strength, therefore, entered largely into their idea of the heroic, and perhaps it was rather policy than dandyism which hindered Alcibiades from learning to play the flute. With us, on the other hand, clothed to the chin in the least graceful costume ever invented by man, and baked half the year with stoves and furnaces, beauty of person has gradually receded from view, and wealth or brain is the essential of the modern novelist's hero. It may not be fanciful to seek in climate, and its resultant effects upon art, the remote cause of that fate-element which entered so largely into the Greek drama. In proportion as sculpture became more perfect, the images of the gods became less and less merely symbolical, and at last presented to the popular mind nothing more than actual representations of an idealized humanity. Before this degradation had taken place, and the divinities had been vulgarized in marble to the common eye, the ideas of the unseen and supernatural came to the assistance of the poet in giving interest to the struggles or connivances between heroes and gods. But presently a new and deeper chord of the imagination must be touched, and the unembodiable shadow of Destiny was summoned up, to move awe and pity as long as the human mind is incapable of familiarizing by precise definition the fearful and the vague. In that more purely objective age, the conflict must be with something external, and the struggles of the mind with itself afforded no sufficient theme for the poet. With us introspection has become a disease, and a poem is a self-dissection.

That Art in America will be modified by circumstances, we have no doubt, though it is impossible to predict the precise form of the moulds into which it will run. New conditions of life will stimulate thought and give new forms to its expression. It may not be our destiny to produce a great literature, as, indeed, our genius seems to find its kindliest development in practicalizing simpler and more perfect forms of social organization. We have yet many problems of this kind to work out, and a continent to subdue with the plough and the railroad, before we are at leisure for æsthetics. Our spirit of adventure will take first a material and practical direction, but will gradually be forced to seek outlet and scope in unoccupied territories of the intellect. In the meantime we may fairly demand of our literature that it should be national to the extent of being as free from out-worn conventionalities, and as thoroughly impregnated with humane and manly sentiment, as is the idea on which our political fabric rests. Let it give a true reflection of our social, political, and household life. The "Poems on Man in the Republic," by Cornelius Mathews, disfigured as they were by gross faults of dialect and metre, had the great merit of presenting the prominent features of our civilization in an American light. The story of "Margaret" is the most emphatically *American* book ever written. The want of plan and slovenliness of construction are characteristic of a new country. The scenery, character, dialect, and incidents mirror New England life as truly as Fresh Pond reflects the sky. The moral, also, pointing forward to a new social order, is the intellectual antitype of that restlessness of disposition, and facility of migration which are among our chief idiosyncrasies. The mistake of our imaginative writers generally is that, though they may take an American subject, they *costume* it in a foreign or antique fashion. The consequence is a painful vagueness and unreality. It is like putting Roman drapery upon a statue of Washington, the absurdity of which does not strike us so forcibly because we are accustomed to it, but which we should recognize at once were the same treatment applied to Franklin. The old masters did exactly the reverse of this. They took ancient or foreign subjects, but selected their models from their own immediate neighborhood. When Shakspeare conceived his Athenian mechanics, he did not cram with Grecian antiquities in order to make them real in speech and manners. Their unconscious prototypes were doubtless walking Stratford streets, and demonstrating to any one who had clear enough eyes, that stupidity and conceit were precisely the same thing on the banks of the Avon and those of the Ilissus. Here we arrive at the truth which is wrapped up and concealed in the demand for nationality in literature. It is neither more nor less than this, that authors should use their own eyes and ears, and not those of other people. We ask of them human nature as it appears in man, not in books; and scenery not at second hand from the canvas of painter or poet, but from that unmatched landscape painted by the Great Master upon the retina of their own eyes. Though a poet should make the bobo-link sing in Attica, the *anachronism* is nothing, provided he can only make it truly sing so that we can hear it. He will have no difficulty in making his peace with posterity. The error of our advocates of nationality lies in their assigning geographical limits to the poet's range of historical char-acters as well as to his natural scenery. There is no time or place in hu-man nature, and Prometheus, Coriolanus, Tasso, and Tell are ours if we can use them, as truly as Washington or Daniel Boone. Let an American author make a living character, even if it be antediluvian, and nationality will take care of itself. The newspaper, the railroad, and the steamship are fast obliterating the externals of distinct and hostile nationality. The Turk-ish soldier has shrunk into coat and pantaloons, and reads Dickens. But human nature is everywhere the same, and everywhere inextinguishable. If we only insist that our authors shall be good, we may cease to feel ner-vous about their being national. Excellence is an alien nowhere. And even if, as we hear it lamented, we have no literature, there are a thousand other ways of making ourselves useful. If the bobolink and mockingbird find no poet to sing them, they can afford, like Kepler, to wait; and in the meantime they themselves will sing as if nothing had happened. For our-selves, we confess, we have hopes. The breed of poets is not extinct, nor has Apollo shot away all the golden, singing arrows in his quiver. We have a very strong persuasion, amounting even to faith, that eyes and ears will yet open on this Western Continent, and find adequate utterance. If some of our birds have a right to feel neglected, yet other parts of our national history have met with due civility; and if the pine tree complain of the tribute which Emerson has paid it, we surrender it to the lumberer and the saw-mill without remorse. It must be an unreasonable tree, wooden at head and heart.

Nay, how are we to know what is preparing for us at this very moment? What herald had Chaucer, singing the matins of that grand cathedral-service whose vespers we have not yet heard, in England? What external circumstance controlled the sweet influence of Spenser? Was Gorboduc a prologue that should have led us to expect Hamlet? Did the Restoration furnish the score for those organ-strains of Milton, breaking in with a somewhat unexpected voluntary to drown the thin song of pander and parasite with its sublime thunders of fervor and ascription? What collyrium of nationality was it that enabled those pleasant Irish eyes of Goldsmith to pierce through the artificial tinsel and frippery of his day to that little clump of primroses at Wakefield? England had long been little better than a province of France in song, when Wordsworth struck the note of independence, and led the people back to the old worship. While we are waiting for our literature, let us console ourselves with the following observation with which Dr. Newman commences his History of the Hebrew Monarchy. "Few nations," he says, "which have put forth a wide and enduring influence upon others, proclaim themselves to have been indigenous on the land of their celebrity." Or, if the worst come, we can steal a literature like the Romans, and thus acquire another point of similarity to that remarkable people, whom we resemble so much, according to the Quarterly Review, in our origin.

Mr. Longfellow has very good-naturedly and pointedly satirized the rigid sticklers for nationality in one of the chapters of his "Kavanagh," which we have taken for the text of some remarks we have long intended to make on this subject. It is time that we should say something about the book itself. . . .

[1849]

⚛ *Melville reviewed Hawthorne's* Mosses *under the guise of "a Virginian Spending July in Vermont," but his remarks on the national letters more properly recall Cornelius Mathews, the Duyckincks, and the other Young Americans of New York. Melville's variation suggests that Sydney Smith's query as to who reads American books was deeply imbedded in contemporary lore some thirty years later. The particular American Goldsmith Melville chides was of course Washington Irving.*

76 ⚛

. . . Some may start to read of Shakespeare and Hawthorne on the same page. They may say that if an illustration were needed, a lesser light might have sufficed to elucidate this Hawthorne, this small man of yesterday. But I am not willingly one of those who, as touching Shakespeare at least exemplify the maxim of Rochefoucauld, that "we exalt the reputation of some, in order to depress that of others"—who, to teach all noble-souled aspirants that there is no hope for them, pronounce Shakespeare absolutely unapproachable. But Shakespeare has been approached. There are minds that have gone as far as Shakespeare into the universe. And hardly a mortal man, who, at some time or other, has not felt as great thoughts in him as any you will find in Hamlet. We must not inferentially malign mankind for the sake of any one man, whoever he may be. This is too cheap a purchase of contentment for conscious mediocrity to make. Besides, this absolute and unconditional adoration of Shakespeare has grown to be a part of our Anglo-Saxon superstitions. The Thirty-Nine Articles are now forty. Intolerance has come to exist in this matter. You must believe in Shakespeare's unapproachability, or quit the country. But what sort of a belief is this for an American, a man who is bound to carry republican progressiveness into Literature as well as into Life? Believe me, my friends, that men not very much inferior to Shakespeare are this day being born on the banks of the Ohio. And the day will come when you shall say, Who reads a book by an Englishman that is a modern? The great mistake seems to be, that even with those Americans who look forward to the coming of a great literary genius among us, they somehow fancy he will come in the costume of Queen Elizabeth's day; be a writer of dramas founded upon old English history or the tales of

Boccaccio. Whereas, great geniuses are parts of the times, they themselves are the times, and possess a corresponding coloring. It is of a piece with the Jews, who, while their Shiloh was meekly walking in their streets, were still praying for his magnificent coming; looking for him in a chariot, who was already among them on an ass. Nor must we forget that, in his own lifetime, Shakespeare was not Shakespeare, but only Master William Shakespeare of the shrewd, thriving business firm of Condell, Shakespeare and Co., proprietors of the Globe Theater in London; and by a courtly author, of the name of Chettle, was looked at as an "upstart crow," beautified "with other birds' feathers." For, mark it well, imitation is often the first charge brought against originality. Why this is so, there is not space to set forth here. You must have plenty of sea-room to tell the Truth in; especially when it seems to have an aspect of newness, as America did in 1492, though it was then just as old, and perhaps older than Asia, only those sagacious philosophers, the common sailors, had never seen it before, swearing it was all water and moonshine there.

Now I do not say that Nathaniel of Salem is a greater man than William of Avon, or as great. But the difference between the two men is by no means immeasurable. Not a very great deal more, and Nathaniel were verily William.

This, too, I mean: that if Shakespeare has not been equaled, give the world time, and he is sure to be surpassed in one hemisphere or the other. Nor will it at all do to say that the world is getting gray and grizzled now, and has lost that fresh charm which she wore of old, and by virtue of which the great poets of past times made themselves what we esteem them to be. Not so. The world is as young today as when it was created; and this Vermont morning dew is as wet to my feet as Eden's dew to Adam's. Nor has nature been all over ransacked by our progenitors, so that no new charms and mysteries remain for this latter generation to find. Far from it. The trillionth part has not yet been said; and all that has been said but multiplies the avenues to what remains to be said. It is not so much paucity as super-abundance of material that seems to incapacitate modern authors.

Let America, then, prize and cherish her writers; yea, let her glorify them. They are not so many in number as to exhaust her goodwill. And while she has good kith and kin of her own to take to her bosom, let her not lavish her embraces upon the household of an alien. For believe it or not, England, after all, is in many things an alien to us. China has more bonds of real love for us than she. But even were there no strong literary individualities among us, as there are some dozens at least, nevertheless, let America first praise mediocrity even, in her children, before she praises (for everywhere merit demands acknowledgment from everyone) the best excellence in the children of any other land. Let her own authors, I say, have the priority of appreciation. I was much pleased with a hot-headed Carolina cousin of mine, who once said, "If there were no other American to stand by, in literature, why, then, I would stand by Pop Emmons and his *Fredoniad,* and till a better epic came along, swear it was not very far behind the *Iliad.*" Take away the words, and in spirit he was sound.

Not that American genius needs patronage in order to expand. For that explosive sort of stuff will expand though screwed up in a vise, and burst it, though it were triple steel. It is for the nation's sake and not for her authors' sake, that I would have America be heedful of the increasing greatness among her writers. For how great the shame, if other nations should be before her, in crowning her heroes of the pen! But this is almost the case now. American authors have received more just and discriminating praise (however loftily and ridiculously given, in certain cases) even from some Englishmen, than from their own countrymen. There are hardly five critics in America; and several of them are asleep. As for patronage, it is the American author who now patronizes his country, and not his country him. And if at times some among them appeal to the people for more recognition, it is not always with selfish motives, but patriotic ones.

It is true that but few of them as yet have evinced that decided originality which merits great praise. But that graceful writer who perhaps of all Americans has received the most plaudits from his own country for his productions—that very popular and amiable writer, however good and self-reliant in many things, perhaps owes his chief reputation to the self-acknowledged imitation of a foreign model, and to the studied avoidance of all topics but smooth ones. But it is better to fail in originality than to succeed in imitation. He who has never failed somewhere, that man cannot be great. Failure is the true test of greatness. And if it be said that continual success is a proof that a man wisely knows his powers, it is only to be added that, in that case, he knows them to be small. Let us believe it, then, once for all, that there is no hope for us in these smooth, pleasing writers that know their powers. Without malice, but to speak the plain fact they but furnish an appendix to Goldsmith and other English authors. And we want no American Goldsmiths, nay, we want no American Miltons. It were the vilest thing you could say of a true American author that he were an American Tompkins. Call him an American and have done, for you cannot say a nobler thing of him. But it is not meant that all American writers should studiously cleave to nationality in their writings; only this, no American writer should write like an Englishman or a Frenchman; let him write like a man, for then he will be sure to write like an American. Let us away with this leaven of literary flunkeyism toward England. If either must play the flunkey in this thing, let England do it, not us. While we are rapidly preparing for that political supremacy among the nations which prophetically awaits us at the close of the present century, in a literary point of view, we are deplorably unprepared for it; and we seem studious to remain so. Hitherto, reasons might have existed why this should be; but no good reason exists now. And all that is requisite to amendment in this matter is simply this: that while fully acknowledging all excellence everywhere, we should refrain from unduly lauding foreign writers, and, at the same time, duly recognize the meritorious writers that are our own; those writers who breathe that unshackled, democratic spirit of Christianity in all things, which now takes the practical lead in this world, though at the same time led by ourselves—us Americans. Let us boldly condemn all imitation, though it comes to us graceful and fragrant as the morning; and foster all originality, though at first it be crabbed and ugly as our own pine knots. And if any of our authors fail, or seem to fail, then, in the words of my Carolina cousin, let us clap him on the shoulder and back him against all Europe for his second round. The truth is, that in one point of view this matter of a national literature has come to such a pass with us, that in some sense we must turn bullies, else the day is lost, or superiority so far beyond us that we can hardly say it will ever be ours.

And now, my countrymen, as an excellent author of your own flesh and blood—an unimitating, and, perhaps, in his way, an inimitable man—whom better can I commend to you, in the first place, than Nathaniel Hawthorne? He is one of the new, and far better generation of your writers. The smell of young beeches and hemlocks is upon him; your own broad prairies are in his soul; and if you travel away inland into his deep and noble nature, you will hear the far roar of his Niagara. . . .

[1850]

✑ *Alexis de Tocqueville's four volumes deal more with equality than democracy, and more with the effects of leveling than with America. America is merely the model used to explore the impact of change on national culture. Nor was Tocqueville's audience initially American. The book is addressed to the older nations of Europe which must face similar changes in a not-too-distant future. But countless translations have established* De la Démocratie en Amérique *among the most authoritative and influential analyses of the young republic. Americans had no doubt that such analysis was the book's aim, and even today the thoughts on aristocratic and democratic literature seem a useful preparation for an understanding of Whitman.*

77 ✑

Various different significations have been given to the word Poetry. It would weary my readers if I were to lead them into a discussion as to which of these definitions ought to be selected: I prefer telling them at once that which I have chosen. In my opinion, Poetry is the search and the delineation of the Ideal.

The Poet is he who, by suppressing a part of what exists, by adding some imaginary touches to the picture, and by combining certain real circumstances, but which do not in fact concurrently happen, completes and extends the work of nature. Thus the object of poetry is not to represent what is true, but to adorn it, and to present to the mind some loftier imagery. Verse, regarded as the ideal beauty of language, may be eminently poetical; but verse does not, of itself, constitute poetry.

I now proceed to inquire whether, among the actions, the sentiments, and the opinions of democratic nations, there are any which lead to a conception of ideal beauty, and which may for this reason be considered as natural sources of poetry.

It must, in the first place, be acknowledged that the taste for ideal beauty, and the pleasure derived from the expression of it, are never so intense or so diffused among a democratic as among an aristocratic people. In aristocratic nations it sometimes happens that the body goes on to act as it were spontaneously, while the higher faculties are bound and burdened by repose. Among these nations the people will very often display poetic tastes, and sometimes allow their fancy to range beyond and above what surrounds them.

But in democracies the love of physical gratification, the notion of bettering one's condition, the excitement of competition, the charm of anticipated success, are so many spurs to urge men onward in the active professions they have embraced, without allowing them to deviate for an instant from the track. The main stress of the faculties is to this point. The imagination is not extinct; but its chief function is to devise what may be useful, and to represent what is real.

The principle of equality not only diverts men from the description of ideal beauty—it also diminishes the number of objects to be described.

Aristocracy, by maintaining society in a fixed position, is favourable to the solidity and duration of positive religions, as well as to the stability of political institutions. It not only keeps the human mind within a certain sphere of belief, but it predisposes the mind to adopt one faith rather than another. An aristocratic people will always be prone to place intermediate powers between God and man. In this respect it may be said that the aristocratic element is favourable to poetry. When the universe is peopled with supernatural creatures, not palpable to the senses but discovered by the mind, the imagination ranges freely, and poets, finding a thousand subjects to delineate, also find a countless audience to take an interest in their productions.

In democratic ages it sometimes happens, on the contrary, that men are as much afloat in matters of belief as they are in their laws. Scepticism then draws the imagination of poets back to earth, and confines them to the real and visible world. Even when the principle of equality does not disturb religious belief, it tends to simplify it, and to divert attention from secondary agents, to fix it principally on the Supreme Power.

Aristocracy naturally leads the human mind to the contemplation of the past, and fixes it there. Democracy, on the contrary, gives men a sort of instinctive distaste for what is ancient. In this respect aristocracy is far more favourable to poetry; for things commonly grow larger and more obscure as they are more remote; and for this twofold reason they are better suited to the delineation of the ideal.

After having deprived poetry of the past, the principle of equality robs it in part of the present. Among aristocratic nations there are a certain number of privileged personages, whose situation is, as it were, without and above the condition of man; to these, power, wealth, fame, wit, refinement, and distinction in all things appear peculiarly to belong. The crowd never sees them very closely, or does not watch them in minute details; and little is needed to make the description of such men poetical. On the other hand, among the same people, you will meet with classes so ignorant, low, and enslaved, that they are no less fit objects for poetry from the excess of their rudeness and wretchedness, than the former are from their greatness and refinement. Besides, as the different classes of which an aristocratic community is composed are widely separated, and imperfectly acquainted with each other, the imagination may always represent them with some addition to, or some subtraction from, what they really are.

In democratic communities, where men are all insignificant and very much alike, each man instantly sees all his fellows when he surveys himself.

The poets of democratic ages can never, therefore, take any man in particular as the subject of a piece; for an object of slender importance, which is distinctly seen on all sides, will never lend itself to an ideal composition.

Thus the principle of equality, in proportion as it has established itself in the world, has dried up most of the old springs of poetry. Let us now attempt to show what new ones it may disclose.

When scepticism has depopulated heaven, and the progress of equality has reduced each individual to smaller and better known proportions, the poets, not yet aware of what they could substitute for the great themes which were departing together with the aristocracy, turned their eyes to inanimate nature. As they lost sight of gods and heroes, they set themselves to describe streams and mountains. Thence originated, in the last century, that kind of poetry which has been called, by way of distinction, the descriptive. Some have thought that this sort of delineation, embellished with all the physical and inanimate objects which cover the earth, was the kind of poetry peculiar to democratic ages; but I believe this to be an error, and that it only belongs to a period of transition.

I am persuaded that in the end democracy diverts the imagination from all that is external to man, and fixes it on man alone. Democratic nations may amuse themselves for a while with considering the productions of nature; but they are only excited in reality by a survey of themselves. Here, and here alone, the true sources of poetry among such nations are to be found; and it may be believed that the poets who shall neglect to draw their inspiration hence, will lose all sway over the minds which they would enchant, and will be left in the end with none but unimpassioned spectators of their transports.

I have shown how the ideas of progression and of the indefinite perfectibility of the human race belong to democratic ages. Democratic nations care but little for what has been, but they are haunted by visions of what will be: in this direction their unbounded imagination grows and dilates beyond all measure. Here then is the widest range open to the genius of poets, which allows them to remove their performances to a sufficient distance from the eye. Democracy shuts the past against the poet, but opens the future before him.

As all the citizens who compose a democratic community are nearly equal and alike, the poet cannot dwell upon any one of them; but the nation itself invites the exercise of his powers. The general similitude of individuals, which renders any one of them taken separately an improper subject of poetry, allows poets to include them all in the same imagery, and to take a general survey of the people itself. Democratic nations have a clearer perception than any others of their own aspect; and an aspect so imposing is admirably fitted to the delineation of the ideal.

I readily admit that the Americans have no poets; I cannot allow that they have no poetic ideas. In Europe people talk a great deal of the wilds of America, but the Americans themselves never think about them: they are insensible to the wonders of inanimate nature, and they may be said not to perceive the mighty forests which surround them till they fall beneath the hatchet. Their eyes are fixed upon another sight: the American people views its own march across these wilds—drying swamps, turning the course of rivers, peopling solitudes, and subduing nature. This magnificent image of themselves does not meet the gaze of the Americans at intervals only; it may be said to haunt every one of them in his least as well as in his most important actions, and to be always flitting before his mind.

Nothing conceivable is so pretty, so insipid, so crowded with paltry interests, in one word so anti-poetic, as the life of a man in the United States. But among the thoughts which it suggests, there is always one which is full of poetry, and that is the hidden nerve which gives vigour to the frame.

In aristocratic ages each people, as well as each individual, is prone to stand separate and aloof from all others. In democratic ages, the extreme fluctuations of men and the impatience of their desires keep them perpetually on the move; so that the inhabitants of different countries intermingle, see, listen to, and borrow from each other's stores. It is not only then the members of the same community who grow more alike; communities are themselves assimilated to one another, and the whole assemblage presents to the eye of the spectator one vast democracy, each citizen of which is a people. This displays the aspect of mankind for the first time in the broadest light. All that belongs to the existence of the human race taken as a whole, to its vicissitudes and to its future, becomes an abundant mine for poetry.

The poets who lived in aristocratic ages have been eminently successful in their delineations of certain incidents in the life of a people or a man; but none of them ever ventured to include within his performances the destinies of mankind—a task which poets writing in democratic ages may attempt.

At the same time at which every man, raising his eyes above his country, begins at length to discern mankind at large, the Divinity is more and more manifest to the human mind in full and entire majesty. If in democratic ages faith in positive religions be often shaken, and the belief in intermediate agents, by whatever name they are called, be overcast; on the other hand men are disposed to conceive a far broader idea of Providence itself, and its interference in human affairs assumes a new and more imposing appearance to their eyes. Looking at the human race as one great whole, they easily conceive that its destinies are regulated by the same design; and in the actions of every individual they are led to acknowledge a trace of that universal and eternal plan on which God rules our race. This consideration may be taken as another prolific source of poetry which is opened in democratic ages.

Democratic poets will always appear trivial and frigid if they seek to invest gods, demons, or angels with corporeal forms, and if they attempt to draw them down from heaven to dispute the supremacy of earth. But if they strive to connect the great events they commemorate with the general providential designs which govern the universe, and, without showing the finger of the Supreme Governor, reveal the thoughts of the Supreme Mind, their works will be admired and understood, for the imagination of their contemporaries takes this direction of its own accord.

It may be foreseen in like manner that poets living in democratic ages will prefer the delineation of passions and ideas to that of persons and achievements. The language, the dress, and the daily actions of men in democracies are repugnant to ideal conceptions. These things are not poetical in themselves; and if it were otherwise, they would cease to be so, because they are too familiar to all those to whom the poet would speak of them. This forces the poet constantly to search below the external surface which is palpable to the senses, in order to read the inner soul: and nothing lends itself more to the delineation of the Ideal than the scrutiny of the hidden depths of the immaterial nature of man. I need not ramble over earth and sky to discover a wondrous object woven of contrasts, of greatness and littleness infinite, of intense gloom and of amazing brightness—capable at once of exciting pity, admiration, terror, contempt. I find that object in myself. Man springs out of nothing, crosses Time, and disappears for ever in the bosom of God: he is seen but for a moment, staggering on the verge of two abysses, and there he is lost.

If man were wholly ignorant of himself, he would have no poetry in him; for it is impossible to describe what the mind does not conceive. If man clearly discerned his own nature, his imagination would remain idle, and would have nothing to add to the picture. But the nature of man is sufficiently disclosed for him to apprehend something of himself; and sufficiently obscure for all the rest to be plunged in thick darkness, in which he gropes for ever—and for ever in vain—to lay hold on some completer notion of his being.

Among a democratic people poetry will not be fed with legendary lays or the memories of old traditions. The poet will not attempt to people the universe with supernatural beings in whom his readers and his own fancy have ceased to believe; nor will he present virtues and vices under the mask of frigid personification, which are better received under their own features. All these resources fail him; but Man remains, and the poet needs no more. The destinies of mankind—man himself, taken aloof from his age and his country, and standing in the presence of Nature and of God, with his passions, his doubts, his rare prosperities and inconceivable wretchedness—will become the chief, if not the sole theme of poetry among these nations.

Experience may confirm this assertion, if we consider the productions of the greatest poets who have appeared since the world has been turned to democracy. The authors of our age who have so admirably delineated the features of [Faust], Childe Harold, Réné, and Jocelyn, did not seek to record the actions of an individual, but to enlarge and to throw light on some of the obscurer recesses of the human heart.

Such are the poems of democracy. The principle of equality does not then destroy all the subjects of poetry: it renders them less numerous, but more vast.

[1840]

Tocqueville's Démocratie *must rival the Bible and Shakespeare's plays as a source of introductory texts. Evert Duyckinck quotes from the book only to repeat the challenge of Young America that the nation's authors were timorous and derivative. More and more the blame would be laid to the culture of New England as literary activity moved from Boston to New York, "a city of the world like London, not a country town of litterateurs and blue-stockings."*

78 ↙

De Tocqueville, in one of the chapters of his work on America, thus characterizes the literature of a democratic state: "There will be more wit than erudition, more imagination than profundity: and literary performances will bear marks of an untutored and rude vigor of thought—frequently of great variety and singular fecundity. The object of authors will be to astonish rather than to please, and to stir the passions more than to charm the taste." Without entering into the question, at present, of what may be yet expected from America, or even of what has been produced honorable to the country, and there is much to exhibit on the positive side, it may be a matter of curiosity to test the peculiar requisitions of the distinguished French critic by a few of the results of actual experience. Our literature has, in fact, been the very opposite of the conditions claimed by de Tocqueville. He demands originality, force, passion, fruitfulness. What have been the accepted productions of American authorship? They disclose, for the most part, just the opposite qualities, of imitation, tameness, want of passion, and poverty.

In place of dramatic power, we find almost altogether descriptive talent; for energy, elaborate elegance; for passion, sentimentality, not even (the very few instances, again, excepted of the best character) sentiment, and so far from fruitfulness in the case of our best writers, they are uncommonly meagre, and easily exhausted. Fecundity is, with us, rather a badge of disgrace, considered a mark of our worst pretenders to authorship.

Imitation is natural, or rather, we should say, was formerly pardonable, from our social and political condition. For to the end of the last century, or even the first quarter (perhaps) of the present, there were good English writers in the country, with no pretence to an American spirit, except in their political speculations. The grave writing of that period, and the lighter efforts as well, were conceived and modelled on English originals. The dependence of the colonies had not yet ceased: our independence was civil only. This was especially the case in New England from the fact of its early settlement by Englishmen. There the English race was kept pure, without the admission of foreign elements. This made New England the stronghold of the English feeling of the country. This kept her, for a long while, the most provincial and colonial part of the union. This made Boston a literary town for English wares, and gave to it its peculiar character and attitude, in respect to English writers, who found their heaven there, when as voyagers they arrived, all prepared for idolatry and man-worship. How different from New York, which is cosmopolitan, and truly a Metropolis, the city of the Dutch and of the English, and of the native American, crossed by the French, German, Welsh, Scottish, and Irish races—a city of the world like London, not a country town of litterateurs and blue-stockings. There can be no doubt of the incalculable moral value of England to us as a means of culture. Our past is hers, and let no man undervalue the sacred influences of Ancient Times, when rivalries are forgotten, jealousies have disappeared, when the drama of life appears to us simple and complete, when evil has perished and good alone remains. The tree of American Literature will be found to have its roots in English soil. But we can only show ourselves capable of receiving those blessed lessons by having in ourselves the virtue to live an independent life. "To him that hath shall be given." . . .

[1847]

American literature, Tocqueville suggests, will never center on the individual hero. The hero of democracy is the mass, a figure for the populace or of the nation itself: "I celebrate myself, and sing myself" seeks to utter the personality of the race. Students of the Leatherstocking Tales *have similarly come to see in Cooper's hero an embodiment of a national myth. In these pages an astute contemporary, William Gilmore Simms, tries to explain Natty's appeal.*

79 ⚑

. . . The success of the "Spy" was very great, and it at once gave Mr. Cooper reputation in Europe. It may be said to have occasioned a greater sensation in Europe than at home;—and there were good reasons for this. At that period America had no literature. Just before this time, or about this time, it was the favourite sarcasm of the British Reviewers that such a thing as an American book was never read. Mr. Irving, it is true, was writing his sweet and delicate essays; but he was not accounted in England an American writer, and he himself,—no doubt with a sufficient policy—his own fortunes alone being the subject of consideration—took no pains to assert his paternity. The publication of the "Spy" may be assumed to have been the first practical reply to a sarcasm, which, since that day, has found its ample refutation. It was immediately republished in England, and soon after, we believe, found its way into half the languages of Europe. Its farther and more important effect was upon the intellect of our own country. It at once opened the eyes of our people to their own resources. It was something of a wonder, to ourselves, that we should be able—(strange, self-destroying humility in a people springing directly from the Anglo-Norman stock)—to produce a writer who should so suddenly, and in his very first work ("Precaution" was not known and scarcely named in that day) rise to such an eminence—equalling most, excelling most, and second to but one, of the great historical romance writers of Britain. This itself was an important achievement—a step gained, without which, no other step could possibly have been taken. It need scarcely be said, that the efforts of a nation at performance,—particularly in letters and the arts,—must first be preceded by a certain consciousness of the necessary resources. This consciousness, in the case of America, was wanting. Our colonial relation to Great Britain had filled us with a feeling of intellectual dependence, of which our success in shaking off her political dominion had in no respect relieved us. We had not then, and, indeed, have not entirely to this day, arrived at any just idea of the inevitable connexion between an ability to maintain ourselves in arts as well as in arms—the ability in both cases arising only from our intellectual resources, and a manly reliance upon the just origin of national strength,—Self-dependence! To Mr. Cooper the merit is due, of having first awakened us to this self-reference,—to this consciousness of mental resources, of which our provincialism dealt, not only in constant doubts, but in constant denials. The first step is half the march, as in ordinary cases, the first blow is half the battle. With what rapidity after that did the American press operate. How many new writers rose up suddenly, the moment that their neighbours had made the discovery that there were such writers—that such writers should be. Every form of fiction, the legend, tale, novel and romance—the poem, narrative and dramatic—were poured out with a prolific abundance, which proved the possession, not only of large resources of thought, but of fancy, and of an imagination equal to every department of creative fiction. It will not matter to show that a great deal of this was crude, faulty, undigested—contracted and narrow in design, and spasmodic in execution. The demand of the country called for no more. The wonder was that, so suddenly, and at such short notice, such resources could be found as had not before been imagined. The sudden rise and progress of German literature seems to have been equally surprising and sudden—equally the result of a national impulse, newly moved in a novel and unexpected direction. The wonderful birth and progress of American letters in the last twenty years—and in every department of thought, art and science, so far from discouraging, because of its imperfections, holds forth the most signal encouragement to industry and hope—showing most clearly, that the deficiency was not in the resource but in the demand, not in the inferior quality, or limited quantity, but in the utter indifference of our people to the possession of the material.

Having struck the vein, and convinced the people not only that there was gold in the land, but that the gold of the land was good, Mr. Cooper proceeded with proper industry to supply the demand which his own genius had occasioned in the markets, as well of Europe as his own country, for his productions. "The Spy" was followed by Lionel Lincoln, the Pioneers, the Last of the Mohicans, the Pilot, Red Rover, Prairie, Water Witch, &c. We speak from memory—we are not so sure that we name these writings in their proper order, nor is this important to us in the plan of this paper, which does not contemplate their examination in detail. All these works were more or less interesting. In most of them, the improvement in style, continuity of narrative, propriety of incident, &c., was obvious. In all of them were obvious, in greater or less degree, the characteristics of the author. The plots were generally simple, not always coherent, and proving either an incapacity for, or an indifference to the exercise of much invention. The reader was led through long and dead levels of dialogue—sensible enough,—sometimes smart, sarcastic or playful,—occasionally marked by depth or originality of thought, and occasionally exhibiting resources of study and reflection in the departments of law and morals, which are not common to the ordinary novel writer. But these things kept us from the story,—to which they were sometimes foreign, and always in some degree, unnecessary. His characters were not often felicitous, and, as in the case of most writers, Mr. Cooper had hobbies on which he rode too often, to the great disquiet of his friends and companions. He rang the changes on words, as Scott once suffered himself to do, in the "Prodigous" of Dominie Sampson, until readers sickened of the stupidity; and occasionally, as in the case of David Gamut, mistaking his own powers of the humorous, he afflicted us with the dispensation of a bore, which qualified seriously the really meritorious in his performance. But, to compensate us for these trials of our tastes and tempers, he gave us the most exquisite scenes of minute artifice, as in his Indian stories,—in which the events were elaborated with a nicety and patience, reminding us of the spider at his web, that curious and complicated spinner, which may well be employed to illustrate by his own labours and ingenuity the subtle frame-work of Indian cunning—the labyrinth of his artifice,—his wily traps and pitfalls, and indomitable perseverance. In these details of Indian art and resource, Mr. Cooper was inimitable. In his pursuits, flights, captures,—in his encounters,—cunning opposed to cunning,—man to man—the trapper and the hunter, against the red man whose life he envies and emulates,—Mr. Cooper has no superior as he has had no master. His conception of the frontier white man, if less true than picturesque, is also not less happy as an artistical conception of great originality and effect. In him, the author embodied his ideal of the philosopher of the foremast—Hawkeye is a sailor in a hunting shirt—and in this respect he committed no error in propriety. The sailor and the forester both derive their philosophies and character from the same sources,—though the one disdains the land, and the other trembles at the sight of the sea. They both think and feel, with a highly individual nature, that has been taught, by constant contemplation, in scenes of solitude. The vast unbroken ranges of forest, to its one lonely occupant, press upon the mind with the same sort of solemnity which one feels condemned to a life of partial isolation upon the ocean. Both are permitted that degree of commerce with their fellow beings, which suffice to maintain in strength the sweet and sacred sources of their humanity. It is through these that they are commended to our sympathies, and it is through the same medium that they acquire that habit of moral musing and meditation which expresses itself finely in the most delightful of all human philosophies. The very isolation to which, in the most successful of his stories, Mr. Cooper subjects his favourite personages, is, alone, a proof of his strength and genius. While the ordinary writer, the man of mere talent, is compelled to look around him among masses for his material, he contents himself with one man, and flings him upon the wilderness. The picture then, which follows, must be one of intense individuality. Out of this one man's nature, his moods and fortunes, he spins his story. The agencies and dependencies are few. With the self-reliance which is only found in true genius, he goes forward into the wilderness, whether of land or ocean; and the vicissitudes of either region, acting upon the natural resources of one man's mind, furnish the whole material of his work-shop. This mode of performance is highly dramatic, and thus it is that his scout, his trapper, his hunter, his pilot, all live to our eyes and thoughts, the perfect ideals of moral individuality. For this we admire them—love them we do not—they are objects not made to love—they do not appeal to our affections so much as to our minds. We admire their progress through sea and forest—their strange ingenuity, the skill with which they provide against human and savage enemies, against cold and hunger, with the same sort of admiration which we feel at watching any novel progress in arts or arms—a noble ship darting like a bird over the deep, unshivering, though the storm threatens to shiver every thing else around it—a splendid piece of machinery which works to the most consummate ends by a *modus operandi,* which we yet fail to detect—any curious and complex invention which dazzles our eyes, confounds our judgment, and mocks the search which would discover its secret principles. Take, for example, the character of the "Pilot," in the rapid and exciting story of that name. Here is a remarkable instance of the sort of interest which Mr. Cooper's writings are chiefly calculated to inspire. Marble could not be more inflexible than this cold, immovable, pulseless personage. He says nothing, shows nothing, promises nothing. Yet we are interested in his very first appearance. Why and how? Naturally enough by the anxiety with which he is sought and looked for;—by the fact that he promises nothing, yet goes to work, without a word, in a manner that promises every thing. We feel, at a glance, that if any mortal man can save the ship, he is the man. Why is this? Simply because he goes to work, without a word, as if it was in him to do so;—as if a calm consciousness of power was his possession; as if he knew just where to lay his hands, and in what direction to expend his strength. He shows *the capacity for work,* and this constitutes the sort of manhood upon which all men rely in moments of doubt or danger. Yet he gives you no process of reasoning—he has no word save that which commands obedience,—he neither storms, implores, nor threatens—he has no books,—he deals in no declamation. He is the ideal of an abstract but innate power, which we acknowledge and perhaps fear, but cannot fathom. All is hidden within himself, and, except when at work, he is nothing—he might as well be stone. Yet, around him,—such a man—a wonderful interest gathers like a halo—bright and inscrutable,—which fills us with equal curiosity and reverence. With him, a man of whom we know nothing,—whom we see now for the first time,—whom we may never see again,—whom we cannot love—whom we should never seek; and with his ship,—timbers, tackle, ropes, spars and cordage,—a frail fabric, such as goes to and fro along our shores, in our daily sight, without awakening a single thought or feeling;—with ship and man we grow fascinated beyond all measure of ordinary attraction. In his hands the ship becomes a being, instinct with life, beauty, sentiment—in danger, and to be saved;—and our interest in her fate, grows from our anxiety to behold the issue, in which human skill, courage and ingenuity, are to contend with storm and sea, rocks and tempest—as it were, man against omnipotence. Our interest springs from our curiosity rather than from our affections. We do not care a straw for the inmates of the vessel. They are very ordinary persons, that one man excepted—and *he* will not suffer us to love him. But *manhood,* true manhood, is a sight, always, of wondrous beauty and magnificence. The courage that looks steadily on the danger, however terrible; the composure that never swerves from its centre under the pressure of unexpected misfortune;—the knowledge that can properly apply its strength, and the adroitness and energy, which, feeling the force of a manly will, flies to their task, in instant and hearty obedience;—these form a picture of singular beauty, and must always rivet the admiration of the spectator. We regard Mr. Cooper's "Pilot"—breasting the storm, tried by, and finally baffling all its powers, as the Prometheus in action—inflexible, ready to endure,—isolated, but still human in a fond loyalty to all the great hopes and interests of humanity.

Hawkeye, the land sailor of Mr. Cooper, is, with certain suitable modifications, the same personage. We see and admire, in him, the qualities of hardihood and endurance, coolness, readiness of resource, keen, clear sighted observation, just reflection, and a sincere, direct, honest heart. He is more human than the other, since, naturally of gentler temperament, the life-conflict has not left upon his mind so many traces of its volcanic fires. He has had more patience, been more easily persuaded; has endured with less struggle if not more fortitude, and, in his greater pliancy, has escaped the greater force of the tempest. But he is, in all substantial respects, the same personage, and inspires us with like feelings. In the hour of danger,—at midnight,—in the green camp of the hunter,—trembling women, timid men, and weeping children, grouped together in doubt,—all eyes turn to him, as, on the sea, in storm, all eyes address themselves to the "Pilot." If any one can save them he is the man. Meanwhile, the shouts of savages are heard on every side,—the fearful whoop of slaughter;—as, on the sea, the wind howls through the ship's cordage, and the storm shrieks a requiem, in anticipation of ultimate triumph, around the shivering inmates. It is only upon true manhood that man can rely, and these are genuine men—not blocks, not feathers—neither dull, nor light of brain,—neither the stubbornly stupid, nor the frothily shallow. Now, as nothing in nature is more noble than a noble-minded, whole-souled man,—however ignorant, however poor, however deficient in imposing costume or imposing person,—so nothing, in nature, is better calculated to win the homage and command the obedience of men, than the presence of such a person in their moments of doubt and danger. It is inevitable, most usually, that such a man will save them, if they are to be saved by human agency. To Mr. Cooper we owe several specimens of this sort of moral manhood. It does not qualify our obligation to him, that they have their little defects,—that he has sometimes failed to hit the true line that divides the simplicity of nature, from the puerility of ignorance or childhood. His pictures are as perfect, of their kind, as the artist of fiction has ever given us. We say this after due reflection.

The Sea and American Forest Tales of Mr. Cooper, were at length superseded, when this gentleman visited Europe, by others of a very different class. Travelling on the continent, with objects of interest and novelty continually before his eyes, it was very natural that he should desire to try his hand at objects of foreign mould and material. The institutions of Europe, where they differed from our own, were also subjects provoking curiosity and calling for examination. These might be discussed in story;—the old traditions and institutions of a country naturally go together, either in connexion or contrast;—and the genius of our countryman conceived the novel idea of so framing his narrative, as to make it illustrate the radical differences, in operation and effect, of the policy of the new world, in opposition to that of the old. There was yet another reason for this change of scene and material. Mr. Cooper entertained a notion, expressed in some one or more of his prefaces, that the literary material of his own country was too limited and too deficient in variety, to admit of frequent employment. He thought it too easily exhausted, and though he did not say so, it was very evident, at that time, that he thought he himself had already exhausted it. . . .

The writer of European romance, unquestionably, possesses greater resources in history than he who confines himself to what is purely American. Time, which hallows all that he touches, had there laid away precious stores for centuries, long before the new world was opened to the eye of European day. The antiquities of the old world are so many treasures of fiction, to attain which, the critic of the American story, must task his invention. . . .

[1842]

≫ *Margaret Fuller looked to the future for a literature based on great national ideas: "We cannot have expression till there is something to be expressed." Her nationalism is romantic: while she can accept earlier American writing only as successful imitation of British models, she yet looks to Wordsworth and Coleridge, Goethe and Kant as prophets of the Ideal and remedies for our overemphasis on intellect and "understanding."*

80 ⋐

. . . Yet, probably, I am too little aware of the difficulties the artist encounters, before he can produce anything excellent, fully to appreciate the greatness he has shown. Here, as elsewhere, I suppose the first question should be, What ought we to expect under the circumstances?

There is no poetical ground-work ready for the artist in our country and time. Good deeds appeal to the understanding. Our religion is that of the understanding. We have no old established faith, no hereditary romance, no such stuff as Catholicism, Chivalry afforded. What is most dignified in the Puritanic modes of thought is not favorable to beauty. The habits of an industrial community are not propitious to delicacy of sentiment.

He, who would paint human nature, must content himself with selecting fine situations here and there; and he must address himself, not to a public which is not educated to prize him, but to the small circle within the circle of men of taste. . . .

[1840]

81 ⋐

Some thinkers may object to this essay, that we are about to write of that which has as yet no existence.

For it does not follow because many books are written by persons born in America that there exists an American literature. Books which imitate or represent the thoughts and life of Europe do not constitute an American literature. Before such can exist, an original idea must animate this nation and fresh currents of life must call into life fresh thoughts along its shores.

We have no sympathy with national vanity. We are not anxious to prove that there is as yet much American literature. Of those who think and write among us in the methods and of the thoughts of Europe, we are not impatient; if their minds are still best adapted to such food and such action. If their books express life of mind and character in graceful forms, they are good and we like them. We consider them as colonists and useful schoolmasters to our people in a transition state; which lasts rather longer than is occupied in passing bodily the ocean which separates the New from the Old World.

We have been accused of an undue attachment to foreign continental literature, and it is true that in childhood we had well nigh "forgotten our English" while constantly reading in other languages. Still what we loved in the literature of continental Europe was the range and force of ideal manifestation in forms of national and individual greatness. A model was before us in the great Latins of simple masculine minds seizing upon life with unbroken power. The stamp both of nationality and individuality was very strong upon them; their lives and thoughts stood out in clear and bold relief. The English character has the iron force of the Latins, but not the frankness and expansion. Like their fruits, they need a summer sky to give them more sweetness and a richer flavor. This does not apply to Shakespeare, who has all the fine side of English genius, with the rich coloring and more fluent life of the Catholic countries. Other poets of England also are expansive more or less, and soar freely to seek the blue sky, but take it as a whole, there is in English literature, as in English character, a reminiscence of walls and ceilings, a tendency to the arbitrary and conventional that repels a mind trained in admiration of the antique spirit. It is only in later days that we are learning to prize the peculiar greatness which a thousand times outweighs this fault, and which has enabled English genius to go forth from its insular position and conquer such vast dominion in the realms both of matter and of mind.

Yet there is often between child and parent a reaction from excessive influence having been exerted, and such a one we have experienced in behalf of our country against England. We use her language and receive in torrents the influence of her thought, yet it is in many respects uncongenial and injurious to our constitution. What suits Great Britain, with her insular position and consequent need to concentrate and intensify her life, her limited monarchy and spirit of trade, does not suit a mixed race continually enriched with new blood from other stocks the most unlike that of our first descent, with ample field and verge enough to range in and leave every impulse free, and abundant opportunity to develop a genius wide and full as our rivers, flowery, luxuriant, and impassioned as our vast prairies, rooted in strength as the rocks on which the Puritan fathers landed.

That such a genius is to rise and work in this hemisphere we are confident; equally so that scarce the first faint streaks of that day's dawn are yet visible. It is sad for those that foresee, to know they may not live to share its glories, yet it is sweet, too, to know that every act and word uttered in the light of that foresight may tend to hasten or ennoble its fulfillment.

That day will not rise till the fusion of races among us is more complete. It will not rise till this nation shall attain sufficient moral and intellectual dignity to prize moral and intellectual no less highly than political freedom, not till the physical resources of the country being explored, all its regions studded with towns, broken by the plow, netted together by railways and telegraph lines, talent shall be left at leisure to turn its energies upon the higher department of man's existence. Nor then shall it be seen till from the leisurely and yearning soul of that riper time national ideas shall take birth, ideas craving to be clothed in a thousand fresh and original forms.

Without such ideas all attempts to construct a national literature must end in abortions like the monster of Frankenstein, things with forms and the instincts of forms, but soulless and therefore revolting. We cannot have expression till there is something to be expressed.

The symptoms of such a birth may be seen in a longing felt here and there for the sustenance of such ideas. At present it shows itself, where felt, in sympathy with the prevalent tone of society by attempts at external action, such as are classed under the head of social reform. But it needs to go deeper before we can have poets, needs to penetrate beneath the springs of action, to stir and remake the soil as by the action of fire.

Another symptom is the need felt by individuals of being even sternly sincere. This is the one great means by which alone progress can be essentially furthered. Truth is the nursing mother of genius. No man can be absolutely true to himself, eschewing cant, compromise, servile imitation, and complaisance, without becoming original, for there is in every creature a fountain of life which, if not choked back by stones and other dead rubbish, will create a fresh atmosphere and bring to life fresh beauty. And it is the same with the nation as with the individual man.

The best work we do for the future is by such truth. By use of that in whatever way, we harrow the soil and lay it open to the sun and air. The winds from all quarters of the globe bring seed enough, and there is nothing wanting but preparation of the soil and freedom in the atmosphere, for ripening of a new and golden harvest.

We are sad that we cannot be present at the gathering-in of this harvest. And yet we are joyous too, when we think that though our name may not be writ on the pillar of our country's fame, we can really do far more towards rearing it than those who come at a later period and to a seemingly fairer task. *Now,* the humblest effort, made in a noble spirit and with religious hope, cannot fail to be even infinitely useful. Whether we introduce some noble model from another time and clime to encourage aspiration in our own, or cheer into blossom the simplest wood-flower that ever rose from the earth, moved by the genuine impulse to grow, independent of the lures of money or celebrity; whether we speak boldly when fear or doubt keep others silent, or refuse to swell the popular cry upon an unworthy occasion, the spirit of truth, purely worshiped, shall turn our acts and forbearances alike to profit, informing them with oracles which the latest time shall bless.

Under present circumstances the amount of talent and labor given to writing ought to surprise us. Literature is in this dim and struggling state, and its pecuniary results exceedingly pitiful. From many well-known causes it is impossible for ninety-nine out of the hundred who wish to use the pen to ransom by its use the time they need. This state of things will have to be changed in some way. No man of genius writes for money; but it is essential to the free use of his powers that he should be able to disembarrass his life from care and perplexity. This is very difficult here; and the state of things gets worse and worse, as less and less is offered in pecuniary meed for works demanding great devotion of time and labor (to say nothing of the ether engaged) and the publisher, obliged to regard the transaction as a matter of business, demands of the author to give him only what will find an immediate market, for he cannot afford to take anything else. This will not do! When an immortal poet was secure only of a few copyists to circulate his works, there were princes and nobles to patronize literature and the arts. Here is only the public, and the public must learn how to cherish the nobler and rarer plants, and to plant the aloe, able to wait a hundred years for its bloom, or its garden will contain presently nothing but potatoes and potherbs. We shall have in the course of the next two or three years a convention of authors to inquire into the causes of this state of things and propose measures for its remedy. Some have already been thought of that look promising, but we shall not announce them till the time be ripe; that date is not distant, for the difficulties increase from day to day in consequence of the system of cheap publication on a great scale.

The ranks that led the way in the first half century of this republic were far better situated than we, in this respect. The country was not so deluged with the dingy page reprinted from Europe, and patriotic vanity was on the alert to answer the question, "Who reads an American book?" And many were the books written as worthy to be read as any out of the first class in England. They were, most of them, except in their subject matter, English books. . . .

[1844–1846]

For Margaret Fuller, as for many other serious writers, Emerson seemed the best candidate for America's prophet of the romantic Ideal. The Emersonian poet would be national because he would be independent, self-reliant, and original. And he would be democratic. You can see from Emerson's own writing, Theodore Parker noted, "that the author lives in a land with free institutions, with town-meetings and ballot boxes. . . ."

82

It is now almost fourteen years since Mr. Emerson published his first book: Nature. A beautiful work it was and will be deemed for many a year to come. In this old world of literature, with more memory than wit, with much tradition and little invention, with more fear than love, and a great deal of criticism upon very little poetry, there came forward this young David, a shepherd, but to be a king, "with his garlands and singing robes about him"; one note upon his new and fresh-strung lyre was "worth a thousand men." Men were looking for something original, they always are; when it came, some said it thundered, others that an angel had spoke. How men wondered at the little book! It took nearly twelve years to sell the five hundred copies of Nature. Since that time Mr. Emerson has said much, and if he has not printed many books, at least has printed much; some things far surpassing the first essay, in richness of material, in perfection of form, in continuity of thought; but nothing which has the same youthful freshness, and the same tender beauty as this early violet, blooming out of Unitarian and Calvinistic sand or snow. Poems and essays of a later date, are there, which show that he has had more time and woven it into life; works which present us with thought deeper, wider, richer, and more complete, but not surpassing the simplicity and loveliness of that maiden flower of his poetic spring. . . .

All of Mr. Emerson's literary works, with the exception of the Poems, were published before they were printed; delivered by word of mouth to various audiences. In frequently reading his pieces, he had an opportunity to see any defect of form and amend it. Mr. Emerson has won by his writings a more desirable reputation, than any other man of letters in America has yet attained. It is not the reputation which brings him money or academic honors, or membership of learned societies; nor does it appear conspicuously in the literary Journals as yet. But he has a high place among thinking men, on both sides of the water; we think no man who writes the English tongue has now so much influence in forming the opinions and character of young men and women. His audience steadily increases, at home and abroad, more rapidly in England than America. It is now with him as it was, at first, with Dr. Channing; the fairest criticism has come from the other side of the water; the reason is that he, like his predecessor, offended the sectarian and party spirit, the personal prejudices of the men about him; his life was a reproach to them, his words an offence, or his doctrines alarmed their sectarian, their party, or their personal pride, and they accordingly condemned the man. A writer who should bear the same relation to the English mind as Emerson to ours, for the same reason would be more acceptable here than at home. Emerson is neither a sectarian nor a partisan, no man less so; yet few men in America have been visited with more hatred,—private personal hatred, which the authors poorly endeavored to conceal, and perhaps did hide from themselves. The spite we have heard expressed against him, by men of the common morality, would strike a stranger with amazement, especially when it is remembered that his personal character and daily life are of such extraordinary loveliness. This hatred has not proceeded merely from ignorant men, in whom it could easily be excused; but more often from men who have had opportunities of obtaining as good a culture as men commonly get in this country. Yet while he has been the theme of vulgar abuse, of sneers and ridicule in public, and in private; while critics, more remarkable for the venom of their poison than the strength of their bow, have shot at him their little shafts, barbed more than pointed, he has also drawn about him some of what old Drayton called "the idle smoke of praise." Let us see what he has thrown into the public fire to cause this incense; what he has done to provoke the immedicable rage of certain other men; let us see what there is in his works, of old or new, true or false, what American and what cosmopolitan; let us weigh his works with such imperfect scales as we have, weigh them by the universal standard of Beauty, Truth and Love, and make an attempt to see what he is worth. . . .

Mr. Emerson is the most American of our writers. The Idea of America, which lies at the bottom of our original institutions, appears in him with great prominence. We mean the idea of personal freedom, of the dignity and value of human nature, the superiority of a man to the accidents of a man. Emerson is the most republican of republicans, the most protestant of the dissenters. Serene as a July sun, he is equally fearless. He looks every thing in the face modestly, but with earnest scrutiny, and passes judgment upon its merits. Nothing is too high for his examination; nothing too sacred. On earth only one thing he finds which is thoroughly venerable, and that is the nature of man; not the accidents, which make a man rich or famous, but the substance, which makes him a man. The man is before the institutions of man; his nature superior to his history. All finite things are only appendages of man, useful, convenient, or beautiful. Man is master, and nature his slave, serving for many a varied use. The results of human experience—the state, the church, society, the family, business, literature, science, art—all of these are subordinate to man: if they serve the individual, he is to foster them, if not, to abandon them and seek better things. He looks at all things, the past and the present, the state and the church, Christianity and the market-house, in the daylight of the intellect. Nothing is allowed to stand between him and his manhood. Hence, there is an apparent irreverence; he does not bow to any hat which Gessler has set up for public adoration, but to every man, canonical or profane, who bears the mark of native manliness. He eats show-bread, if he is hungry. While he is the most American, he is almost the most cosmopolitan of our writers, the least restrained and belittled by the popular follies of the nation or the age.

In America, writers are commonly kept in awe and subdued by fear of the richer class, or that of the mass of men. Mr. Emerson has small respect for either; would bow as low to a lackey as a lord, to a clown as a scholar, to one man as a million. He spurns all constitutions but the law of his own nature, rejecting them with manly scorn. The traditions of the churches are no hindrances to his thought; Jesus or Judas were the same to him, if either stood in his way and hindered the proportionate development of his individual life. The forms of society and the ritual of scholarship are no more effectual restraints. His thought of today is no barrier to freedom of thought tomorrow, for his own nature is not to be subordinated, either to the history of man, or his own history. "Tomorrow to fresh fields and pastures new," is his motto.

Yet, with all this freedom, there is no wilful display of it. He is so confident of his freedom, so perfectly possessed of his rights, that he does not talk of them. They appear, but are not spoken of. With the hopefulness and buoyant liberty of America, he has none of our ill-mannered boasting. He criticizes America often; he always appreciates it; he seldom praises, and never brags of our country. The most democratic of democrats, no disciple of the old régime is better mannered, for it is only the vulgar democrat or aristocrat who flings his follies in your face. While it would be difficult to find a writer so uncompromising in his adhesion to just principles, there is not in all his works a single jeer or ill-natured sarcasm. None is less addicted to the common forms of reverence, but who is more truly reverential?

While his Idea is American, the form of his literature is not less so. It is a form which suits the substance, and is modified by the institutions and natural objects about him. You see that the author lives in a land with free institutions, with town-meetings and ballot-boxes; in the vicinity of a decaying church; amongst men whose terrible devils are Poverty and Social Neglect, the only devils whose damnation is much cared for. His geography is American. Catskill and the Alleghenies, Monadnock, Wachusett, and the uplands of New Hampshire, appear in poetry or prose; Contocook and Agiochook are better than the Ilyssus, or Pactolus, or "smooth-sliding Mincius, crowned with vocal reeds." New York, Fall River, and Lowell have a place in his writings, where a vulgar Yankee would put Thebes or Paestum. His men and women are American—John and Jane, not Coriolanus and Persephone. He tells of the rhodora, the club-moss, the blooming clover, not of the hibiscus and the asphodel. He knows the bumblebee, the blackbird, the bat, and the wren, and is not ashamed to say or sing of the things under his own eyes. He illustrates his high thought by common things out of our plain New England life—the meeting in the church, the Sunday school, the dancing-school, a huckleberry party, the boys and girls hastening home from school, the youth in the shop, beginning an unconscious courtship with his unheeding customer, the farmers about their work in the fields, the bustling trader in the city, the cattle, the new hay, the voters at a town-meeting, the village brawler in a tavern full of tipsy riot, the conservative who thinks the nation is lost if his ticket chance to miscarry, the bigot worshipping the knot hole through which a dusty beam of light has looked in upon his darkness, the radical who declares that nothing is good if established, and the patent reformer who screams in your ears that he can finish the world with a single touch,—and out of all these he makes his poetry, or illustrates his philosophy. Now and then he wanders off to other lands, reports what he has seen, but it is always an American report of what an American eye saw. Even Mr. Emerson's recent exaggerated praise of England is such a panegyric as none but an American could bestow. . . .

From what has been said, notwithstanding the faults we have found in Emerson, it is plain that we assign him a very high rank in the literature of mankind. He is a very extraordinary man. To no English writer since Milton can we assign so high a place; even Milton himself, great genius though he was, and great architect of beauty, has not added so many thoughts to the treasury of the race; no, nor been the author of so much loveliness. Emerson is a man of genius such as does not often appear, such as has never appeared before in America, and but seldom in the world. He learns from all sorts of men, but no English writer, we think, is so original. We sincerely lament the want of logic in his method, and his exaggeration of the intuitive powers, the unhappy consequences of which we see in some of his followers and admirers. They will be more faithful than he to the false principle which he lays down, and will think themselves wise because they do not study, learned because they are ignorant of books, and inspired because they say what outrages common sense. In Emerson's poetry there is often a ruggedness and want of finish which seems wilful in a man like him. This fault is very obvious in those pieces he has put before his several essays. Sometimes there is a seed-corn of thought in the piece, but the piece itself seems like a pile of rubbish shot out of a cart which hinders the seed from germinating. His admirers and imitators not unfrequently give us only the rubbish and probably justify themselves by the example of their master. Spite of these defects, Mr. Emerson, on the whole, speaks with a holy power which no other man possesses who now writes the English tongue. Others have more readers, are never sneered at by respectable men, are oftener praised in the Journals, have greater weight in the pulpits, the cabinets and the councils of the nation; but there is none whose words so sink into the mind and heart of young men and maids; none who work so powerfully to fashion the character of the coming age. Seeing the power which he exercises, and the influence he is likely to have on generations to come, we are jealous of any fault in his matter, or its form, and have allowed no private and foolish friendship to hinder us from speaking of his faults.

This is his source of strength: his intellectual and moral sincerity. He looks after Truth, Justice, and Beauty. He has not uttered a word that is false to his own mind or conscience; has not suppressed a word because he thought it too high for men's comprehension, and therefore dangerous to the repose of men. He never compromises. He sees the chasm between the ideas which come of man's nature and the institutions which represent only his history; he does not seek to cover up the chasm, which daily grows wider between Truth and Public Opinion, between Justice and the State, between Christianity and the Church; he does not seek to fill it up, but he asks men to step over and build institutions commensurate with their ideas. He trusts himself, trusts man, and trusts God. He has confidence in all the attributes of infinity. Hence he is serene; nothing disturbs the even poise of his character, and he walks erect. Nothing impedes him in his search for the true, the lovely and the good; no private hope, no private fear, no love of wife or child, of gold, or ease, or fame. He never seeks his own reputation; he takes care of his Being, and leaves his seeming to take care of itself. Fame may seek him; he never goes out of his way a single inch for her.

He has not written a line which is not conceived in the interest of mankind. He never writes in the interest of a section, of a party, of a church, of a man, always in the interest of mankind. Hence comes the ennobling influence of his works. Most of the literary men of America, most of the men of superior education, represent the ideas and interests of some party; in all that concerns the welfare of the Human Race, they are proportionably behind the mass who have only the common cultures; so while the thought of the people is democratic, putting man before the accidents of a man, the literature of the nation is aristocratic, and opposed to the welfare of mankind. Emerson belongs to the exceptional literature of the times—and while his culture joins him to the history of man, his ideas and his whole life enable him to represent also the nature of man, and so to write for the future. He is one of the rare exceptions amongst our educated men, and helps redeem American literature from the reproach of imitation, conformity, meanness of aim, and hostility to the progress of mankind. No faithful man is too low for his approval and encouragement; no faithless man too high and popular for his rebuke.

A good test of the comparative value of books, is the state they leave you in. Emerson leaves you tranquil, resolved on noble manhood, fearless of the consequences; he gives men to mankind, and mankind to the laws of God. His position is a striking one. Eminently a child of Christianity and of the American idea, he is out of the Church and out of the State. In the midst of Calvinistic and Unitarian superstition, he does not fear God, but loves and trusts Him. He does not worship the idols of our time—Wealth and Respectability, the two calves set up by our modern Jeroboam. He fears not the damnation these idols have the power to inflict—neither poverty nor social disgrace. In busy and bustling New England comes out this man serene and beautiful as a star, and shining like "a good deed in a naughty world." Reproached as an idler, he is active as the sun, and pours out his radiant truth on Lyceums at Chelmsford, at Waltham, at Lowell, and all over the land. Out of a cold Unitarian Church rose this most lovely light. Here is Boston, perhaps the most humane city in America, with its few noble men and women, its beautiful charities, its material vigor, and its hardy enterprise; commercial Boston, where honor is weighed in the public scales, and justice reckoned by the dollars it brings; conservative Boston, the grave of the Revolution, wallowing in its wealth, yet grovelling for more, seeking only money, careless of justice, stuffed with cotton yet hungry for tariffs, sick with the greedy worm of avarice, loving money as the end of life, and bigots as the means of preserving it; Boston, with toryism in its parlors, toryism in its pulpits, toryism in its press, itself a tory town, preferring the accidents of man to man himself—and amidst it all there comes Emerson, graceful as Phoebus-Apollo, fearless and tranquil as the sun he was supposed to guide, and pours down the enchantment of his light, which falls where'er it may, on dust, on diamonds, on decaying heaps to hasten their rapid rot, on seeds new sown to quicken their ambitious germ, or virgin minds of youth and maids to waken the natural seed of nobleness therein, and make it grow to beauty and to manliness. Such is the beauty of his speech, such the majesty of his ideas, such the power of the moral sentiment in men, and such the impression which his whole character makes on them, that they lend him, everywhere, their ears, and thousands bless his manly thoughts.

[1850]

◈ The remarks which preface Emerson's support for the poems of the younger William Ellery Channing have proven more durable than Channing's verses. Emerson's faith in intuition and in the untutored wisdom of the common man led him naturally to the celebration of unlettered genius and the poet buried in each of us.

83 ◈

The tendencies of the times are so democratical, that we shall soon have not so much as a pulpit or raised platform in any church or townhouse, but each person, who is moved to address any public assembly, will speak from the floor. The like revolution in literature is now giving importance to the portfolio over the book. Only one man in the thousand may print a book, but one in ten or one in five may inscribe his thoughts, or at least with short commentary his favorite readings in a private journal. The philosophy of the day has long since broached a more liberal doctrine of the poetic faculty than our fathers held, and reckons poetry the right and power of every man to whose culture justice is done. We own that, though we were trained in a stricter school of literary faith, and were in all our youth inclined to the enforcement of the straitest restrictions on the admission of candidates to the Parnassian fraternity, and denied the name of poetry to every composition in which the workmanship and the material were not equally excellent, in our middle age we have grown lax, and have learned to find pleasure in verses of a ruder strain,—to enjoy *verses of society,* or those effusions which in persons of a happy nature are the easy and unpremeditated translation of their thoughts and feelings into rhyme. This new taste for a certain private and household poetry, for somewhat less pretending than the festal and solemn verses which are written for the nations, really indicates, we suppose, that a new style of poetry exists. The number of writers has increased. Every child has been taught the tongues. The universal communication of the arts of reading and writing has brought the works of the great poets into every house, and made all ears familiar with the poetic forms. The progress of popular institutions has favored self-respect, and broken down that terror of the great, which once imposed awe and hesitation on the talent of the masses society. A wider epistolary intercourse ministers to the ends of sentiment and reflection than ever existed before; the practice of writing diaries is becoming almost general; and every day witnesses new attempts to throw into verse the experiences of private life.

What better omen of true progress can we ask than an increasing intellectual and moral interest of men in each other? What can be better for the republic than that the Capitol, the White House, and the Court House are becoming of less importance than the farm-house and the book-closet? If we are losing our interest in public men, and finding that their spell lay in number and size only, and acquiring instead a taste for the depths of thought and emotion, as they may be sounded in the soul of the citizen or the countryman, does it not replace man for the state, and character for official power? Men should be treated with solemnity; and when they come to chant their private griefs and doubts and joys, they have a new scale by which to compute magnitude and relation. Art is the noblest consolation of calamity. The poet is compensated for his defects in the street and in society, if in his chamber he has turned his mischance into noble numbers.

Is there not room then for a new department in poetry, namely, *Verses of the Portfolio?* We have fancied that we drew greater pleasure from some manuscript verses than from printed ones of equal talent. For there was herein the charm of character; they were confessions; and the faults, the imperfect parts, the fragmentary verses, the halting rhymes, had a worth beyond that of a high finish; for they testified that the writer was more man than artist, more earnest than vain; that the thought was too sweet and sacred to him, than that he should suffer his ears to hear or his eyes to see a superficial defect in the expression.

The characteristic of such verses is, that being not written for publication, they lack that finish which the conventions of literature require of authors. But if poetry of this kind has merit, we conceive that the prescription which demands a rhythmical polish may be easily set aside; and when a writer has outgrown the state of thought which produced the poem, the interest of letters is served by publishing it imperfect, as we preserve studies, torsos, and blocked statues of the great masters. For though we should be loath to see the wholesome conventions, to which we have alluded, broken down by a general incontinence of publication, and every man's and woman's diar/ flying into the bookstores, yet it is to be considered, on the other hand, that men of genius are often more incapable than others of that elaborate execution which criticism exacts. Men of genius in general are, more than others, incapable of any perfect exhibition, because, however agreeable it may be to them to act on the public, it is always a secondary aim. They are humble, self-accusing, moody men, whose worship is toward the Ideal Beauty, which chooses to be courted not so often in perfect hymns, as in wild ear-piercing ejaculations, or in silent musings. Their face is forward, and their heart is in this heaven. By so much are they disqualified for a perfect success in any particular performance to which they can give only a divided affection. But the man of talents has every advantage in the competition. He can give that cool and commanding attention to the thing to be done, that shall secure its just performance. Yet are the failures of genius better than the victories of talent; and we are sure that some crude manuscript poems have yielded us a more sustaining and a more stimulating diet, than many elaborated and classic productions.

We have been led to these thoughts by reading some verses, which were lately put into our hands by a friend with the remark, that they were the production of a youth, who had long passed out of the mood in which he wrote them, so that they had become quite dead to him. Our first feeling on reading them was a lively joy. So then the Muse is neither dead nor dumb, but has found a voice in these cold Cisatlantic States. Here is poetry which asks no aid of magnitude or number, of blood or crime, but finds theatre enough in the first field or brookside, breadth and depth enough in the flow of its own thought. Here is self-repose, which to our mind is stabler than the Pyramids; here is self-respect which leads a man to date from his heart more proudly than from Rome. Here is love which sees through surface, and adores the gentle nature and not the costume. Here is religion, which is not of the Church of England, nor of the Church of Boston. Here is the good wise heart, which sees that the end of culture is strength and cheerfulness. In an age too which tends with so strong an inclination to the philosophical muse, here is poetry more purely intellectual than any American verses we have yet seen, distinguished from all competition by two merits; the fineness of perception; and the poet's trust in his own genius to that degree, that there is an absence of all conventional imagery, and a bold use of that which the moment's mood had made sacred to him, quite careless that it might be sacred to no other, and might even be slightly ludicrous to the first reader. . . .

[1840]

The superficial nationalism of Cornelius Mathews and Young America invited the ridicule it received. But when similar impulses throbbed through the theoretical manifestos of Transcendentalism, American literature had at last found one firm base on which to stand. Emerson was primarily a religious writer. He looked to literature and to the poet for the same thing he required of the state: an "argument" which would liberate the human spirit. The central document is the short book, Nature, *and it should be complemented by the essays on "Self-Reliance" and "The American Scholar." Here are a few well-known lines from this last.*

84 🖾

. . . I look upon the discontent of the literary class as a mere announcement of the fact that they find themselves not in the state of mind of their fathers, and regret the coming state as untried; as a boy dreads the water before he has learned that he can swim. If there is any period one would desire to be born in, is it not the age of Revolution; when the old and the new stand side by side and admit of being compared; when the energies of all men are searched by fear and by hope; when the historic glories of the old can be compensated by the rich possibilities of the new era? This time, like all times, is a very good one, if we but know what to do with it.

I read with some joy of the auspicious signs of the coming days, as they glimmer already through poetry and art, through philosophy and science, through church and state.

One of these signs is the fact that the same movement which effected the elevation of what was called the lowest class in the state, assumed in literature a very marked and as benign an aspect. Instead of the sublime and beautiful, the near, the low, the common, was explored and poetized. That which had been negligently trodden under foot by those who were harnessing and provisioning themselves for long journeys into far countries, is suddenly found to be richer than all foreign parts. The literature of the poor, the feelings of the child, the philosophy of the street, the meaning of household life, are the topics of the time. It is a great stride. It is a sign—is it not?—of new vigor when the extremities are made active, when currents of warm life run into the hands and the feet. I ask not for the great, the remote, the romantic; what is doing in Italy or Arabia;

what is Greek art, or Provençal minstrelsy; I embrace the common, I explore and sit at the feet of the familiar, the low. Give me insight into to-day, and you may have the antique and future worlds. What would we really know the meaning of? The meal in the firkin; the milk in the pan; the ballad in the street; the news of the boat; the glance of the eye; the form and the gait of the body; show me the ultimate reason of these matters; show me the sublime presence of the highest spiritual cause lurking, as always it does lurk, in these suburbs and extremities of nature; let me see every trifle bristling with the polarity that ranges it instantly on an eternal law; and the shop, the plough, and the ledger referred to the like cause by which light undulates and poets sing; and the world lies no longer a dull miscellany and lumber-room, but has form and order; there is no trifle, there is no puzzle, but one design unites and animates the farthest pinnacle and the lowest trench.

This idea has inspired the genius of Goldsmith, Burns, Cowper, and, in a newer time, of Goethe, Wordsworth, and Carlyle. This idea they have differently followed and with various success. In contrast with their writing, the style of Pope, of Johnson, of Gibbon, looks cold and pedantic. This writing is blood-warm. Man is surprised to find that things near are not less beautiful and wondrous than things remote. The near explains the far. The drop is a small ocean. A man is related to all nature. This perception of the worth of the vulgar is fruitful in discoveries. . . .

[1837]

⚞ *"The Poet" is the* Preface *to the* Lyrical Ballads *and* Biographia Litteraria *of American romanticism. It is addressed, as Emerson says, "to the poet concerning his art," and it has a good deal to say about organic form, symbolism, and the poet's use of language. For Emerson the poet's vocation is a high one; he is called to be prophet and seer, a "liberating god"; like Brownson and Margaret Fuller, Emerson believed that great poems are possible only to one who lives a great life.*

He had found no such poetry as yet in America. But the challenge he issued and the advice he offered was soon to be accepted in painstaking detail by Walt Whitman: the lists, the place of industrial change, the role of sex as a symbol for vitality, the art of "terrible simplicity" and the life which hopefully might itself be made an artistic whole.

"The Poet" seems, until its last pages, to discuss a general theory of literature. But its diction should not obscure its nativist implications: "I am not wise enough for a national criticism, and must use the old largeness a little longer, to discharge my errand from the muse to the poet concerning his art." The roots of Emerson's essay lie deep in the American assumption that art has a moral purpose and that even the artist must in some way "bear witness." Emerson means to bring Idealism and the aesthetics of English romanticism to the parched American literary scene; as its influence was to demonstrate, his essay was more local in its implications than its language might at first suggest.

85 ⚞

Those who are esteemed umpires of taste are often persons who have acquired some knowledge of admired pictures or sculptures, and have an inclination for whatever is elegant; but if you inquire whether they are beautiful souls, and whether their own acts are like fair pictures, you learn that they are selfish and sensual. Their cultivation is local, as if you should rub a log of dry wood in one spot to produce fire, all the rest remaining cold. Their knowledge of the fine arts is some study of rules and particulars, or some limited judgment of color or form, which is exercised for amusement or for show. It is a proof of the shallowness of the doctrine of beauty as it lies in the minds of our amateurs, that men seem to have lost the perception of the instant dependence of form upon soul. There is no doctrine of forms in our philosophy. We were put into our bodies, as fire is put into a pan to be carried about; but there is no accurate adjustment between the spirit and the organ, much less is the latter the germination of the former. So in regard to other forms, the intellectual men do not believe in any essential dependence of the material world on thought and volition. Theologians think it a pretty air-castle to talk of the spiritual meaning of a ship or a cloud, of a city or a contract, but they prefer to come again to the solid ground of historical evidence; and even the poets are contented with a civil and conformed manner of living, and to write poems from the fancy, at a safe distance from their own experience. But the highest minds of the world have never ceased to explore the double meaning, or shall I say the quadruple or the centuple or much more manifold meaning, of every sensuous fact; Orpheus, Empedocles, Heraclitus, Plato, Plutarch, Dante, Swedenborg, and the masters of sculpture, picture and poetry. For we are not pans and barrows, nor even porters of the fire and torch-bearers, but children of the fire, made of it, and only the same divinity transmuted and at two or three removes, when we know least about it. And this hidden truth, that the fountains whence all this river of Time and its creatures floweth are intrinsically ideal and beautiful, draws us to the consideration of the nature and functions of the Poet, or the man of Beauty; to the means and materials he uses, and to the general aspect of the art in the present time.

The breadth of the problem is great, for the poet is representative. He stands among partial men for the complete man, and apprises us not of his wealth, but of the common wealth. The young man reveres men of genius, because, to speak truly, they are more himself than he is. They receive of the soul as he also receives, but they more. Nature enhances her beauty, to the eye of loving men, from their belief that the poet is beholding her shows at the same time. He is isolated among his contemporaries by truth and by his art, but with this consolation in his pursuits, that they will draw all men sooner or later. For all men live by truth and stand in need of expression. In love, in art, in avarice, in politics, in labor, in games, we study to utter our painful secret. The man is only half himself, the other half is his expression.

Notwithstanding this necessity to be published, adequate expression is rare. I know not how it is that we need an interpreter, but the great majority of men seem to be minors, who have not yet come into possession of their own, or mutes, who cannot report the conversation they have had with nature. There is no man who does not anticipate a supersensual utility in the sun and stars, earth and water. These stand and wait to render him a peculiar service. But there is some obstruction or some excess of phlegm in our constitution, which does not suffer them to yield the due effect. Too feeble fall the impressions of nature on us to make us artists. Every touch should thrill. Every man should be so much an artist that he could report in conversation what had befallen him. Yet, in our experience, the rays or appulses have sufficient force to arrive at the senses, but not enough to reach the quick and compel the reproduction of themselves in speech. The poet is the person in whom these powers are in balance, the man without impediment, who sees and handles that which others dream of, traverses the whole scale of experience, and is representative of man, in virtue of being the largest power to receive and to impart.

For the Universe has three children, born at one time, which reappear under different names in every system of thought, whether they be called cause, operation and effect; or, more poetically, Jove, Pluto, Neptune; or, theologically, the Father, the Spirit and the Son; but which we will call here the Knower, the Doer and the Sayer. These stand respectively for the love of truth, for the love of good, and for the love of beauty. These three are equal. Each is that which he is, essentially, so that he cannot be surmounted or analyzed, and each of these three has the power of the others latent in him and his own, patent.

The poet is the sayer, the namer, and represents beauty. He is a sovereign, and stands on the centre. For the world is not painted or adorned, but is from the beginning beautiful; and God has not made some beautiful things, but Beauty is the creator of the universe. Therefore the poet is not any permissive potentate, but is emperor in his own right. Criticism is infested with a cant of materialism, which assumes that manual skill and activity is the first merit of all men, and disparages such as say and do not, overlooking the fact that some men, namely poets, are natural sayers, sent into the world to the end of expression, and confounds them with those whose province is action but who quit it to imitate the sayers. But Homer's words are as costly and admirable to Homer as Agamemnon's victories are to Agamemnon. The poet does not wait for the hero or the sage, but, as they act and think primarily, so he writes primarily what will and must be spoken, reckoning the others, though primaries also, yet, in respect to him, secondaries and servants; as sitters or models in the studio of a painter, or as assistants who bring building-materials to an architect.

For poetry was all written before time was, and whenever we are so finely organized that we can penetrate into that region where the air is music, we hear those primal warblings and attempt to write them down, but we lose ever and anon a word or a verse and substitute something of our own, and thus miswrite the poem. The men of more delicate ear write down these cadences more faithfully, and these transcripts, though imperfect, become the songs of the nations. For nature is as truly beautiful as it is good, or as it is reasonable, and must as much appear as it must be done, or be known. Words and deeds are quite indifferent modes of the divine energy. Words are also actions, and actions are a kind of words.

The sign and credentials of the poet are that he announces that which no man foretold. He is the true and only doctor; he knows and tells; he is the only teller of news, for he was present and privy to the appearance which he describes. He is a beholder of ideas and an utterer of the necessary and causal. For we do not speak now of men of poetical talents, or of industry and skill in metre, but of the true poet. I took part in a conversation the other day concerning a recent writer of lyrics, a man of subtle mind, whose head appeared to be a music-box of delicate tunes and rhythms, and whose skill and command of language we could not sufficiently praise. But when the question arose whether he was not only a lyrist but a poet, we were obliged to confess that he is plainly a contemporary, not an eternal man. He does not stand out of our low limitations, like a Chimborazo under the line, running up from a torrid base through all the climates of the globe, with belts of the herbage of every latitude on its high and mottled sides; but this genius is the landscape-garden of a modern house, adorned with fountains and statues, with well-bred men and women standing and sitting in the walks and terraces. We hear, through all the varied music, the ground-tone of conventional life. Our poets are men of talents who sing, and not the children of music. The argument is secondary, the finish of the verses is primary.

For it is not metres, but a metre-making argument that makes a poem,—a thought so passionate and alive that like the spirit of a plant or an animal it has an architecture of its own, and adorns nature with a new thing. The thought and the form are equal in the order of time, but in the order of genesis the thought is prior to the form. The poet has a new thought; he has a whole new experience to unfold; he will tell us how it was with him, and all men will be the richer in his fortune. For the experience of each new age requires a new confession, and the world seems always waiting for its poet. I remember when I was young how much I was moved one morning by tidings that genius had appeared in a youth who sat near me at table. He had left his work and gone rambling none knew whither, and had written hundreds of lines, but could not tell whether that which was in him was therein told; he could tell nothing but that all was changed,—man, beast, heaven, earth and sea. How gladly we listened! how credulous! Society seemed to be compromised. We sat in the aurora of a sunrise which was to put out all the stars. Boston seemed to be at twice the distance it had the night before, or was much farther than that. Rome,—what was Rome? Plutarch and Shakspeare were in the yellow leaf, and Homer no more should be heard of. It is much to know that poetry has been written this very day, under this very roof, by your side. What! that wonderful spirit has not expired! These stony moments are still sparkling and animated! I had fancied that the oracles were all silent, and nature had spent her fires; and behold! all night, from every pore, these fine auroras have been streaming. Every one has some interest in the advent of the poet, and no one knows how much it may concern him. We know that the secret of the world is profound, but who or what shall be our interpreter, we know not. A mountain ramble, a new style or face, a new person, may put the key into our hands. Of course the value of genius to us is in the veracity of its report. Talent may frolic and juggle; genius realizes and adds. Mankind in good earnest have availed so far in understanding themselves and their work, that the foremost watchman on the peak announces his news. It is the truest word ever spoken, and the phrase will be the fittest, most musical, and the unerring voice of the world for that time.

All that we call sacred history attests that the birth of a poet is the principal event in chronology. Man, never so often deceived, still watches for the arrival of a brother who can hold him steady to a truth until he has made it his own. With what joy I begin to read a poem which I confide in as an inspiration! And now my chains are to be broken; I shall mount above these clouds and opaque airs in which I live,—opaque, though they seem transparent,—and from the heaven of truth I shall see and comprehend my relations. That will reconcile me to life and renovate nature, to see trifles animated by a tendency, and to know what I am doing. Life will no more be a noise; now I shall see men and women, and know the signs by which they may be discerned from fools and satans. This day shall be better than my birthday: then I became an animal; now I am invited into the science of the real. Such is the hope, but the fruition is postponed. Oftener it falls that this winged man, who will carry me into the heaven, whirls me into mists, then leaps and frisks about with me as it were from cloud to cloud, still affirming that he is bound heavenward; and I, being myself a novice, am slow in perceiving that he does not know the way into the heavens; and is merely bent that I should admire his skill to rise like a fowl or a flying fish, a little way from the ground or the water; but the all-piercing, all-feeding and ocular air of heaven that man shall never inhabit. I tumble down again soon into my old nooks, and lead the life of exaggerations as before, and have lost my faith in the possibility of any guide who can lead me thither where I would be.

But, leaving these victims of vanity, let us, with new hope, observe how nature, by worthier impulses, has insured the poet's fidelity to his office of announcement and affirming, namely by the beauty of things, which becomes a new and higher beauty when expressed. Nature offers all her creatures to him as a picture-language. Being used as a type, a second wonderful value appears in the object, far better than its old value; as the carpenter's stretched cord, if you hold your ear close enough, is musical in the breeze. "Things more excellent than every image," says Jamblichus, "are expressed through images." Things admit of being used as symbols because nature is a symbol, in the whole, and in every part. Every line we can draw in the sand has expression; and there is no body without its spirit or genius. All form is an effect of character; all condition, of the quality of the life; all harmony, of health; and for this reason a perception of beauty should be sympathetic, or proper only to the good. The beautiful rests on the foundations of the necessary. The soul makes the body, as the wise Spenser teaches:—

> "So every spirit, as it is more pure,
> And hath in it the more of heavenly light,
> So it the fairer body doth procure
> To habit in, and it more fairly dight,
> With cheerful grace and amiable sight.
> For, of the soul, the body form doth take,
> For soul is form, and doth the body make."

Here we find ourselves suddenly not in a critical speculation but in a holy place, and should go very warily and reverently. We stand before the secret of the world, there where Being passes into Appearance and Unity into Variety.

The Universe is the externization of the soul. Wherever the life is, that bursts into appearance around it. Our science is sensual, and therefore superficial. The earth and the heavenly bodies, physics and chemistry, we sensually treat, as if they were self-existent; but these are the retinue of that Being we have. "The mighty heaven," said Proclus, "exhibits, in its transfigurations, clear images of the splendor of intellectual perceptions; being moved in conjunction with the unapparent periods of intellectual natures." Therefore science always goes abreast with the just elevation of the man, keeping step with religion and metaphysics; or the state of science is an index of our self-knowledge. Since every thing in nature answers to a moral power, if any phenomenon remains brute and dark it is because the corresponding faculty in the observer is not yet active.

No wonder then, if these waters be so deep, that we hover over them with a religious regard. The beauty of the fable proves the importance of the sense; to the poet, and to all others; or, if you please, every man is so far a poet as to be susceptible of these enchantments of nature; for all men have the thoughts whereof the universe is the celebration. I find that the fascination resides in the symbol. Who loves nature? Who does not? Is it only poets, and men of leisure and cultivation, who live with her? No; but also hunters, farmers, grooms and butchers, though they express their affection in their choice of life and not in their choice of words. The writer wonders what the coachman or the hunter values in riding, in horses and dogs. It is not superficial qualities. When you talk with him he holds these at as slight a rate as you. His worship is sympathetic; he has no definitions, but he is commanded in nature by the living power which he feels to be there present. No imitation or playing of these things would content him; he loves the earnest of the north wind, of rain, of stone and wood and iron. A beauty not explicable is dearer than a beauty which we can see to the end of. It is nature the symbol, nature certifying the supernatural, body overflowed by life which he worships with coarse but sincere rites.

The inwardness and mystery of this attachment drive men of every class to the use of emblems. The schools of poets and philosophers are not more intoxicated with their symbols than the populace with theirs. In our political parties, compute the power of badges and emblems. See the great ball which they roll from Baltimore to Bunker Hill! In the political processions, Lowell goes in a loom, and Lynn in a shoe, and Salem in a ship. Witness the cider-barrel, the log-cabin, the hickory-stick, the palmetto, and all the cognizances of party. See the power of national emblems. Some stars, lilies, leopards, a crescent, a lion, an eagle, or other figure which came into credit God knows how, on an old rag of bunting, blowing in the wind on a fort at the ends of the earth, shall make the blood tingle under the rudest or the most conventional exterior. The people fancy they hate poetry, and they are all poets and mystics!

Beyond this universality of the symbolic language, we are apprised of the divineness of this superior use of things, whereby the world is a temple whose walls are covered with emblems, pictures and command-ments of the Deity,—in this, that there is no fact in nature which does not carry the whole sense of nature; and the distinctions which we make in events and in affairs, of low and high, honest and base, disappear when nature is used as a symbol. Thought makes everything fit for use. The vocabulary of an omniscient man would embrace words and images excluded from polite conversation. What would be base, or even obscene, to the obscene, becomes illustrious, spoken in a new connection of thought. The piety of the Hebrew prophets purges their grossness. The circumcision is an example of the power of poetry to raise the low and offensive. Small and mean things serve as well as great symbols. The meaner the type by which a law is expressed, the more pungent it is, and the more lasting in the memories of men; just as we choose the smallest box or case in which any needful utensil can be carried. Bare lists of words are found suggestive to an imaginative and excited mind; as it is related of Lord Chatham that he was accustomed to read in Bailey's Dictionary when he was preparing to speak in Parliament. The poorest experience is rich enough for all the purposes of expressing thought. Why covet a knowledge of new facts? Day and night, house and garden, a few books, a few actions, serve us as well as would all trades and all spectacles. We are far from having exhausted the significance of the few symbols we use. We can come to use them yet with a terrible simplicity. It does not need that a poem should be long. Every word was once a poem. Every new relation is a new word. Also we use defects and deformities to a sacred purpose, so expressing our sense that the evils of the world are such only to the evil eye. In the old mythology, mythologists observe, defects are ascribed to divine natures, as lameness to Vulcan, blindness to Cupid, and the like,—to signify exuberances.

For as it is dislocation and detachment from the life of God that makes things ugly, the poet, who re-attaches things to nature and the Whole,—re-attaching even artificial things and violation of nature, to nature, by a deeper insight,—disposes very easily of the most disagreeable facts. Readers of poetry see the factory-village and the railway, and fancy that the poetry of the landscape is broken up by these; for these works of art are not yet consecrated in their reading; but the poet sees them fall within the great Order not less than the beehive or the spider's geometrical web. Nature adopts them very fast into her vital circles, and the gliding train of cars she loves like her own. Besides, in a centred mind, it signifies nothing how many mechanical inventions you exhibit. Though you add millions, and never so surprising, the fact of mechanics has not gained a grain's weight. The spiritual fact remains unalterable, by many or by few particulars; as no mountain is of any appreciable height to break the curve of the sphere. A shrewd country-boy goes to the city for the first time, and the complacent citizen is not satisfied with his little wonder. It is not that he does not see all the fine houses and know that he never saw such before, but he disposes of them as easily as the poet finds place for the railway. The chief value of the new fact is to enhance the great and constant fact of Life, which can dwarf any and every circumstance, and to which the belt of wampum and the commerce of America are alike.

The world being thus put under the mind for verb and noun, the poet is he who can articulate it. For though life is great, and fascinates and absorbs; and though all men are intelligent of the symbols through which it is named; yet they cannot originally use them. We are symbols and inhabit symbols; workmen, work, and tools, words and things, birth and death, all are emblems; but we sympathize with the symbols, and being infatuated with the economical uses of things, we do not know that they are thoughts. The poet, by an ulterior intellectual perception, gives them a power which makes their old use forgotten, and puts eyes and a tongue into every dumb and inanimate object. He perceives the independence of the thought on the symbol, the stability of the thought, the accidency and fugacity of the symbol. As the eyes of Lyncæus were said to see through the earth, so the poet turns the world to glass, and shows us all things in their right series and procession. For through that better perception he stands one step nearer to things, and sees the flowing or metamorphosis; perceives that thought is multiform; that within the form of every creature is a force impelling it to ascend into a higher form; and following with his eyes the life, uses the forms which express that life, and so his speech flows with the flowing of nature. All the facts of the animal economy, sex, nutriment, gestation, birth, growth, are symbols of the passage of the world into the soul of man, to suffer there a change and reappear a new and higher fact. He uses forms according to the life, and not according to the form. This is true science. The poet alone knows astronomy, chemistry, vegetation and animation, for he does not stop at these facts, but employs them as signs. He knows why the plain or meadow of space was strown with these flowers we call suns and moons and stars; why the great deep is adorned with animals, with men, and gods; for in every word he speaks he rides on them as the horses of thought.

By virtue of this science the poet is the Namer or Language-maker, naming things sometimes after their appearance, sometimes after their essence, and giving to every one its own name and not another's, thereby rejoicing the intellect, which delights in detachment or boundary. The poets made all the words, and therefore language is the archives of history, and, if we must say it, a sort of tomb of the muses. For though the origin of most of our words is forgotten, each word was at first a stroke of genius, and obtained currency because for the moment it symbolized the world to the first speaker and to the hearer. The etymologist finds the deadest word to have been once a brilliant picture. Language is fossil poetry. As the limestone of the continent consists of infinite masses of the shells of animalcules, so language is made up of images of tropes, which now, in their secondary use, have long ceased to remind us of their poetic origin. But the poet names the thing because he sees it, or comes one step nearer to it than any other. This expression or naming is not art, but a second nature, grown out of the first, as a leaf out of a tree. What we call nature is a certain self-regulated motion or change; and nature does all things by her own hands, and does not leave another to baptize her but baptizes herself; and this through the metamorphosis again. I remember that a certain poet described it to me thus:—

Genius is the activity which repairs the decays of things, whether wholly or partly of a material and finite kind. Nature, through all her kingdoms, insures herself. Nobody cares for planting the poor fungus; so she shakes down from the gills of one agaric countless spores, any one of which, being preserved, transmits new billions of spores to-morrow or next day. The new agaric of this hour has a chance which the old one had not. This atom of seed is thrown into a new place, not subject to the accidents which destroyed its parent two rods off. She makes a man; and having brought him to ripe age, she will no longer run the risk of losing this wonder at a blow, but she detaches from him a new self, that the kind may be safe from accidents to which the individual is exposed. So when the soul of the poet has come to ripeness of thought, she detaches and sends away from it its poems or songs,—a fearless, sleepless, deathless progeny, which is not exposed to the accidents of the weary kingdom of time; a fearless, vivacious offspring, clad with wings (such was the virtue of the soul out of which they came) which carry them fast and far, and infix them irrecoverably into the hearts of men. These wings are the beauty of the poet's soul. The songs, thus flying immortal from their mortal parent, are pursued by clamorous flights of censures, which swarm in far greater numbers and threaten to devour them; but these last are not winged. At the end of a very short leap they fall plump down and rot, having received from the souls out of which they came no beautiful wings. But the melodies of the poet ascend and leap and pierce into the deeps of infinite time.

So far the bard taught me, using his freer speech. But nature has a higher end, in the production of new individuals, than security, namely *ascension,* or the passage of the soul into higher forms. I knew in my younger days the sculptor who made the statute of the youth which stands in the public garden. He was, as I remember, unable to tell directly what made him happy or unhappy, but by wonderful indirections he could tell. He rose one day, according to his habit, before the dawn, and saw the morning break, grand as the eternity out of which it came, and for many days after, he strove to express this tranquillity, and lo! his chisel had fashioned out of marble the form of a beautiful youth, Phosphorus, whose aspect is such that it is said all persons who look on it become silent. The poet also resigns himself to his mood, and that thought which agitated him is expressed, but *alter idem,* in a manner totally new. The expression is organic, or the new type which things themselves take when liberated. As, in the sun, objects paint their images on the retina of the eye, so they, sharing the aspiration of the whole universe, tend to paint a far more delicate copy of their essence in his mind. Like the metamorphosis of things into higher organic forms is their change into melodies. Over everything stands its dæmon or soul, and, as the form of the thing is reflected by the eye, so the soul of the thing is reflected by a melody. The sea, the mountain-ridge, Niagara, and every flower-bed, pre-exist, or super-exist, in pre-cantations, which sail like odors in the air, and when any man goes by with an ear sufficiently fine, he overhears them and endeavors to write down the notes without diluting or depraving them. And herein is the legitimation of criticism, in the mind's faith that the poems are a corrupt version of some text in nature with which they ought to be made to tally. A rhyme in one of our sonnets should not be less pleasing than the iterated nodes of a seashell, or the resembling difference of a group of flowers. The pairing of the birds is an idyl, not tedious as our idyls are; a tempest is a rough ode, without falsehood or rant; a summer, with its harvest sown, reaped and stored, is an epic song, subordinating how many admirably executed parts. Why should not the symmetry and truth that modulate these, glide into our spirits, and we participate the invention of nature?

This insight, which expresses itself by what is called Imagination, is a very high sort of seeing, which does not come by study, but by the intellect being where and what it sees; by sharing the path or circuit of things through forms, and so making them translucid to others. The path of things is silent. Will they suffer a speaker to go with them? A spy they will not suffer; a lover, a poet, is the transcendency of their own nature,—him they will suffer. The condition of true naming, on the poet's part, is his resigning himself to the divine *aura* which breathes through forms, and accompanying that.

It is a secret which every intellectual man quickly learns, that beyond the energy of his possessed and conscious intellect he is capable of a new energy (as of an intellect doubled on itself), by abandonment to the nature of things; that beside his privacy of power as an individual man, there is a great public power on which he can draw, by unlocking, at all risks, his human doors, and suffering the ethereal tides to roll and circulate through him; then he is caught up into the life of the Universe, his speech is thunder, his thought is law, and his words are universally intelligible as the plants and animals. The poet knows that he speaks adequately then only when he speaks somewhat wildly, or "with the flower of the mind;" not with the intellect used as an organ, but with the intellect released from all service and suffered to take its direction from its celestial life; or as the ancients were wont to express themselves, not with intellect alone but with the intellect inebriated by nectar. As the traveller who has lost his way throws his reins on his horse's neck and trusts to the instinct of the animal to find his road, so must we do with the divine animal who carries us through this world. For if in any manner we can stimulate this instinct, new passages are opened for us into nature; the mind flows into and through things hardest and highest, and the metamorphosis is possible.

This is the reason why bards love wine, mead, narcotics, coffee, tea, opium, the fumes of sandalwood and tobacco, or whatever other procurers of animal exhilaration. All men avail themselves of such means as they can, to add this extraordinary power to their normal powers; and to this end they prize conversation, music, pictures, sculpture, dancing, theatres, travelling, war, mobs, fires, gaming, politics, or love, or science, or animal intoxication,—which are several coarser or finer *quasi*-mechanical substitutes for the true nectar, which is the ravishment of the intellect by coming nearer to the fact. These are auxiliaries to the centrifugal tendency of a man, to his passage out into free space, and they help him to escape the custody of that body in which he is pent up, and of that jail-yard of individual relations in which he is enclosed. Hence a great number of such as were professionally expressers of Beauty, as painters, poets, musicians and actors, have been more than others wont to lead a life of pleasure and indulgence; all but the few who received the true nectar; and, as it was a spurious mode of attaining freedom, as it was an emancipation not into the heavens but into the freedom of baser places, they were punished for that advantage they won, by a dissipation and deterioration. But never can any advantage be taken of nature by a trick. The spirit of the world, the great calm presence of the Creator, comes not forth to the sorceries of opium or of wine. The sublime vision comes to the pure and simple soul in a clean and chaste body. That is not an inspiration, which we owe to narcotics, but some counterfeit excitement and fury. Milton says that the lyric poet may drink wine and live generously, but the epic poet, he who shall sing of the gods and their descent unto men, must drink water out of a wooden bowl. For poetry is not 'Devil's wine,' but God's wine. It is with this as it is with toys. We fill the hands and nurseries of our children with all manner of dolls, drums and horses; withdrawing their eyes from the plain face and sufficing objects of nature, the sun and moon, the animals, the water and stones, which should be their toys. So the poet's habit of living should be set on a key so low that the common influences should delight him. His cheerfulness should be the gift of the sunlight; the air should suffice for his inspiration, and he should be tipsy with water. That spirit which suffices quiet hearts, which seems to come forth to such from every dry knoll of sere grass, from every pine stump and half-imbedded stone on which the dull March sun shines, comes forth to the poor and hungry, and such as are of simple taste. If thou fill thy brain with Boston and New York, with fashion and covetousness, and wilt stimulate thy jaded senses with wine and French coffee, thou shalt find no radiance of wisdom in the lonely waste of the pine woods.

If the imagination intoxicates the poet, it is not inactive in other men. The metamorphosis excites in the beholder an emotion of joy. The use of symbols has a certain power of emancipation and exhilaration for all men. We seem to be touched by a wand which makes us dance and run about happily, like children. We are like persons who come out of a cave or cellar into the open air. This is the effect on us of tropes, fables, oracles and all poetic forms. Poets are thus liberating gods. Men have really got a new sense, and found within their world another world, or nest of worlds; for, the metamorphosis once seen, we divine that it does not stop. I will not now consider how much this makes the charm of algebra and the mathematics, which also have their tropes, but it is felt in every definition; as when Aristotle defines *space* to be an immovable vessel in which things are contained;—or when Plato defines a *line* to be a flowing point; or *figure* to be a bound of solid; and many the like. What a joyful sense of freedom we have when Vitruvius announces the old opinion of artists that no architect can build any house well who does not know something of anatomy. When Socrates, in Charmides, tells us that the soul is cured of its maladies by certain incantations, and that these incantations are beautiful reasons, from which temperance is generated in souls; when Plato calls the world an animal, and Timæus affirms that the plants also are animals; or affirms a man to be a heavenly tree, growing with his root, which is his head, upward; and, as George Chapman, following him, writes,

> "So in our tree of man, whose nervie root
> Springs in his top;"—

when Orpheus speaks of hoariness as "that white flower which marks extreme old age;" when Proclus calls the universe the statue of the intellect; when Chaucer, in his praise of 'Gentilesse,' compares good blood in mean condition to fire, which, though carried to the darkest house betwixt this and the mount of Caucasus, will yet hold its natural office and burn as bright as if twenty thousand men did it behold; when John saw, in the Apocalypse, the ruin of the world through evil, and the stars fall from heaven as the fig tree casteth her untimely fruit; when Æsop reports the whole catalogue of common daily relations through the masquerade of birds and beasts;—we take the cheerful hint of the immortality of our essence and its versatile habit and escapes, as when the gypsies say of themselves "it is in vain to hang them, they cannot die."

The poets are thus liberating gods. The ancient British bards had for the title of their order, "Those who are free throughout the world." They are free, and they make free. An imaginative book renders us much more service at first, by stimulating us through its tropes, than afterward when we arrive at the precise sense of the author. I think nothing is of any value in books excepting the transcendental and extraordinary. If a man is inflamed and carried away by his thought, to that degree that he forgets the authors and the public and heeds only this one dream which holds him like an insanity, let me read his paper, and you may have all the arguments and histories and criticism. All the value which attaches to Pythagoras, Paracelsus, Cornelius Agrippa, Cardan, Kepler, Swedenborg, Schelling, Oken, or any other who introduces questionable facts into his cosmogony, as angels, devils, magic, astrology, palmistry, mesmerism, and so on, is the certificate we have of departure from routine, and that here is a new witness. That also is the best success in conversation, the magic of liberty, which puts the world like a ball in our hands. How cheap even the liberty then seems; how mean to study, when an emotion communicates to the intellect the power to sap and upheave nature; how great the perspective! nations, times, systems, enter and disappear like threads in tapestry of large figure and many colors; dream delivers us to dream, and while the drunkenness lasts we will sell our bed, our philosophy, our religion, in our opulence.

There is good reason why we should prize this liberation. The fate of the poor shepherd, who, blinded and lost in the snow-storm, perishes in a drift within a few feet of his cottage door, is an emblem of the state of man. On the brink of the waters of life and truth, we are miserably dying. The inaccessibleness of every thought but that we are in, is wonderful. What if you come near to it; you are as remote when you are nearest as when you are farthest. Every thought is also a prison; every heaven is also a prison. Therefore we love the poet, the inventor, who in any form, whether in an ode or in an action or in looks and behavior, has yielded us a new thought. He unlocks our chains and admits us to a new scene.

This emancipation is dear to all men, and the power to impart it, as it must come from greater depth and scope of thought, is a measure of intellect. Therefore all books of the imagination endure, all which ascend to that truth that the writer sees nature beneath him, and uses it as his exponent. Every verse or sentence possessing this virtue will take care of its own immortality. The religions of the world are the ejaculations of a few imaginative men.

But the quality of the imagination is to flow, and not to freeze. The poet did not stop at the color or the form, but read their meaning; neither may he rest in this meaning, but he makes the same objects exponents of his new thought. Here is the difference betwixt the poet and the mystic, that the last nails a symbol to one sense, which was a true sense for a moment, but soon becomes old and false. For all symbols are fluxional; all language is vehicular and transitive, and is good, as ferries and horses are, for conveyance, not as farms and houses are, for homestead. Mysticism consists in the mistake of an accidental and individual symbol for an universal one. The morning-redness happens to be the favorite meteor to the eyes of Jacob Behmen, and comes to stand to him for truth and faith; and, he believes, should stand for the same realities to every reader. But the first reader prefers as naturally the symbol of a mother and child, or a gardener and his bulb, or a jeweller polishing a gem. Either of these, or of a myriad more, are equally good to the person to whom they are significant. Only they must be held lightly, and be very willingly translated into the equivalent terms which others use. And the mystic must be steadily told,—All that you say is just as true without the tedious use of that symbol as with it. Let us have a little algebra, instead of this trite rhetoric,—universal signs, instead of these village symbols,—and we shall both be gainers. The history of hierarchies seems to show that all religious error consisted in making the symbol too stark and solid, and was at last nothing but an excess of the organ of language.

Swedenborg, of all men in the recent ages, stands eminently for the translator of nature into thought. I do not know the man in history to whom things stood so uniformly for words. Before him the metamorphosis continually plays. Everything on which his eye rests, obeys the impulses of moral nature. The figs become grapes whilst he eats them. When some of his angels affirmed a truth, the laurel twig which they held blossomed in their hands. The noise which at a distance appeared like gnashing and thumping, on coming nearer was found to be the voice of disputants. The men in one of his visions, seen in heavenly light, appeared like dragons, and seemed in darkness; but to each other they appeared as men, and when the light from heaven shone into their cabin, they complained of the darkness, and were compelled to shut the window that they might see.

There was this perception in him which makes the poet or seer an object of awe and terror, namely that the same man or society of men may wear one aspect to themselves and their companions, and a different aspect to higher intelligences. Certain priests, whom he describes as conversing very learnedly together, appeared to the children who were at some distance, like dead horses; and many the like misappearances. And instantly the mind inquires whether these fishes under the bridge, yonder oxen in the pasture, those dogs in the yard, are immutably fishes, oxen and dogs, or only so appear to me, and perchance to themselves appear upright men; and whether I appear as a man to all eyes. The Brahmins and Pythagoras propounded the same question, and if any poet has witnessed the transformation he doubtless found it in harmony with various experiences. We have all seen changes as considerable in wheat and caterpillars. He is the poet and shall draw us with love and terror, who sees through the flowing vest the firm nature, and can declare it.

I look in vain for the poet whom I describe. We do not with sufficient plainness or sufficient profoundness address ourselves to life, nor dare we chaunt our own times and social circumstance. If we filled the day with bravery, we should not shrink from celebrating it. Time and nature yield us many gifts, but not yet the timely man, the new religion, the reconciler, whom all things await. Dante's praise is that he dared to write his auto-biography in colossal cipher, or into universality. We have yet had no genius in America, with tyrannous eye, which knew the value of our incomparable materials, and saw, in the barbarism and materialism of the times, another carnival of the same gods whose picture he so much ad-mires in Homer; then in the Middle Age; then in Calvinism. Banks and tariffs, the newspaper and caucus, Methodism and Unitarianism, are flat and dull to dull people, but rest on the same foundations of wonder as the town of Troy and the temple of Delphi, and are as swiftly passing away. Our log-rolling, our stumps and their politics, our fisheries, our Negroes and Indians, our boats and our repudiations, the wrath of rogues and the pusillanimity of honest men, the northern trade, the southern planting, the western clearing, Oregon and Texas, are yet unsung. Yet America is a poem in our eyes; its ample geography dazzles the imagina-tion, and it will not wait long for metres. If I have not found that excellent combination of gifts in my countrymen which I seek, neither could I aid myself to fix the idea of the poet by reading now and then in Chalmers's collection of five centuries of English poets. These are wits more than poets, though there have been poets among them. But when we adhere to the ideal of the poet, we have our difficulties even with Milton and Homer. Milton is too literary, and Homer too literal and historical.

But I am not wise enough for a national criticism, and must use the old largeness a little longer, to discharge my errand from the muse to the poet concerning his art.

Art is the path of the creator to his work. The paths or methods are ideal and eternal, though few men ever see them; not the artist himself for years, or for a lifetime, unless he come into the conditions. The painter, the sculptor, the composer, the epic rhapsodist, the orator, all partake one desire, namely to express themselves symmetrically and abundantly, not dwarfishly and fragmentarily. They found or put themselves in certain conditions, as, the painter and sculptor before some impressive human figures; the orator into the assembly of the people; and the others in such scenes as each has found exciting to his intellect; and each presently feels the new desire. He hears a voice, he sees a beckoning. Then he is apprised, with wonder, what herds of dæmons hem him in. He can no more rest; he says, with the old painter, "By God it is in me and must go forth of me." He pursues a beauty, half seen, which flies before him. The poet pours out verses in every solitude. Most of the things he says are conventional, no doubt; but by and by he says something which is original and beautiful. That charms him. He would say nothing else but such things. In our way of talking we say 'That is yours, this is mine;' but the poet knows well that it is not his; that it is as strange and beautiful to him as to you; he would fain hear the like eloquence at length. Once having tasted this immortal ichor, he cannot have enough of it, and as an admirable creative power exists in these intellections, it is of the last importance that these things get spoken. What a little of all we know is said! What drops of all the sea of our science are baled up! and by what accident it is that these are exposed, when so many secrets sleep in nature! Hence the necessity of speech and song; hence these throbs and heart-beatings in the orator, at the door of the assembly, to the end namely that thought may be ejaculated as Logos, or Word.

Doubt not, O poet, but persist. Say 'It is in me, and shall out,' Stand there, balked and dumb, stuttering and stammering, hissed and hooted, stand and strive, until at last rage draw out of thee that *dream*-power which every night shows thee is thine own; a power transcending all limit and privacy, and by virtue of which a man is the conductor of the whole river of electricity. Nothing walks, or creeps, or grows, or exists, which must not in turn arise and walk before him as exponent of his meaning. Comes he to that power, his genius is no longer exhaustible. All the creatures by pairs and by tribes pour into his mind as into a Noah's ark, to come forth again to people a new world. This is like the stock of air for our respiration or for the combustion of our fireplace; not a measure of gallons, but the entire atmosphere if wanted. And therefore the rich poets, as Homer, Chaucer, Shakspeare, and Raphael, have obviously no limits to their works except the limits of their lifetime, and resemble a mirror carried through the street, ready to render an image of every created thing.

O poet! a new nobility is conferred in groves and pastures, and not in castles or by the sword-blade any longer. The conditions are hard, but equal. Thou shalt leave the world, and know the muse only. Thou shalt not know any longer the times, customs, graces, politics, or opinions of men, but shalt take all from the muse. For the time of towns is tolled from the world by funeral chimes, but in nature the universal hours are counted by succeeding tribes of animals and plants, and by growth of joy on joy. God wills also that thou abdicate a manifold and duplex life, and that thou be content that others speak for thee. Others shall be thy gentlemen and shall represent all courtesy and worldly life for thee; others shall do the great and resounding actions also. Thou shalt lie close hid with nature, and canst not be afforded to the Capitol or the Exchange. The world is full of renunciations and apprenticeships, and this is thine; thou must pass for a fool and a churl for a long season. This is the screen and sheath in which Pan has protected his well-beloved flower, and thou shalt be known only to thine own, and they shall console thee with tenderest love. And thou shalt not be able to rehearse the names of thy friends in thy verse, for an old shame before the holy ideal. And this is the reward; that the ideal shall be real to thee, and the impressions of the actual world shall fall like summer rain, copious, but not troublesome to thy invulnerable essence. Thou shalt have the whole land for thy park and manor, the sea for thy bath and navigation, without tax and without envy; the woods and the rivers thou shalt own, and thou shalt possess that wherein others are only tenants and boarders. Thou true land-lord! sea-lord! air-lord! Wherever snow falls or water flows or birds fly, wherever day and night meet in twilight, wherever the blue heaven is hung by clouds or sown with stars, wherever are forms with transparent boundaries, wherever are outlets into celestial space, wherever is danger, and awe, and love,—there is Beauty, plenteous as rain, shed for thee, and though thou shouldst walk the world over, thou shalt not be able to find a condition inopportune or ignoble.

[1844]

One solution to the problem of American literature was making its way during the middle years of the century almost unnoticed, although the license to exaggerate claimed by the romancers might well seem an implicit admission that ordinary American materials were of little use to the writer of narrative fiction. Hawthorne was not, of course, the first to write romance. Edward Tyrell Channing's essay of 1819 (q.v.) describes the work of C. B. Brown in terms which retain their validity in our own day, and when Simms sought to define the romance, he decided that "The Romance is of loftier origin than the Novel. It approximates the poem. It may be described as an amalgam of the two." The second selection here may serve to introduce Hawthorne's familiar prefaces; his picture of the Master Genius anticipates Melville's remarks in "Hawthorne and His Mosses" (q.v.). Hawthorne's prefaces should be read in their entirety; the lengthy Custom-House sketch in particular can be viewed as an essay on the theory of fiction. His statements here seem coherent enough, and yet in practice Hawthorne rarely mastered the American problem of form. The point becomes well-nigh explicit in his discussion of The Marble Faun: *his romance demanded the excision of excessive novelistic detail, but his attraction to the Rome of fact and history proved irresistible. In the concluding item here, Trollope casts his novelist's eye over the flawed* Faun. *He attempts sympathy with an American literature built on dreams, but his taste proves in the end dominated by the realism of beef and ale.*

86 &

. . . You will note that I call "The Yemassee" a romance, and not a novel. You will permit me to insist upon the distinction. I am unwilling that the story shall be examined by any other than those standards which have governed me in its composition; and unless the critic is prepared to adopt with me those leading principles, in accordance with which the book has been written, the sooner we part company the better.

Supported by the authority of common sense and practice, to say nothing of Pope—

> "In every work regard the writer's end,
> Since none can compass more than they intend—"

I have surely a right to insist upon this particular. It is only when an author departs from his own standard (speaking of his labours as a work of art), that he offends against propriety and merits censure. Reviewing "Atalantis," a fairy tale, full of fanciful machinery, and without a purpose, save the embodiment to the mind's eye of some of those

> "Gay creatures of the element,
> That, in the colour of the rainbow live,
> And play i' the flighted clouds—"

one of my critics—then a very distinguished writer—gravely remarked, in a very popular periodical, "Magic is now beyond the credulity of eight years;" and yet the author *set out* to make a tale of magic, *knowing* it to be thus beyond the range of the probable—knowing that all readers were equally sagacious—and never, for a moment, contemplated the deception of any sober citizen.

The question briefly is—What are the standards of the modern Romance? What is the modern Romance itself? The reply is immediate. The modern Romance is the substitute which the people of the present day offer for the ancient epic. The form is changed; the matter is very much the same; at all events, it differs much more seriously from the English novel than it does from the epic and the drama, because the difference is one of material, even than of fabrication. The reader who, reading Ivanhoe, keeps Richardson and Fielding beside him, will be at fault in every step of his progress. The domestic novel of those writers, confined to the felicitous narration of common and daily occurring events, and the grouping and delineation of characters in ordinary conditions of society, as altogether a different sort of composition; and if, in a strange doggedness, or simplicity of spirit, such a reader happens to pin his faith to such writers alone, circumscribing the boundless horizon of art to the domestic circle, the Romances of Maturin, Scott, Bulwer, and others of the present day, will be little better than rhapsodical and intolerable nonsense.

When I say that our Romance is the substitute of modern times for the epic or the drama, I do not mean to say that they are exactly the same things, and yet, examined thoroughly . . . the differences between them are very slight. These differences depend on the material employed, rather than upon the particular mode in which it is used. The Romance is of loftier origin than the Novel. It approximates the poem. It may be described as an amalgam of the two. It is only with those who are apt to insist upon poetry as verse, and to confound rhyme with poetry, that the resemblance is unapparent. The standards of the Romance—take such a story, for example, as the Ivanhoe of Scott, or the Salathiel of Croly,—are very much those of the epic. It invests individuals with an absorbing interest—it hurries them rapidly through crowding and exacting events, in a narrow space of time—it requires the same unities of plan, of purpose, and harmony of parts, and it seeks for its adventures among the wild and wonderful. It does not confine itself to what is known, or even what is probable. It grasps at the possible; and, placing a human agent in hitherto untried situations, it exercises its ingenuity in extricating him from them, while describing his feelings and his fortunes in his progress. The task has been well or ill done, in proportion to the degree of ingenuity and knowledge which the romancer exhibits in carrying out the details, according to such proprieties as are called for by the circumstances of the story. These proprieties are the standards set up at his starting, and to which he is required religiously to confine himself.

"The Yemassee" is proposed as an *American* romance. It is so styled as much of the material could have been furnished by no other country. Something too much of extravagance—so some may think,—even beyond the usual license of fiction—may enter into certain parts of the narrative. On this subject, it is enough for me to say, that the popular faith yields abundant authority for the wildest of its incidents. The natural romance of our country has been my object, and I have not dared beyond it. For the rest—for the general peculiarities of the Indians, in their undegraded condition—my authorities are numerous in all the writers who have written from their own experience. My chief difficulty, I may add, has risen rather from the discrimination necessary in picking and choosing, than from any deficiency of the material itself. It is needless to add that the historical events are strictly true, and that the outline is to be found in the several chronicles devoted to the region of country in which the scene is laid. A slight anachronism occurs in one of the early chapters, but it has little bearing upon the story, and is altogether unimportant.

But I must not trespass upon your patience, if I do upon your attention. If you read "The Yemassee" *now*, with such changes of mood and judgment as I must acknowledge in my own case, I can hardly hope that it will please you as it did twenty years ago. And yet, my friend, could we both read it as we did then! Ah! how much more grateful our faith than our knowledge! How much do we lose by our gains—how much do our acquisitions cost us!

[1853]

87 ✍

A man of fancy made an entertainment at one of his castles in the air, and invited a select number of distinguished personages to favor him with their presence. The mansion, though less splendid than many that have been situated in the same region, was, nevertheless, of a magnificence such as is seldom witnessed by those acquainted only with terrestrial architecture. Its strong foundations and massive walls were quarried out of a ledge of heavy and sombre clouds, which had hung brooding over the earth, apparently as dense and ponderous as its own granite, throughout a whole autumnal day. Perceiving that the general effect was gloomy—so that the airy castle looked like a feudal fortress, or a monastery of the middle ages, or a state-prison of our own times, rather than the home of pleasure and repose which he intended it to be—the owner, regardless of expense, resolved to gild the exterior from top to bottom. Fortunately, there was just then a flood of evening sunshine in the air. This being gathered up and poured abundantly upon the roof and walls, imbued them with a kind of solemn cheerfulness; while the cupolas and pinnacles were made to glitter with the purest gold, and all the hundred windows gleamed with a glad light, as if the edifice itself were rejoicing in its heart. And now, if the people of the lower world chanced to be looking upward, out of the turmoil of their petty perplexities, they probably mistook the castle in the air for a heap of sunset clouds, to which the magic of light and shade had imparted the aspect of a fantastically constructed mansion. To such beholders it was unreal, because they lacked the imaginative faith. Had they been worthy to pass within its portal, they would have recognized the truth, that the dominions which the spirit conquers for itself among unrealities, become a thousand times more real than the earth whereon they stamp their feet, saying, "This is solid and substantial!—this may be called a fact!"

At the appointed hour, the host stood in his great saloon to receive the company. It was a vast and noble room, the vaulted ceiling of which was supported by double rows of gigantic pillars, that had been hewn entire out of masses of variegated clouds. So brilliantly were they polished, and so exquisitely wrought by the sculptor's skill, as to resemble the finest specimens of emerald, porphyry, opal, and chrysolite, thus producing a delicate richness of effect, which their immense size rendered not incompatible with grandeur. To each of these pillars a meteor was suspended. Thousands of these ethereal lustres are continually wandering about the firmament, burning out to waste, yet capable of imparting a useful radiance to any person who has the art of converting them to domestic purposes. As managed in the saloon, they are far more economical than ordinary lamp-light. Such, however, was the intensity of their blaze, that it has been found expedient to cover each meteor with a globe of evening mist, thereby muffling the too potent glow, and soothing it into a mild and comfortable splendor. It was like the brilliancy of a powerful, yet chastened, imagination; a light which seemed to hide whatever was unworthy to be noticed, and give effect to every beautiful and noble attribute. The guests, therefore, as they advanced up the centre of the saloon, appeared to better advantage than ever before in their lives. . . .

But now appeared a stranger, whom the host had no sooner recognized, than, with an abundance of courtesy unlavished on any other, he hastened down the whole length of the saloon, in order to pay him emphatic honor. Yet he was a young man in poor attire, with no insignia of rank or acknowledged eminence, nor anything to distinguish him among the crowd except a high, white forehead, beneath which a pair of deep-set eyes were glowing with warm light. It was such a light as never illuminates the earth, save when a great heart burns as the household fire of a grand intellect. And who was he? Who but the Master Genius, for whom our country is looking anxiously into the mist of time, as destined to fulfil the great mission of creating an American literature, hewing it, as it were, out of the unwrought granite of our intellectual quarries. From him, whether moulded in the form of an epic poem, or assuming a guise altogether new, as the spirit itself may determine, we are to receive our first great original work, which shall do all that remains to be achieved for our glory among the nations. How this child of a mighty destiny had been discovered by the Man of Fancy, it is of little consequence to mention. Suffice it, that he dwells as yet unhonored among men, unrecognized by those who have known him from his cradle;—the noble countenance which should be distinguished by a halo diffused around it, passes daily amid the throng of people, toiling and troubling themselves about trifles of a moment—and none pay reverence to the work of immortality. Nor does it matter much to him, in his triumph over all the ages, though a generation or two of his own times shall do themselves the wrong to disregard him.

By this time, Monsieur On-Dit had caught up the stranger's name and destiny, and was busily whispering the intelligence among the other guests.

"Pshaw!" said one, "there can never be an American Genius."

"Pish!" cried another, "we have already as good poets as any in the world. For my part, I desire to see no better."

And the Oldest Inhabitant, when it was proposed to introduce him to the Master Genius, begged to be excused, observing that a man who had been honored with the acquaintance of Dwight, Freneau, and Joel Barlow, might be allowed a little austerity of taste. . . .

[1844]

88 ✍

. . . Either of these stern and black-browed Puritans would have thought it quite a sufficient retribution for his sins, that, after so long a lapse of years, the old trunk of the family tree, with so much venerable moss upon it, should have borne, as its topmost bough, an idler like myself. No aim, that I have ever cherished, would they recognize as laudable; no success of mine—if my life, beyond its domestic scope, had ever been brightened by success—would they deem otherwise than worthless, if not positively disgraceful. "What is he?" murmurs one gray shadow of my forefathers to the other. "A writer of story-books! What kind of a business in life,—what mode of glorifying God, or being serviceable to mankind in his day and generation,—may that be? Why, the degenerate fellow might as well have been a fiddler!"

On Hester Prynne's story, therefore, I bestowed much thought. It was the subject of my meditations for many an hour, while pacing to and fro across my room, or traversing, with hundredfold repetition, the long extent from the front-door of the Custom-House to the side-entrance, and back again. Great were the weariness and annoyance of the old Inspector and the Weighers and Gaugers, whose slumbers were disturbed by the unmercifully lengthened tramp of my passing and returning footsteps. Remembering their own former habits, they used to say that the Surveyor was walking the quarter-deck. They probably fancied that my sole object—and, indeed, the sole object for which a sane man could ever put himself into voluntary motion—was, to get an appetite for dinner. And to say the truth, an appetite, sharpened by the east-wind that generally blew along the passage, was the only valuable result of so much indefatigable exercise. So little adapted is the atmosphere of a Custom-House to the delicate harvest of fancy and sensibility, that, had I remained there through ten Presidencies yet to come, I doubt whether the tale of "The Scarlet Letter" would ever have been brought before the public eye. My imagination was a tarnished mirror. It would not reflect, or only with miserable dimness, the figures with which I did my best to people it. The characters of the narrative would not be warmed and rendered malleable, by any heat that I could kindle at my intellectual forge. They would take neither the glow of passion nor the tenderness of sentiment, but retained all the rigidity of dead corpses, and stared me in the face with a fixed and ghastly grin of contemptuous defiance. "What have you to do with us?" that expression seemed to say. "The little power you might once have possessed over the tribe of unrealities is gone! You have bartered it for a pittance of the public gold. Go, then, and earn your wages!" In short, the almost torpid creatures of my own fancy twitted me with imbecility, and not without fair occasion.

It was not merely during the three hours and a half which Uncle Sam claimed as his share of my daily life, that this wretched numbness held possession of me. It went with me on my sea-shore walks and rambles into the country, whenever—which was seldom and reluctantly—I bestirred myself to seek that invigorating charm of Nature, which used to give me such freshness and activity of thought, the moment that I stepped across the threshold of the Old Manse. The same torpor, as regarded the capacity for intellectual effort, accompanied me home, and weighed upon me in the chamber which I most absurdly termed my study. Nor did it quit me, when, late at night, I sat in the deserted parlour, lighted only by the glimmering coal-fire and the moon, striving to picture forth imaginary scenes, which, the next day, might flow out on the brightening page in many-hued description.

If the imaginative faculty refused to act at such an hour, it might well be deemed a hopeless case. Moonlight, in a familiar room, falling so white upon the carpet, and showing all its figures so distinctly,—making every object so minutely visible, yet so unlike a morning or noontide visibility,—is a medium the most suitable for a romance-writer to get acquainted with his illusive guests. There is the little domestic scenery of the well-known apartment; the chairs, with each its separate individuality; the centre-table, sustaining a work-basket, a volume or two, and an extinguished lamp; the sofa; the book-case; the picture on the wall;—all these details, so completely seen, are so spiritualized by the unusual light, that they seem to lose their actual substance, and become things of intellect. Nothing is too small or too trifling to undergo this change, and acquire dignity thereby. A child's shoe; the doll, seated in her little wicker carriage; the hobby-horse;—whatever, in a word, has been used or played with, during the day, is now invested with a quality of strangeness and remoteness, though still almost as vividly present as by daylight. Thus, therefore, the floor of our familiar room has become a neutral territory, somewhere between the real world and fairy-land, where the Actual and the Imaginary may meet, and each imbue itself with the nature of the other. Ghosts might enter here, without affrighting us. It would be too much in keeping with the scene to excite surprise, were we to look about us and discover a form, beloved, but gone hence, now sitting quietly in a streak of this magic moonshine, with an aspect that would make us doubt whether it had returned from afar, or had never once stirred from our fireside.

The somewhat dim coal-fire has an essential influence in producing the effect which I would describe. It throws its unobtrusive tinge throughout the room, with a faint ruddiness upon the walls and ceiling, and a reflected gleam from the polish of the furniture. This warmer light mingles itself with the cold spirituality of the moonbeams, and communicates, as it were, a heart and sensibilities of human tenderness to the forms which fancy summons up. It converts them from snow-images into men and women. Glancing at the looking-glass, we behold—deep within its haunted verge—the smouldering glow of the half-extinguished anthracite, the white moonbeams on the floor, and a repetition of all the gleam and shadow of the picture, with one remove farther from the actual, and nearer to the imaginative. Then, at such an hour, and with this scene before him, if a man, sitting all alone, cannot dream strange things, and make them look like truth, he need never try to write romances.

But, for myself, during the whole of my Custom-House experience, moonlight and sunshine, and the glow of firelight, were just alike in my regard; and neither of them was of one whit more avail than the twinkle of a tallow-candle. An entire class of susceptibilities, and a gift connected with them,—of no great richness or value, but the best I had,—was gone from me.

It is my belief, however, that, had I attempted a different order of composition, my faculties would not have been found so pointless and inefficacious. I might, for instance, have contented myself with writing out the narratives of a veteran shipmaster, one of the Inspectors, whom I should be most ungrateful not to mention; since scarcely a day passed that he did not stir me to laughter and admiration by his marvellous gifts as a story-teller. Could I have preserved the picturesque force of his style, and the humorous coloring which nature taught him how to throw over his descriptions, the result, I honestly believe, would have been something new in literature. Or I might readily have found a more serious task. It was a folly, with the materiality of this daily life pressing so intrusively upon me, to attempt to fling myself back into another age; or to insist on creating the semblance of a world out of airy matter, when, at every moment, the impalpable beauty of my soap-bubble was broken by the rude contact of some actual circumstance. The wiser effort would have been, to diffuse thought and imagination through the opaque substance of to-day, and thus to make it a bright transparency; to spiritualize the burden that began to weigh so heavily; to seek, resolutely, the true and indestructible value that lay hidden in the petty and wearisome incidents, and ordinary characters, with which I was now conversant. The fault was mine. The page of life that was spread out before me seemed dull and commonplace, only because I had not fathomed its deeper import. A better book than I shall ever write was there; leaf after leaf presenting itself to me, just as it was written out by the reality of the flitting hour, and vanishing as fast as written, only because my brain wanted the insight and my hand the cunning to transcribe it. At some future day, it may be, I shall remember a few scattered fragments and broken paragraphs, and write them down, and find the letters turn to gold upon the page. . . .

[1850]

89 ✍

When a writer calls his work a Romance, it need hardly be observed that he wishes to claim a certain latitude, both as to its fashion and material, which he would not have felt himself entitled to assume, had he professed to be writing a Novel. The latter form of composition is presumed to aim at a very minute fidelity, not merely to the possible, but to the probable and ordinary course of man's experience. The former—while, as a work of art, it must rigidly subject itself to laws, and while it sins unpardonably, so far as it may swerve aside from the truth of the human heart—has fairly a right to present that truth under circumstances, to a great extent, of the writer's own choosing or creation. If he think fit, also, he may so manage his atmospherical medium as to bring out or mellow the lights and deepen and enrich the shadows of the picture. He will be wise, no doubt, to make a very moderate use of the privileges here stated, and, especially, to mingle the Marvellous rather as a slight, delicate, and evanescent flavor, than as any portion of the actual substance of the dish offered to the Public. He can hardly be said, however, to commit a literary crime, even if he disregard this caution.

In the present work, the Author has proposed to himself (but with what success, fortunately, it is not for him to judge) to keep undeviatingly within his immunities. The point of view in which this Tale comes under the Romantic definition, lies in the attempt to connect a by-gone time with the very Present that is flitting away from us. It is a Legend, pro-longing itself, from an epoch now gray in the distance, down into our own broad daylight, and bringing along with it some of its legendary mist, which the Reader, according to his pleasure, may either disregard, or allow it to float almost imperceptibly about the characters and events, for the sake of a picturesque effect. The narrative, it may be, is woven of so humble a texture as to require this advantage, and, at the same time, to render it the more difficult of attainment.

Many writers lay very great stress upon some definite moral purpose, at which they profess to aim their works. Not to be deficient, in this par-ticular, the Author has provided himself with a moral;—the truth, namely, that the wrong-doing of one generation lives into the successive ones, and, divesting itself of every temporary advantage, becomes a pure and uncontrollable mischief;—and he would feel it a singular gratifica-tion, if this Romance might effectually convince mankind (or, indeed, any one man) of the folly of tumbling down an avalanche of ill-gotten gold, or real estate, on the heads of an unfortunate posterity, thereby to maim and crush them, until the accumulated mass shall be scattered abroad in its original atoms. In good faith, however, he is not sufficiently imagina-tive to flatter himself with the slightest hope of this kind. When romances do really teach anything, or produce any effective operation, it is usually through a far more subtle process than the ostensible one. The Author has considered it hardly worth his while, therefore, relentlessly to impale the story with its moral, as with an iron rod—or rather, as by sticking a pin through a butterfly—thus at once depriving it of life, and causing it to stiffen in an ungainly and unnatural attitude. A high truth, indeed, fairly, finely, and skilfully wrought out, brightening at every step, and crowning the final development of a work of fiction, may add an artistic glory, but is never any truer, and seldom any more evident, at the last page than at the first.

The Reader may perhaps choose to assign an actual locality to the imaginary events of this narrative. If permitted by the historical connec-tion, (which, though slight, was essential to his plan,) the Author would very willingly have avoided anything of this nature. Not to speak of other objections, it exposes the Romance to an inflexible and exceedingly dangerous species of criticism, by bringing his fancy-pictures almost into positive contact with the realities of the moment. It has been no part of his object, however, to describe local manners, nor in any way to meddle with the characteristics of a community for whom he cherishes a proper respect and a natural regard. He trusts not to be considered as unpardon-ably offending, by laying out a street that infringes upon nobody's private rights, and appropriating a lot of land which had no visible owner, and building a house, of materials long in use for constructing castles in the air. The personages of the Tale—though they give themselves out to be of ancient stability and considerable prominence—are really of the Author's own making, or, at all events, of his own mixing; their virtues can shed no lustre, nor their defects redound, in the remotest degree, to the discredit of the venerable town of which they profess to be inhabitants. He would be glad, therefore, if—especially in the quarter to which he alludes—the book may be read strictly as a Romance, having a great deal more to do with the clouds overhead, than with any portion of the actual soil of the County of Essex.

[1851]

90 ✍

In the "BLITHEDALE" of this volume many readers will, probably, suspect a faint and not very faithful shadowing of BROOK FARM, in Roxbury, which (now a little more than ten years ago) was occupied and cultivated by a company of socialists. The author does not wish to deny that he had this community in his mind, and that (having had the good fortune, for a time, to be personally connected with it) he has occasionally availed himself of his actual reminiscences, in the hope of giving a more life-like tint to the fancy-sketch in the following pages. He begs it to be understood, however, that he has considered the institution itself as not less fairly the subject of fictitious handling than the imaginary personages whom he has introduced there. His whole treatment of the affair is altogether incidental to the main purpose of the romance; nor does he put forward the slightest pretensions to illustrate a theory, or elicit a conclusion, favorable or otherwise, in respect to socialism.

In short, his present concern with the socialist community is merely to establish a theatre, a little removed from the highway of ordinary travel, where the creatures of his brain may play their phantasmagorical antics, without exposing them to too close a comparison with the actual events of real lives. In the old countries, with which fiction has long been conversant, a certain conventional privilege seems to be awarded to the romancer; his work is not put exactly side by side with nature; and he is allowed a license with regard to every-day probability, in view of the improved effects which he is bound to produce thereby. Among ourselves, on the contrary, there is as yet no such Faery Land, so like the real world, that, in a suitable remoteness, one cannot well tell the difference, but with an atmosphere of strange enchantment, beheld through which the inhabitants have a propriety of their own. This atmosphere is what the American romancer needs. In its absence, the beings of imagination are compelled to show themselves in the same category as actually living mortals; a necessity that generally renders the paint and pasteboard of their composition but too painfully discernible. With the idea of partially obviating this difficulty (the sense of which has always pressed very heavily upon him), the author has ventured to make free with his old and affectionately remembered home at BROOK FARM, as being certainly the most romantic episode of his own life,—essentially a day-dream, and yet a fact,—and thus offering an available foothold between fiction and reality. Furthermore, the scene was in good keeping with the personages whom he desired to introduce. . . .

[1852]

91 ✍

. . . This Romance was sketched out during a residence of considerable length in Italy, and has been rewritten and prepared for the press in England. The author proposed to himself merely to write a fanciful story, evolving a thoughtful moral, and did not purpose attempting a portraiture of Italian manners and character. He has lived too long abroad not to be aware that a foreigner seldom acquires that knowledge of a country at once flexible and profound, which may justify him in endeavoring to idealize its traits.

Italy, as the site of his Romance, was chiefly valuable to him as affording a sort of poetic or fairy precinct, where actualities would not be so terribly insisted upon as they are, and must needs be, in America. No author, without a trial, can conceive of the difficulty of writing a romance about a country where there is no shadow, no antiquity, no mystery, no picturesque and gloomy wrong, nor anything but a commonplace prosperity, in broad and simple daylight, as is happily the case with my dear native land. It will be very long, I trust, before romance writers may find congenial and easily handled themes, either in the annals of our stalwart republic, or in any characteristic and probable events of our individual lives. Romance and poetry, ivy, lichens, and wall-flowers, need ruin to make them grow.

In rewriting these volumes, the author was somewhat surprised to see the extent to which he had introduced descriptions of various Italian objects, antique, pictorial, and statuesque. Yet these things fill the mind everywhere in Italy, and especially in Rome, and cannot easily be kept from flowing out upon the page when one writes freely and with self-enjoyment. And, again, while reproducing the book, on the broad and dreary sands of Redcar, with the gray German Ocean tumbling in upon me, and the northern blast always howling in my ears, the complete change of scene made these Italian reminiscences shine out so vividly that I could not find it in my heart to cancel them. . . .

[1860]

92 🖎

The creations of American literature generally are no doubt more given to the speculative,—less given to the realistic,—than are those of English literature. On our side of the water we deal more with beef and ale, and less with dreams. Even with the broad humor of Bret Harte, even with the broader humor of Artemus Ward and Mark Twain, there is generally present an undercurrent of melancholy, in which pathos and satire are intermingled. There was a touch of it even with the simple-going Cooper and the kindly Washington Irving. Melancholy and pathos, without the humor, are the springs on which all Longfellow's lines are set moving. But in no American writer is to be found the same predominance of weird imagination as in Hawthorne. There was something of it in M. G. Lewis—our Monk Lewis as he came to be called, from the name of a tale which he wrote; but with him, as with many others, we feel that they have been weird because they have desired to be so. They have struggled to achieve the tone with which their works are pervaded. With Hawthorne we are made to think that he could not have been anything else if he would. . . .

I have space to mention but one other of our author's works; "The Marble Faun," as it is called in America, and published in England under the name of "Transformation; or, The Romance of Monte Beni." The double name, which has given rise to some confusion, was, I think, adopted with the view of avoiding the injustice to which American and English authors are subjected by the want of international copyright. Whether the object was attained, or was in any degree attainable by such means, I do not know.

In speaking of "The Marble Faun," as I will call the story, I hardly know whether, as a just critic, to speak first of its faults or of its virtues. As one always likes to keep the sweetest bits for the end of the banquet, I will give priority of place to my caviling. The great fault of the book lies in the absence of arranged plot. The author, in giving the form of a novel to the beautiful pictures and images which his fancy has enabled him to draw, and in describing Rome and Italian scenes as few others have described them, has in fact been too idle to carry out his own purpose of constructing a tale. We will grant that a novelist may be natural or supernatural. Let us grant, for the occasion, that the latter manner, if well handled, is the better and the more efficacious. And we must grant also that he who soars into the supernatural need not bind himself by any of the ordinary trammels of life. His men may fly, his birds may speak. His women may make angelic music without instruments. His cherubs may sit at the piano. This wide latitude, while its adequate management is much too difficult for ordinary hands, gives facility for the working of a plot. But there must be some plot, some arrangement of circumstances, with an intelligible conclusion, or the reader will not be satisfied. If, then, a ghost, who,—shall I say which?—is made on all occasions to act as a *Deus ex machina,* and to create and to solve every interest, we should know something of the ghost's antecedents, something of the causes which have induced him, or it, to meddle in the matter under discussion. The ghost of Hamlet's father had a manifest object, and the ghost of Banquo a recognized cause. In "The Marble Faun" there is no ghost, but the heroine of the story is driven to connive at murder, and the hero to commit murder, by the disagreeable intrusion of a personage whose *raison d'être* is left altogether in the dark. "The gentle reader," says our author as he ends his narrative, "would not thank us for one of those minute elucidations which are so tedious and after all so unsatisfactory in clearing up the romantic mysteries of a story." There our author is, I think, in error. His readers will hardly be so gentle as not to require from him some explanation of the causes which have produced the romantic details to which they have given their attention, and will be inclined to say that it should have been the author's business to give an explanation neither tedious nor unsatisfactory. The critic is disposed to think that Hawthorne, as he continued his narrative, postponed his plot till it was too late, and then escaped from his difficulty by the ingenious excuse above given. As a writer of novels, I am bound to say that the excuse can not be altogether accepted. . . .

[1879]

➢ The Universal Review *of Great Britain took the publication of Hawthorne's* The Marble Faun *as an occasion for discussing both his career and his nation's literary achievement. The writer for the* Review *has read Hawthorne carefully and well, but he is yet forced to insist that America has no literature which can properly be called her own. The length to which the* Westminster *went to document an American literary tradition might seem to make the opposite case, but the reviewer has such a slight grasp of his material that his enthusiasm is hardly convincing.*

93 ↞

American literature is always an interesting subject, not only because it is literature, but because it is one of the elements in the solution of a problem which is important in a greater or less degree to the whole world—the moral and intellectual influence of democratic government. Political philosophers have sometimes wished that the sphere of their data was not limited to the province of observation only but was capable of including the results of experiment as well. They would be glad of the power of those Eastern despots who sometimes transplanted a whole nation, and who would doubtless have subjected it to any other mental or physical process if they had thought it worth while to do so. The resources of science have not hitherto been sufficient to compass a similar end for us; but, to compensate for this want, we have before our eyes a spectacle which, to an instructed vision, is scarcely less fraught with momentous lessons than the trials which such philosophers have imagined for us. We see a nation, one of the mightiest on the earth, in the yet early years of its existence, and undergoing the process of formation and self-development under influences scarcely less various than those which could have been invented for it by the most imaginative speculator. If we look at one aspect of the United States, we may see many things which constitute an admirable success, and which may make us emulous, if not envious, of the means by which results are achieved which, with us, seem as distant as they are confessedly desirable. If we look on another, we are reminded of a child who has possessed himself of a handful of powerful drugs, and perched himself out of reach of any one who can control him. We know that he will make experiments for himself much more extraordinary than any we should have courage to make on his constitution, and we await the issue with feelings in which sympathy and compassion are not without their alloy of scientific curiosity. Thus we are not forced, as in most instances of historic speculation, to search out, by more or less imperfect means, the obscure and latent causes which have originated what we see before us. In almost all other cases we have to draw our conclusions from the results—to argue from effects to causes. We look upon the present state of old societies and nations as the geologist does upon a formation—and speculate on the forces which have upheaved it from its primeval bed,—which have studded it with innumerable fossils, telling some strange and unknown story of forgotten cataclysms—which have covered these ancient ruins with the alluvial soil, the trees, the grass, and the flowers, with which Nature delights to smooth over and efface former convulsions. But in America the traces of all that has contributed to form her state and shape her destiny, are patent to the view. It is like observing, beneath the surface of the ocean, the coral insects as they build up their reef—or like watching bees at work in their glass hive.

An imaginative mind—such as that of Mr. Hawthorne himself, for instance—might discern in both the illustrations we have used, some analogy to the elements of national life. In the rocky or coralline strata of the earth—in the wavy structure, compacted with infinite though instinctive skill by successive myriads of workers—he might trace the semblance of institutions and laws which are the matrix of the social development which forms their visible outgrowth. In the flora and fauna of the terrestrial surface—in the sweet contents of the hive—he might fancy a representation of the positive productions of physical and intellectual industry, and of the blossoms of art, poetry, and literature; since it is these, as much as the stronger foundation which underlies them, that one generation leaves for a heritage to its successors. Whether, however, we look at the matter in this fanciful light or from a purely rational point of view, all would agree in thinking that that efflorescence of a nation's being which finds its expression in its literature is as well worthy of attention for what it points to, even if not for its own positive merit, as any other product of its institutions. And, especially at the present day, when social topics have become elevated, in the philosopher's consideration, to an equality with purely political ones, no view of a people could be considered complete which did not include some estimate of the manner in which they regarded such problems of life as are not directly connected with material interests, and the method they took of expressing it (*sic*) their solution of them.

In the case of America, the light which art and literature throw on the character of a nation has been to a great extent denied, because the country can hardly be said to possess in this respect any thing peculiarly and distinctively its own. For, though it be a legitimate philosophic generalization to look at these things as natural results of general progress, it does not follow that their magnitude bears any proportion to the other constituents of a nation's being. The Roman literature, characteristic though it might be as far as it went, would have occupied but a meagre place in the literature of the world but for the impulse and the material which it derived from Greece. And, if Rome had been from the earliest times of her history in as constant communication with the Hellenic mind as she was after her conquest of its country, it may be a question whether even that amount of purely Latin literature which we know to have existed would have sprung up at all. What the Greeks were to the Romans in a literary point of view, that the English are to the Americans. We have long supplied them with the greater part of what they require in this respect. Not that there is any deficiency of printed books in the United States, but the part which is not a reflection of something in the old country appears to be very small indeed. For almost every work of note which has been produced there, the mother nation can show a better counterpart. How can a national literature flourish when this is the case? It can scarcely do so, until the nation undergoes so great a change that the literature it imports no longer finds anything responsive to it in the national mind. By the time that such a result is accomplished, something also will have arisen which will find its appropriate literary vent. Till then, probably, the most distinctive feature of American literature will be that which has often been pointed out as its most remarkable feature now—the element of humor. Humor is universal enough in itself; but the manner of its expression is so dependent upon local peculiarities that it will hardly bear to travel. The best part of its aroma is lost, like that of tea, in crossing salt water. Hence every nation has had to make its humorous literature at home, if it required any. We do not require to remind the reader of the indigenous origin of Roman satire, Fescennine verses, ancient lays, and Atellane fables. It was not without a certain appropriateness that the witty authors of Bon Gaultier's *Ballads* chose for their American subjects to parody some of the verses in which Macaulay tried to set before us some notion of what ancient Roman poetry might have been. If we wished to preserve for posterity some idea of what the Americans are, and how they differ from us, we should choose not Irving or Longfellow, but Lowell and Sam Slick.

Are there, then, no signs of a national American literature in any department except that of humor? It must be confessed there are but few. If we exclude from consideration all who have not gained sufficient fame to be read beyond their own limits, the number of American writers who are any thing more than Englishmen in America does not amount to much. Irving dealt with national traditions, and devoted himself to national subjects. But his whole cast of thought, and of the dress of his thought, was formed upon English models. Longfellow is equally indebted to Germany; and the poem in which he is sometimes said to be most original is a homage to the traditions of the red man rather than of his own white brethren. About Emerson, indeed, there is something which one does not think would have been written in Europe, but it is not his strongest part. Poe seems altogether incapable of being classified; and if his works (omitting the American phrases and positive local allusions) had been published as translations from the French, German, or Danish, we do not think any one would have disbelieved in their assumed origin. This is not quite the case with the writer before us. Mr. Hawthorne is, we are inclined to think, the most national writer, of a serious kind, whom the country has yet produced in the department of fiction. He seems to us to reflect many of the characteristics of the American mind more exactly than any of his predecessors. He has evidently a warm as well as an enlightened love for his country. He likes to dwell on the picturesque part of its early struggles, just as we like to hover about the region of the civil war. The primitive habits of the first settlers—the stern Puritanic training of the infant states—the conflict of asceticism with the old jovial English spirit—the legends which cluster, like bats around a ruined tower, about the decaying period of the English rule—are all familiar denizens of his mind, and the channels through which many of his ideas spontaneously flow. He reflects more unconsciously, perhaps, some of the, perhaps transitional, characteristics of the America that is; the contrasts which are always presenting themselves between the material and the moral side of civilization, and the singular combination of knowingness and superstition, which some at least of the present phases of American life offer to our notice.

[1860?]

94 ✍

We propose in this article to enter on no proper discussion of American literature, but merely to present such an array of carefully-ascertained and interesting facts, with brief and hastily written but deliberately-formed opinions, as will guide the intelligent reader to a just estimate of the general intellectual activity in the United States; reserving for a separate article an account of the books that have recently issued from the American press. We have been over the field with some care, having in the last few months examined with more or less attention a larger number of American books in the various departments of literature than a majority of our readers would be apt to believe were ever written. The library of the British Museum contains an immense number of American Histories, Biographies, Reviews, &c., and is by no means deficient in what with more propriety may be called American Literature, though the privilege that we enjoy, while occupied with these pages, of consulting a library in which there are thirteen thousand works composed in the United States, leaves on our mind an impression that Mr. Panizzi might, with some advantage to British students, suggest the bestowal of a few hundred guineas more on the speculation, the poetry, romance, and aesthetical dissertation of the cultivators of their language across the Atlantic.

We cannot but think, despite the contrary judgment of some wise persons who have debated this point, that the distinct history of the American mind should be commenced, far back, in the times of the first Puritans in New England. There is a national character in America; it is seen, very decided and strongly marked, in the free northern States; and making every proper allowance for the Dutch element and its influence in New York, that national character was born in England, cast out from thence, because it was not agreeable to a majority of the people, and has remained until now, unchanged in its essentials, where it first found a home, in the area of civilization ever widening from the British settlements on this continent. The history of American literature begins in the good old days of the Dudleys, the Cottons, Nortons, and Mathers, or earlier still, in those of John Milton, who has been claimed as the "most American author that ever lived." And with justice. For what has that stern and sublime intelligence in common with kingly domination, or hierarchical despotism, against both of which he made "all Europe ring from side to side"? And are not his immortal books on State and Church polities the very fixed and undecaying expression of the American ideas on these subjects? . . .

It is frequently, but we think most erroneously, asserted that the Americans are deficient in humour. The writings of Franklin, "Modern Chivalry," written half a century ago by Judge Breckenridge, Trumbull's M'Fingal, and a dozen other works of the last age, abound with original and for the most part national comedy; and Irving may certainly be ranked with the first humourists who have written in the English language; while Paulding, Judge Longstreet, the late Robert C. Sands, Halleck, Hawthorne (in the "Twice-Told Tales"), Mr. Davis and Seba Smith (in the "Jack Downing Letters"), John P. Kennedy (in "Swallow Barn"), Willis Gaylord Clark (in "Ollapodiana"), John Sanderson, Charles F. Briggs, and Mrs. Kirkland (in a "New Home"), may well be said to have given American literature a fair infusion of this quality. But a school of comic writers in the southern and western states, amply represented in a series of volumes published in Philadelphia under the direction of William T. Porter, editor of the chief sporting journal in the Union, would quite redeem the fame of the Americans in this respect, though all the rest of their books were grim and stern as the most fanatical preacher in their pulpits. In this school T. B. Thorpe of New Orleans, author of "Mysteries in the Backwoods," and Johnson J. Hooper of Alabama, author of "Capt. Simon Suggs," are most conspicuous; and we know not where to turn for anything more rich, original, and indigenous, than much of the racy mockery and grotesque extravagance in their pages. We have not room for quotations, but let the reader turn for illustrations to pages 548–9 of Mr. Griswold's "Prose Writers." In the satirical vein the Americans have not succeeded so well, though the "Fable for Critics" and the "Bigelow Papers" and a few pieces by Holmes, have remarkable merit.

Among the novelists Washington Irving cannot very justly be included, as his exquisite productions do not in any case quite conform to the novel's description. It was his intention, however, when a young man, to devote himself to the novel of American life, and he had half finished a work referring to the time of King Philip of the Wampanoags, when the reading of one of Cooper's earlier tales convinced him, as the reading of Byron convinced Scott, that he must change his rôle or occupy a secondary position. The freshness and abounding power of Cooper carried the day on the large canvas; but in refinement, grace, tenderness, and humour, the cabinet productions of Geoffrey Crayon are masterpieces. Cooper died a few weeks ago, exactly sixty years of age; comparatively poor, we believe, but his family, (to one of whom, his daughter Susan, we are indebted for the charming book entitled "Rural Hours,") are able to retain his beautiful seat at Cooperstown. In the last month, the memory of Cooper has received the highest honours that could be offered by the literary class in his country; a committee, of which Washington Irving was chairman, and Fitz-Greene Halleck and Rufus W. Griswold were secretaries, and among the members of which were all the distinguished literary men of New York, was formed some time in September, and pursuant to its arrangements, Mr. Bryant was, on the 24th of December, to deliver in the Metropolitan Hall, an immense edifice capable of receiving six thousand persons, a discourse on the illustrious author's life and genius. Daniel Webster, Everett, Bancroft, Prescott, Kennedy, Hawthorne, Paulding, and indeed all the distinguished writers of the country were to be present. A colossal statue of Mr. Cooper, by his friend Greenough, is likewise to be placed in one of the parks of New York.

Mr. Irving lives in lettered ease at his delightful place on the Hudson, the patriarchal genius of his country's literature, enjoying the grateful and affectionate reverence of the Anglo-Saxon race. Since he was ambassador to Spain he has been chiefly occupied with a careful revision of his various works, of which fourteen large volumes have already been published, and he will conclude the series with a personal history of General Washington, which is now nearly completed.

Of the deceased American novelists the most celebrated were Brown, Allston (the painter), and Timothy Flint; but the names Paulding, Kennedy, Neal, Fay, Ware, Simms, and Bird, belong almost to the last generation. The new writers who have been heard of in England are, Hawthorne, first and greatest; Kimball, best known by his fine metaphysical romance of "St. Leger," but deserving highest praises for his finely-conceived shorter domestic tales; Sylvester Judd, an eccentric Unitarian minister, whose original, peculiar, and very American stories of "Margaret" and "Richard Edney," have excited at home a great deal of attention and criticism; Melville, a man of unquestionable genius, who struck out for himself a new path in Typee, Omoo, and his last book "The Whale;" Dr. Mayo, whose remarkable novels of "Kaloolah" and "The Berber," are well known in England; and Mr. Mitchell, who, under the *nom de plume* of Ik. Marvel, has written the "Lorgnette" (in the class of the Spectator), "Fresh Gleanings" (a "sentimental journey through France and Italy"), the "Reveries of a Bachelor" (a graceful romance of reflection, sentiment, and humour, which has had an extraordinary success in America), and "Dream-Life" (a work of the same character), which has just reached us.

Among the writers of magazine stories, of whom there are a large number, Richard H. Dana, N. P. Willis, C. F. Hoffman, and the late Edgar A. Poe, besides the novelists already mentioned, deserve particular praise, for various and generally for very eminent abilities.

We can but allude to the scholarship of Robinson, Conant, Sears,

Felton, Anthon, Woolsey, and several others, who deserve honourable mention for their labours in ancient literature. With the same brevity we must dismiss Livingston, Wheaton, Marshall, Parsons, Kent, and Story. And in the criticism of literature and life we have no room for characterization of Legaré, Wilde, Dana, Verplanck, or the younger writers, Whipple, Hudson, and others who have recently begun to attract attention.

We offer here no criticism of the American poets. Their works demand a separate and elaborate discussion. Pre-eminent among them unquestionably stands Bryant. Longfellow is more read in England, as Mr. Martin Farquhar Tupper has a larger audience than any British bard, from Shakespeare to Browning, in the United States. Dana, Percival, Halleck, Brainard, Sands, Pinckney, Emerson, Hoffman, Willis, Whittier, Pike, Poe, Parsons, Lowell, Street, Taylor, Stoddard, and Boker, have each a good right to be considered at some length. The last three have just published volumes, of which we have seen only Bayard Taylor's and R. H. Stoddard's, each of which embraces a portion of the most excellent verse produced in this decade.

We close this too hasty article with a brief paragraph respecting American literary women. The intellectual activity of the sex in that country constitutes a remarkable feature of its civilization. We do not think Southey overpraised Mrs. Brooks when he declared her the most impassioned and imaginative of all poetesses; and for her genius and her character, but most for her beautiful character, the late Mrs. Osgood's name should move men's hearts as the moon moves the sea. No living American woman has evinced in prose or verse anything like the genius of Alice Carey; but next to her, in poetry, must be ranked Edith May, of whose writings an edition has just appeared with a preface by N. P. Willis; and following, Mrs. Hewitt, Mrs. Whitman, Mrs. Welby, Mrs. Green, Mrs. Sigourney, Miss Gould, and Miss Townsend. Among the female prose-writers of America, a conspicuous rank must be awarded to the late Margaret Fuller d'Ossoli (whose memoirs are soon to be published by R. W. Emerson), Mrs. Kirkland (the amusing and sensible "Mary Clavers"), Miss Sedgwick, Miss M'Intosh, Mrs. Lee, Mrs. Robinson ("Talvi"), and Mrs. Oakes Smith, a voluminous writer in poetry, prose, fiction, criticism, and the philosophy of society, whose late book, "Woman and her Needs," is the most powerful assertion that has appeared of the necessity of a change in the legal and social condition of women.

[1852]

Brownson seems to echo The Universal Review *in assessing the nation's literary achievement: "Our American literature wants . . . originality, freedom, and freshness. It lacks spontaneity, is imitative, and, for the most part, imitative of the English." But although Brownson attests to their durability by repeating many of the familiar explanations for American failure, he nevertheless persists in the confidence echoed by Thoreau in the succeeding passage and sounded ever more frequently as the century entered its final quarter. America might not yet have a national literature, but it must have one ere long; it has the materials and the spirit—"The West is preparing to add its fables to those of the East."*

95

. . . Literature is frequently taken by modern writers in the sense of polite literature, or what the French call *belles-lettres*. In this more restricted sense, it does not include professional works, or works devoted specially to science or the sciences. It must express something universal, and be addressed to the common understanding and common sentiments of all cultivated readers. There is, if we may so speak, a certain universal mind in all men who think, and certain sentiments common to all men who feel. It is to these common sentiments and this universal mind that polite literature is addressed, and these it must aim to embody or express in its creations. Not that the literary man is not free to express individualities, or to describe local manners, usages, habits, and customs, but he must do it always under some relation to the common and the universal. The common and the universal are the sources of his inspiration and the principles of his judgments. These common sentiments and this universal mind embrace what goes ordinarily under the name of common sense, good sense, taste, or good taste. To determine their basis, their existence, or their authority beyond human nature as we find it, is the province of science, not of general or polite literature.

The philosopher knows that in this universal mind, and in these common sentiments, there is the intuition of an ideal that transcends human nature, that transcends all created nature, identical with Him who is "First True, First Good, and First Fair;" without which the human mind could neither exist nor operate, the human soul neither feel nor aspire, neither know nor love. But the literary man, as such, takes no account of this, and is contented to express human nature and its ideal without looking beyond it, and to embody the best he can the intuition, the sentiments, the beliefs, the convictions which he finds to be common to all men. He practises art without giving its philosophy. He who is truest to this common and universal human nature, and expresses it with the most vividness, clearness, distinctness, vigor, and energy, is the prince of literature, as the homage rendered by all men who read them, to Homer, Dante, and Shakspeare amply testifies.

As this common and universal nature is in every living and full-grown man, the true artist, whether he writes or paints, sings or sculptures, pronounces an oration or designs a temple, is he who best expresses what is truest, deepest, richest, and broadest in his own human nature. He who only copies the convictions, sentiments, or ideals of others, without having found them in himself, or made them his own by his life and experience, is unworthy of the noble name of artist, however successful he may be as a copyist or an imitator. He must draw from the well within himself, from his own inspiration, his own life and experience, his own ideal, or an ideal that he has really assimilated and made his own. So of the literary man. A literature which is simply copied or imitated from a foreign model is no literature at all in its artistic sense. Hence, we can assign no high rank to the Italian Sannazar, notwithstanding the exquisite beauty, rhythm, and polish of his Latin verse, for he is only a servile imitator of Virgil, and Virgil himself ranks below Lucretius, and even Ovid, to say nothing of Horace and Catullus, for he servilely copies Homer and other Greek poets.

It is not meant by this, that the literary man, to be original, must say nothing that has been said before him, for that would imply that no modern can be original. It is doubtful if there remains any thing to be said that has not been said a thousand times over already, and better said than any one can now say it. The author often finds, on extending his reading, that even in the very passages in which he honestly believed that he was saying something new, he had been anticipated ages ago. You can find little even in Shakspeare that is not, in some form, to be found in his predecessors. Originality does not consist in saying things absolutely new, or which no one has said before, but in expressing in our own way, from our own mind, what we ourselves have really thought, felt, or lived.

Our American literature wants, generally speaking, originality, free-dom, and freshness. It lacks spontaneity, is imitative, and, for the most part, imitative of the English. Those of our writers who are free, racy, original, as some of them are, lack culture, polish, are rude and extravagant. We, as a people, are educated up to a certain point, better educated up to that point, perhaps, than any European people, but we are not a highly cultivated people. A certain number of our scholars, historians, poets, and novel writers have a mental and social culture that places them on a level with the cultivated men of Europe; but, in general, our easy classes have more instruction than cultivation, while our poorer classes, excluding those of European birth, if better informed, are less well trained than those even of England. In literature and art we are provincials, striving to ape metropolitan fashions. Hence our literature is constrained and stiff, and has a certain vulgar air and tone. Like the American people themselves, it lacks free, manly, independent thought. It is licentious enough, at times, in doctrine and speculation, but there is all the difference in the world between license and freedom. In many sections we can find impudence enough, not unfrequently taken for independence; but, as a people, we have very little real independence of character, far less, in fact, than we had before 1776. *What will they say?* has more influence with us than with any other people on earth. My wife has constantly the fear of Mrs. Grundy before her eyes, and is afraid to consult her own taste, convenience, or means in furnishing her house, or in selecting and shaping her dresses. In politics we go with our party, and never dare think beyond it or differently from it; and hence it would be difficult to find a civilized nation on earth so destitute of scientific and thorough-bred statesmen as our own. Not a man amongst us was found, at the breaking out of the present formidable rebellion, able to solve a single one of the great problems it presented for practical solution. We have seen no statesmanship in either the administration or congress, or even in any of the leading journals and periodicals of the country. In religion we believe, or do not believe, with our sect, denomination, or church, accept, or reject its symbols alike without thought, without reason, and without any perception of their meaning. In literature we copy, or try to copy, the English, the French, or the German, seldom venturing to give free play to our own original powers, or even suspecting that we have any. There is even in our best literature a constant effort to conform to a foreign standard, to write or sing, not as we want to write or sing, but as somebody else has written or sung. Ralph Waldo Emerson is almost the only original writer of distinction that we can boast. His friend, Theodore Parker, thought and wrote as a sectarian, and was a rhetorician and sometimes a declaimer, but never a free, original thinker, and has produced nothing that will live.

We have any quantity of fictitious literature, fictitious in all the senses of the term, produced chiefly by women, and therefore weak, sentimental, preventing instead of aiding high national culture. We prize woman as highly as do any of our contemporaries, but we have no great liking for feminine literature, whichever sex has produced it. Woman has a noble and important intellectual mission, but she performs it by her conversational rather than by literary gifts. Her genius may emit flashes which penetrate even further into the surrounding darkness than the slower intellect of man, but the light is not steady enough, and is too transient, to enable us to see even the outlines of the objects it momentarily illumines. Man can penetrate further and rise higher by her aid than without it. Yet even the light she flashes, and which is so serviceable to him, has been struck out by her collision with the masculine intellect, and the problems she helps to solve she could never have conceived if man had not first suggested them and prepared her to grasp them. She can aid man, but can do nothing without him. She was made for him, and in herself is only an inchoate man. The effort of "our strong-minded women" to raise their sex from the position of drudge, plaything, or an article of luxury, is praiseworthy and well deserving our sympathy and coöperation; but when they go further, and attempt to make her as independent of man as he is of her, they forget the respective provinces of the sexes, and simply attempt to reverse the laws of nature, and assign to the female of the species the office of the male. It is not conventionalism, but God, that has made the man the head of the woman, and not the woman the head of the man, and every day's experience proves that the men who lend themselves to the silly woman's rights movement are precisely the men the least acceptable to women. A woman wants a man, not a woman, for her husband, and a man wants a woman, not a man, for his wife.

The curse of the age is its femininity, its lack, not of barbarism, but of virility. It is the age of woman-worship. Women are angels; men are demons. Our modern literature, not our brave old English tongue, makes all the virtues feminine and all the vices masculine. A well-formed, fair-faced, sweet-tempered and gentle-spoken woman, if young and accomplished, is an angel; her sentimental tears are angel's tears, though her heart is cold, selfish, incapable of a single generous emotion or heroic virtue,—an angel, though utterly regardless of the misery she needlessly inflicts on an accepted lover, if her caprice only calls her to suffer also. Sweet angels are the dear creatures, if we may believe modern literature, though they make all connected with them thoroughly wretched, if they have gentle manners, pretty faces, and sweet voices. Yet it must be conceded that we have no class of writers who draw so much from themselves, in their writings, as our literary women. They draw from themselves, and draw themselves, and present woman, under the veil of pretended female modesty, which prevents her from being open, frank, truthful, honest, as self-willed, capricious, passionate, rash, artful, artificial, false, servile, tyrannical, exaggerating mole-hills into mountains, and seeing every thing through the distorting medium of a morbid sensibility. Their fault, a feminine fault is, that they exaggerate, and write themselves down infinitely worse than they are. Though moderately well read in feminine literature, we cannot call to mind a single heroine, drawn by a female hand, that is really frank and truthful, unless it be Jane Eyre, and Dinah in *Adam Bede,* and no one that a sensible man could love or wish for his wife.

But literature is the exponent of the life and character of the people who produce it. The stream cannot rise higher than its fountain. Our authors, whether male or female, have labored, and still labor, under many disadvantages. The American people have the germs of romance in them as have every people, but they have not as yet been developed. Our country is new, and our people, as a distinct, free, and independent people, have hardly, as yet, attained to a consciousness of their own existence. The materials of romance have not yet been furnished us. We are removed from the old homestead, have lost its legends, traditions, and associations, and have too recently settled in the wilderness to have created them anew for ourselves. There is little mystery in our ordinary life, and we have, save in the southern Atlantic states, acquired no deep attachment to the soil, and are, if not a nomadic race, at least a moving, and a migratory, rather than a sedentary people. We have rich, varied, and magnificent natural scenery, though rarely equalling that of Europe, Mexico, or South America; but no human memories hallow it, and render it either poetical or romantic, and, as a people, we are not nature-worshippers. We have not that intense love of external nature which the English have, or affect to have. We are too familiar from our childhood up with woods and fields, pastures and meadows, winding brooks, water-falls, precipices, sheep feeding, lambs frolicking, cattle browsing, partridges whirring, quails whistling, birds singing, to go into ecstasies over them. If we are capable of being impressed by them, we have seen and felt more than the poet can express in his song, or the romancer seize and embody in his description. We have our rivers, our lakes, our forests, our mountains; but these, to serve the purpose of literature, must be associated with man, and consecrated by human joy or sorrow, human affections, or the fierce struggle of human passions. The wild Indian was a resource, but it has been exhausted by Cooper; and, besides, the Indian is himself the least romantic of mortals, and the memory of his treachery, his cruelty, and the fierce struggle for life which our pioneer settlers have had to sustain with him, is too recent to be poetical or romantic. We have a glorious nature, no doubt, but it is barren of legends, traditions, and human associations, unpeopled with fairies, even with dwarfs; descriptions of it soon become wearisome to the mind, fatiguing to the soul, as do our immense and treeless prairies to the eye. In traversing these prairies, we long for a hill, a tree, or any thing that can break the monotony. Nature, without man, or human association, as Byron well maintained, is not poetical, and cannot sustain a literature that does not soon become fatiguing and repulsive. We have never been able to admire Cole's picture of *The Voyage of Life;* for, though the human is there, it is dwarfed and crushed beneath the wild and massive nature overhanging it. The human is too feeble to transform it, or to clothe it with the bright and unfading hues of its own immortal spirit.

Most of us even, who live in cities, have been born and brought up in the country, and our cockney class, to whom nature is a novelty, is very small. Our cities themselves are mostly huge market-towns, where people congregate to trade, not to live. They are, with two or three exceptions, of which New York is not one, provincial in their tastes, manners, and habits; looking to some foreign city, chiefly London or Paris, as their metropolis. The commercial spirit dominates, and the commercial spirit is always and everywhere the most positive spirit in the world, so positive and hard, that it is only by a figure of speech that we can call it a *spirit* at all. The commercial classes, engrossed in business, intent on making, increasing, or retrieving their fortunes, have little leisure, and less taste for general literature, and absorb whatever of poetry or romance they may have in their nature in business operations or hazardous speculations. Our country residents are mostly country people. They have some education, but the mass of them, even when great readers, though characterized by much natural shrewdness and quickness of apprehension have not much mental culture, or intellectual development or refinement. Their tastes are crude and coarse, and after the journals, become a necessity of American life, crave yellow-covered literature, what are called "sensation novels," or works addressed specially to the sentiments, emotions, or passions. The more cultivated, but much smaller portion, who have wealth, leisure, and taste for polite literature of a higher order, rely principally on the supply from England, France, Italy, and Germany, or content themselves with reperusing the classics.

The Americans as a people are colonists and *parvenus*. We have never yet felt that we are a nation, with our own national metropolis. Washington is only a village where are the government offices, and where congress meets; it gives no tone to our literature, and only partially even to our politics. Boston is more of a literary capital than Washington, but it is the capital of New England rather than of the nation. New York and Philadelphia are great book-manufacturing cities, but no great literary centres, like London or Paris. New York especially is the Leipsig of America, but the population of which it is the business centre, is hardly counted by the trade in their calculations of the sale of a book. New York subscribed for just one-eighth as many copies of Agassiz's great work on the Natural History of the United States as Boston. In our cities, so numerous and so wealthy before the breaking out of the rebellion, and so marked by their hurry and bustle, luxurious tastes, and frightful extravagance, the great majority of the wealthy citizens have become rich by their own exertions and successful speculations. They had sometimes, and sometimes had not, a good business education to begin with, but in general as little mental culture or refinement as wealth. Engrossed in money-getting, they have had little time and less disposition to supply their early literary deficiencies. Their brains exhausted in their business pursuits they cannot find relaxation in a literature that makes any demand on their intellects. They must seek their relaxation either in light, flashy, emotional novels, or in gross sensual pleasures. As parvenus, we seek rather to forget than to recall our own past. We are in a position which we were not born to, which we were not brought up to, and which we feel that we may at any moment lose. We do not feel ourselves at home, or settled for life; we are ill at ease; care sits on our brow, anxiety contracts and sharpens our features. We have no freedom, no leisure to cultivate the mind, to develop and purify our tastes, to find enjoyment in intellectual and spiritual pleasures. With fine original mental constitutions, with an unequalled cerebral activity, which unhappily tells on our bills of mortality, save in special or professional studies, there is perhaps no civilized people that is not above us in the higher intellectual culture, and in the development of thought. We are in this respect below Great Britain, and Great Britain is below most of the continental nations. Even the Irish and German peasants who migrate hither soon come to leave our old American population in the lurch, and to govern the country.

Such a public is not favorable to high literary culture, and it is no wonder that American literature is no great thing. In these days, when the public are the only literary patrons, literature of a high, generous, and ennobling character cannot be produced without a high, generous, and cultivated literary public, that finds its amusement and relaxation from business or dissipation in literature, in works of taste, in the creations of thought and imagination. As yet we have as a people no real artistic culture. The literary man is not independent of his medium. He can never be formed, by himself alone, without living, breathing, and moving in a literary atmosphere. Man cultivates man, and cultivated society is essential to the production and growth of a genuine, high-toned literature. The society and conversation of virtuous, refined, and cultivated women are also indispensable. Woman cannot be a literary man herself; but no literary man of correct taste, and of broad, elevated, and generous views and sentiments can be formed without her.

Some of these disadvantages are, no doubt, common to all modern society, so universally pervaded by what the late Emperor Nicholas so justly stigmatized as the "mercantile spirit," which makes all things venal, and estimates a man by what he has, not by what he is. Worth, now-a-days, means hard cash, or what can be exchanged for hard cash. But this "mercantile spirit," which turns even religion into speculation, and coins genius into money—of which Barnum, if a vulgar, is yet a real impersonation—is more rife in our country, and finds less to counteract or temper it than elsewhere. Here it coins the blood of our brave and heroic defenders, the widow's desolation, the mother's grief, and the orphan's wail into money, which our shoddy nabobs display in the form of silks, laces, and jewellery, with which they deck out their vulgar wives and daughters, as we are learning by an experience that will, in the end, be as bitter as it has hitherto seemed sweet. It is hard for genuine literary men to be formed in such a medium, and still harder for them to find a larger appreciative public. Nevertheless, our literary artists must not despair; they must struggle manfully against the false taste and false tendencies of the age and the nation, not by preaching against them and scolding them, as we do in our capacity of critic, or as Cooper did in his later novels; but by laboring to produce fitting and attractive examples of what literature should be, by careful self-culture, by acquiring habits of independence, and by avoiding all servile imitation—not study—of foreign models, whether ancient or modern. No man writes well unless he writes freely from his own life. Above all, let them bear in mind that a literature destined to live, and to exert an ennobling influence on the national character, must entertain the ideal, be replete with thought, inspired by an earnest purpose, and addressed to the understanding as well as to the affections, passions, and emotions. Truth has a bottom of its own, and can stand by itself; but beauty cannot, for it exists only in the relation of the

406 THE NATIVE MUSE

true to our sensibility or imagination, as a combination of intellect and sense. The form of ancient classic literature is unsurpassable, but that literature finds its vital principle, that which preserves it as a living literature to-day, chiefly in its thought, in the truth which it expresses to the understanding, though under the form of the beautiful to our sensitive nature. Hence all efforts to exclude the study of the classics from our schools and colleges have failed and will fail. The neglect of the ancient classics marks simply the advance of barbarism.

Some of the remarks we have made have been suggested by reading *Hannah Thurston,* a story of American life, by Bayard Taylor, late secretary of the American legation at the court of St. Petersburg. Mr. Taylor enjoys a high reputation as a literary man. He is said to be a poet; but whether so or not we are unable to judge, for, to our loss, no doubt, we have read only two or three of his occasional songs, of which we did not think much. He has been a great traveller, has seen much, and relates well what he has seen. But we really know him only by his *Hannah Thurston,* and can judge him only as the author of that work. As the author of *Hannah Thurston,* he has most of the faults of American writers in general, and very few of the merits of such writers as Irving, Cooper, Hawthorne, Kennedy, Bird, and Gilmore Simms; and he even ranks below several of our female writers, such as Miss Sedgwick and the author of *Miriam* and *Husks.* He strikes us as a feminine man. The virile element in him, apparently, is weak, and he writes more as a man of sentiment than as a man of thought. His story is well conceived, and is conducted with artistic skill to its conclusion. His intention has been good, and he deserves high praise for it. His book may be read once, if not with intense interest, without fatigue; but we broke down in our attempt to read it a second time. It is unlike Thackeray's novels, which interest more on a second than on a first perusal. His book shows some experience of life, fine powers of observation, some humor, and now and then, unobtrusive wit; but it lacks strength—free, vigorous, masculine thought. It is called "A Story of American Life," and American it is, and none but an American could have written it; for none but an American could have shown us the same evident effort to write like an Englishman, without ever attaining to the real English manner. The American who does not try to write like an Englishman, and is contented to write as a man whose mother tongue is English, will catch more of the English manner than the one who does.

Mr. Taylor is unmistakably American. His style has the peculiarly American nasal twang. We, Americans, lack the English *aplomb,* the

English *Selbstständigkeit,* and the English round and full pronunciation. We do not feel ourselves full-blooded Englishmen, are afraid to be ourselves, and seldom speak out, like men, our own mother tongue in a full round voice. We speak through the nose, in a thin, sharp voice, as if afraid to speak with an open mouth. This is especially true of us in the northern states; in the South and the West we find more individual independence. As a rule we both write and speak our common language with more grammatical correctness than do the English, but rarely with the same ease, fluency, and idiomatic grace. Our writers have as much genius, ability, and knowledge as the English, but less mental culture and less self-confidence, as any can feel who compares the *North American* with the *Quarterly,* or the *Atlantic* with *Blackwood.* There is almost always something of the plebeian and the provincial about us, and we act as if afraid of committing some solecism, or of neglecting some conventional usage which we have heard of but are unfamiliar with. This is easily explained by the fact that English writers themselves had, at the epoch of the founding of the Anglo-American colonies, very little of that high-bred and metropolitan air which the better class of them have now; and by the further fact that the first settlers of the colonies were chiefly provincials, plebeians, and dissenters from the national church, to which adhered the aristocratic and ruling classes of the mother country. The American people have sprung, in so far as of English blood, chiefly from the middle and lower classes of England, for, as Mr. Bancroft has justly remarked, royalty and nobility did not emigrate, and the larger portion of the colonial gentry, such as we had, abandoned the colonies when they declared their independence of Great Britain. The objections to the air and tone of our literature, apply more especially to New England and the middle states; the writers of the southern states have the temper and tone of a slaveholding community, are independent enough, but are too florid, too wordy, and incline to the pompous; western writers are free enough, but inflated, turgid, bombastic, and neglectful of the graces and proprieties of our mother tongue. Indeed, we are daily losing throughout the Union the purity, the simplicity, and directness demanded by the English genius, as is also the fact in England, owing to the extraordinary development of journalistic and periodical literature, and to the influence of Hibernian and feminine writers. The writers for our leading journals are in no small proportion Irishmen, and for our popular magazines women, or, what is far worse, feminine men, who have great fluency and little thought.

Mr. Taylor has a touch of the nasal twang of the middle states, which is very distinguishable from that of New England, but not a whit more agreeable or manly. The real "Down East" vernacular has been rendered classic by our excellent friend Seba Smith, in his famous Jack Downing letters, the only man who has yet written it. Haliburton, in his Sam Slick, Davis of this city in his counterfeit Jack Downing, and Professor Lowell, of Cambridge, in his Biglow Papers, write it as a language they have learned, as many Americans, ourselves especially, do English, never as their mother tongue. With Mr. Smith the language of "Down East" is really vernacular, and he writes it as naturally, as gracefully, as idiomatically as Burns or Scott writes broad Scotch, or Gerald Griffin the Munster brogue. We ought to be a good judge in this matter, for the Down East dialect was our mother tongue, and we never heard any other spoken till we were a right smart lad. Mr. Taylor writes English, very correct English, but with an American twang, all the more remarkable, for he evidently tries to write English as an Englishman. We find no fault with any writer for writing according to his own national character. Americans are not inferior to Englishmen, as we may one day prove, by a fierce war on the sea and on the land, if we have not done it already, and the inferiority of our literature is due to our fear to be ourselves. Human nature is as broad, as rich, as living in us as in Englishmen; their mother tongue is ours, and we can write it as well as they, if we only write as they do, from our own minds and hearts, and learn to express our own thoughts and sentiments in our own way, with frankness, directness, naturalness, and simplicity. Mr. Taylor's fault is, being an American, in trying to play the Englishman. . . .

[1864]

⊰ *The chasm of the Civil War made the later work of Thoreau and Whitman appear a final gasp of nineteenth-century literary romanticism. The mind of Concord would enter the new century through philosophy, educational and political theory, and art— through James, Dewey, and Louis Sullivan. Recent students of the national culture have come to see in Thoreau's western* Wild *a basic element of American thought and in Whitman's "Leaves" the central literary statement of his time.*

96 ⊱

I wish to speak a word for Nature, for absolute freedom and wildness, as contrasted with a freedom and culture merely civil—to regard man as an inhabitant, or a part and parcel of Nature, rather than a member of society. I wish to make an extreme statement, if so I may make an emphatic one, for there are enough champions of civilization: the minister and the school-committee, and every one of you will take care of that. . . .

What is it that makes it so hard sometimes to determine whither we will walk? I believe that there is subtle magnetism in Nature, which, if we unconsciously yield to it, will direct us aright. It is not indifferent to us which way we walk. There is a right way; but we are very liable from heedlessness and stupidity to take the wrong one. We would fain take that walk, never yet taken by us through this actual world, which is perfectly symbolical of the path which we love to travel in the interior and ideal world; and sometimes, no doubt, we find it difficult to choose our direction, because it does not yet exist distinctly in our idea.

When I go out of the house for a walk, uncertain as yet whither I will bend my steps, and submit myself to my instinct to decide for me, I find, strange and whimsical as it may seem, that I finally and inevitably settle southwest, toward some particular wood or meadow or deserted pasture or hill in that direction. My needle is slow to settle—varies a few degrees, and does not always point due southwest, it is true, and it has good authority for this variation, but it always settles between west and south-southwest. The future lies that way to me, and the earth seems more unexhausted and richer on that side. The outline which would bound my walks would be, not a circle, but a parabola, or rather like one of those cometary orbits which have been thought to be non-returning curves, in this case opening westward, in which my house occupies the place of the sun. I turn round and round irresolute sometimes for a quarter of an hour, until I decide, for a thousandth time, that I will walk into the southwest or west. Eastward I go only by force; but westward I go free. Thither no business leads me. It is hard for me to believe that I shall find fair landscapes or sufficient wildness and freedom behind the eastern horizon. I am not excited by the prospect of a walk thither; but I believe that the forest which I see in the western horizon stretches uninterruptedly toward the setting sun, and there are no towns nor cities in it of enough consequence to disturb me. Let me live where I will, on this side is the city, on that the wilderness, and ever I am leaving the city more and more, and withdrawing into the wilderness. I should not lay so much stress on this fact, if I did not believe that something like this is the prevailing tendency of my countrymen. I must walk toward Oregon, and not toward Europe. And that way the nation is moving, and I may say that mankind progresses from east to west. Within a few years we have witnessed the phenomenon of a southeastward migration, in the settlement of Australia; but this affects us as a retrograde movement, and, judging from the moral and physical character of the first generation of Australians, has not yet proved a successful experiment. The eastern Tartars think that there is nothing west beyond Thibet. "The world ends there," say they: beyond there is nothing but a shoreless sea." It is unmitigated East where they live.

We go eastward to realize history and study the works of art and literature, retracing the steps of the race; we go westward as into the future, with a spirit of enterprise and adventure. The Atlantic is a Lethean stream, in our passage over which we have had an opportunity to forget the Old World and its institutions. If we do not succeed this time, there is perhaps one more chance for the race left before it arrives on the banks of the Styx; and that is the Lethe of the Pacific, which is three times as wide. . . . Some months ago I went to see a panorama of the Rhine. It was like a dream of the Middle Ages. I floated down its historic stream in something more than imagination, under bridges built by the Romans, and repaired by later heroes, past cities and castles whose very names were music to my eyes, and each of which was the subject of a legend. . . .

Soon after, I went to see a panorama of the Mississippi, and as I worked my way up the river in the light of today, and saw the steam-boats wooding up, counted the rising cities, gazed on the fresh ruins of Nauvoo, beheld the Indians moving west across the stream, and, as before I had looked up the Moselle now looked up the Ohio and the Missouri, and heard the legends of Dubuque and of Wenona's Cliff—still thinking more of the future than of the past or present—I saw that this was a Rhine stream of a different kind; that the foundations of castles were yet to be laid, and the famous bridges were yet to be thrown over the river; and I felt that this was the heroic age itself, though we know it not, for the hero is commonly the simplest and obscurest of men.

The West of which I speak is but another name for the Wild; and what I have been preparing to say is, that in Wilderness is the preservation of the World. Every tree sends its fibres forth in search of the Wild. The cities import it at any price. Men plow and sail for it. From the forest and wilderness come the tonics and barks which brace mankind. Our ancestors were savages. The story of Romulus and Remus being suckled by a wolf is not a meaningless fable. The founders of every state which has risen to eminence have drawn their nourishment and vigor from a similar wild source. It was because the children of the Empire were not suckled by the wolf that they were conquered and displaced by the children of the northern forests who were.

I believe in the forest, and in the meadow, and in the night in which the corn grows. We require an infusion of hemlock spruce or arbor-vitae in our tea. There is a difference between eating and drinking for strength and from mere gluttony. The Hottentots eagerly devour the marrow of the koodoo and other antelopes raw, as a matter of course. Some of our northern Indians eat raw the marrow of the Arctic reindeer, as well as various other parts, including the summits of the antlers, as long as they are soft. And herein, perchance, they have stolen a march on the cooks of Paris. They get what usually goes to feed the fire. This is probably better than stall-fed beef and slaughter-house pork to make a man of. Give me a wildness whose glance no civilization can endure—as if we live on the marrow of koodoos devoured raw. . . .

In literature it is only the wild that attracts us. Dullness is but another name for tameness. It is the uncivilized free and wild thinking in *Hamlet* and the *Iliad,* in all the scriptures and mythologies, not learned in the schools, that delights us. As the wild duck is more swift and beautiful than the tame, so is the wild—the mallard—thought, which 'mid falling dews wings its way above the fens. A truly good book is something as natural, and as unexpectedly and unaccountably fair and perfect, as a wild-flower discovered on the prairies of the West or in the jungles of the East.

Genius is a light which makes the darkness visible, like the lightning's flash, which perchance shatters the temple of knowledge itself—and not a taper lighted at the hearth-stone of the race, which pales before the light of common day.

English literature, from the days of the minstrels to the Lake Poets— Chaucer and Spenser and Milton, and even Shakespeare, included— breathes no quite fresh and, in this sense, wild strain. It is essentially tame and civilized literature, reflecting Greece and Rome. Her wilderness is a greenwood, her wild man a Robin Hood. There is plenty of genial love of Nature, but not so much of Nature herself. Her chronicles inform us when her wild animals, but not when the wild man in her, became extinct.

The science of Humboldt is one thing, poetry is another thing. The poet to-day, nothwithstanding all the discoveries of science, and the accumulated learning of mankind, enjoys no advantage over Homer.

Where is the literature which gives expression to Nature? He would be a poet who could impress the winds and streams into his service, to speak for him; who nailed words to their primitive senses, as farmers drive down stakes in the spring, which the frost has heaved; who derived his words as often as he used them—transplanted them to his page with earth adhering to their roots; whose words were so true and fresh and natural that they would appear to expand like the buds at the approach of spring, though they lay half smothered between two musty leaves in a library— aye, to bloom and bear fruit there, after their kind, annually, for the faithful reader, in sympathy with surrounding Nature.

I do not know of any poetry to quote which adequately expresses this yearning for the Wild. Approached from this side, the best poetry is tame. I do not know where to find in any literature, ancient or modern, any account which contents me of that Nature with which even I am acquainted. You will perceive that I demand something which no Augustan nor Elizabethan age, which no *culture,* in short, can give. Mythology comes nearer to it than anything. How much more fertile a Nature, at least, has Grecian mythology its root in than English literature! Mythology is the crop which the Old World bore before its soil was exhausted, before the fancy and imagination were affected with blight; and which it still bears, wherever its pristine vigor is unabated. All other literatures endure only as the elms which overshadow our houses; but this is like the great dragon-tree of the Western Isles, as old as mankind, and, whether that does or not, will endure as long; for the decay of other literatures makes the soil in which it thrives.

The West is preparing to add its fables to those of the East. The valleys of the Ganges, the Nile, and the Rhine having yielded their crop, it remains to be seen what the valleys of the Amazon, the Plate, the Orinoco, the St. Lawrence, and the Mississippi will produce. Perchance, when, in the course of ages, American liberty has become a fiction of the past—as it is to some extent a fiction of the present—the poets of the world will be inspired by American mythology.

[1862]

⊁ *There is a sense in which Whitman's entire life and work should appear here as an appropriate conclusion to this volume. As has often been asserted in challenge to his actual poetic achievement, his verse deals almost exclusively with America's need for a national literature and with the materials such writing will draw upon when it appears. He writes of America and its mission, and he makes of his country and himself a model of Emersonian art. From the many suitable selections I have chosen two: an uncommonly clear and uncharacteristically brief essay on "The Poetry of the Future" from the* North American Review *and the retrospective "Backward Glance" of 1888. By that date it was clear to Whitman that he would not live to see his aesthetic values either understood or adopted as basic to the national letters. "My volume is a candidate for the future," he concludes; "As America fully and fairly construed is the legitimate result and evolutionary outcome of the past, so I would dare to claim for my verse." The claim has been recognized and the romantic aesthetic has established itself at the center of our native mind and art, but although a literary tradition was taking effective shape the debate over its nature and prospect showed no sign of waning.*

97 ⧏

Strange as it may seem, the topmost proof of a race is its own born poetry. The presence of that, or the absence, each tells its story. As the flowering rose or lily, as the ripened fruit to a tree, the apple or the peach, no matter how fine the trunk, or copious or rich the branches and foliage, here waits *sine qua non* at last. The stamp of entire and finished greatness to any nation, to the American Republic among the rest, must be sternly withheld till it has expressed itself, and put what it stands for in the blossom of original, first-class poems. No imitations will do.

And though no *esthetik* worthy the present condition or future certainties of the New World seems to have been even outlined in men's minds,* or has been generally called for, or thought needed, I am clear

---

* In 1850, Emerson said earnestly to Miss Bremer, in response to her praises: "No, you must not be too good-natured. We have not yet any poetry which can be said to represent the mind of our world. The poet of America is not yet come. When he comes, he will sing quite differently."

that until the United States have just such definite and native expressers in the highest artistic fields, their mere political, geographical, wealth-forming, and even intellectual eminence, however astonishing and pre-dominant, will constitute (as I have before likened it)a more and more expanded and well-appointed body, and perhaps brain, with little or no soul. Sugar-coat the grim truth as we may, and ward off with outward plausible words, denials, explanations, to the mental inward perception of the land this blank is plain. A barren void exists. For the meanings and maturer purposes of these States are not the constructing of a new world of politics merely, and physical comforts for the million, but even more determinedly, in range with science and the modern, of a new world of democratic sociology and imaginative literature. If the latter were not carried out and established to form their only permanent tie and hold, the first-named would be of little avail.

With the poems of a first-class land are twined, as weft with warp, its types of personal character, of individuality, peculiar, native, its own physiognomy, man's and woman's, its own shapes, forms, and manners, fully justified under the eternal laws of all forms, all manners, all times.

I say the hour has come for democracy in America to inaugurate itself in the two directions specified,—autochthonic poems and personalities,—born expressers of itself, its spirit alone, to radiate in subtle ways, not only in art, but the practical and familiar, in the transactions between employers and employed persons, in business and wages, and sternly in the army and navy, and revolutionizing them.

I find nowhere a scope profound enough, and radical and objective enough, either for aggregates or individuals. The thought and identity of a poetry in America to fill, and worthily fill, the great void, and enhance these aims, involves the essence and integral facts, real and spiritual, of the whole land, the whole body. What the great sympathetic is to the congeries of bones and joints, and heart and fluids and nervous system, and vitality, constituting, launching forth in time and space a human being—aye, an immortal soul—in such relation, and no less, stands true poetry to the single personality or to the nation.

Here our thirty-eight States stand to-day, the children of past prece-dents, and, young as they are, heirs of a very old estate. One or two we will consider, out of the myriads presenting themselves. The feudalism of the British Islands, illustrated by Shakespeare, and by his legitimate fol-lowers, Walter Scott and Alfred Tennyson, with all its tyrannies, supersti-tions, evils, had most superb and heroic permeating veins, poems, manners

—even its errors fascinating. It almost seems as if only that feudalism in Europe, like slavery in our own South, could outcrop types of tallest, noblest personal character yet—strength and devotion and love better than elsewhere—invincible courage, generosity, aspiration, the spines of all. Here is where Shakespeare and the others I have named perform a service incalculably precious to our America. Politics, literature, and everything else centers at last in perfect *personnel* (as democracy is to find the same as the rest); and here feudalism is unrivaled—here the rich and highest-rising lessons it bequeaths us—a mass of precious, though foreign, nutriment, which we are to work over, and popularize, and enlarge, and present again in Western growths.

Still, there are pretty grave and anxious drawbacks, jeopardies, fears. Let us give some reflections on the subject, a little fluctuating, but starting from one central thought, and returning there again. Two or three curious results may plow up. As in the astronomical laws, the very power that would seem most deadly and destructive turns out to be latently conservative of longest, vastest future births and lives.

Let us for once briefly examine the just-named authors solely from a Western point of view. It may be, indeed, that we shall use the sun of English literature, and the brightest current stars of his system, mainly as pegs to hang some cogitations on, for home inspection.

As depicter and dramatist of the passions at their stormiest outstretch, though ranking high, Shakespeare (spanning the arch wide enough) is equaled by several, and excelled by the best old Greeks (as Æschylus). But in portraying the mediæval lords and barons, the arrogant port and stomach so dear to the inmost human heart (pride! pride! dearest, perhaps, of all—touching us, too, of the States closest of all—closer than love), he stands alone, and I do not wonder he so witches the world.

From first to last, also, Walter Scott and Tennyson, like Shakespeare, exhale that principle of caste which we Americans have come on earth to destroy. Jefferson's criticism on the Waverly novels was that they turned and condensed brilliant but entirely false lights and glamours over the lords, ladies, courts, and aristocratic institutes of Europe, with all their measureless infamies, and then left the bulk of the suffering, down-trodden people contemptuously in the shade. Without stopping to answer this hornet-stinging criticism, or to repay any part of the debt of thanks I owe, in common with every American, to the noblest, healthiest, cheeriest romancer that ever lived, I pass on to Tennyson and his works.

Poetry here of a very high (perhaps the highest) order of verbal melody, exquisitely clean and pure, and almost always perfumed, like the tuberose, to an extreme of sweetness—sometimes not, however, but even then a camellia of the hot-house, never a common flower—the verse of elegance and high-life, and yet preserving amid all its super-delicatesse a smack of outdoors and outdoor folk—the old Norman lordhood quality here, too, crossed with that Saxon fiber from which twain the best current stock of England springs—poetry that revels above all things in traditions of knights and chivalry, and deeds of derring-do. The odor of English social life in its highest range—a melancholy, affectionate, very manly, but dainty breed—pervading the books like an invisible scent; the idleness, the traditions, the mannerisms, the stately *ennui;* the yearning of love, like a spinal marrow inside of all; the costumes, old brocade and satin; the old houses and furniture,—solid oak, no mere veneering,—the moldy secrets everywhere; the verdure, the ivy on the walls, the moat, the English landscape outside, the buzzing fly in the sun inside the window pane. Never one democratic page; nay, not a line, not a word; never free and *naïve* poetry, but involved, labored, quite sophisticated—even when the theme is ever so simple or rustic (a shell, a bit of sedge, the commonest love-passage between a lad and lass), the handling of the rhyme all showing the scholar and conventional gentleman; showing the Laureate, too, the *attaché* of the throne, and most excellent, too; nothing better through the volumes than the dedication "To the Queen" at the beginning, and the other fine dedication, "These to his Memory" (Prince Albert's), preceding "Idylls of the King."

Such for an off-hand summary of the mighty three that now, by the women, men, and young folk of the fifty millions given these States by their late census, have been and are more read than all others put together.

We hear it said, both of Tennyson and the other current leading literary illustrator of Great Britain, Carlyle,—as of Victor Hugo in France,—that not one of them is personally friendly or admirant toward America; indeed, quite the reverse. *N'importe.* That they (and more good minds than theirs) cannot span the vast revolutionary arch thrown by the United States over the centuries, fixed in the present, launched to the endless future; that they cannot stomach the high-life-below-stairs coloring all our poetic and genteel social status so far—the measureless viciousness of the great radical republic, with its ruffianly nominations and elections; its loud, ill-pitched voice, utterly regardless whether the verb agrees with the nominative; its fights, errors, eructations, repulsions, dishonesties, audacities; those fearful and varied and long continued storm and stress stages (so offensive to the well-regulated college-bred mind) wherewith nature, history, and time block out nationalities more powerful than the past, and to upturn it and press on to the future;—that they cannot understand and fathom all this, I say, is it to be wondered at? Fortunately, the gestation of our thirty-eight empires (and plenty more to come) proceeds on its course, on scales of area and velocity immense and absolute as the globe, and, like the globe itself, quite oblivious even of great poets and thinkers. But we can by no means afford to be oblivious of them.

The same of feudalism, its castles, courts, etiquettes, wars, personalities. However they, or the spirits of them hovering in the air, might scowl and glower at such removes as current Kansas or Kentucky life and forms, the latter may by no means repudiate or leave out the former. Allowing all the evil that it did, we get, here and to-day, a balance of good out of its reminiscence almost beyond price.

Am I content, then, that the general interior chyle of our republic should be supplied and nourished by wholesale from foreign and antagonistic sources such as these? Let me answer that question briefly:

Years ago I thought Americans ought to strike out separate, and have expressions of their own in highest literature. I think so still, and more decidedly than ever. But those convictions are now strongly tempered by some additional points (perhaps the results of advancing age, or the reflections of invalidism). I see that this world of the West, as part of all, fuses inseparably with the East, and with all, as time does—the ever new, yet old, old human race—"the same subject continued," as the novels of our grandfathers had it for chapter-heads. If we are not to hospitably receive and complete the inaugurations of the old civilizations, and change their small scale to the largest, broadest scale, what on earth are we for?

The currents of practical business in America, the rude, coarse, tussling facts of our lives, and all their daily experiences, need just the precipitation and tincture of this entirely different fancy world of lulling, contrasting, even feudalistic, anti-republican poetry and romance. On the enormous outgrowth of our unloosed individualities, and the rank self-assertion of humanity here, may well fall these grace-persuading, *recherché* influences. We first require that individuals and communities shall be free; then surely comes a time when it is requisite that they shall not be too free. Although to such result in the future I look mainly for a great poetry native to us, these importations till then will have to be accepted, such as they are, and thankful they are no worse.

The inmost spiritual currents of the present time curiously revenge and check their own compelled tendency to democracy, and absorption in it, by marked leanings to the past—by reminiscences in poems, plots, operas, novels, to a far-off, contrary, deceased world, as if they dreaded the great vulgar gulf tides of to-day. Then what has been fifty centuries growing, working in, and accepted as crowns and apices for our kind, is not going to be pulled down and discarded in a hurry.

It is, perhaps, time we paid our respects directly to the honorable party, the real object of these preambles. But we must make *reconnaissance* a little further still. Not the least part of our lesson were to realize the curiosity and interest of friendly foreign experts,* and how our situation looks to them. "American poetry," says the London "Times,"† "is the poetry of apt pupils, but it is afflicted from first to last with a fatal want for raciness. Bryant has been long passed as a poet by Professor Longfellow; but in Longfellow, with all his scholarly grace and tender feeling, the defect is more apparent than it was in Bryant. Mr. Lowell can overflow with American humor when politics inspire his muse; but in the realm of pure poetry he is no more American than a Newdigate prizeman. Joaquin Miller's verse has fluency and movement and harmony, but as for the thought, his songs of the sierras might as well have been written in Holland."

Unless in a certain very slight contingency, the "Times" says:

> "American verse, from its earliest to its latest stages, seems an exotic, with an exuberance of gorgeous blossom, but no principle of reproduction. That is the very note and test of its inherent want. Great poets are tortured and massacred by having their flowers of fancy gathered and gummed down in the *hortus siccus* of an anthology. American poets show better in an anthology than in the collected volumes of their works. Like their audience, they have been unable to resist the attraction of the vast orbit

* A few years ago I saw the question, "Has America produced any great poet?" announced as prize-subject for the competition of some university in Northern Europe. I saw the item in a foreign paper, and made note of it; but being taken down with paralysis, and prostrated for a long season, the matter slipped away, and I have never been able since to get hold of any essay presented for the prize, or report of the discussion, nor to learn for certain whether there was any essay or discussion, nor can I remember the place. It may have been Upsala, or possibly Heidelberg. Perhaps some German or Scandinavian can give particulars. I think it was in 1872.

† In a long and prominent editorial, at the time, on the death of William Cullen Bryant.

of English literature. They may talk of the primeval forest, but it would generally be very hard from internal evidence to detect that they were writing on the banks of the Hudson rather than on those of the Thames. . . . In fact, they have caught the English tone and air and mood only too faithfully, and are accepted by the superficially cultivated English intelligence as readily as if they were English born.

"Americans themselves confess to a certain disappointment that a literary curiosity and intelligence so diffused [as in the United States] have not taken up English literature at the point at which America has received it, and carried it forward and developed it with an independent energy. But like reader like poet. Both show the effects of having come into an estate they have not earned. A nation of readers has required of its poets a diction and symmetry of form equal to that of an old literature like that of Great Britain, which is also theirs. No ruggedness, however racy, would be tolerated by circles which, however superficial their culture, read Byron and Tennyson."

The English critic, though a gentleman and a scholar, and friendly withal, is evidently not altogether satisfied (perhaps he is jealous) and winds up by saying:

"For the English language to have been enriched with a national poetry which was not English but American, would have been a treasure beyond price."

With which, as whet and foil, we shall proceed to ventilate more definitely certain no doubt willful opinions.

Leaving unnoticed at present the great masterpieces of the antique, or anything from the middle ages, the prevailing flow of poetry for the last fifty or eighty years, and now at its height, has been and is (like the music) an expression of mere surface melody, within narrow limits, and yet, to give it its due, perfectly satisfying to the demands of the ear, of wondrous charm, of smooth and easy delivery, and the triumph of technical art. Above all things it is fractional and select. It shrinks with aversion from the sturdy, the universal, and the democratic.

The poetry of the future (the phrase is open to sharp criticism, and is not satisfactory to me, but is significant, and I will use it)—the poetry of the future aims at the free expression of emotion (which means far, far more than appears at first), and to arouse and initiate more than to define or finish. Like all modern tendencies, it has direct or indirect reference continually to the reader, to you or me, to the central identity of everything, the mighty Ego. (Byron's was a vehement dash, with plenty of impatient democracy, but lurid and introverted amid all its magnetism;

not at all the fitting, lasting song of a grand, secure, free, sunny race.) It is more akin, likewise, to outside life and landscape (returning mainly to the antique feeling), real sun and gale, and woods and shores—to the elements themselves—not sitting at ease in parlor or library listening to a good tale of them, told in good rhyme. Character, a feature far above style or polish,—a feature not absent at any time, but now first brought to the fore,—gives predominant stamp to advancing poetry. Its born sister, music, already responds to the same influences:

> "The music of the present, Wagner's, Gounod's, even the later Verdi's, all tends toward this free expression of poetic emotion, and demands a vocalism totally unlike that required for Rossini's splendid roulades, or Bellini's suave melodies."

Is there not even now, indeed, an evolution, a departure from the masters? Venerable and unsurpassable after their kind as are the old works, and always unspeakably precious as studies (for Americans more than any other people), is it too much to say that by the shifted combinations of the modern mind the whole underlying theory of first-class verse has changed? "Formerly, during the period termed classic," says Sainte-Beuve, "when literature was governed by recognized rules, he was considered the best poet who had composed the most perfect work, the most beautiful poem, the most intelligible, the most agreeable to read, the most complete in every respect,—the Æneid, the Gerusalemme, a fine tragedy. To-day, something else is wanted. For us, the greatest poet is he who in his works most stimulates the reader's imagination and reflection, who excites him the most himself to poetize. The greatest poet is not he who has done the best; it is he who suggests the most; he, not all of whose meaning is at first obvious, and who leaves you much to desire, to explain, to study, much to complete in your turn."

The fatal defects our American singers labor under are subordination of spirit, an absence of the concrete and of real patriotism, and in excess that modern æsthetic contagion a queer friend of mine calls the *beauty disease*. "The immoderate taste for beauty and art," says Charles Baudelaire, "leads men into monstrous excesses. In minds imbued with a frantic greed for the beautiful, all the balances of truth and justice disappear. There is a lust, a disease of the art faculties, which eats up the moral like a cancer."

Of course, by our plentiful verse-writers there is plenty of service performed, of a kind. Nor need we go far for a tally. We see, in every polite circle, a class of accomplished, good-natured persons ("society," in fact, could not get on without them), fully eligible for certain problems, times, and duties—to mix eggnog, to mend the broken spectacles, to decide whether the stewed eels shall precede the sherry or the sherry the stewed eels, to eke out Mrs. A. B.'s parlor-tableaux with monk, Jew, Turk, lover, Romeo, Puck, Prospero, Caliban, or what not, and to generally contribute and gracefully adapt their flexibilities and talents, in those ranges, to the world's service. But for real crises, great needs and pulls, moral or physical, they might as well have never been born.

Or the accepted notion of a poet would appear to be a sort of male odalisque, singing or piano-playing a kind of spiced ideas, second-hand reminiscences, or toying late hours at entertainments, in rooms stifling with fashionable scent. I think I haven't seen a new-published healthy, bracing, simple lyric in ten years. Not long ago, there were verses in each of three fresh monthlies, from leading authors, and in every one the whole central *motif* (perfectly serious) was the melancholiness of a marriageable young woman who didn't get a rich husband, but a poor one!

Besides its tonic and *al fresco* physiology, relieving such as this, the poetry of the future will take on character in a more important respect. Science, having extirpated the old stock-fables and superstitions, is clearing a field for verse, for all the arts, and even for romance, a hundred-fold ampler and more wonderful, with the new principles behind. Republicanism advances over the whole world. Liberty, with Law by her side, will one day be paramount—will at any rate be the central idea. Then only—for all the splendor and beauty of what has been, or the polish of what is—then only will the true poets appear, and the true poems. Not the satin and patchouly of to-day, not the glorification of the butcheries and wars of the past, nor any fight between Deity on one side and somebody else on the other—not Milton, not even Shakespeare's plays, grand as they are. Entirely different and hitherto unknown classes of men, being authoritatively called for in imaginative literature, will certainly appear. What is hitherto most lacking, perhaps most absolutely indicates the future. Democracy has been hurried on through time by measureless tides and winds, resistless as the revolution of the globe, and as far-reaching and rapid. But in the highest walks of art it has not yet had a single representative worthy of it anywhere upon the earth.

Never had real bard a task more fit for sublime ardor and genius than to sing worthily the songs these States have already indicated. Their origin, Washington, '76, the picturesqueness of old times, the war of 1812 and the sea-fights; the incredible rapidity of movement and breadth of area—to fuse and compact the South and North, the East and West, to express the native forms, situations, scenes, from Montauk to California, and from the Saguenay to the Rio Grande—the working out on such gigantic scales, and with such a swift and mighty play of changing light and shade, of the great problems of man and freedom,—how far ahead of the stereotyped plots, or gem-cutting, or tales of love, or wars of mere ambition! Our history is so full of spinal, modern, germinal subjects—one above all. What the ancient siege of Ilium, and the puissance of Hector's and Agamemnon's warriors proved to Hellenic art and literature, and all art and literature since, may prove the war of attempted secession of 1861-5 to the future æsthetics, drama, romance, poems of the United States.

Nor could utility itself provide anything more practically serviceable to the hundred millions who, a couple of generations hence, will inhabit within the limits just named, than the permeation of a sane, sweet, autochthonous national poetry—must I say of a kind that does not now exist? but which, I fully believe, will in time be supplied on scales as free as Nature's elements. (It is acknowledged that we of the States are the most materialistic and money-making people ever known. My own theory, while fully accepting this, is that we are the most emotional, spiritualistic, and poetry-loving people also.)

Infinite are the new and orbic traits waiting to be launched forth in the firmament that is, and is to be, America. Lately I have wondered whether the last meaning of this cluster of thirty-eight States is not only practical fraternity among themselves—the only real *union* (much nearer its accomplishment, too, than appears on the surface)—but for fraternity over the whole globe—that dazzling, pensive dream of ages! Indeed, the peculiar glory of our lands, I have come to see, or expect to see, not in their geographical or republican greatness, nor wealth or products, nor military or naval power, nor special, eminent names in any department, to shine with, or outshine, foreign special names in similar departments,— but more and more in a vaster, saner, more splendid Comradeship, uniting closer and closer not only the American States, but all nations, and all humanity. That, O poets! is not that a theme worth chanting, striving for? Why not fix your verses henceforth to the gauge of the round globe? the whole race?

Perhaps the most illustrious culmination of the modern may thus prove to be a signal growth of joyous, more exalted bards of adhesiveness, identically one in soul, but contributed by every nation, each after its distinctive kind. Let us, audacious, start it. Let the diplomates, as ever, still deeply plan, seeking advantages, proposing treaties between governments, and to bind them, on paper: what I seek is different, simpler. I would inaugurate from America, for this purpose, new formulas—international poems. I have thought that the invisible root out of which the poetry deepest in, and dearest to, humanity grows, is Friendship. I have thought that both in patriotism and song (even amid their grandest shows past) we have adhered too long to petty limits, and that the time has come to enfold the world.

Not only is the human and artificial world we have established in the West a radical departure from anything hitherto known,—not only men and politics, and all that goes with them,—but Nature itself, in the main sense, its construction, is different. The same old font of type, of course, but set up to a text never composed or issued before. For Nature consists not only in itself objectively, but at least just as much in its subjective reflection from the person, spirit, age, looking at it, in the midst of it, and absorbing it—faithfully sends back the characteristic beliefs of the time or individual—takes, and readily gives again, the physiognomy of any nation or literature—falls like a great elastic veil on a face, or like the molding plaster on a statue.

What is Nature? What were the elements, the invisible backgrounds and eidolons of it, to Homer's heroes, voyagers, gods? What all through the wanderings of Virgil's Æneas? Then to Shakespeare's characters— Hamlet, Lear, the English-Norman kings, the Romans? What was nature to Rousseau, to Voltaire, to the German Goethe in his little classical court gardens? In those presentments in Tennyson (see the "Idylls of the King"—what sumptuous, perfumed, arras-and-gold nature, inimitably described, better than any, fit for princes and knights and peerless ladies— wrathful or peaceful, just the same—Vivien and Merlin in their strange dalliance, or the death-float of Elaine, or Geraint and the long journey of his disgraced Enid and himself through the wood, and the wife all day driving the horses), as in all the great imported art-works, treaties, systems, from Lucretius down, there is a constantly lurking, often pervading something that will have to be eliminated, as not only unsuited to modern democracy and science in America, but insulting to them, and disproved by them.

Still, the rule and demesne of poetry will always be not the exterior, but interior; not the macrocosm, but microcosm; not Nature, but Man. I haven't said anything about the imperative need of a race of giant bards in the future, to hold up high to eyes of land and race the eternal antiseptic models, and to dauntlessly confront greed, injustice, and all forms of that wiliness and tyranny whose roots never die (my opinion is, that after all the rest is advanced, *that* is what first-class poets are for, as, to their days and occasions, the Hebrew lyrists, Roman Juvenal, and doubtless the old singers of India and the British Druids),—to counteract dangers, immensest ones, already looming in America—measureless corruption in politics; what we call religion a mere mask of wax or lace; for *ensemble,* that most cankerous, offensive of all earth's shows—a vast and varied community, prosperous and fat with wealth of money and products and business ventures,—plenty of mere intellectuality too,—and then utterly without the sound, prevailing, moral, and æsthetic health-action beyond all the money and mere intellect of the world.

Is it a dream of mine that, in times to come, West, South, East, North, will silently, surely arise a race of such poets, varied, yet one in soul—nor only poets, and of the best, but newer, larger prophets—larger than Judea's, and more passionate—to meet and penetrate those woes, as shafts of light the darkness?

As I write, the last fifth of the nineteenth century is entered upon, and will soon be waning. Now, and for a long time to come, what the United States most need, to give purport, definiteness, reason why, to their unprecedented material wealth, industrial products, education by rote merely, great populousness and intellectual activity, is the central, spinal reality (or even the idea of it) of such a democratic band of native-born-and-bred teachers, artists, *littérateurs,* tolerant and receptive of importations, but entirely adjusted to the West, to ourselves, to our own days, purports, combinations, differences, superiorities. Indeed, I am fond of thinking that the whole series of concrete and political triumphs of the republic are mainly as bases and preparations for half a dozen first-rate future poets, ideal personalities, referring not to a special class, but to the entire people, four to five millions of square miles.

Long, long are the processes of the development of a nationality. Only to the rapt vision does the seen become the prophecy of the unseen.*

* Is there not such a thing as the philosophy of American history and politics? And if so—what is it? . . . Wise men say there are two sets of wills to nations and to persons—one set that acts and works from explainable motives—from teaching, intelligence, judgment, circumstance, caprice, emulation, greed, etc.—and then another set, perhaps deep, hidden, unsuspected, yet often more potent than the first, refusing to be argued with, rising as it were out of abysses, resistlessly urging on speakers, doers, communities, unwitting to themselves—the poet to his fieriest words—the race to pursue its loftiest ideal. . . . Indeed, the paradox of a nation's life and career, with all its wondrous contradictions, can probably only be explained from these two wills, sometimes conflicting, each operating in its sphere, combining in races or in persons, and producing strangest results.

Democracy, so far attending only to the real, is not for the real only, but the grandest ideal—to justify the modern by that, and not only to equal, but to become by that superior to the past. On a comprehensive summing up of the processes and present and hitherto condition of the United States with reference to their future and the indispensable precedents to it, I say I am fully content. My point, below all surfaces, and subsoiling them, is, that the basis and prerequisites of a leading nationality are, first, at all hazards, freedom, worldly wealth and products on the largest and most varied scale, common education and intercommunication, and, in general, the passing through of just the stages and crudities we have passed or are passing through in the United States.

Then, perhaps, as weightiest factor of the whole business, and of the main outgrowths of the future, it remains to be definitely avowed that the native-born middle-class population of quite all the United States,—the average of farmers and mechanics everywhere,—the real, though latent

---

Let us hope there is (indeed, can there be any doubt there is?) this great, unconscious, and abysmic second will also running through the average nationality and career of America. Let us hope that, amid all the dangers and defections of the present, and through all the processes of the conscious will, it alone is the permanent and sovereign force, destined to carry on the New World to fulfill its destinies in the future—to resolutely pursue those destinies, age upon age; to build, far, far beyond its past vision, present thought; to form and fashion, and for the general type, men and women more noble, more athletic than the world has yet seen; to gradually, firmly blend, from all the States, with all varieties, a friendly, happy, free, religious nationality—a nationality not only the richest, most inventive, most productive and materialistic the world has yet known, but compacted indissolubly, and out of whose ample and solid bulk, and giving purpose and finish to it, conscience, morals, and all the spiritual attributes, shall surely rise, like spires above some group of edifices, firm-footed on the earth, yet scaling space and heaven.

Great as they are, and greater far to be, the United States, too, are but a series of steps in the eternal process of creative thought. And here is, to my mind, their final justification, and certain perpetuity. There is in that sublime process, in the laws of the universe—and, above all, in the moral law—something that would make unsatisfactory, and even vain and contemptible, all the triumphs of war, the gains of peace, and the proudest worldly grandeur of all the nations that have ever existed, or that (ours included) now exist, except that we constantly see, through all their worldly career, however struggling and blind and lame, attempts, by all ages, all peoples, according to their development, to reach, to press, to progress on, and farther on, to more and more advanced ideals.

The glory of the republic of the United States, in my opinion, is to be that, emerging in the light of the modern and the splendor of science, and solidly based on the past, it is to cheerfully range itself, and its politics are henceforth to come, under those universal laws, and embody them, and carry them out, to serve them. . . .

and silent bulk of America, city or country, presents a magnificent mass of material, never before equalled on earth. It is this material, quite unexpressed by literature or art, that in every respect insures the future of the republic. During the secession war I was with the armies, and saw the rank and file, North and South, and studied them for four years. I have never had the least doubt about the country in its essential future since.

Meantime, we can (perhaps) do no better than saturate ourselves with, and continue to give imitations, yet a while, of the æsthetic models, supplies, of that past and of those lands we spring from. Those wondrous stores, reminiscences, floods, currents! Let them flow on, flow hither freely. And let the sources be enlarged, to include not only the works of

---

And as only that individual becomes truly great who understands well that, while complete in himself in a certain sense, he is but a part of the divine, eternal scheme, and whose special life and laws are adjusted to move in harmonious relations with the general laws of nature, and especially with the moral law, the deepest and highest of all, and the last vitality of man or State—so those nations, and so the United States, may only become the greatest and the most continuous, by understanding well their harmonious relations with entire humanity and history, and all their laws and progress, and sublimed with the creative thought of Deity, through all time, past, present, and future. Thus will they expand to the amplitude of their destiny, and become splendid illustrations and culminating parts of the cosmos, and of civilization.

No more considering the States as an incident, or series of incidents, however vast, coming accidentally along the path of time, and shaped by casual emergencies as they happen to arise, and the mere result of modern improvements, vulgar and lucky, ahead of other nations and times, I would finally plant, as seeds, these thoughts or speculations in the growth of our republic—that it is the deliberate culmination and result of all the past—that here, too, as in all departments of the universe, regular laws (slow and sure in acting, slow and sure in ripening) have controlled and governed, and will yet control and govern; and that those laws can no more be baffled or steered clear of, or vitiated, by chance, or any fortune or opposition, than the laws of winter and summer, or darkness and light.

The summing up of the tremendous moral and military perturbations of 1861-5, and their results—and indeed of the entire hundred years of the past of our national experiment, from its inchoate movement down to the present day (1780-1881)—is, that they all now launch the United States fairly forth, consistently with the entirety of civilization and humanity, and in main sort the representative of them, leading the van, leading the fleet of the modern and democratic, on the seas and voyages of the future.

And the real history of the United States—starting from that great convulsive struggle for unity, the secession war, triumphantly concluded, and *the South* victorious, after all—is only to be written at the remove of hundreds, perhaps a thousand, years hence.—*From my "Memoranda of the War."*

British origin, as now, but stately and devout Spain, courteous France, profound Germany, the manly Scandinavian lands, Italy's art race, and always the mystic Orient.

Remembering that at present, and doubtless long ahead, a certain humility would well become us. The course through time of highest civilization, does it not wait the first glimpse of our contribution to its cosmic train of poems, bibles, structures, perpetuities—Egypt and Palestine and India—Greece and Rome and mediæval Europe—and so onward? The shadowy procession is not a meager one, and the standard not a low one. All that is mighty or precious in our kind seems to have trod the road. Ah, never may America forget her thanks and reverence for samples, treasures such as these—that other life-blood, inspiration, sunshine, hourly in use to-day, all days, forever, throughout her broad demesne!

All serves our New World progress, even the bafflers, head-winds, cross-tides. Through many perturbations and squalls, and much backing and filling, the ship, upon the whole, makes unmistakably for her destination. Shakespeare has served, and serves, may be, the best of any.

For conclusion, a passing thought, a contrast, of him who, in my opinion, continues and stands for the Shakespearean cultus at the present day among all English-writing peoples—of Tennyson, his poetry. I find it impossible, as I taste the sweetness of these lines, to escape the flavor, the conviction, the lush-ripening culmination, and last honey of decay (I dare not call it rottenness) of that feudalism which the mighty English dramatist painted in all the splendors of its noon and afternoon. And how they are chanted—both poets! Happy those kings and nobles to be so sung, so told! To run their course—to get their deeds and shape in lasting pigments—the very pomp and dazzle of the sunset!

Meanwhile, democracy waits the coming of its bards in silence and in twilight—but 'tis the twilight of the dawn.

[1881]

98 ✍

Perhaps the best of songs heard, or of any and all true love, or life's fairest episodes, or sailors', soldiers' trying scenes on land or sea, is the *résumé* of them, or any of them, long afterwards, looking at the actualities away back past, with all their practical excitations gone. How the soul loves to float amid such reminiscences!

So here I sit gossiping in the early candle-light of old age—I and my book—casting backward glances over our travel'd road. After completing, as it were, the journey—(a varied jaunt of years, with many halts and gaps of intervals—or some lengthen'd ship-voyage, wherein more than once the last hour had apparently arrived, and we seem'd certainly going down—yet reaching port in a sufficient way through all discomfitures at last)—after completing my poems, I am curious to review them in the light of their own (at the time unconscious, or mostly unconscious) intentions, with certain unfoldings of the thirty years they seek to embody. These lines, therefore, will probably blend the weft of first purposes and speculations, with the warp of that experience afterwards, always bringing strange developments.

Results of seven or eight stages and struggles extending through nearly thirty years, (as I nigh my three-score-and-ten I live largely on memory,) I look upon *Leaves of Grass,* now finish'd to the end of its opportunities and powers, as my definitive *carte de visite* to the coming generations of the New World,* if I may assume to say so. That I have not gain'd the acceptance of my own time, but have fallen back on fond dreams of the future—anticipations—("still lives the song, though Regnar dies")—that from a worldly and business point of view *Leaves of Grass* has been worse than a failure—that public criticism on the book and myself as author of it yet shows mark'd anger and contempt more than anything else—("I find a solid line of enemies to you everywhere,"—letter from W. S. K., Boston, May 28, 1884)—and that solely for publishing it I have been the object of two or three pretty serious special official buffetings—is all probably no more than I ought to have expected. I had my choice when I commenc'd. I bid neither for soft eulogies, big money returns, nor the approbation of existing schools and conventions. As fulfill'd or partially fulfill'd, the best comfort of the whole business (after a small band of the dearest friends and upholders ever vouchsafed to man or cause—doubtless all the more faithful and uncompromising—this little phalanx!—for being so few) is that, unstopp'd and unwarp'd by any influence outside the soul within me, I have had my say entirely my own way, and put it unerringly on record—the value thereof to be decided by time.

In calculating that decision, William O'Connor and Dr. Bucke are far

* When Champollion, on his death-bed, handed to the printer the revised proof of his *Egyptian Grammar,* he said gayly, "Be careful of this—it is my *carte de visite* to posterity."

more peremptory than I am. Behind all else that can be said, I consider *Leaves of Grass* and its theory experimental—as, in the deepest sense, I consider our American republic itself to be, with its theory. (I think I have at least enough philosophy not to be too absolutely certain of anything, or any results.) In the second place, the volume is a *sortie*—whether to prove triumphant, and conquer its field of aim and escape and construction, nothing less than a hundred years from now can fully answer. I consider the point that I have positively gain'd a hearing, to far more than make up for any and all other lacks and withholdings. Essentially, *that* was from the first, and has remain'd throughout, the main object. Now it seems to be achiev'd, I am certainly contented to waive any otherwise momentous drawbacks, as of little account. Candidly and dispassionately reviewing all my intentions, I feel that they were creditable—and I accept the result, whatever it may be.

After continued personal ambition and effort, as a young fellow, to enter with the rest into competition for the usual rewards, business, political, literary, &c.—to take part in the great *mêlée,* both for victory's prize itself and to do some good—after years of those aims and pursuits, I found myself remaining possess'd, at the age of thirty-one to thirty-three, with a special desire and conviction. Or rather, to be quite exact, a desire that had been flitting through my previous life, or hovering on the flanks, mostly indefinite hitherto, had steadily advanced to the front, defined itself, and finally dominated everything else. This was a feeling or ambition to articulate and faithfully express in literary or poetic form, and uncompromisingly, my own physical, emotional, moral, intellectual, and æsthetic Personality, in the midst of, and tallying, the momentous spirit and facts of its immediate days, and of current America—and to exploit that Personality, identified with place and date, in a far more candid and comprehensive sense than any hitherto poem or book.

Perhaps this is in brief, or suggests, all I have sought to do. Given the nineteenth century, with the United States, and what they furnish as area and points of view, *Leaves of Grass* is, or seeks to be, simply a faithful and doubtless self-will'd record. In the midst of all, it gives one man's—the author's—identity, ardors, observations, faiths, and thoughts, color'd hardly at all with any decided coloring from other faiths or other identities. Plenty of songs had been sung—beautiful, matchless songs—adjusted to other lands than these—another spirit and stage of evolution; but I would sing, and leave out or put in, quite solely with reference to America and to-day. Modern science and democracy seem'd to be throwing out their challenge to poetry to put them in its statements in contradistinction to the songs and myths of the past. As I see it now (perhaps too late), I have unwittingly taken up that challenge and made an attempt at such statements—which I certainly would not assume to do now, knowing more clearly what it means.

For grounds for *Leaves of Grass,* as a poem, I abandon'd the conventional themes, which do not appear in it: none of the stock ornamentation, or choice plots of love or war, or high, exceptional personages of Old-World song; nothing, as I may say, for beauty's sake—no legend, or myth, or romance, nor euphemism, nor rhyme. But the broadest average of humanity and its identities in the now ripening nineteenth century, and especially in each of their countless examples and practical occupations in the United States to-day.

One main contrast of the ideas behind every page of my verses, compared with establish'd poems, is their different relative attitude towards God, towards the objective universe, and still more (by reflection, confession, assumption, &c.) the quite changed attitude of the ego, the one chanting or talking, towards himself and towards his fellow-humanity. It is certainly time for America, above all, to begin this readjustment in the scope and basic point of view of verse; for everything else has changed. As I write, I see in an article on Wordsworth, in one of the current English magazines, the lines, "A few weeks ago an eminent French critic said that, owing to the special tendency to science and to its all-devouring force, poetry would cease to be read in fifty years." But I anticipate the very contrary. Only a firmer, vastly broader, new area begins to exist—nay, is already form'd—to which the poetic genius must emigrate. Whatever may have been the case in years gone by, the true use for the imaginative faculty of modern times is to give ultimate vivification to facts, to science, and to common lives, endowing them with the glows and glories and final illustriousness which belong to every real thing, and to real things only. Without that ultimate vivification—which the poet or other artist alone can give—reality would seem incomplete, and science, democracy, and life itself, finally in vain.

Few appreciate the moral revolutions, our age, which have been profounder far than the material or inventive or war-produced ones. The nineteenth century, now well towards its close (and ripening into fruit the seeds of the two preceding centuries*)—the uprisings of national masses

---

* The ferment and germination even of the United States to-day, dating back to, and in my opinion mainly founded on, the Elizabethan age in English history, the age of Francis Bacon and Shakspere. Indeed, when we pursue it, what growth or advent is there that does not date back, back, until lost—perhaps its most tantalizing clues lost—in the receded horizons of the past?

and shiftings of boundary-lines—the historical and other prominent facts of the United States—the war of attempted Secession—the stormy rush and haste of nebulous forces—never can future years witness more excitement ar.d din of action—never completer change of army front along the whole line, the whole civilized world. For all these new and evolutionary facts, meanings, purposes, new poetic messages, new forms and expressions, are inevitable.

My Book and I—what a period we have presumed to span! those thirty years from 1850 to '80—and America in them! Proud, proud indeed may we be, if we have cull'd enough of that period in its own spirit to worthily waft a few live breaths of it to the future!

Let me not dare, here or anywhere, for my own purposes, or any purposes, to attempt the definition of Poetry, nor answer the question what it is. Like Religion, Love, Nature, while those terms are indispensable, and we all give a sufficiently accurate meaning to them, in my opinion no definition that has ever been made sufficiently encloses the name Poetry; nor can any rule or convention ever so absolutely obtain but some great exception may arise and disregard and overturn it.

Also it must be carefully remember'd that first-class literature does not shine by any luminosity of its own; nor do its poems. They grow of circumstances, and are evolutionary. The actual living light is always curiously from elsewhere—follows unaccountable sources, and is lunar and relative at the best. There are, I know, certain controlling themes that seem endlessly appropriated to the poets—as war, in the past—in the Bible, religious rapture and adoration—always love, beauty, some fine plot, or pensive or other emotion. But, strange as it may sound at first, I will say there is something striking far deeper and towering far higher than those themes for the best elements of modern song.

Just as all the old imaginative works rest, after their kind, on long trains of presuppositions, often entirely unmention'd by themselves, yet supplying the most important bases of them, and without which they could have had no reason for being, so *Leaves of Grass,* before a line was written, presupposed something different from any other, and, as it stands, is the result of such presupposition. I should say, indeed, it were useless to attempt reading the book without first carefully tallying that preparatory background and quality in the mind. Think of the United States to-day—the facts of these thirty-eight or forty empires solder'd in one—sixty or seventy millions of equals, with their lives, their passions, their future—these incalculable, modern, American, seething multitudes around us, of which we are inseparable parts! Think, in comparison, of the petty environage and limited area of the poets of past or present Europe, no matter how great their genius. Think of the absence and ignorance in all cases hitherto, of the multitudinousness, vitality, and the unprecedented stimulants of to-day and here. It almost seems as if a poetry with cosmic and dynamic features of magnitude and limitlessness suitable to the human soul, were never possible before. It is certain that a poetry of absolute faith and equality for the use of the democratic masses never was.

In estimating first-class song, a sufficient Nationality, or, on the other hand, what may be call'd the negative and lack of it, (as in Goethe's case it sometimes seems to me), is often, if not always, the first element. One needs only a little penetration to see, at more or less removes, the material facts of their country and radius, with the coloring of the moods of humanity at the time, and its gloomy or hopeful prospects, behind all poets and each poet, and forming their birth-marks. I know very well that my *Leaves* could not possibly have emerged or been fashion'd or completed, from any other era than the latter half of the nineteenth century, nor any other land than democratic America, and from the absolute triumph of the National Union arms.

And whether my friends claim it for me or not, I know well enough, too, that in respect to pictorial talent, dramatic situations, and especially in verbal melody and all the conventional technique of poetry, not only the divine works that to-day stand ahead in the world's reading, but dozens more, transcend (some of them immeasurably transcend) all I have done, or could do. But it seem'd to me, as the objects in Nature, the themes of æstheticism, and all special exploitations of the mind and soul, involve not only their own inherent quality, but the quality, just as inherent and important, of *their point of view,** the time had come to reflect all themes and things, old and new, in the lights thrown on them by the advent of America and democracy—to chant those themes through the utterance of one, not only the grateful and reverent legatee of the past, but the born child of the New World—to illustrate all through the genesis and ensemble of to-day; and that such illustration and ensemble are the chief demands of America's prospective imaginative literature. Not to carry out, in the approved style, some choice plot of fortune or misfortune, or fancy, or fine thoughts, or incidents, or courtesies—all of which has been done overwhelmingly and well, probably never to be excell'd—but that while in

---

* According to Immanuel Kant, the last essential reality, giving shape and significance to all the rest.

such aesthetic presentation of objects, passions, plots, thoughts, &c., our lands and days do not want, and probably will never have, anything better than they already possess from the bequests of the past, it still remains to be said that there is even towards all those a subjective and contemporary point of view appropriate to ourselves alone, and to our new genius and environments, differing from anything hitherto; and that such conception of current or gone-by life and art is for us the only means of their assimilation consistent with the Western world.

Indeed, and anyhow, to put it specifically, has not the time arrived when, (if it must be plainly said, for democratic America's sake, if for no other) there must imperatively come a readjustment of the whole theory and nature of Poetry? The question is important, and I may turn the argument over and repeat it: Does not the best thought of our day and Republic conceive of a birth and spirit of song superior to anything past or present? To the effectual and moral consolidation of our lands (already, as materially establish'd, the greatest factors in known history, and far, far greater through what they prelude and necessitate, and are to be in future)—to conform with and build on the concrete realities and theories of the universe furnish'd by science, and henceforth the only irrefragable basis for anything, verse included—to root both influences in the emotional and imaginative action of the modern time, and dominate all that precedes or opposes them—is not either a radical advance and step forward, or a new verteber of the best song indispensable?

The New World receives with joy the poems of the antique with European feudalism's rich fund of epics, plays, ballads—seeks not in the least to deaden or displace those voices from our ear and area—holds them indeed as indispensable studies, influences, records, comparisons. But though the dawn-dazzle of the sun of literature is in those poems for us of to-day—though perhaps the best parts of current character in nations, social groups, or any man's or woman's individuality, Old World or New, are from them—and though if I were ask'd to name the most precious bequest to current American civilization from all the hitherto ages, I am not sure but I would name those old and less old songs ferried hither from east and west—some serious words and debits remain; some acrid considerations demand a hearing. Of the great poems receiv'd from abroad and from the ages, and to-day enveloping and penetrating America, is there one that is consistent with these United States, or essentially applicable to them as they are and are to be? Is there one whose underlying basis is not a denial and insult to democracy? What a comment it forms, anyhow, on this era of literary fulfilment, with the splendid day-rise of science and resuscitation of history, that our chief religious and poetical works are not our own, nor adapted to our light, but have been furnish'd by far-back ages out of their arrière and darkness, or, at most, twilight dimness! What is there in those works that so imperiously and scornfully dominates all our advanced civilization and culture?

Even Shakspere, who so suffuses current letters and art (which indeed have in most degrees grown out of him) belongs essentially to the buried past. Only he holds the proud distinction for certain important phases of that past, of being the loftiest of the singers life has yet given voice to. All, however, relate to and rest upon conditions, standards, politics, sociologies, ranges of belief, that have been quite eliminated from the Eastern Hemisphere, and never existed at all in the Western. As authoritative types of song they belong in America just about as much as the persons and institutes they depict. True, it may be said, the emotional, moral, and æsthetic natures of humanity have not radically changed—that in these the old poems apply to our times and all times, irrespective of date; and that they are of incalculable value as pictures of the past. I willingly make those admissions, and to their fullest extent; then advance the points herewith as a serious, even paramount importance.

I have indeed put on record elsewhere my reverence and eulogy for those never-to-be-excell'd poetic bequests, and their indescribable preciousness as heirlooms for America. Another and separate point must now be candidly stated. If I had not stood before those poems with uncover'd head, fully aware of their colossal grandeur and beauty of form and spirit, I could not have written *Leaves of Grass*. My verdict and conclusions as illustrated in its pages are arrived at through the temper and inculcation of the old works as much as through anything else—perhaps more than through anything else. As America fully and fairly construed is the legitimate result and evolutionary outcome of the past, so I would dare to claim for my verse. Without stopping to qualify the averment, the Old World has had the poems of myths, fictions, feudalism, conquest, caste, dynastic wars, and splendid exceptional characters and affairs, which have been great; but the New World needs the poems of realities and science and of the democratic average and basic equality, which shall be greater. In the centre of all, and object of all, stands the Human Being, towards whose heroic and spiritual evolution poems and everything directly or indirectly tend, Old World or New.

Continuing the subject, my friends have more than once suggested—or may be the garrulity of advancing age is possessing me—some further embryonic facts of *Leaves of Grass,* and especially how I enter'd upon them. Dr. Bucke has, in his volume, already fully and fairly described the preparation of my poetic field, with the particular and general plowing, planting, seeding, and occupation of the ground, till everything was fertilized, rooted, and ready to start its own way for good or bad. Not till after all this, did I attempt any serious acquaintance with poetic literature. Along in my sixteenth year I had become possessor of a stout, well-cramm'd one thousand page octavo volume (I have it yet,) containing Walter Scott's poetry entire—an inexhaustible mine and treasury of poetic forage (especially the endless forests and jungles of notes)—has been so to me for fifty years, and remains so to this day.*

Later, at intervals, summers and falls, I used to go off, sometimes for a week at a stretch, down in the country, or to Long Island's sea-shores—there, in the presence of outdoor influences, I went over thoroughly the Old and New Testaments, and absorb'd (probably to better advantage for me than in any library or indoor room—it makes such difference *where* you read,) Shakspere, Ossian, the best translated versions I could get of Homer, Eschylus, Sophocles, the old German "Nibelungen," the ancient Hindoo poems, and one or two other masterpieces, Dante's among them. As it happen'd, I read the latter mostly in an old wood. The *Iliad* (Buckley's prose version) I read first thoroughly on the peninsula of Orient, northeast end of Long Island, in a shelter'd hollow of rocks and sand, with the sea on each side. (I have wonder'd since why I was not overwhelm'd by those mighty masters. Likely because I read them, as described, in the full presence of Nature, under the sun, with the far-spreading landscape and vistas, or the sea rollong in.)

Toward the last I had among much else look'd over Edgar Poe's poems—of which I was not an admirer, tho' I always saw that beyond their limited range of melody (like perpetual chimes of music bells, ringing from lower *b* flat up to *g*) they were melodious expressions, and perhaps never excell'd ones, of certain pronounc'd phases of human

---

* Sir Walter Scott's *Complete Poems;* especially including "Border Minstrelsy"; then "Sir Tristrem"; "Lady of the Last Minstrel"; "Ballads from the German"; "Marmion"; "Lady of the Lake"; "Vision of Don Roderick"; "Lord of the Isles"; "Rokeby"; "Bridal of Triermain"; "Field of Waterloo"; "Harold the Dauntless"; all the Dramas; various Introductions, endless interesting Notes, and Essays on Poetry, Romance, &c.

Lockhart's 1833 (or '34) edition with Scott's latest and copious revisions and annotations. (All the poems were thoroughly read by me, but the ballads of the "Border Minstrelsy" over and over again.)

morbidity. (The Poetic area is very spacious—has room for all—has so many mansions!) But I was repaid in Poe's prose by the idea that (at any rate for our occasions, our day) there can be no such thing as a long poem. The same thought had been haunting my mind before, but Poe's argument, though short, work'd the sum and proved it to me.

Another point had an early settlement, clearing the ground greatly. I saw, from the time my enterprise and questionings positively shaped themselves (how best can I express my own distinctive era and surroundings, America, Democracy?) that the trunk and centre whence the answer was to radiate, and to which all should return from straying however far a distance, must be an identical body and soul, a personality—which personality, after many considerations and ponderings, I deliberately settled should be myself—indeed could not be any other. I also felt strongly (whether I have shown it or not) that to the true and full estimate of the Present both the Past and the Future are main considerations.

These, however, and much more might have gone on and come to naught (almost positively would have come to naught,) if a sudden, vast, terrible, direct and indirect stimulus for new and national declamatory expression had not been given to me. It is certain, I say, that, although I had made a start before, only from the occurrence of the Secession War, and what it show'd me as by flashes of lightning, with the emotional depths it sounded and arous'd (of course, I don't mean in my own heart only, I saw it just as plainly in others, in millions)—that only from the strong flare and provocation of that war's sights and scenes the final reasons-for-being of an autochthonic and passionate song definitely came forth.

I went down to the war fields in Virginia (end of 1862), lived thenceforward in camp—saw great battles and the days and nights afterward—partook of all the fluctuations, gloom, despair, hopes again arous'd, courage evoked—death readily risk'd—*the cause,* too—along and filling those agonistic and lurid following years, 1863-'64-'65—the real parturition years (more than 1776-'83) of this henceforth homogeneous Union. Without those three or four years and the experiences they gave, *Leaves of Grass* would not now be existing.

But I set out with the intention also of indicating or hinting some point-characteristics which I since see (though I did not then, at least not definitely) were bases and object-urgings toward those *Leaves* from the first. The word I myself put primarily for the description of them as they stand at last, is the word Suggestiveness. I round and finish little, if anything; and could not, consistently with my scheme. The reader will always have his or her part to do, just as much as I have had mine. I seek less to state or display any theme or thought, and more to bring you, reader, into the atmosphere of the theme or thought—there to pursue your own flight. Another impetus-word is Comradeship as for all lands, and in a more commanding and acknowledg'd sense than hitherto. Other word signs would be Good Cheer, Content, and Hope.

The chief trait of any given poet is always the spirit he brings to the observation of Humanity and Nature—the mood out of which he contemplates his subjects. What kind of temper and what amount of faith report these things? Up to how recent a date is the song carried? What the equipment, and special raciness of the singer—what his tinge of coloring? The last value of artistic expressers, past and present—Greek æsthetes, Shakspere—or in our own day Tennyson, Victor Hugo, Carlyle, Emerson—is certainly involv'd in such questions. I say the profoundest service that poems or any other writings can do for their reader is not merely to satisfy the intellect, or supply something polish'd and interesting, nor even to depict great passions, or persons or events, but to fill him with vigorous and clean manliness, religiousness, and give him *good heart* as a radical possession and habit. The educated world seems to have been growing more and more ennuyéd for ages, leaving to our time the inheritance of it all. Fortunately there is the original inexhaustible fund of buoyancy, normally resident in the race, forever eligible to be appeal'd to and relied on.

As for native American individuality, though certain to come, and on a large scale, the distinctive and ideal type of Western character (as consistent with the operative political and even money-making features of United States' humanity in the nineteenth century as chosen knights, gentlemen and warriors were the ideals of the centuries of European feudalism) it has not yet appear'd. I have allow'd the stress of my poems from beginning to end to bear upon American individuality and assist it—not only because that is a great lesson in Nature, amid all her generalizing laws, but as counterpoise to the leveling tendencies of Democracy—and for other reasons. Defiant of ostensible literary and other conventions, I avowedly chant "the great pride of man in himself," and permit it to be more or less a *motif* of nearly all my verse. I think this pride indispensable to an American. I think it not inconsistent with obedience, humility, deference, and self-questioning.

Democracy has been so rewarded and jeopardized by powerful per-

sonalities, that its first instincts are fain to clip, conform, bring in strag-
glers, and reduce everything to a dead level. While the ambitious thought
of my song is to help the forming of a great aggregate Nation, it is,
perhaps, altogether through the forming of myriads of fully develop'd and
enclosing individuals. Welcome as are equality's and fraternity's doctrines
and popular education, a certain liability accompanies them all, as we see.
That primal and interior something in man, in his soul's abysms, coloring all, and, by exceptional fruitions, giving the last majesty to him—
something continually touch'd upon and attain'd by the old poems and
ballads of feudalism, and often the principal foundation of them—modern
science and Democracy appear to be endangering, perhaps eliminating.
But that forms an appearance only; the reality is quite different. The new
influences, upon the whole, are surely preparing the way for grander
individualities than ever. To-day and here personal force is behind everything, just the same. The times and depictions from the *Iliad* to Shakspere
inclusive can happily never again be realized—but the elements of cou-
rageous and lofty manhood are unchanged.

Without yielding an inch the working-man and working-woman were
to be in my pages from first to last. The ranges of heroism and loftiness
with which Greek and feudal poets endow'd their god-like or lordly born
characters—indeed prouder and better based and with fuller ranges than
those—I was to endow the democratic averages of America. I was to show
that we, here and to-day, are eligible to the grandest and the best—more
eligible now than any times of old were. I will also want my utterances (I
said to myself before beginning) to be in spirit the poems of the morning. (They have been founded and mainly written in the sunny forenoon
and early midday of my life.) I will want them to be the poems of women
entirely as much as men. I have wish'd to put the complete Union of the
States in my songs without any preference or partiality whatever. Henceforth, if they live and are read, it must be just as much South as North—
just as much along the Pacific as Atlantic—in the valley of the Mississippi,
in Canada, up in Maine, down in Texas, and on the shores of Puget
Sound.

From another point of view *Leaves of Grass* is avowedly the song of
Sex and Amativeness, and even Animality—though meanings that do
not usually go along with those words are behind all, and will duly
emerge; and all are sought to be lifted into a different light and atmosphere. Of this feature, intentionally palpable in a few lines, I shall only
say the espousing principle of those lines so gives breath of life to my
whole scheme that the bulk of the pieces might as well have been left

unwritten were those lines omitted. Difficult as it will be, it has become, in my opinion, imperative to achieve a shifted attitude from superior men and women towards the thought and fact of sexuality, as an element in character, personality, the emotions, and a theme in literature. I am not going to argue the question by itself; it does not stand by itself. The vitality of it is altogether in its relations, bearings, significance—like the clef of a symphony. At last analogy the lines I allude to, and the spirit in which they are spoken, permeate all *Leaves of Grass,* and the work must stand or fall with them, as the human body and soul must remain as an entirety.

Universal as are certain facts and symptoms of communities or individuals all times, there is nothing so rare in modern conventions and poetry as their normal recognizance. Literature is always calling in the doctor for consultation and confession, and always giving evasions and swathing suppressions in place of that "heroic nudity"* on which only a genuine diagnosis of serious cases can be built. And in respect to editions of *Leaves of Grass* in time to come (if there should be such) I take occasion now to confirm those lines with the settled convictions and deliberate renewals of thirty years, and to hereby prohibit, as far as word of mine can do so, any elision of them.

Then still a purpose enclosing all, and over and beneath all. Ever since what might be call'd thought, or the budding of thought, fairly began in my youthful mind, I had had a desire to attempt some worthy record of that entire faith and acceptance ("to justify the ways of God to men" is Milton's well-known and ambitious phrase) which is the foundation of moral America. I felt it all as positively then in my young days as I do now in my old ones; to formulate a poem whose every thought or fact should directly or indirectly be or connive at an implicit belief in the wisdom, health, mystery, beauty of every process, every concrete object, every human or other existence, not only consider'd from the point of view of all, but of each.

While I cannot understand it or argue it out, I fully believe in a clue and purpose in nature, entire and several; and that invisible spiritual results, just as real and definite as the visible, eventuate all concrete life and all materialism, through Time. My book ought to emanate buoyancy and gladness legitimately enough, for it was grown out of those elements, and has been the comfort of my life since it was originally commenced.

One main genesis-motive of the *Leaves* was my conviction (just as

---

* *Nineteenth Century,* July, 1883.

strong to-day as ever) that the crowning growth of the United States is to be spiritual and heroic. To help start and favor that growth—or even to call attention to it, or the need of it—is the beginning, middle, and final purpose of the poems. (In fact, when really cipher'd out and summ'd to the last, plowing up in earnest the interminable average fallows of humanity—not "good government" merely, in the common sense—is the justification and main purpose of these United States.)

Isolated advantages in any rank or grace or fortune—the direct or indirect threads of all the poetry of the past—are in my opinion distasteful to the republican genius, and offer no foundation for its fitting verse. Establish'd poems, I know, have the very great advantage of chanting the already perform'd, so full of glories, reminiscences dear to the minds of men. But my volume is a candidate for the future. "All original art," says Taine, anyhow, "is self-regulated, and no original art can be regulated from without; it carries its own counterpoise, and does not receive it from elsewhere—lives on its own blood"—a solace to my frequent bruises and sulky vanity.

As the present is perhaps mainly an attempt at personal statement or illustration, I will allow myself as further help to extract the following anecdote from a book, *Annals of Old Painters,* conn'd by me in youth. Rubens, the Flemish painter, in one of his wanderings through the galleries of old convents, came across a singular work. After looking at it thoughtfully for a good while, and listening to the criticisms of his suite of students, he said to the latter, in answer to their questions, (as to what school the work implied or belong'd,)"I do not believe the artist, unknown and perhaps no longer living, who has given the world this legacy, ever belong'd to any school, or ever painted anything but this one picture, which is a personal affair—a piece out of a man's life."

Leaves of Grass indeed (I cannot too often reiterate) has mainly been the outcropping of my own emotional and other personal nature—an attempt, from first to last, to put *a Person,* a human being (myself, in the latter half of the nineteenth century, in America,) freely, fully and truly on record. I could not find any similar personal record in current literature that satisfied me. But it is not on *Leaves of Grass* distinctively as *literature,* or a specimen thereof, that I feel to dwell, or advance claims. No one will get at my verses who insists upon viewing them as a literary performance, or attempt at such performance, or as aiming mainly toward art or æstheticism.

I say no land or people or circumstances ever existed so needing a race of singers and poems differing from all others, and rigidly their own, as the land and people and circumstances of our United States need such singers and poems to-day, and for the future. Still further, as long as the States continue to absorb and be dominated by the poetry of the Old World, and remain unsupplied with autochthonous song, to express, vitalize and give color to and define their material and political success, and minister to them distinctively, so long will they stop short of first-class Nationality and remain defective.

In the free evening of my day I give to you, reader, the foregoing garrulous talk, thoughts, reminiscences,

> As idly drifting down the ebb,
> Such ripples, half-caught voices, echo from the shore.

Concluding with two items for the imaginative genius of the West, when it worthily rises—First, what Herder taught to the young Goethe, that really great poetry is always (like the Homeric or Biblical canticles) the result of a national spirit, and not the privilege of a polish'd and select few; Second, that the strongest and sweetest songs yet remain to be sung.

[1888]

Biographical Notes

Prepared by HERBERT ZAROV

HUGH HENRY BRACKENRIDGE
[1748–1816]

Lawyer, politician, editor, essayist, teacher, preacher, and novelist, Hugh Henry Brackenridge was a veritable model of the self-made American man. A Princeton classmate of Philip Freneau, Brackenridge spent his young manhood as a teacher, poet, and frequent contributor of magazine articles and stories. His most important contribution to literature was his *Modern Chivalry* (1792–1819), a multivolume picaresque novel. Strongly influenced by Cervantes, Sterne, and Fielding, *Modern Chivalry* is a loosely structured and episodic novel which gently satirizes American democracy and its abuses.

CHARLES BROCKDEN BROWN
[1771–1810]

Born to a Philadelphia Quaker family and trained for the law, Charles Brockden Brown went on to become America's first significant novelist and the first purveyor of the classic American literary myth: the moral drama of the innocent child-man confronting experience in a strange world of preternatural evil and Gothic horror. His four major novels—*Wieland, Ormand, Edgar Huntly,* and *Arthur Mervyn*—were all written between 1797 and 1801. Brown completed four other novels, composed a quantity of short fiction, and edited the *Monthly Magazine and American Review*. In his last years he abandoned novel writing for magazine work and political and historical studies, but he was known primarily as a novelist. Margaret Fuller praised him as "by far our first in point of genius and instruction as to the soul of things."

ORESTES BROWNSON
[1803-1876]

Orestes Brownson was a clergyman, political radical (until a late conversion to Catholicism), and man of letters who contributed much to the intellectual ferment of the 1830's and 1840's in America. For a time he was connected with the socialist schemes of Robert Dale Owen and Fanny Wright—a connection which led to his attack, in the January, 1838, edition of his own *Quarterly Review,* on organized Christianity, the inheritance of wealth, and the existing penal code. During the early 1840's he was influenced by Coleridge, Carlyle, and especially Cousin, and contributed much to the Transcendentalist movement. His most important literary work was *The Convert: or, Leaves from My Experience* (1857), an autobiographical record of his five religious conversions and an excellent account of the Boston literary world of the 1830's.

MATHER BYLES
[1706/7-1788]

Nephew of Cotton Mather and lifelong friend of Benjamin Franklin, Mather Byles found himself attracted both to his uncle's piety and his friend's worldly pragmatism. A study in paradox, he was both a Congregational minister and a poet, a spiritual leader and a bon vivant, an author of orthodox theological tracts and a creator of poetry imitative of Pope and Thomson. His loyalty to the Crown during the Revolution led the victorious patriots to dismiss him from his pulpit and banish him from Boston.

EDWARD TYRELL CHANNING
[1790-1856]

In the winter of 1814-1815 Edward Tyrell Channing and others planned the launching of the *New England Magazine and Review.* When news came of William Tudor's projected *North American Review,* however, the group switched its support to that journal, and Channing edited the *Review* with the assistance of his cousin Richard Dana from May of 1818 to October, 1819. He resigned to become Boylston Professor of Rhetoric and Oratory at Harvard—where he taught Thoreau, Emerson, and Holmes, and "probably trained as many conspicuous authors as all other American instructors put together" (T. W. Higginson).

WILLIAM DUNLAP
[1766-1839]

William Dunlap was a playwright and manager who dominated the first years of American theater. In addition to producing most of his own plays,

Dunlap translated and produced many contemporary French and German dramas, wrote a biography of his friend Charles Brockden Brown, and composed a comprehensive history of American theater. Most of his own plays were sentimental comedies, but he also attempted tragedy and Gothic romance. Mindful of the traditional American hostility to theater, he justified his work by arguing that the stage was a vehicle for moral instruction and that his plays were efforts "to make Pleasure subservient to the cause of Virtue."

EVERT AUGUSTUS DUYCKINCK
[1816–1878]

Evert Augustus Duyckinck was a New York critic. In addition to editing American editions of Thackeray's *Confessions of Fitz-Boodle* (1852), Sydney Smith's *Wit and Wisdom* (1856), and Philip Freneau's *Poems Relating to the American Revolution,* he founded the *Literary World, a Journal of American and Foreign Literature, Science and Art* and coedited, with Cornelius Mathews, *Arcturus, a Journal of Books and Opinion.* He also wrote, with his brother George, the comprehensive two volume *Cyclopedia of American Literature* (1855), a biographical dictionary of American literary figures.

NATHANIEL EVANS
[1742–1767]

Nathaniel Evans was an Anglican clergyman and lyric poet who struggled to develop a viable art in America. Conscious of the difficulties of writing poetry in a country where art was suspect and where there was no established tradition, he celebrated literature cautiously and diffidently. In his own work he was content to imitate Cowley, Milton, and Gray and in his criticism he justified literature on the grounds that it was "innocent," that it could "instruct as well as entertain," and that "of all others" it was "the cheapest entertainment."

ALEXANDER EVERETT
[1790–1847]

Alexander Everett was a member of that first generation of Unitarians which sought to substitute literature for theology as the dominant intellectual activity of New England. At various times a diplomat to Russia, Spain, and the Netherlands, he knew Europe well and worked to disseminate European ideas in America. His own writings include *Critical and Miscellaneous Essays* (1845), a collection of his contributions to the *North American Review* (which he edited from 1830–1835), *Poems* (1845), a series of imitations and translations, and *New Ideas on Population,* an optimistic refutation of Malthusian economic theory.

EDWARD EVERETT
[1794–1865]

In 1815, at the age of twenty-one, Edward Everett left his position as pastor of Boston's fashionable Brattle Street Church to accept an appointment as Professor of Greek Literature at Harvard. He traveled to Germany to prepare himself, receiving at Göttingen in 1817 the first Ph.D. bestowed upon an American and returning in 1819 to assume his professorship and to become editor of the *North American Review*. In the years that followed he was a Congressman (1825–1835), Governor of Massachusetts (1836–1839), Minister to the Court of St. James (1841–1845), President of Harvard (1846–1849), Secretary of State (for four months between 1852–1853), Senator (1853–1854), and unsuccessful Vice-Presidential candidate of the Constitutional Union Party (1860).

PHILIP FRENEAU
[1752–1832]

Sailor, journalist, and poet, Philip Freneau was an ardent patriot, an energetic defender of the American Revolution, and a prolific opponent of the Hamiltonianism he felt betrayed that revolution. As a poet he felt the impulse of two important literary currents—he wrote neoclassical political satire and nature poetry which anticipated nineteenth-century Romantic verse. His journalistic and literary endeavors were usually financial failures, but later readers continue to number him among the more interesting poets of early America.

MARGARET FULLER
[1810–1850]

Before she reached her teens, Margaret Fuller had read Ovid, Shakespeare, Cervantes, and Molière. The promise of her precocious first years was later realized in a brilliant career as journalist, critic, social reformer, and leading feminine member of the Transcendentalist movement. In the course of her literary career she edited *The Dial* (1840–1842), served as a literary critic for Horace Greeley's *New York Tribune,* and published the feminist tract, *Woman in the Nineteenth Century* (1845). Her posthumous *Memoirs* (1852) were published in an elaborate two-volume edition by her friends Emerson, James Freeman Clarke, and W. H. Channing.

WILLIAM HOWARD GARDINER
[1797–1882]

W. H. Gardiner was a frequent contributor to the *North American Review* and well known for his acerbic reviews of contemporary novels. The tenor of his nationalistic criticism is perhaps best represented by his attack, in an 1822 review of Cooper's *The Spy,* on those who believed that America lacked Romantic materials and that sharply defined classes were necessary for the production of fiction. "In no country on the face of the globe," he argued, "can there be found a greater variety of specific character than is at this moment developed in this United States of America."

G. S. HILLARD
[1808–1879]

Clergyman, politician, critic, and friend of Hawthorne, George Stillman Hillard was for thirty years an important contributor to periodicals like the *Christian Examiner,* the *North American Review,* and the *New England Magazine.* In addition to his essays and book reviews, he produced an edition of Spenser in five volumes (1839), a *Selection from the Writings of Landor* (1856), and a biography of Captain John Smith for Jared Sparks's *Library of American Biography* (1834).

DAVID HUMPHREYS
[1752–1818]

Farmer, soldier, statesman and "Connecticut Wit," David Humphreys celebrated in verse imitative of Pope the eighteenth-century myth of the versatile, practical, productive American. Himself a living embodiment of that myth, he wrote overtly didactic poems which urged his countrymen to labor industriously for the greater glory of America. By giving poetic expression to such topics as "the moral effect of industry on constitution and character," "in what manner labor embellishes the land," and "the fabrication of maple syrup dwelt upon, as having a gradual tendency to the abolition of slavery," he demonstrated that poetry, like farming, politics, and commerce, could be employed for utilitarian and patriotic purposes.

FRANCIS JEFFREY
[1773–1850]

Francis Jeffrey founded the *Edinburgh Review*—along with Smith, Brougham, and Horner—and served from 1803 to 1829 as editor of that influential journal. Although Carlyle called him the first of the English critics of his day, he had little sympathy for Romantic poetry and believed that Rogers and Campbell were the only contemporary poets likely to win lasting fame. When he left the *Review* to devote his energies to law and politics, he gave up his literary life as well—he published only four articles between 1829 and his death in 1850.

SAMUEL LORENZO KNAPP
[1783–1838]

Samuel Lorenzo Knapp was a lawyer, newspaper editor, and writer of miscellaneous essays on literary and cultural history. His most important work was *Lectures on American Literature* (1829), a panoramic "history of the American mind" which lawyer Knapp intended as "the opening argument of junior counsel . . . to establish the claims of the United States to that intellectual, literary and scientific eminence which . . . she deserves to have and ought to maintain." Knapp's literary nationalism found expression also in biographies of historical figures like Lafayette, Webster, and Burr, in two volumes of short tales, and in the Revolutionary War romance, *Polish Chiefs* (1832). He is also thought to have had a hand in *Miriam Coffin* (1834), an anonymously published whaling novel which influenced Melville.

RICHARD LEWIS
[1699?–1733?]

"As to who R. Lewis was," the Maryland Historical Society remarks, "we know nothing." In the Preface to his translation of Edward Holdsworth's "Muscipula," Lewis tells us that he is a teacher of language, and his commentary reveals a learned man. The translation itself, in mock heroic lines frankly imitative of Pope, was the first literary production of the Maryland Press and, as the author tells us, a conscious attempt "to cultivate Polite Literature in Maryland."

CORNELIUS MATHEWS
[1817–1889]

In addition to contributing to periodicals like the *American Monthly Magazine*, the *New York Review*, and the *Knickerbocker Magazine*, Cornelius Mathews wrote several romances, a number of dramas—including the immensely successful *Witchcraft, or the Martyrs of Salem* (1846)—and *Poems on Man in His Various Aspects under the American Republic* (1834). His interest in "original" materials led him to attempt projects as various as "a fossil romance" about an ante-Indian culture's battle with a mastodon, a novel comparing Indian life before the settlement of New York with the later Dutch culture, and an essay on "The Ethics of Eating." He was also editor of *Yankee Doodle* (1846–1847) and coeditor with his friend Evert Duyckinck of *Arcturus, a Journal of Books and Opinion.*

GRENVILLE MELLEN
[1799–1841]

Grenville Mellen spent most of his adult life in North Yarmouth, Maine, where he was a fellow townsman of Longfellow and a literary figure in his own right. In addition to contributing poems, tales, and essays to the *United States Literary Gazette* and the *North American Review,* he wrote a volume of Byronic verse, *The Martyr's Triumph; and Other Poems* (1833), and a collection of *Sad Tales and Glad Tales* (1828), one of the first American ventures in short-story writing.

JOHN GORHAM PALFREY
[1796–1881]

John Gorham Palfrey was a Unitarian clergyman, editor, politician, and historian whose major contribution to American culture was his five-volume *History of New England.* Like so many of the influential literary figures of his day, he was closely associated with the *North American Review,* which he served variously between 1817 and 1843 as owner, editor, and frequent contributor. He was also, from 1831 to 1839, Dexter Professor of Sacred Literature at Harvard and, in 1847, Representative to Congress and leader of the Free Soil Party.

THEODORE PARKER
[1810–1860]

Theologian, Unitarian clergyman, and publicist, Theodore Parker was, according to Perry Miller, "the man who next only to Emerson . . . was to give shape and meaning to the Transcendental movement in America." His most important contributions to Transcendental theory were "A Discourse on the Transient and Permanent in Christianity" (1842) and "A Discourse of Matters Pertaining to Religion" (1842), both of which attacked what Parker called the "truncated supernaturalism" of Unitarianism. In 1848 he wrote his *Letter to the People of the United States Touching the Matter of Slavery* and devoted the last years of his life to the support of abolition.

THEOPHILUS PARSONS
[1797–1882]

Theophilus Parsons was a prominent Professor of Law at Harvard who dabbled in literature. Although he devoted most of his energy to producing numerous volumes on legal theory, he also edited, for a time, the *United States Literary Gazette* and the *New England Galaxy* and contributed frequently to the *North American Review.* His books on nonliterary affairs include three series of essays (1845, 1856, 1862), a volume on the slavery question (1863), and an *Outline of the Religion and Philosophy of Swedenborg* (1875).

JAMES KIRKE PAULDING
[1778–1860]

In James Kirke Paulding the cultural nationalism which had been slowly simmering during the previous literary generation came to a full and tempestuous boil. An 1814 issue of the *British Quarterly Review* contained a savage attack on his own narrative poem, *The Lay of the Scottish Fiddle,* and a stupidly prejudiced traveler's account of the United States. Paulding was furious, and he set off to redress his and America's grievances in a single lengthy volume. The result was *The United States and England,* the first of five books in which Paulding celebrated American virtue and attacked British vice. Before his involvement in the English-American literary wars, Paulding was known primarily for his collaboration with William and Washington Irving on *Salmagundi.* In later years he devoted himself to realistic fiction; he published over seventy tales, most of them subscribing to his theory that American art should concern itself with American subjects.

WILLIAM BOURN OLIVER PEABODY
[1799–1847]

W. B. O. Peabody spent his entire adult life as pastor of the Third Congregational (Unitarian) Church of Springfield, Massachusetts. He was also, however, a man of letters who wrote four volumes for Jared Sparks's *Library of American Biography* and who over a twenty-year period contributed frequent articles—many of them expounding his theory that the historical romance was the ideal form for the novel—to periodicals like the *North American Review* and the *Christian Examiner.*

JOHN PICKERING
[1777–1846]

John Pickering earned his living practicing law, but he is best remembered for his pioneering work in American philology. A student of language who knew twenty tongues, his *Vocabulary or Collection of Words Which Have Been Supposed to be Peculiar to the United States of America* was the first study of the English language as spoken in America. According to Van Wyck Brooks, Pickering's spelling of American Indian languages inspired worldwide interest in the study of all the primitive languages.

WILLIAM GILMORE SIMMS
[1806–1870]

Often described as "the Southern Cooper," William Gilmore Simms was a prolific South Carolina man of letters. He wrote poetry, drama, criticism, and biography, but he concentrated his considerable energies on the romance. "Modern romance," he argued, "is the substitute which the people of the present day offer for the ancient epic." Of Simms's own popular border romances, *The Yemassee* (1835) has proven most durable.

SYDNEY SMITH
[1771–1845]

Sydney Smith was canon of St. Paul's, London, founder, along with Jeffrey, Brougham, and Horner of the *Edinburgh Review,* and probably the most famous wit of his generation. During the Anglo-American literary war which raged during the first quarter of the nineteenth century, Smith frequently demonstrated his sincere affection for America by praising American institutions—he once described himself as a "Philoyankeeist." His skepticism about this country's claims to a worthy national literary tradition, however, earned him the unreasoning and seemingly unending enmity of American cultural defenders. As late as 1963 a CBS television special was introduced as a reply to Smith's comments on American culture, and *Webster's Biographical Dictionary* still describes him as "a denouncer of everything American."

WILLIAM JOSEPH SNELLING
[1804–1848]

W. J. Snelling was a journalist, satirist, and adventurer who, among other things, lived with the Dakota Indians as a young man, helped put down the Winnebago Indian revolt of 1827, and served a short term for drunkenness in a Boston prison. Out of these experiences came two long narratives: *Tales of the Northwest; or, Sketches of Indian Life and Character* (1830) and *The Rat-Trap; or, Cogitations of a Convict in the House of Correction* (1837). His most famous work, however, was a verse satire on contemporary poets, *Truth: A New Year's Gift for Scribblers* (1831), which aimed its most pointed barbs at the pretensions of the Boston literary establishment.

JARED SPARKS
[1789–1866]

Jared Sparks devoted his life to reclaiming the American past for his generation. In addition to editing *The Correspondence of George Washington*

(12 volumes, 1834–1837), *The Works of Benjamin Franklin* (10 volumes, 1836–1840), *The Diplomatic Correspondence of the American Revolution* (12 volumes, 1829–1830), and *The Library of American Biography* (first series 10 volumes, 1834–1838), he also served as owner and editor of the *North American Review,* as Professor of Ancient and Modern History at Harvard (the first chair in nontheological history in America), and as that university's president (1849–1853).

EBENEEZER SYME
[1826–1860]

Syme was an evangelist, journalist and literary man. He contributed frequently to the *Westminster Review* between 1848 and 1852, and then emigrated to Australia where he purchased the *Melbourne Review.* Under his direction this journal became Australia's leading liberal magazine.

WILLIAM TUDOR
[1779–1830]

William Tudor was a merchant, a lawyer, a politician, and a writer who was, during the first quarter of the nineteenth century, a central figure in the cultural life of Boston. In addition to his own writing—which ranged from a biography of James Otis to essays on cranberry sauce and purring cats—he helped found the Boston Athenaeum, was an active member of the Massachusetts Historical Society, and founded and edited the influential *North American Review.*

ROYALL TYLER
[1757–1826]

In March of 1787 Royall Tyler, a young Boston lawyer in New York on a mission for the Governor of Massachusetts, paid his first visit to the legitimate theater. Three weeks later he had completed *The Contrast,* the first comedy (and only the second play) written by a native American and produced by a professional company. Despite the enormous success of his work—*The Contrast* was repeated five times in New York and soon after was produced in Baltimore, Philadelphia, Boston, and Charleston—Tyler continued to think of himself as a lawyer with a literary avocation. His major contribution to literature remains *The Contrast,* but he also wrote several other comic plays, a good deal of satiric verse, and two fictional narratives. His work in the law culminated in his appointment to the Supreme Court of Vermont in 1807.

ROBERT WALSH
[1784–1859]

Lawyer, journalist, and literary entrepreneur, Robert Walsh founded *The American Review of History and Politics* (1811), America's first quarterly; *The National Gazette and Literary Review* (1820), a successful liberal tri-weekly; and *The American Quarterly Review* (1827), a literary journal which he personally conducted for ten years. His most important individual work was *An Appeal to the Judgments of Great Britain Respecting the United States of America* (1819), a polemic in which he attempted "to repel actively, and if possible to arrest, the war which is waged without stint or intermission, upon our national character." His contemporary reputation is reflected in Edgar Allan Poe's description of him as "one of the finest writers, one of the most accomplished scholars, and when not in too great a hurry one of the most accurate thinkers in the country."

MICHAEL WIGGLESWORTH
[1631–1705]

Michael Wigglesworth was born in England and came to Massachusetts Bay with his parents in 1638. A minister and author, his most famous work was "The Day of Doom," a poem in ballad meter which "versified" the Puritan concept of the day of the last judgment (and led Paul Elmer More to dub him "the doggerel Dante of the New England meeting house"). In-significant as poetry (Wigglesworth's primary poetic concern was probably to compose a poem which could be easily memorized), "The Day of Doom" remains an excellent example of the Puritan attempt to use art as a vehicle for theology.

ABOUT THE EDITOR

Richard Ruland is Professor of English at Washington University, St. Louis, Missouri. He was born in Detroit in 1932 and has degrees from the University of Western Ontario, the University of Detroit, and the University of Michigan. He has taught at Yale, the University of Leeds, where he was a Bruern Fellow, and at Groningen, as a Fulbright Fellow. *The Rediscovery of American Literature,* his first book, was published by the Harvard University Press in 1967. He has also edited *Walden: A Collection of Critical Essays* (Prentice-Hall 1968) and has contributed essays and articles to a variety of journals. He lives in St. Louis with his wife, Barbara Nolan, a specialist in mediaeval literature who also teaches at Washington University.